"Supported by research at seventeen archives in North America and across Europe, Beorn's effort is impressive, and, at times, brilliant. . . . Highly recommended."

—D. R. SNYDER, *Choice*

"*Between the Wires* is original, finely researched and written, and a deeply compelling account of a place of terrible crimes. . . . I hope this book might induce others to take the steps in the city of Lviv to recognize the full extent of what happened."

—PHILIPPE SANDS, author of *East West Street: On the Origins of "Genocide" and "Crimes Against Humanity"*

"This history of the Janowska camp and the atrocities committed there as well as in the nearby Sand execution site is based on profound expert knowledge. These parts of the book enrich the research available with a wealth of details about perpetrators, victims, and practices of violence. Where possible the author takes a micro-historical and biographical approach in order to condense and vividly present the complexity of the events."

—THOMAS SANDKÜHLER, professor in the Department of History of Humboldt University in Berlin

"A remarkable book. . . . The range of sources *Between the Wires* consults is outstanding, giving it a panoptic feel. It has used the trial testimony to excellent effect, and it also includes local histories, victim diaries, survivor memories, and more."

—MARK ROSEMAN, author of *Lives Reclaimed: A Story of Rescue and Resistance in Nazi Germany*

"This outstanding book resurrects the history of one of the most notorious and least-known sites of slave labor and genocide in World War II. The Janowska camp, located in Lviv, Ukraine, witnessed the mass murder of up to eighty thousand people, mostly Jews, between 1941 and 1944. A place of extraordinary inhumanity, even by Nazi standards, it was also a transition point for hundreds of thousands of Jews in Galicia transported to the Belzec extermination camp. And yet, until Waitman Beorn took it upon himself to reconstruct the horrors that occurred there, it largely disappeared from historiography and memory. This is not an easy book to read, but a necessary one, and we should all be thankful to its author for his tenacious research and unflinching, courageous narrative of atrocity, resistance, and survival."

—OMER BARTOV, author of *Anatomy of a Genocide: The Life and Death of a Town Called Buczacz*

Between the Wires

Between the Wires

The Janowska Camp
and the Holocaust in Lviv

WAITMAN WADE BEORN

University of Nebraska Press   Lincoln

© 2024 by Waitman Wade Beorn

All rights reserved

The University of Nebraska Press is part of a land-grant institution with campuses and programs on the past, present, and future homelands of the Pawnee, Ponca, Otoe-Missouria, Omaha, Dakota, Lakota, Kaw, Cheyenne, and Arapaho Peoples, as well as those of the relocated Ho-Chunk, Sac and Fox, and Iowa Peoples.

First Nebraska Paperback printing: 2026

For customers n the EU with safety/GPSR concerns, contact:
gpsr@mare-nostrum.co.uk
Mare Nostrum Group BV
Mauritskade 21D
1091 GC Amsterdam
The Netherlands

Library of Congress Cataloging-in-Publication Data
Names: Beorn, Waitman Wade, 1977– author.
Title: Between the wires: the Janowska camp and the Holocaust in Lviv / Waitman Wade Beorn.
Other titles: Janowska camp and the Holocaust in Lviv
Description: [Lincoln]: [University of Nebraska Press], [2024] | Includes bibliographical references and index.
Identifiers: LCCN 2023034425
ISBN 9781496237590 (hardback)
ISBN 9781496246387 (paperback)
ISBN 9781496239778 (epub)
ISBN 9781496239785 (pdf)
Subjects: LCSH: Janowska (Concentration camp) | Holocaust, Jewish (1939–1945)—Ukraine—Lviv. | Jewish ghettos—Ukraine—Lviv—History—20th century. | Jews—Persecutions—Ukraine—Lviv—History—20th century. | Lviv (Ukraine)—History—20th century. | BISAC: SOCIAL SCIENCE / Jewish Studies | HISTORY / Wars & Conflicts / World War II / European Theater
Classification: LCC D805.5.J36 B46 2024 | DDC 940.53/18094779 23/eng/20231—dc09
LC record available at https://lccn.loc.gov/2023034425

Designed and set in Arno by L. Welch.

For Emmaline:
May she grow up in a world
where genocide is truly history

Contents

List of Illustrations — ix
Acknowledgments — xi

Prologue — 1
Introduction — 3
1. City of Lions — 15
2. Ein Furioso — 29
3. The Devil's Workshop — 53
4. A Tragic Life — 79
5. Cerberus Awakens — 109
6. Behind the Wires — 141
7. Here Be Monsters — 165
8. The Spider's Web — 189
9. Holokaustos — 203
10. Testify for Us All — 233
Conclusion — 263

Notes — 269
Bibliography — 321
Index — 339

Illustrations

Following page 108
1. Luftwaffe aerial photograph, June 6, 1944
2. Map of German-occupied Poland
3. July Days pogrom in Lviv, July 1941
4. Public notice of ghettoization in Lviv
5. Staff of the DAW-L, ca. 1941–42
6. Staff of the DAW in the SS living area, ca. 1941–42
7. Janowska camp SS with Ukrainian guards
8. German troops entering downtown Lviv on June 29, 1941
9. Lviv Jews being deported to the Janowska camp or Kleparów station
10. Gustav Willhaus with wife, Liesel, and daugher, Heike
11. The camp headquarters building in an early postwar photograph
12. Workers load destroyed tombstones for use as building material
13. Janowska prisoners doing paving work in the camp
14. Looted Jewish property in the camp, postliberation
15. SS men carry out an execution in the ravines behind the Janowska camp
16. Photograph of the camp orchestra, by Herman Lewinter
17. Zeev Porath, a trained architect who was imprisoned at Janowska
18. Zeev Porath drawing of SS man Adolf Kolonko abusing prisoners
19. Zeev Porath drawing capturing the torture and humiliation of two rabbis from Jaworow
20. Drawing by Zeev Porath depicting the geography of the camp
21. View of the commandant's house in Janowska
22. Postwar mugshot of Peter Blum

23. The first commandant of the Janowska camp, Gustav Willhaus
24. SS man Richard Rokita relaxing at his quarters in the camp
25. Heinrich Himmler tours a camp along the Durchgangstrasse IV
26. SS man Adolf Kolonko
27. A social network diagram of Janowska SS men during the war
28. Postwar photograph of Walter Schallock, who commanded the Lviv SK 1005
29. Death Brigade members pose with the bone grinder in Janowska
30. One of the many ravines where thousands were shot to death
31. The Łyczaków Forest today
32. Defendants in the dock during the Lviv Trial, 1966
33. Jewish tombstone uncovered in Lviv, where it had been used as paving material
34. The terrain of Janowska today

TABLES

1. Lviv city population by religious denomination, 1910 — 17
2. Food allowances in the Lviv ghetto — 87
3. Janowska DAW and ZAL SS staff deployed to other camps and ghettos — 197
4. Lviv Trial verdicts, 1968 — 254

Acknowledgments

I began this project in 2013 by returning to look at a German Army motor pool unit (HKP 547) that I had come across in earlier research; HKP 547 had used Jewish labor from a place called Janowska, which I had never heard of. Over a decade later, this book has come to fruition, and it absolutely would not have been possible without the support and generosity of a diverse array of institutions and individuals.

First and foremost, I must thank the families of both Janowska survivors and perpetrators for their willingness to share documents and memories with me. I should start with the only two Janowska survivors I was able to speak with: Michael Katz and Janine Oberrotman. I am also incredibly thankful for conversations with Rachel Hennoch, Zeev Porath's daughter, as well as with Eve and Helen Ash, daughters of Feliks Ash who provided me with his unpublished interviews. The family of Herman Lewinter (Keith Lewinter and Mimi Werner) gave me access to Herman's photographs of the camp, which are reproduced here and are continuing to prove invaluable to my research. I am also grateful for the cooperation of Derek Niemann and Rüdiger Schallock, who helpfully provided important elements of their family history.

Archivists and museum professionals are the unsung heroes of scholarly research; without them, we would be unable to do our work. I am particularly appreciative of the support of those at the United States Holocaust Memorial Museum (USHMM), Yad Vashem, the Ghetto Fighters' House Museum, and the Central Office for the Investigation of Nazi Crimes in Ludwigsburg. In Ludwigsburg, I am indebted as always to Dr. Tobias Hermann and Sidar Toptanci for their assistance. At the USHMM, I want to recognize the help and guidance given me by Elizabeth Anthony, Peter

Black, Ron Coleman, Jo-Ellyn Decker, Rebecca Erbelding, Steven Feldman, Suzanne Brown-Fleming, Nicole Frechette, Krista Hegburg, Vincent Slatt, Elliott Wrenn, Megan Lewis, and Judy Cohen.

My institutional home changed three times over the course of this project, but each institution contributed in critical ways to the success of this endeavor. I want to thank my colleagues at the University of Nebraska–Omaha, especially in the History Department, for their collegiality and support. The department's Martin Fund also supported this research. My research assistant, Chad Gibbs (now a Holocaust Studies professor), provided invaluable assistance, including retrieving documents from Yad Vashem. He also spurred me to consider the utility of a social network approach to the Janowska perpetrators. At the University of Virginia, I am grateful for the material support of the History Department, especially from Jeff Rossman and Brian Owensby. Gabriel Finder also contributed to this project in meaningful ways, as did Kyrill Kunakhovich. The Criss Library staff deserve special mention as without their tireless response to seemingly endless requests for esoteric texts, this book would never have come about. As a digital humanist, I would not be where I am today without the collaboration of the UVA Scholars' Lab and the tutelage of Drew MacQueen and Chris Gist, whose visualizations and maps I continue to use today. Last, I want to highlight the amazing experience enabled by the Faulty Global Research with Undergraduates grant that enabled me to work with UVA students Jesse Ginn, Ryan Wolfe, and Matthew Poliakoff. All assisted me in the research for this book, and Ryan and Matt accompanied me to Lviv to on-site research. At my current home, I must, again, thank the Northumbria University library staff for their help and also my excellent colleagues in History who have been incredibly welcoming and supportive. I especially thank Brian Ward for his feedback on the manuscript over pints.

I owe more than I can possibly repay to the Lviv Center for Urban History. My Ukrainian partners continue to be vital to my work. Harald Binder and Sofia Dyak have been generous partners in inviting me to share my research at the center and attend events. Taras Martynenko served as an excellent guide through the Ukrainian archival system. My friend Taras Nazaruk is a tireless partner whose contributions to this book are legion... even if he was unable to convert me to drinking kvass. I am also thankful for the staff members of the Territory of Terror: Memorial Museum of Totalitarian Regimes in Lviv who also contributed to this project, especially Oleksandr Pahiria who literally took the time to write me from the front. Even amid the ongoing war in their country, the scholars at both places have found the time to graciously assist me with a project whose importance pales in comparison.

Over a decade of researching, I have amassed quite a number of debts large and small to various individuals who shaped this project as it evolved. David Domina and David Blinka were instrumental in giving me access to the Kalymon case files. Tarik Cyril Amar, Robin O'Neill, Claudia Koonz, Henning Pieper, Stephen Tyas, Sara Berger, Marla Raucher Osborn, and Brianna Burdetsky also provided me with source material for this book. Joanna Sliwa and Gershom Gorenberg provided translation help. Christopher Browning has been, as always, an insightful and invaluable source of advice. Deep conversations with Paul Jaskot and Anne Knowles have also shaped not only this project but the trajectory of my research moving forward. The two reviewers of this manuscript, Thomas Sandkühler and Mark Roseman, graciously shared their time and expertise to suggest ways to improve this book, and I am indebted to them for their insightful feedback. Much of the writing took place in two coffee shops where I became more than a regular and which very much felt like home, so I must recognize C'ville Coffee and Café 1901 in Jesmond.

I would like to thank my agent, Joelle Delbourgo, for her insights and quest to find the best home for this book. I also must thank my editors, Heather Stauffer and Ann Baker, for shepherding the manuscript through the publication process. Thanks also to Natalie Jones for some truly meticulous editing and Varsha Venkatasubramian for a comprehensive index. All remaining errors and omissions are mine alone.

Between the Wires

Prologue

> How doth the city sit solitary, that was full of people!
> How is she become as a widow!
> —Book of Eicha (Lam. 1:1)

If you step onto tram number 7 in front of the grand yellow neoclassical Maria Zankovetska Theatre in downtown Lviv, it will take you to the end of the line on the western outskirts of the city along Shevchenka Street in about twenty minutes.[1] And if you get off one stop before the terminus, you arrive at the Yanivski cemetery. Walking through this forested necropolis laid out on a neat grid, you are also entering the former "New" Jewish cemetery, founded in 1855. An art nouveau–style funereal building (Beth Tahara) was built in 1912 but it was destroyed along with almost all of the Jewish cemetery complex under the shadow of the swastika.[2] The distinctive neo-Romanesque fence still stands, but now marks the border of a Christian cemetery.[3] Only a few Jewish tombstones (*matzevot*) from the postwar period remain, distinctive in their rounded shape, Stars of David, and Hebrew lettering. Protective fencing surrounds them, as if guarding them against their neighbors. The oldest Jewish tombstones found in the city date to 1348.[4] Citizens of Lviv often bring the fragments of old matzevot to the cemetery when they are found in the city where the Nazis used them as building materials.

Two such fragments laid at the entrance to the cemetery when I visited in 2017. One belonged to Izak Kroch, "an enlightened and educated man" who died on January 10 or 11, 1919. A blessing could be seen on the stone: "May his soul be bound in the bond of life." The other tombstone was fragmented, violently ripped in half, leaving only a jagged diagonal top portion. The surviving inscription reads: "Here lies an esteemed woman," who died on September 14 or 15, 1893. Beneath a three-armed candelabra, the rest of the *matzevah* is gone, leaving only the fragment and the words "and upright." The place of her burial and even her name have been erased forever.[5]

Deeper into the now almost entirely Christian cemetery, the path leads up a hill into the newest section, where unfinished mausoleums rather haphazardly populate either side of a muddy road. Breaking through the trees into the tall grass at the top of the ridge, the terrain of the former *Zwangsarbeitslager-Lemberg* (ZAL-L) or Forced Labor Camp-Lviv comes into view. This was the Janowska camp, a place where perhaps eighty thousand Jews were murdered. Below, in the shadow of the curving cliffs, is what remains of this sinister place. Perhaps fittingly, it is still a prison: the Lychakivska Penal Colony Number 30. Often shrouded in fog and smoke, the complex still occupies almost precisely the footprint of the old Nazi camp. Though many new buildings have been added, the place still evokes a palpable feeling of desolation and despair. The icy wind through the barren trees and the snow heavy on the ground only reinforces an almost visceral feeling that this is defiled ground, a truly cursed place.

And the very ground *is* defiled. Walking west down a narrow forest trail, one can still clearly see the natural draws and ravines known as "the Sands," a name once whispered with terror by the Jews of the city, where thousands of men, women, and children were shot to death and later burned. Just north of the prison's walls lies a small field where the Jews of Lviv and other surrounding communities awaited their turn to be murdered in these hills. This circuit ends at approximately where the monumental entrance to the Janowska camp once stood. Indeed, the former camp headquarters building remains, lying just outside of the modern prison; it is now a multifamily home. Guard dogs bark from within the prison yard. More recent guard towers and wire blend with rusted wartime wire and long-dark drooping lights from the Nazi era. A simple sign in this neighborhood (which also used to be part of the camp complex) explains that this is the grounds of the Janowska concentration camp. It says, "This is a site of memory of the Holocaust." Yet, few have heard of this camp and fewer still remember it. Like the tombstones at the cemetery's entrance and those buried throughout the city, the terrible history of the Janowska camp is fragmented, scattered, and unexcavated.

Introduction

> In all of my work I have never begun by asking the big questions, because I was always afraid that I would come up with small answers; and I have preferred to address these things which are minutiae or details in order that I might then be able to put together in a gestalt a picture which, if not an explanation, is at least a description, a more full description, of what transpired.
> —Raul Hilberg, 1985

Fall–Winter 1941–42
DEUTSCHE AUSRÜSTUNGSWERKE-LEMBERG (DAW-L)
49°51′8.76″N, 23°59′28.98″E

In August 1941, SS-Hauptsturmführer Fritz Gebauer appeared in the chaotically busy offices of the Jewish Labor Office in Lviv. At this early point, it was likely still under control of the Jewish Council (Judenrat) whose officials struggled daily to fulfill the occupiers' endless demands for labor. On July 14 and 15, 1941, the military commander of the city and the mayor had issued a series of anti-Jewish measures including forced labor for all males aged fourteen to sixty.[1] Jews seeking steady work to avoid random abduction off the street thronged the Labor Office (*Arbeitsamt*). Gebauer shoved his way through the crowd and demanded five hundred workers for his still-unborn DAW labor camp, promising they would get documentation signed by the proper authorities.

A morally bankrupt Jewish office assistant, Sylvia Schapira, who would later extort bribes from her own people, put out the word that work at the DAW would be a "brilliant job" to have. Those Jews seeking security volunteered. Bernard Hirschhorn, a fifty-seven-year-old engineer, signed up as one of the first hundred fifty. Along with other specialists, and unskilled laborers (*Schwarzarbeiter*), he arrived at an abandoned compound at 134 Janowskastrasse. As other Jews heard of the relatively good working conditions, commandant Gebauer soon had his first five hundred laborers.

The first task was to build the means of their own exploitation and incarceration, much as it had been for the first prisoners of the very first concentration camps in Germany eight years earlier. Hirschhorn recalled that workers scrambled "at breakneck speed" to build the first barracks.[2] At his age, Bernard's life was probably saved by his profession as an engineer; it secured him a place in the Technical Office, protected from the elements. Even years after the war, the Nazi civilian overseer Hugo Bleines noted coldly that the "most intelligent Jews were workshop and office supervisors."[3] The Schwarzarbeitern were not as lucky. As the weather turned, construction continued. The winter of 1941/42 raged as prisoners hacked at the frozen earth for twelve hours a day. Guards beat them constantly.[4] Eventually, barracks rose on the abandoned lot, but the unskilled workers found theirs to be so cold that they could not sleep at night.[5]

Soon, the workshops became operational, though construction work never ceased, particularly once the Zwangsarbeitslager-Lemberg (ZAL-L, forced labor camp) was born next door. The slave labor varied widely. Eugenia Maas worked as a maid for the Gebauer family, for example, while Chaim Rosen worked repairing sewing machines.[6] As Janowska evolved, however, the quantity and variety of slave labor exponentially increased. And it was brutal from the beginning. One day, a work detail returned to the camp carrying the broken body of a Mr. Jagid from the Kleparów station who had been crushed between two railcars.[7] Nor was the work itself the only danger. Hirschhorn witnessed Gebauer catching a prisoner resting; the commandant threw the man to the ground and stood on his throat until he died.[8] The work continued for the next four years.

PIASKI, SUMMER 1942   49°51′30.29″N, 23°59′16.52″E

From the earliest days of the camp, the shadowy draws and ravines north of Janowska haunted the ghetto. "You'll end up in the dunes!" Lviv's Jews would warn each other.[9] The ravines symbolized the dreadful scriptural monster Moloch, devouring Jews in fire and blood. Lviv Jews themselves connected the Holocaust more generally with this biblical fiend.[10] It was "the German Moloch," "the insatiable jaws of the Nazi Moloch," that "crushed everything."[11] The *Piaski* (Polish for "sands") were John Milton's "Moloch, horrid king besmear'd with blood / of human sacrifice, and parents' tears."[12] They were the Moloch of Ginsburg: "Moloch whose breast is a cannibal dynamo! Moloch whose ear is a smoking tomb!"[13] One historian described the camp itself as a "ravenous Moloch."[14]

Chaim Rosen, twenty-seven, stood within reach of Moloch's jaws on the *Appellplatz* in the ZAL-L (Zwangsarbeitslager-Lemberg) in the 4:00 a.m. darkness. He waited as SS man Adolf Kolonko conducted a selection of prisoners deemed too weak to live. Because he apparently enjoyed the "dirty work," Kolonko often escorted the victims into the hills himself. One morning, a prisoner refused to go, and Kolonko shot him on the spot.[15] In addition to these constant routine camp killings, mass executions often took place in the sands. Women, children, and the elderly arrived from the city alone for the first time on June 2, 1942. These eleven hundred to twelve hundred Jews waited on the *Sammelplatz* (assembly area) overnight. In the morning, the camp SS took them to the ravines and shot them.[16]

The killing sites were so permanent that signs in Polish, German, and Ukrainian were erected stating: "To enter this place is strictly forbidden. Anyone nearing this site at a distance of less than 150 feet of the sign will be shot."[17] Shootings here predated even the Great Aktion of August 1942, with the "Gestapo delivering 60–100 Jews almost daily to the camp, the vast majority of whom were shot."[18] Many Jews did not go quietly, but the killings continued and the smoke of burning bodies wafted frequently over the city.

SAMMELPLATZ, AUGUST 1942   49°51'18.49"N, 23°59'10.96"E

Tram cars and open trucks loaded with Jews—men, women, and children— constantly charted their course through the streets of the "Vienna of the East." Those traveling down Zamarstynówka Street would pass the ruins of the Tempel synagogue, the first reformed synagogue in Galicia (built in 1846), torched and dynamited the previous summer. An onlooker had noted approvingly that "it just collapsed on the spot, sinking down smoothly."[19] Once they passed behind the monumental city opera house, the passengers would know that they were headed for the Janowska camp. Now trundling along Janowska Street (renamed Weststrasse by the Nazis), many of them would have recognized the site of the Hasidic Aguda Shalom synagogue. The last thing these people would see before arriving at the camp would be the Cemetery Brigade from the ZAL-L breaking tombstones in the Jewish cemetery and tossing them into the back of trucks from various German businesses. And then they were at the entrance: a massive square stone arch supported by rectangular pillars, each topped with German eagle and a swastika. The iron gates were crudely decorated. The passengers had all heard of this place and knew it augured nothing good.

SS men counted each Jew as they dismounted from each truck or tram and entered the outer precinct of the camp.[20] From his window in the camp technical bureau overlooking the camp, architect and prisoner Zeev Porath watched the new arrivals sorted into those "capable of work and those incapable."[21] One prisoner estimated that 90 percent of the Jews were selected for deportation.[22] SS men stormed throughout the throng, lashing out with clubs, and shouting, "Anyone who won't give up the money will be shot immediately. There will be a strict inspection, and anyone found with gold or valuables will be shot." Steady streams of Jews poured their remaining valuables into buckets or baskets. A brave few, in a last act of resistance, "buried valuables in the sand, in order to at least avoid giving it up to *them*."[23]

The men, women, and children who arrived at the camp during the Great Aktion of August 1942 were then ordered to sit down in the outer square of the camp. When there were too many, as often happened, guards crowded them onto a field just north of the women's camp. Frequently, they would have to wait days without moving on the Sammelplatz before they would be loaded onto trains, suffering in the hot summer sun without food or water. Spotlights from the administration building crisscrossed the inner courtyard at night. Deputy camp commander SS-*Unterscharführer* (Sergeant) Richard Rokita hunted prey in these groups. Apparently blinded by the searchlight, he shouted to the commandant, "Gustav, dim those lights!" He then searched for those making the loudest noise and shot them. He continued shooting until all was quiet, often enough that he had to go back to the building to retrieve more ammunition.[24] On August 12, Porath recognized his former landlady, Mrs. Ebel, and her twenty-seven-year-old daughter among those nonworkers on the Sammelplatz. Before he could pass them some food, Rokita shot them both to death.²⁵

These temporary stays in the camp ended with fear and despair, either through death as Porath witnessed or through wrenching goodbyes. The Nazis divided families into those destined to labor and those destined to die. In the latter group that August was Rudolf Reder. He remembered, "At six o'clock in the morning, we were ordered to get up from the wet grass, and a long column of the doomed marched to the Kleparów railway station."²⁶ The Sammelplatz was empty except for the bodies of those shot by men like Rokita.

During the Great Aktion alone, around fifty thousand Jews from Lviv arrived in the Janowska camp, waited, walked the short distance to the nearby Kleparów station, were forced into cattle cars, and transported to the gas chambers of Bełżec where they were murdered on arrival. The camp was but a stop on the path to death, a path from which of the approximately five hundred thousand who traveled to Bełżec only two returned—including Reder.

THE BUNKER, 1943–44　　　　　　　49°51'12.55"N, 23°59'12.38"E

Sometime in late 1943, Joseph Wind fell into Nazi hands for the second time, recaptured after managing to escape from the infamous "Death Brigade" responsible for burning bodies. He arrived back at the camp, his footsteps falling on the road made of *matzevot* from the Jewish cemetery. But Wind and his group of strangers—another man and five women—did not make it past the gates. Instead, the SS men locked them in the "bunker": two small concrete rooms built into the gate itself.²⁷ Seven people, including a seventy-five-year-old woman, stood in the dark four-foot-by-four-foot cell, awaiting their fate.

Camp authorities had expanded the gate in autumn 1942, building these rectangular concrete detention cells with "grill door[s] facing into the camp." The cells were tiny; one witness said the cells could only accommodate two people.²⁸ The location and design of the "bunkers" was no accident. No prisoner could enter or leave the ZAL-L without knowing that they were incarcerated, under the total control of the Nazis. A survivor

Introduction　7

wrote, "It is precisely for this that these bunkers are here and designed in this manner: a view of the condemned should serve as a moral warning for the passing columns."²⁹ Having passed through these gates themselves, arrivals knew they had passed beyond the boundaries of humanity. Philosopher Giorgio Agamben could have been describing Janowska when he observed that "whoever entered the camp moved in a zone of indistinction between outside and inside, exception and rule, licit and illicit, in which the very concepts of subjective right and juridical protection no longer made any sense."³⁰

Of course, the suffering was not theoretical but was made flesh. Camp authorities used the bunker mostly for escapees and Jews caught hiding in Lviv after liquidations, often keeping them naked in the cold and damp of the claustrophobic darkness or simply leaving them to die. The record for survival was twelve days, held by an escapee who had been caught hiding in the ghetto.³¹ Most prisoners were taken out after a few days and shot to death. Only Wind survived of his group. A day after their arrival, a guard led them to an execution area behind the camp kitchen. Wind was standing on the edge of death when he was spared because as an electrician he was needed to repair the camp's air raid sirens. He had to wait, though, while the other six were executed.³² Some were never the same after this stay in the prison within a prison. Herman Lewinter recognized the wife of his best friend among the captives standing in the bunker. She was eventually released to the women's camp but was forever damaged. She could not work or function, and her fellow women prisoners did her work and covered for her as best they could.³³ Bronia Lubasz was caught passing as a Pole in June 1943 and her twenty-one-year-old son, Marcel, had to march past her in the bunker daily on his way to work. She was shot shortly thereafter.³⁴

This book is a history of a place—a place of imprisonment, of slave labor, of suffering, of murder, of theft, of resistance. It is also a history of the prisoners, the slave laborers and their overseers, the murderers, the thieves, the resisters, and the ordinary people who inhabited it. But the story of this place, the Janowska camp, is also the story of a city, a colony, and an empire. It is a story whose scale ranges from the trails into "the Sands" to Nazi decision-makers in Berlin. It is also a story of networks and connections, the individual movements of killers and the mass movement of Jews through a landscape of killing, enslavement, and death. But this is also an analysis of the *meaning* that these diverse individuals gave to the places they inhabited, meanings that evolved over time through changing circumstances and perspectives. This book is a history of a place that most have never heard of.

The Janowska camp in Lviv in what is now Ukraine offers the opportunity to craft what the great Holocaust historian Saul Friedländer has called "an integrative and integrated history."[35] In short, it opens "a window into the individual communities destroyed [and] to ... the interaction of Jews and perpetrators at the micro level," while not developing historical tunnel vision.[36] Yet this recognition of place also requires an exploration of its connections at a variety of scales without becoming a sterile recitation of bureaucratic crime. This book, then, seeks to provide a comprehensive approach highlighting the importance of this camp for understanding the nature of experience within its walls, its connections to the regional genocide of which it was a part, and the ways in which it represents both continuity with and divergence from similar organizations during the Holocaust.

Janowska (which is really a blanket term for the Zwangsarbeitslager-Lemberg [ZAL-L] or Forced Labor Camp-Lviv and the Deutsche Ausrüstungswerke-Lemberg [DAW-L] or German Equipment Works) stands out in the history of the Holocaust first and foremost for its hybrid nature, seen in the historical vignettes at the beginning of this introduction. One of the leading researchers on the camp, Thomas Sandkühler, has called it "an integral component of the annihilation of the Jews, both in its initial phase and during its execution."[37] Janowska was not officially a concentration camp as it did not fall under the Nazi Inspectorate of Camps, but it served a similar function. The complex played, almost from its inception, three distinct roles simultaneously. First, it was a slave labor camp designed to hold primarily Jews—both those who had violated Nazi anti-Jewish policies and those who had done nothing. In this way it also functioned as an instrument of terror for the city of Lviv, given its proximity and the fact that the majority of its prisoners were locals. In its role as a forced labor camp, Janowska served the German colonial economy. This took several forms: the construction of the camp, the workshops within it, the brigades of prisoners leased to local businesses who left the camp in the morning and returned each day, and those who were transferred to other sites of labor such as the important Durchgangstrasse IV (DG IV) or Highway 4 intended to be a main military artery across Ukraine.

Second, this small plot of land two miles from the city center functioned as a transit camp for hundreds of thousands of Jews from both Lviv and the surrounding area who would be sent on to further labor and suffering or to death in the gas chambers of Bełżec fifty miles away. It stood at the center of a network of deportations bringing in Jews from the countryside and also serving as the city's collection point for Jews destined to die. City streetcars brought Lviv Jews from the nearby ghetto to the camp where they were marched to the Kleparów train station, a small freight station only three hundred yards from the main entrance of the camp. It facilitated the movement of Jewish labor throughout the region. The camp also took in and sent out perpetrators. This kind of network has not been investigated, yet it was pivotal to the Holocaust in Galicia (Western Ukraine) and elsewhere. SS men often began their service in Janowska and then left to command their own ghettos and work camps in the local environs. Often, the men assigned to these locations returned to the Janowska camp again. Groups of SS also left the camp to assist in the liquidation of these same Jewish populations. These personnel movements carried modes of behavior, procedures, experiences, and relationships along with them. These men knew each other and often had for extended periods of time.

Finally, and perhaps most importantly, the Janowska camp operated as a site for the extermination of Jews (and others) almost from its inception. This is an important distinction from other camps that also certainly murdered prisoners. Janowska SS not only killed sick prisoners or those incapable of labor; they also carried out mass shootings of Jews that resembled *Einsatzgruppen* killings more than the routine individual murders of other camps. In addition, once the extermination center for the region, the Bełżec camp, ceased operation in December 1942, all killing operations for the area shifted to Janowska. Tens of thousands met their deaths in the sandy ravines north of the camp. Janowska thus was very much "an integral element in the destruction of the Jews both in its start-up phase and during its execution, above all in 1942 [during the] so-called 'Operation

Reinhard."[38] In his book on mass shootings, Father Patrick Desbois writes that "in Ukraine there were no extermination camps, no barbed wire to separate the condemned from their assassins."[39] He is wrong here. While Janowska was not an extermination center like the *Operation Reinhard* camps, it *was* a dedicated, continuously operational killing site whose death toll raises its profile above most other camps that participated in dedicated killing operations.

Thus, this relatively unknown camp played a disproportionate role in the Holocaust in Galicia. Thomas Sandkühler has estimated that perhaps as many as eighty thousand people, mainly Jews, were murdered in or around the camp.[40] This exceeds the number killed at the Majdanek concentration camp, which is commonly considered part of the canon of extermination centers. Indeed, one scholar has written that "although there were no gas chambers in Janowska, it is likely that more people were murdered there, mostly by shooting than at Majdanek."[41] Wendy Lower describes the camp as "the biggest Jewish labor and transit camp in Ukraine."[42] If we consider those directly murdered there as well as those who passed through on their way to the gas chambers, and those Jews murdered by Janowska men throughout the region, the deadly footprint of the camp grows considerably.[43]

Janowska's influence did not end with the war either. In 1966, the camp formed a significant part of the Lemberg (Lviv) Trial in Stuttgart, lasting 18 months with 214 witnesses and 15 defendants. Simon Wiesenthal predicted in 1967 that "the scope of the forthcoming Galicia trial [of which Janowska was a part] will surpass the Auschwitz trial in Frankfurt."[44] He was wrong in that, but only barely; the Stuttgart Lviv Trial *was* the second longest in German history, second only to that Frankfurt Trial. In addition, investigations and trials of Janowska criminals dragged on throughout the 1960s and 1970s. The postwar search for justice yields chilling insights into not only the perpetrators themselves but also the attempts by the German people to confront or ignore their Nazi past.

Yet no major study of the camp has been written. This is perhaps not surprising given general trends in the history of the Holocaust. As one scholar notes, "although Soviet Ukraine's Jews represented the second largest Jewish community in Europe prior to the Second World War, scholars have largely neglected the history of this community's destruction (and even more so the destruction of the Russian Federation's Jews)."[45] This is not to say Janowska is unknown to scholars. One of the earliest Holocaust historians, Philip Friedman, himself a survivor from Lviv, discussed it in his history of the Holocaust as early as 1945. It receives mention in studies of the Holocaust in Lviv and in larger histories of the city itself, but rarely with the detail and focus it deserves.[46] There are many reasons for this beginning with the general absence of the Soviet Union from writings on the Holocaust until its collapse in the 1990s. Another is the (relatively) low number of survivors from Lviv itself, let alone the camp. A third is the fate of the ground itself. The camp never ceased being a prison; it just changed hands from Germans to Soviets to Ukrainians. It never became a museum or a memorial, had there even been any real interest in making it one. Last, like Poles, Ukrainians have a difficult relationship with World War II and the Holocaust. The actions of Ukrainians as collaborators both with the Nazis in general and in the murder of the Jews complicate narratives of Jewish suffering. Thus, Ukrainian nationalists tend to minimize or avoid altogether both the Holocaust and their own role in it. So, for most outside of the academic community, the Janowska camp disappeared into the fog of its own small valley in Lviv and into the mists of time.

In spite of all this, abundant source material regarding the camp exists. Multiple survivors of the camp and the Holocaust in Lviv (not least Simon Wiesenthal) have written memoirs of their experience. Though most of the original camp records have been lost, the Lviv Trial, given its length and scope, created a simply massive chronicle of the camp both in its rare verbatim transcription and in the extensive media coverage it received. Volumes of witness statements from survivors, perpetrators, Ukrainian collaborators, onlookers, and investigators add another source layer in Hebrew, German, Polish, Yiddish, Ukrainian, and Russian. These testimonies exist along a lengthy chronological arc, from those taken by the Soviets in 1944 to the Eichmann Trial in 1961 to the video testimonies of the 1990s. Maps and photographs, often underutilized by scholars, provide important spatial evidence. An even less examined source is the body of drawings, both artistic and architectural, done by prisoners themselves, which provide factual evidence and human insight into the experience and operations of the camp. What is unique about this history, however, is that it must be reconstructed with almost no wartime German documents from the camp. In the case of Janowska, the usually helpful Nazi obsession with documentation has left us with little.

However, what has not been attempted thus far is a detailed and integrated study of the unique characteristics of the camp and daily life there as well as of its relationship to local, regional, and national policy. Compiling and analyzing the travels and experiences of the SS in the camp along with the qualitative evidence of their behavior also allows for the analysis of a social network that reveals the significance of movement, even in the history of a stationary organization. The history of the camp cannot be viewed in isolation from the history of Lviv during World War II any more than it can be separated from Nazi policy in Galicia and the *Generalgouvernement* (General Government). At these scales, the history of the camp and the Holocaust in Lviv provides insight into how Nazi policy evolved and changed over time and space.

At the level of the camp itself, there is much to be learned as well. Maps (both traditional and those drawn by witnesses), aerial photographs, and drawings of the camp by prisoners provide a framework on which to hang an immense amount of testimony. These allow us to then examine the camp as a collection of spaces imbued with emotion (fear, safety) and the imprint of behaviors associated with them (killing, resistance, sexual violence). Adding testimony to landscape allows a mapping of experience and emotion onto the more traditional, empirical depictions of space. The ground and the built environment do not remain neutral; they impact our lives daily. If, as one historian argues, "what we (humanity) share is the experience of both choice and necessity, agency and restraint," then we also share the tyranny and benevolence of the environment impacting that experience.[47] For both prisoners and guards, the terrain and construction of the camp played a determinative factor in their lives. This history recognizes that and incorporates a spatial sensitivity.

Good histories are stories, and stories are about specific people and places. The best histories use the lives of particular people in particular places at particular times to give us critical insights about the larger experience of an event. Investigating broader historical moments from a local perspective is often called "microhistory," and it is the preferred approach in this book. This perspective "leads in and of itself to comparative queries and, more generally, to connections that are otherwise but dimly perceived."[48] If we are to avoid in Holocaust studies the "tendency toward 'encylopedism'" and the risk of the "sacrifice of analytic depth on the altar of detail," then such microhistory must speak to a larger argument, must fit in to more universal discussion, and must demonstrate its relevance to the critical questions we ask of the past.[49]

This book, then, immerses us in the difficult and painful history of the camp at 134 Janowska Street. But it also incorporates the experience and influence of the city of Lviv with its large Jewish population. It strives to avoid indiscriminate description by relating the lived experience in the camp to the changes in Nazi policy at larger scales and to pivotal moments across the continent whose aftershocks were felt in the camp. The excavation of networked connections between the camp and the Holocaust writ large helps place Janowska in the larger context of the Nazi genocidal project. Likewise, this book personalizes the generic Holocaust identities of perpetrators, victim, and bystander in the actors connected with the camp. This allows, for example, the voice of the survivors and the victims "by its eloquence or its clumsiness, by the immediacy of the cry of terror, or by the naivety of unfounded hope, [to] tear through the fabric of the 'detached' and 'objective' historical rendition."[50] The Janowska camp serves as a specific lens through which to observe and analyze not only the unfolding of policy but also the diverse ways that individuals negotiated the extraordinary historical moments in which they lived. Finally, it provides a lens through which to explore the seemingly exceptional violence of the place in order to perhaps understand how aberrant behavior becomes normal.

City of Lions 1

> This city lies in the arms of two enemies, and each wants
> to dominate it. Subterranean enmity and violence are
> fermenting in the background.
> —Alfred Döblin, *Reise in Polen*, 1924

In 1845, Ukrainian poet Taras Shevchenko asked of his own people "Who are we? Whose sons? Of what sires?"[1] He might well have been speaking of Lviv specifically, for the city was certainly born of many fathers. It was a border city and a multicultural landscape before that terminology entered our lexicon. Before we encounter the Holocaust in Lviv, we must examine this "Paris of the East," and the vibrant Jewish life that was forever destroyed or damaged by the years 1941–44. Throughout its history, Lviv also reflected the policies of the various empires to which it belonged; as a result, it not infrequently witnessed the fermenting violence that Döblin observed in the interwar period.

Prince Danylo of Galicia founded the city in 1256, naming it after Lev, King of Rus'. Upon Lev's death in 1301, the city came under the control of Poland for the next four hundred years, which helped solidify its multiethnic composition.[2] Straddling two important medieval trade routes, it became an important economic center in eastern Europe.[3] The constant passage of merchants and goods brought together the Poles, Ukrainians, and Jews who would make up most of the city's population until 1944. Other groups such as Germans and Roma arrived also. The three main ethnicities (Poles, Ukrainians, and Jews) settled into a sometimes tense but generally workable relationship. Polish supremacy was, in many ways, welcomed by the Jews of Galicia, particularly as Poland encouraged their settlement in its lands as a path to economic modernization.

A Jewish Quarter was established in the city by 1356, and its Jewish residents enjoyed the relative autonomy of the kahal system of self-government. Though seen by many as the "golden age" of Jewry in eastern Europe, the medieval and early modern periods were not without violence, particularly for the Jewish community. Between 1498 and 1500, Christian crusaders attacked in Jews in Lviv on their way to fight the Turks.[4] Above all, the seventeenth-century bloodletting by the Cossack chief (and Ukrainian folk hero) Bohdan Khmelnytsky left an indelible scar on the Jews of Galicia as they found themselves caught in the middle of a violent revolt against Polish rule.[5] Khmelnytsky's Cossacks targeted and massacred Jews throughout the region both as a group privileged by the Poles and a religious group. Estimates of the number of Jews murdered during the Khmelnytsky massacres range from 40,000 to 100,000.

The terror unleashed by Khmelnytsky's Cossacks introduced many of the political frictions that characterized life in Lviv (and Ukraine) before World War II. Polish control and Ukrainian nationalist aspirations caused constant tension with Jews often caught in the middle. Even when Poland ceased to exist during the three partitions of the eighteenth century, tensions remained, as did yearnings for independence. Antisemitism in its religious and other forms continued manifesting itself both through violence and discrimination. Simultaneously, the city became ever more metropolitan and diverse under the Poles and later Habsburgs. But its position as a borderland city, an entangling "swamp" in Joseph Roth's words, would not change until the end of World War II.[6]

"Paris of the East": Lviv from the Habsburgs to 1918

With the first partition of Poland in 1772, Lviv became part of the Austro-Hungarian Empire, which controlled it until 1918. The Austrians rechristened the city with the more Germanic-sounding "Lemberg" and honored it as the capital of the Kingdom of Galicia. Under Habsburg rule, the population increased from 87,000 in 1869 to 212,000 in 1914.[7] This period transformed the city into the "Paris of the East," and was responsible for an architectural style (much of which remains today) as well as a cosmopolitan and diverse population (which largely does not).

A glance at the city's population by religious denomination in 1910 gives us some idea of the national makeup as well: Catholics were almost always Poles, and Greek Catholics were often, but not always, Ukrainian.[8] Of course, these identities were not always fixed and did not always reflect ethnicity. Even under Austrian control, Poles carried out a successful program of Polonization that would make Lviv very much a Polish city until 1945. The Austrian Empire "always appointed a *Polish* politician as governor of Galicia" from 1848 to 1915, demonstrating their preference for Poles over Ukrainians in local government.[9]

Table 1. Lviv city population by religious denomination, 1910

POP.	ROMAN CATHOLIC	% OF POP.	GREEK CATHOLIC	% OF POP.	JEWISH	% OF POP.	OTHER	% OF POP.
206,100	105,200	51.2	39,300	19.2	57,400	27.8	3,900	1.8

Despite ethnic tensions simmering beneath the surface, the city's grandeur shown through clearly to any visitor. One could take in an opera (arias in Italian, choruses in Polish) at the beautiful Lviv Opera House, crowned by statues of Glory, Poetry, and Music, which opened in 1900.[10] Or join 1,459 other theatergoers for a play at the Skarbek Theater founded by the Polish noble Count Stanisław Marcin Skarbek, who created the building's foundations with 16,000 oak logs from his own estate.[11]

A leisurely stroll in the evening carried one down large boulevards, past statues of the famous Polish poet Adam Mickiewicz; the great Polish king Jan Sobieski III; and Stanisław Jabłonowksi, a Polish nobleman who beat back the Ottomans during the Battle of Vienna in 1683. Of course, the statues of Ukrainian folk heroes like King Danylo in modern-day Lviv were absent. The city hall sat in a spacious market square, with fountains at the four points honoring Greek gods. Two recumbent lions guarded the entrance to the municipal building.[12] Past the grand promenades, one could explore winding cobblestone streets filled with shops and restaurants from which voices and music spilled into the crisp night air. The city's cafés and coffeehouses were "more like social institutions: neutral places where people meet people" much as one would find in Paris or Vienna.[13]

At the time of World War I, Lviv boasted a musical conservatory with lineage back to Mozart's son, two major universities (Lviv Polytechnic and Franz I University of Lviv), a medical school, multiple seminaries, and the only military academy in Galicia. The Rappaport Jewish hospital as well as several others, a children's clinic, an orphanage, several sanatoriums and asylums provided for the health of the community. Multiple parks offered peaceful retreats from bustling city life. Holocaust survivor Arnon Rubin remembered his time as a child wandering in the Łyczaków (Lychakiv) forest, feeding squirrels and playing games with his friends there.[14] The future of the forest would be as dark as the shadows in which he played.

Jewish life blossomed in the vibrant city—the home of the great Jewish philosopher Martin Buber. Imperial Austria offered more freedom for Jews and a "progressive integration into political life."[15] It was home to forty synagogues from Hasidic to Reform, a hundred fifty prayer houses, as well as Jewish schools and newspapers. The Gimpel Theater Troupe performed Yiddish plays and music at the Colosseum Theater, the second-largest theater in Lviv. Directors of Jewish theater from around the world sent promising actors to Gimpel's group for training.[16] Yiddish literature flourished. In the renowned Rubin antiquarian bookshop, across from the Carmelite convent on Batorego Street, rabbi David Kahane and future historian of the Holocaust in Lviv Tadeusz Zaderecki discussed the Talmud and Judaism.[17]

For sports fans, the Jewish Hasmonea Lwów sports club provided a competitive soccer team that played in the topflight Polish First League. Its stadium was the largest in the city. Hometown hero Zygmunt Steuermann also played for the Polish National team where he set a record as one of only two players to notch a hat trick in their first appearance.[18]

By 1900, 20 percent of students in Lviv's universities were Jews. By 1914, 60 percent of the city's doctors were Jewish and 70 percent of its "lawyers and members of the chamber of trade and commerce."[19] In many ways, the period of Habsburg rule represented a second "golden age" for the Jews of Lviv. Still, despite cultural and legal freedoms, Austrians, Poles, and, later, Ukrainians controlled the political destiny of the city. And, as always, riches did not fall on all equally. Grinding poverty, among other factors, drove three hundred fifty thousand Jews to leave Galicia between 1880 and 1914.[20] And in the years before World War I, general ethnic tension flared in Lviv. In 1908, a Ukrainian student assassinated the Polish Governor Potocki in retaliation for a decline in Ukrainian representation in parliament.[21] Two years later, violence flared over the status of Ukrainian representation, this time in Lviv's universities—one Ukrainian student was killed and a hundred thirty were arrested on July 1, 1910.[22]

World War I brought suffering, distrust, and fear while fanning the flames of ethnic tensions. The city's Jewish population found itself caught in the middle. Two weeks after the war started, by August 17, forty-seven Russian divisions headed for Galicia, with the aim of capturing its capital.[23] Soon fighting raged throughout the region. Russian Cossacks cut down a "crazy-brave" Austrian regimental commander and 12 percent of his men in a meaningless skirmish over the nearby town of Bełżec, a place that had only begun to see blood spilled and which would host the gas chambers that murdered the Jews of Lviv.[24] Incompetence ruled as Austrian and Russian forces stood toe to toe like exhausted heavyweight boxers.

The Russians captured the city on September 3, 1914, bringing with them a hundred thousand refugees including forty thousand Jews "with memories of pogroms still in their bones."[25] Among those who had fled in 1914 fearing antisemitic pogroms were future Polish national team striker Zygmunt Steuermann and his family; Steuermann later served as an artilleryman in the Austrian army on the Italian front.[26] Russian entry into the city brought looting and violence. On September 27, shots were fired in downtown Lviv, supposedly at Russian soldiers. An alternate rumor blamed Russian soldiers shooting at their own officers.[27] A swift, violent, and sadly predictable reaction followed. Rumors immediately circulated blaming the Jews. Russian soldiers and Cossacks surged toward the Jewish Quarter. Cossacks shot out windows on Walowa Street, home to Jewish "professionals and tradesmen." They were joined by Russian soldiers and a local mob that "broke into Jewish apartments and wine warehouses, and after imbibing, began to shoot indiscriminately."[28] Bodies, including those of children, lay on the sidewalks. Galicia's Russian governor general, Count Vladimir Bobrinskiy, arrested over four hundred Jews "as an insurance against Jewish denunciation and spying." By spring 1915, that number had increased to five thousand from the city itself.²⁹ Foreshadowing later victimization of Jews, "local residents guided soldiers to Jewish apartments and participated in the looting." All told, between twenty and fifty Jews were murdered in this first, irrational spasm of violence.³⁰ Unfortunately, this was not an isolated event. A Russian officer placed the violence in historical context, describing the "shadow of pogroms" that accompanied the Russian army on the Eastern Front. "People might say that these are just 'anecdotes,'" he wrote, "but they're much more than that; they are monuments to our modern history."³¹ In times of crisis and upheaval, non-Jews seemed to turn on their Jewish neighbors.

The Russian stay in Lviv was brief as they were thrown out by the Austrians (stiffened by German support) in the spring of 1915. The city would remain in Austrian hands until the end of the war, but its liberation did not end the city's suffering. Throughout the war, shortages of food and essential items plagued its residents. In a story repeated throughout history, uncertainty, privation, and unrest led to an increase in antisemitism as well. Lviv newspaper *Słowo Polskie* (The Polish Word) printed antisemitic accusations that the Jews had been supporters of the Tsar. This claim even found its way into official reports from the military; General Riml informed Vienna that "the behavior of the Jews of Lviv during the Russian invasion gave great offense to the rest of the population, generating a previously unknown degree of antisemitism."³² Jews were also accused of attempting to "evade military service using all sorts of tricks and deceits."³³

Beyond just antisemitism, the war exacerbated other rivalries. As one scholar noted, "the worst result of the war ... was the irreparable harm done to interethnic relationships."³⁴ As the Austro-Hungarian Empire collapsed in on itself and the new Soviet Union struggled to its feet in 1918, a window of opportunity opened in Galicia, a moment both Poles and Ukrainians seized in attempts to assert their dominance and independence. For the next three years, Poles, Ukrainians, and the Soviets would battle in a bitter civil war and Lviv would be one of the battlefields. Polish and Ukrainian factions clashed in the streets.

The civil war in Lviv reminded the Jews again of their precarious situation. At the very beginning, in an extraordinary show of unity, all Jewish organizations, regardless of political or religious stripes set up a "security committee... to maintain order and preserve the public peace in the Jewish districts." Lviv's Jewish leaders realized that aligning with either side would open them to violence from the other. The best course seemed to be avoiding any participation in the conflict. Thus, the kahal adhered to a position of "strict neutrality" and set up a militia unit of "Jewish soldiers from the Habsburg Army" to maintain order and protect Jewish property.[35] Neutrality did not spare the Jews of Lviv from bloodshed, however. Rumors flew that the Jewish militias had attacked Polish troops, even that they had "poured boiling water on them."[36] Non-Jews saw betrayal rather than an impossible situation for Jews. Stoked by existing antisemitism, Polish fighters engaged in a three-day pogrom of arson, looting, assaulting, raping, and killing Jewish residents. Jews reported that ordinary Polish citizens had taken part. As one noted: "It is an interesting and sad business that in addition to members of the military, persons from the so-called 'superior middle classes' also joined in the attacks, the women wearing fur coats and gloves; among those doing the plundering you could see civil servants, high school teachers, persons who were attending university, etc."[37] In yet another meeting of past, present, and future, non-Jews took advantage of an uncertain situation to victimize their Jewish neighbors while simultaneously accusing them of disloyalty. In the end, the Allies backed the reborn Poland in 1919 and Lviv now became (for Poles) a "stronghold of the Polish state in the hostile environment of the eastern 'borderlands.'"[38]

However, the life of the Second Polish Republic began with yet another war, almost immediately after the Polish-Ukrainian conflict as the Soviet Union sought to bring western Galicia under its control. The Polish-Soviet War was, at times, a close-run affair, but an audacious counterattack by Marshal Piłsudski near Warsaw known as the "Miracle on the Vistula" shattered Soviet military hopes. Among the Polish soldiers driving the Soviets back was future Polish soccer star Zygmunt Steuermann who had returned to Lviv from Vienna.[39] According to the 1921 Treaty of Riga, Lviv would remain a Polish city, even if "an 'island' in a Ukrainian 'sea.'"[40]

Lviv in Poland

Conditions varied in the interwar years, as they did across Poland but turbulence was never far away. A startling diversity of vocal parties electrified the world of Polish politics, representing nationalists, antisemites, Communists, Ukrainians, Germans, and multiple Jewish constituencies. Marshal Piłsudski's time as leader of Poland exhibited a unique mixture of authoritarianism and democracy. In the end, Jews, in particular, remembered Piłsudski's era fondly, if perhaps nostalgically. Samuel Drix in Lviv remembered that Piłsudski "curbed the influence of the nationalists" and that "anti-Semitism was rarely violent."[41] But sporadic incidents continued to mar the twenties. Polish university students attacked a Jewish Zionist student—ironically enough near the café De La Paix (Of the Peace)—on Legionów Street on May 29, 1923. They beat him with a stick until a policeman (badge number 30278) intervened, but refused to make an arrest, explaining, "I cannot, after all, arrest a Pole." The Jewish newspaper *Chwila* reported this and many other incidents to its concerned readers.[42] When reflecting on his time as a student in Lviv, Frank Stiffel quipped that he saw Poland in black and blue, not the national red and white.[43]

Ukrainians were less likely to remember Piłsudski with fondness. In 1930, the Ukrainian Military Organization (UVO) brazenly declared that "by means of individual assassinations and occasional mass actions, we will attract large numbers of the population to the idea of liberation and into the revolutionary ranks."[44] By 1934, the UVO had merged into the Organization of Ukrainian Nationalists (OUN) led by Stepan Bandera. The OUN carried out more than two hundred attacks on Poles between July and November 1930 alone. Three years later in Lviv, it assassinated the Soviet consul in retaliation for the manmade famine (the Holodomor) in Ukraine.[45]

Things deteriorated for Jews as well when Roman Dmowski's Far-Right Endek Party took control. The ironically titled National Democracy Party did not shrink from openly pursuing antisemitic policies and demanding assimilation from minorities rather than protecting them. In Lviv, the government's funding priorities signaled a turn to the Right. The local government slashed the 1935 allotment for Jewish welfare services, even though Jewish taxes represented a considerable percentage of overall revenue.[46] The national government's increasingly heavy-handed attempts at Polonization, solidifying Polish culture as dominant, led to attacks on Jews, often led by university students as universities became hotbeds of antisemitism between 1921 and 1939. The percentage of Jewish students in all Polish universities dropped from 24.6 to 8.2 percent as a result.[47] In November and December 1932, students in Lviv attacked Jews in the streets and cafés, leading to arrests. Angry Poles, mostly students, beat a Jewish postal official to death. They looted Jewish homes and burned the Hasmonai sports house to the ground. Officials closed the Lviv University in an attempt to restore order.[48] In this time period, Polish students beat Samuel Drix with a stick while a professor witnessed and did nothing.[49] The Lviv Polytechnic University continued to be at the center of both Polish nationalism and accompanying antisemitism. Raphael Lemkin, who would go on to coin the term "genocide," had attended law school there a few years earlier where he had argued with his professors that "sovereignty cannot be conceived as the right to kill millions of innocent people."[50] The same university earned the dubious distinction of being the first university in Poland to reintroduce the "ghetto benches," requiring Jewish students to set on special benches in the backs of classrooms.[51]

Violence peaked in 1938 and 1939 when two Jewish students were murdered on campus. One victim, Markus Landesberg, was honored at his funeral by a demonstration of twelve thousand locals, including many Poles attending in solidarity.[52] In 1939, a man and a woman beat and scratched a Jewish man and were arrested. However, by the time of the trial, the man, a Polish law student, had escaped Lviv and the woman did not appear in court, citing illness. This apparently ended the prosecution.[53] One month later, however, the violence of the "ghetto benches" and bigoted students was overshadowed by the coming of the war that would change life in Lviv forever.

The Soviet Occupation

During the night of August 31, 1939, an SS squad crept through the dark woods toward the radio station in the small eastern German town of Gleiwitz (Gliwice). They "attacked" the station, killing a politically "unreliable" ethnic German in the process. Trucks arrived with the corpses of murdered inmates from the Dachau concentration camp who were then dressed in Polish uniforms and spread around the building as "evidence" of this Polish provocation. It was the quintessential false-flag attack. Among the perpetrators was thirty-four-year-old ethnic German Josef Grzimek, an SS man who would later command the remnants of the Lviv ghetto.⁵⁴ All along the frontier, similar faked provocations took place. Lviv citizens had already begun digging antitank trenches on August 29 with, according to one Jewish newspaper, "ostentatious participation of the Jewish population."⁵⁵ The next day, the German Army crossed the border and the greatest cataclysm in European history began. The Second World War came as quickly to Lviv as the first. German bombs began raining down on the train station and airport within hours. Ten days later, artillery shells started falling in the city.⁵⁶

For the briefest of moments, German troops occupied parts of the city, attacking from the southwest on September 12. Hasty barricades choked the broad Gródecka Street, which ran past the grand train station.⁵⁷ Elements of the German 1st Mountain Division fought their way down Janowska Street but Polish forces halted their advance; a small but solid defense also stopped them at the main train station.⁵⁸ However, in accordance with the secret portion of the Nazi-Soviet Pact of August 1939, the Soviets, not the Germans, accepted the Polish surrender of the city and entered Lviv on September 22, ushering in another period of climactic change for both the city and the parts of Poland the Soviets had gained through their deal with the devil.

Many Jews in Lviv (and Poland) welcomed the Soviets as conquerors, given that the Nazis were the alternative. One of them was Arnon Rubin. As he and his family watched Soviet tanks rolling into Lviv, they "embraced each other and ... wept from joy. [They] were saved from the Nazi beasts."⁵⁹ Yet Jewish responses occupied both ends of the spectrum. A Jew in Tarnopol, seventy miles from Lviv, expressed the mood succinctly: "The unexpected events were met by the Jewish population with mixed feelings. First of all, there was a sense of relief, we were spared the agonies of Hitlerism.... The truth is that the communist regime also presented its own dangers, but these were of a different kind."⁶⁰ Regardless, the *appearance* of overwhelming support for the Soviets would have devastating repercussions when a more permanent Nazi occupation returned.

Chaos reigned in the first days of the occupation. Seventy thousand refugees fleeing the Germans arrived in Lviv in "streams of human wreckage," finding not sanctuary but Soviet attempts to force them back. The Red Army looted shops and killed shopkeepers who resisted.⁶¹ So, too, did the local population. Opportunistic citizens ransacked abandoned train cars full of food and supplies standing at the Kleparów station.⁶² The decision of which side of the border to run to left no good options. The Jews of Lviv grimly shared a joke about passengers from two trains, one heading east (to the Soviets) and one west (to the Germans): each group looked at the other and exclaimed in Yiddish "Bist a mishige? (Have you gone out of your mind?)."⁶³

Once order was restored, Soviet policy in Lviv (and throughout Poland) aimed at incorporating the new territory into the Soviet state. A stocky new head of the Ukrainian Communist Party named Nikita Khrushchev arrived from Moscow to oversee the transition in the new UKRSSR. The Soviet culture wars swept through the city. Polish symbols were torn down, streets renamed, Soviet imagery liberally spread throughout the city. The clocks were set to Moscow time. For religious citizens of Lviv (Jewish, Catholic, or Orthodox), the Soviet occupation was almost uniformly a time of ruin. Prohibitive taxation targeted religious institutions of all faiths, and failure to pay could result in closure.

Soviet economic policies almost immediately ushered in a period of greater hardship. The Red Army and Soviet carpetbaggers descended like locusts on local retail. Out of eighty-five hundred shops in Lviv, sixty-four hundred sold out their entire inventory in the first weeks of the occupation. Because the Soviets imported little of value, most shop owners were unable to restock and "were effectively bankrupted." This run on the stores disproportionately affected Jews, given their overrepresentation in this sector.⁶⁴ More official theft through nationalization followed. In October 1939, "banks, land, heavy industries and other large enterprises" in Lviv were nationalized. Fortunate owners were allowed to stay on as foremen in their own factories.⁶⁵ Even the Lviv Opera House building itself became the property of the UKRSSR.⁶⁶ One of the businesses nationalized and shuttered was the Steinhaus Company, which occupied open ground on the western outskirts of the city, at 134 Janowskastrasse. This territory would become the Janowska camp two years later.⁶⁷ Families were affected as well. Samuel Drix's family lost their small business to the state and was left to look for work elsewhere.⁶⁸ Leon Wells's father had moved his family to Lviv after financial success in a rural village and had invested in an apartment building but was reduced to working as its caretaker.

Worse was to come. Without a doubt, the violent Soviet repression and deportation of Polish citizens dominates the memory of their occupation. Throughout Poland, the Soviet secret police apparatus rounded up or executed thousands of Poles, Jews, and Ukrainians. Lviv was not immune from this program. Indeed, the memory and effects of this violence would have a significant impact on the Holocaust there.

Repression began rapidly as Soviet officials sought to reshape Poland into a Soviet state by removing both real and imagined political enemies. However, as the mask of the "worker's paradise" quickly slipped, arrest and imprisonment became the true face of occupation. A law professor from Lviv gave the famous Polish resistance agent Jan Karski the following report for his superiors: "There is one thing you must understand and tell the men in Warsaw. Conditions here are very different, indeed. For one thing, the Gestapo and GPU [Soviet Secret Police] are two entirely different organisations. The men of the Russian secret police are more clever and better trained. Their police methods are superior. They are less crude, more scientific and systematic."[69] Meanwhile, under Khrushchev's watchful eye, the deportation apparatus of the Soviet Union swung into motion as well. Pacifying a region by removing "unreliable" elements of the population was a tried-and-true tactic for Stalin's men. The Soviets deported between 309,000 and 980,000 Polish citizens from occupied Poland between 1939 and 1941.[70] Ten days after the Soviet invasion, the secret police had arrested almost 1,000 people in the Lviv region and had recruited 130 informants in the city itself. Among the arrested were Lviv's mayor and his administration. Two hundred twenty-six Polish officers in Lviv were arrested in one night. A convoy containing two hundred of perhaps these same Polish officers left Lviv headed for Jeziorna, where elements of the Soviet terror apparatus shot them all near a small stream.

By the end of the Soviet occupation, the Lviv secret police had "processed" 20,450 prisoners.[71] They arrested Moritz Grünbart in the spring of 1941 and took him to the eighteenth-century Brygidki Prison just three hundred yards west of the Lviv Opera House.[72] In the former Polish military prison Zamarstynów, Aleksander Wat shared a ten-foot-by-ten-foot cell with twenty-eight other prisoners.[73] A prisoner in a Lviv jail described the misery of the situation: "Every night they call out some of the condemned:

some of them are given hard labor for life, others are taken into the cellars where the executioners carry out the death sentence with a shot in the back of the skull. If you stay in the death cell for a month it gives you hope that your sentence will be changed."[74]

Deportations and arrests struck Lviv in waves. Between April 9 and 14, 1940, approximately 12,000 people were deported from the city, including Jews and Polish family members of military and police officers.[75] Nazi authorities sent a commission to the city in May 1940 ostensibly to offer refugees the option of returning to German-occupied Poland. Seventy-five percent of refugees (mostly Poles) registered to return.[76] Unable to process so many, the Germans left mostly empty-handed. The Soviets then hunted down those who had so clearly rejected the new order and deported them. Refugees without Soviet passports or with transient status found themselves on trains to the interior of the Soviet Union as well. Many of these deportees boarded boxcars at a small freight station named Kleparów on the outskirts of the city across from the grounds of the former Steinhaus Company. The arrests and deportations terrorized the population, including the Wells family. Leon's father hid every night in the basement of the apartment building he once owned until he decided that if they were to be deported, they should go as a family and he returned to the apartment to await his fate.[77]

On June 22, 1941, almost two years exactly after the Soviets arrived in Lviv, the Nazis turned on their erstwhile allies and launched the largest military operation in history. That Sunday morning, three million German soldiers drove into the Soviet Union as part of Operation Barbarossa, named after a long-dead German king who would rise from the dead to save Germany in its hour of need. It was, in the end, an inauspicious name as Frederick Barbarossa had fallen from his horse during the Third Crusade and drowned in waist-deep water. But for the moment it caught the Red Army completely unawares. One Russian unit radioed its headquarters that it was under attack and was told: "You must be insane and why is your signal not in code?"[78] A stunned Stalin failed to appear before his embattled nation, leaving Foreign Minister Molotov the difficult task of both addressing the people and overcoming his stutter. "Let Molotov do it," the shaken dictator repeated.[79] The first days of the invasion shattered the confidence of the "Man of Steel," who withdrew to his private dacha for some time. Meanwhile, the Wehrmacht slashed deep into Soviet territory, surrounding hundreds of thousands of Red Army troops in massive "cauldrons" to be eliminated by follow-on forces. It would reach Lviv within a week.

The invasion threw the city's administration into a panic. The speed of the Nazi advance and the disintegration of Red Army forces on the border made it clear that the city would soon fall. Less than twenty-four hours after the bombs fell on the airfield, the Soviet Sixth Army ordered the city to be evacuated.[80] While ashes from burning documents filled the air near government buildings, the Soviet system of repression accelerated rather than slowed.

Precisely how many civilians the Soviets murdered in the last days of June 1941 remains somewhat unclear. Official Soviet documents state that 2,464 prisoners were murdered, 808 officially released, and 1,546 abandoned.[81] This must be seen as the lowest estimate; certainly, more than 3,000 were killed. When the Soviets withdrew from the city, an eerie silence fell upon the streets of the "Paris of the East." Moritz Grünbart emerged cautiously from his cell in the Brygidki prison and stumbled across a courtyard full of "at least several hundred" bodies.[82] If the Soviet occupation's first act had to been to fill Lviv's prisons with prisoners, its last act was to fill them with corpses. Helene Kaplan, a Jewish teenager, watched a "seemingly endless line" of trucks carrying Russian troops crawling out of the city. Their faces were "somber, showing fear, and to a certain degree, hatred." Recognizing a Russian schoolmate in one of the cars, she ran toward him, only to hear him shout, "You all hated us so much. Now you will have the Germans here."[83] And so they would.

Ein Furioso 2

> To stop an elderly man peacefully walking in the street and then to force him to stand at attention while slamming his face for no reason and without pity, is something one has to learn. A diligent student soon masters the game on his own, his peasant greed bidding him to combine amusement with practicality.
>
> —Edmund Kessler, Lviv

On Sunday morning, June 30, Lviv changed hands for the second time in as many years. German reconnaissance troops on motorcycles with sidecars roared into the city from the west, down Janowska Street, past the Steinhaus factory grounds at 134 and the Jewish cemetery, and down Grodecka Street past the main train station as they converged on the city center. Tanks clattered toward the citadel and downtown along Sapieha Street. More and more troops began to arrive, some by train at the Kleparów station. By that afternoon, German soldiers had bivouacked in the Jewish cemetery on Janowska Street.[1] Some of these troops were entering Lviv again, having reached its outskirts during the invasion of Poland in 1939.[2] Yellow and gold *Edelweiss* blossoms on their soldiers marked them as elite mountain infantry of the 1st *Gebirgsjäger* Division, Regiments 98 and 99.

Accompanying them was the Nachtigall (Nightingale) Battalion made up of Ukrainian nationalist volunteers under German command. In Wehrmacht uniforms with ribbons of Ukrainian blue and yellow, these troops followed the motorcycles down Grodecka Street before turning at the opera house onto the grand Legionow Street on their way to the city hall.[3] They sang Ukrainian songs, and cheering crowds greeted them as they returned to what they and their leaders hoped would be an independent Ukraine. The head of army counterintelligence, Admiral Canaris, had considered using Ukrainians to instigate pogroms as early as 1939 due to existing relationships between exiled Ukrainian nationalists and the Weimar *Reichswehr*.[4] Though under the command of a German officer, Theodor Oberländer, the Nachtigall Battalion really followed its Ukrainian nationalist leader Roman Shukhevych. Shukhevych was a true believer and an experienced assassin from the interwar years and had participated in the failed assassination attempt of the Soviet consul in Lviv in 1933. His men of the Nachtigall returned to Lviv from German protection chanting, "Death to the Muscovite-Jewish commune!"[5]

The arrival of the Germans spawned varying reactions from the city's inhabitants, much as the Soviet arrival had two years earlier. Adolf Folkmann recalled that "thousands of better-situated Poles and Ukrainians welcomed the German troops as liberators and cheered them through the streets. Most of the people on the streets showed beaming faces. Those who felt no pleasure at the arrival of the Germans preferred to remain in their homes."[6] Ukrainian blue and yellow banners appeared along with nationalist slogans like "Ukraine for Ukrainians." Stanisława Gogołowska watched in shock as a housewife across the street unfurled a Nazi flag from her balcony.[7]

Most of the city's Jews were understandably worried and many tried to stay out of sight. Refugees from Nazi-occupied Poland had brought with them tales of the horrors of Nazi occupation. Others were less worried, at least initially. Abraham Goldberg recalled, "I must say, personally I was not nearly as upset because the Russian period had not appealed to me and I hoped that when the Germans came to Lviv there would at least be a little order."[8] Marek Redner ran into his friend, Dr. Perec Gleich, at a streetcar stop and found him "full of optimism and good feelings." Gleich was convinced that the Germans would "demonstrate their cultural superiority over the Soviets" and "not permit any excesses." As a World War I veteran of the Austrian Army, he believed that the German Army was "strongly disciplined and honorable." Dr. Gleich climbed onto the streetcar smiling and carrying his Austrian military documents just in case.[9]

Meanwhile, the Wehrmacht immediately set about controlling the city. The 17th Army commander tasked General Ludwig Kübler, commander of the 49th Corps, with the "maintenance of security, discipline, and order" in Lviv.¹⁰ Military government and civil-military relations in the city was the purview of Oberfeldkommandantur 365, commanded by Generalmajor Edwin Graf von Rothkirch.¹¹ He was assisted by a subordinate unit, Feldkommandantur 603. Together, these units began organizing the city for war: managing traffic, combating looting, putting up road signs, scouting housing and office space, and "preventing excesses of any kind by Army troops."¹² Yet it was the Wehrmacht, not the SS, that first required that all Jews wear a white armband.¹³

More sinister organizations also began entering the city. One of these was Einsatzgruppe C, a Nazi mobile killing unit that eventually murdered 118,341 Jews in the East.¹⁴ Elements of EG C would also murder 33,771 Jews in Kiev, in the ravine at Babi Yar in the largest single-day mass shooting during the Holocaust. For the only time in the war, all 700 members of EG C would be together, in Lviv.¹⁵ Following on the heels of the army, EG C commander, SS *Brigadeführer* Otto Rasch, led his men into Lviv. Rasch was no brute; he was a former mayor and holder of two doctoral degrees, in law and political economy. Yet he was also a ruthless killer who demanded that each of his men participate in the murder of the Jews. As commander of the subordinate Sonderkommando 4a, the forty-seven-year-old Paul Blöbel also arrived to begin his work in Lviv; he would find his way back again at the end, this time to conceal Nazi crimes, including those at the Janowska camp.

Pogrom: Prison Aktions, July Days, and Other Atrocities

As Rasch's Einsatzgruppe C and the future military government was still closing on Lviv, its citizens slowly emerged from their houses and apartments. Many of them already knew that something terrible had happened in the last hours and days of the Soviet occupation. They had heard gunshots and smelled the foul smoke drifting up from the Soviet prisons. What relatives and the curious discovered when they began entering the abandoned buildings was a slaughter that likely exceeded their worst suspicions. What happened next was a combination of spontaneous mob violence, pogrom, and organized murder.

The non-Jewish civilian population of Lviv immediately blamed the Jews for the atrocities discovered in the prisons. As one Polish witness remembered, "the prisons that the Soviets left behind opened and dozens, hundreds of mutilated bodies of political prisoners were revealed.... Who carried out the murders? The Jews! The fact that the murdered prisoners included Jews made no difference to anyone."[16] There were four official NKVD prisons in Lviv: Prison #1 (Brygidki), Prison #2 (former military prison on Zamarstynówska Street), Prison #3 (Lviv Oblast prison), and Prison #4 (NKGB prison on Lackiego Street).[17] These spaces provided the initial flashpoints for the deadly violence that engulfed the city from June 30 until the end of July. The timeline is more than a little unclear, but it seems the first action taken was the rounding up of Jews to recover and/or bury the bodies of the Soviet victims. The Judeo-Bolshevist myth of close historical ties between Jews and communism stoked the anger and desire for revenge felt by the locals, notwithstanding that many of those bodies lying in the yards of the city's prisons belonged to Jews as well. Most German forces that would become involved as well were not yet established in the city. Thus, private citizens, a hastily organized Ukrainian militia, and members of the Nachtigall Battalion began the violence.

Even before the Nazis reached Lviv, Ukrainian nationalist leader Yaroslav Stets'ko had declared that "we are creating a *militsiya* that will help remove the Jews and protect the population."[18] By early July, at least some of this militia had already taken shape. As one survivor recalled, the Nazis "started by giving the Ukrainians two days for them to dance, as they themselves called it later. So they danced."[19] Militiamen captured Joseph Wind on the street and led him to one of the city's prisons. On the way, they beat him. At the prison, he worked removing the bodies of the Soviet victims. He recalled Germans taking pictures. At 6:00 p.m., the militia took him home; he had to be led, however, because his eyes had swollen shut as a result of the continuous beating.[20] Abraham Goldberg, who had been hoping for some restoration of order from the German occupiers, instead found himself forced to exhume bodies as well. He identified his captors as members of the Ukrainian Nachtigall Battalion. After digging up the corpses in the yard of the KGB prison (Prison #4), Goldberg barely survived running the gauntlet of soldiers beating Jews with rifle butts and stabbing them with bayonets. He fell beneath a pile of Jewish victims and was able later to join a working party loading bodies onto trucks.[21] As time passed, the army began supervising work in the prisons. Soldiers wore gas masks to ward off the vile odors and "strolled among the Jewish workers with taunting cries such as 'sweet is the vengeance.'"[22] The pattern soon became clear: Ukrainians rounded up Jews, brought them to the prisons, and forced them to exhume bodies. Then, quite often, they killed them, though at this early stage they also released them.

The violence surrounded everyone in the city, including the Wehrmacht. As a group of officers from the First Mountain Division held a meeting at the Citadel on July 1, the sounds of gunfire from the prisons below provided a chilling backdrop.[23] German officers and soldiers, however, also observed the proceedings up close. One officer visiting Brygidki described what he called "conflict among the population" and learned that it concerned Jews who were denounced as having collaborated with the Russians and had earned the "hatred" of the locals. He also claimed that German military police had been stationed outside the prison to "restore peace and order."[24] But the military police did not restore calm; to the contrary, the violence escalated and spread to the streets.

Here, Ukrainian civilians and militia seized Jews who had ventured out in search of food and abused them in a myriad of ways. They arrested many Jewish citizens and confined them in a variety of locations throughout the city. A Ukrainian policeman caught Rabbi David Kahane. Ignoring Kahane's attempts to explain, the policeman sneered, "I'll show you, you damned Jews, how to walk down the street without escort. Dogs are led on a leash." When he had captured eight Jews, he drove them to a Ukrainian police station whose courtyard was "filled to overflowing with detained Jews." At short intervals, Ukrainian police brought in more and more hapless victims.[25]

The outpouring of hatred and abuse on Jews in the streets moved beyond what one historian has called a "Nazi edition of a Soviet text."[26] Instead, the reactions toward the Jews of Lviv became a communal atrocity whose roots lay much further back in history than the idea of genocide. The early July mass killing and abuse of Jews was a pogrom. And as the rumors flew like smoke on the wind from the former Soviet prisons, the killing and victimization became dispersed across the city. Jewish men and women were attacked, harassed, beaten, and often killed in the streets. A July 7 report on the mass violence from the German military police relayed the mood of Ukrainian nationalists, stating that they "were of the opinion that every Jew should be clubbed to death immediately."²⁷ A series of horrific images caught by the camera's unflinching eye from July 1941 conveys only a small portion of the terror that reigned in the street. Yet these images are terrifying enough. A newsreel found in an abandoned SS barracks in Augsburg shows the violence in motion. A man in a fedora beats a naked woman. Another woman is dragged through a crowd by her hair.²⁸ Onlookers are everywhere, among them German soldiers.

Not content with catching unlucky Jewish pedestrians, the Ukrainian militia, civilians, and sometimes Nachtigall men entered homes and dragged Jews out onto the street. Nachtigall members and leaders later denied any organized participation, contending that if their soldiers had participated it was on their own time. Ukrainian police dragged Mendel Gerner from his apartment on July 4 to a nearby train station where they loaded him onto a truck to another location in the city. He found himself imprisoned with three thousand others. Deprived of food and water for two days, they were robbed and, after a selection apparently based on profession, twenty-five hundred Jews disappeared, sent to an unknown location. The guards then abused the remainder for two hours, forcing them to run, beating them, and dowsing them with water. Then, Mendel's group was simply freed.²⁹

Many of the more amateur killers appear to have come into the city from the countryside specifically to take part in the pogrom. Marek Redner recalled that "thousands of Ukrainian hoodlums, mostly young peasants between 14 and 30 years old, armed with heavy wooden sticks and steel bars, appeared from nowhere, simultaneously in all the Jewish neighborhood streets." A Polish witness "watched as 'a rabble of drunken farmers flowed in from the countryside to Lvov.' 'Something,' he predicted darkly, 'was about to happen and it was planned.'"³⁰ These killers broke into houses, beat Jews to death, and looted, with the crowds following them and picking through Jewish goods after. Survivors were driven to the former Soviet prisons and often killed there.³¹ Redner's friend, Dr. Gleich, so optimistic and proud of his service in the Austrian army, was also dead only hours later, executed in the Brygidki prison. According to Redner, he was the first Jewish doctor in Lviv to die.

Nazi propagandists immediately sought to capitalize on the propaganda value of the pogroms. German officials escorted a group of international journalists, including a *New York Times* correspondent, to the prisons.[32] Reich propaganda minister Joseph Goebbels sent twenty journalists and radiomen to the city.[33] Nazi propaganda units quickly began filming the "Prison Aktion." Raw footage shows Jewish men beaten by Ukrainians as they carry bodies into a courtyard where Jewish women use brooms to brush away the dirt so that families can attempt to identify them. The Brygidki prison, pockmarked with bullets and with smoke still pouring out of the windows, appears to be the setting.[34]

The Nazi propaganda machine released this footage to the world as part of *Die Deutsche Wochenschau* (newsreel) #566 on July 9. It showed viewers the German mountain troops entering Lviv, welcomed with flowers by joyful Ukrainian crowds. As the narrator describes the atrocities committed by "Jewish agents of the GPU," a German soldier comforts an elderly Ukrainian woman. Images of Jews removing bodies and laying them in rows fill the screen while the voice-over narrates the brutal ways in which the victims were murdered. The camera follows crowds into the streets as they round up "Jewish murderers" and hand them over to German troops for punishment. Finally, "Soviet-types . . . mainly Jews" are displayed and blamed for the atrocities.[35]

Nazi propagandists had anticipated this kind of mass violence before the invasion of the Soviet Union and had issued guidelines for messaging. Some excerpts from a policy text from the office of the administrator for the occupied Soviet Union, Alfred Rosenberg, are both enlightening and eerily prescient. "The entire population surely will welcome our understandable portrayal of the Jews as the chief culprits. The Jewish question can be solved to a significant extent by giving the population free rein for a certain length of time after we occupy the country. The propaganda should emphasize that the clique in the Kremlin is nothing but a group of Jewish criminal despots who are exploiting the peoples of the Soviet Union."[36] The events of July 1941 in Lviv no doubt delighted the Nazis as they played right into their hands. Even those in the lofty realms of the Nazi elite took notice. According to Goebbels, the Führer himself was "thrilled about the propaganda opportunities presented by these pictures out of Lemberg."

Specifically, he wrote in his diary on July 8 that the *Wochenschau* covering Lviv was "Ein Furioso!" referring to a musical term meaning "movement which requires a wildness of character in the execution."[37] He scribbled exuberantly that Hitler himself had called to tell him that "that was the best *Wochenschau* that we have made so far."[38] The Prison Aktion slowly evolved into a month-long storm of violence that became known as the "July Days." And in early July, the Germans took a more active role as the killers of Einsatzgruppe C arrived in Lviv.

Himmler had established Einsatzgruppen as early as 1938, mainly to seize important documents from Czechoslovakia and Austria. However, they changed fundamentally in nature and mission during the invasion of Poland where they were responsible for the murder of present and imagined future enemies of the Reich—including Polish nationalists, Polish politicians, military officers, Jewish leaders, priests, and Communists. By the invasion of the Soviet Union, Reinhard Heydrich, head of the Reich Security Main Office and the man who would plan the Final Solution, issued expanded targeting guidelines. He ordered his killers to execute "officials of the Comintern (together with professional Communist politicians in general), top and medium-level officials and radical lower-level officials of the Party, Central Committee and district and sub-district committees People's Commissars, Jews in Party and State employment and other radical elements (saboteurs, propagandists, snipers, assassins, inciters, etc.)."[39] These categories, particularly regarding Jews, rapidly expanded. Four Einsatzgruppen entered the Soviet Union (A-D) from north to south, each following an Army Group as they plunged into Russia.

Rasch's Einsatzgruppe C followed Army Group South, pausing briefly in Lviv. EG C was made up initially of seven hundred fifty men recruited somewhat haphazardly from the Gestapo, other police, and the Waffen-SS. EG C was further subdivided into four units: Sonderkommando 4a, Sonderkommando 4b, Einsatzkommando 5, and Einsatzkommando 6. These units arrived shortly after the German occupation started and began their bloody work. Himmler and Heydrich had hoped that, with a little encouragement, locals would eliminate the Jews themselves in precisely the kinds of pogroms that EG C had walked into. Heydrich directed that "no obstacle is to be placed in the way of the 'self-cleansing efforts' of anticommunist and anti-Jewish circle in the newly occupied territories. On the contrary, they are to be intensified and if necessary pointed in the right direction."[40] However, Rasch and his counterparts across the east found that spontaneous local killings would never be systematic enough, and they began their own killing operations.

Einsatzgruppe C encamped near the Lviv Sportplatz at the beginning of July.[41] It began killing in earnest. The Wehrmacht knew about and assisted in these operations. The operations officer of the 17th Army dutifully recorded in the unit's reports the murder of over four hundred Jews by Einsatzkommando 6 as "reprisal actions for murdered Ukrainians." He further noted that an additional two hundred were killed but that a hundred fifty thousand Jews remained in Lviv.[42] EG C commander Rasch had explained the mission in Lviv shortly after their arrival. According to a subordinate, "Dr. Rasch informed us that Jewish officials and Jewish inhabitants of Lvov had taken part in the killings. The military command had already organized a local Ukrainian militia in the town. Dr. Rasch, who cooperated closely with the militia, ordered Company 4B and afterwards Company 6 to help the militia."[43] The Lviv stadium served as the holding area for these victims. A tragic footnote to these mass killings is that the Metropolitan of the Greek Catholic Church Andrei Sheptytsky refused to condemn the murder of Lviv's Jews when approached by the prominent rabbi David Kahane.[44]

While EG C only stayed in the city for a brief period of time, perhaps little more than a week, it carried out one particularly notorious aktion in addition to the other mass killings. Rasch's killers targeted Lviv's intelligentsia (predominantly Poles and Jews). Decapitation had long been Nazi policy, emanating from the Führer himself. In 1940, Hitler had proclaimed that "all members of the Polish intelligentsia must be killed."[45] Indeed, Einsatzgruppen had already carried out the so-called A-B Aktion in Poland in which practically the entire faculty of the Jagiellonian University in Kraków was sent to concentration camps in Germany. In Lviv, Einsatzgruppen and Gestapo units skipped intermediate steps and simply began murdering their targets.

SS *Brigadeführer* Karl Eberhard Schöngarth (who would later participate in the 1942 Wannsee Conference) led a designated team to murder the leading minds of the city. Working off prepared lists, his men rounded up and murdered the city's university professors. One witness blamed Ukrainian nationalists for denouncing Lviv's intelligentsia, many of whom were Polish.[46] The Nazis arrested and murdered at least forty of them on July 3 and 4. One resident remembered that the aktion also targeted Jewish lawyers, doctors, and engineers who were taken to a forest outside the city and shot.[47] A professor who managed to escape recalled being taken with a group to the Bursa Abrahamowitschew boarding school at Nr. 8 Arzyschewski Street where Germans interrogated and beat them.[48] Behind the six Ionic columns of this former orphanage, the SS men collected around twenty scientists, specialists, and other professionals.[49] There, the Nazis forced them to wash seven flights of stairs with their tongues. After this humiliation, five of them were taken out of town and later shot.[50] Some were taken with their wives. Among those who disappeared into the void was geometry professor and former Polish prime minister Kazimierz Bartel. At least a hundred students were also murdered during this aktion.

The last outburst of rage against Lviv's Jews may have been partially the result of the kind of instigation that Himmler and Heydrich hoped the Einsatzgruppen would spark. Its origins remain a bit unclear, but from July 24 to approximately July 28, the local population again turned its anger on the Jews, this time allegedly in retaliation for the murder of a Ukrainian nationalist fifteen years earlier. Symon Petliura had been a leader in Ukrainian paramilitary forces in the aftermath of World War I and had at best condoned and at worst ordered pogroms against Jews, including in Proskurov where a local commander carried out the murder of perhaps two thousand Jews.[51] A Ukrainian Jewish anarchist (whose family were themselves victims of pogroms) assassinated Petliura in Paris in 1926. Oddly, as the assassination took place on May 25, the pogroms were two months too late to allegedly commemorate his death. One scholar of the city argues that "German authorities approved a period of three days—July 25 to July 27—during which it was permissible to torture, kill and rob Jews without fear of reprisal" and that "these so-called Petljura days—the name given to them by the occupiers—were not spontaneous outbursts."[52] This time the SS, Gestapo, and SD allegedly "instructed [the Ukrainian police and militia] to arrest hostages among the Jewish intelligentsia." The Ukrainians involved shouted, "All of this is for our ataman [leader], Semyon Petliura!" as they beat and killed their victims. The killing was centered on five predominantly Jewish streets: Kazimierzowska, Sloneczna, Peltewna, Zamarstynówska, and Zolkiewska. Many victims ended up at the former KGB prison on Lackiego Street.⁵³ Once again, villagers from the countryside flocked to the city to join in the violence. Ukrainians and the new occupiers murdered at least one thousand Jews during the "Petliura Days."⁵⁴ It was also during this period that the Nazis destroyed many of the city's synagogues. They torched the five-hundred-year-old Golden Rose synagogue, and the SS detonated the great Tempel Progressive synagogue. Edmund Kessler witnessed the destruction; he writes that "the Jews, sad-eyed and full of tears, looked on from the windows of the surrounding buildings, as the flames consumed these ancient buildings together with their decorations and sacred relics" and that many Jews "entered the burning synagogues to rescue the Torahs, the most sacred of relics, despite being shot at by the police and, in the end, perishing in the flames."⁵⁵ Local firefighters arrived on the scene . . . to ensure that neighboring buildings did not catch fire.

How do we explain the "furioso" of anti-Jewish violence in the early days of occupation? Certainly, revenge for Soviet crimes (which locals erroneously blamed on Jews) motivated some of the perpetrators, as did simple antisemitism or opportunism. Nazi propaganda and encouragement fanned these flames further. There was organization to this chaos as well. Behind the scenes, German forces orchestrated violence, and Ukrainian organizations like the police, militias, and members of the Nachtigall Battalion mobilized to both exact vengeance and to please "their new masters, whether or not they believed that the Jews were responsible for their own woes" and thus "confirming the Nazi worldview."⁵⁶ The prospect of an independent Ukraine and the accompanying nationalistic fervor also spurred many Ukrainians to kill and abuse their Jewish neighbors. One scholar estimates that more than twelve thousand Jews were murdered in similar acts of communal genocide across Eastern Galicia.⁵⁷ From the beginning of the German occupation to the end of July 1941, the Einsatzgruppen murdered between three thousand and seven thousand Jews in Lviv, with the assistance of Ukrainian police and militias.⁵⁸

Despite the carnage they had partially enabled, the Nazis realized that "spontaneous" local pogroms would not solve the "Jewish Question." Otto

Rasch's Einsatzgruppe C admitted as much, reporting at the beginning of August that "carefully planned attempts made at an earlier date to incite pogroms against Jews have unfortunately not shown the results hoped for."[59] The Germans had signed their guestbook entry in Lviv with blood, but as a certain calm took hold, some Jews hoped that worst had passed. Adolf Folkmann spoke for many when he wrote, "we hoped, now that the outbursts of mass anger and the pogroms had ceased, that our life would gradually revert to its normal course in time, and we could see no reason why it should not. It had always been like that before. Why shouldn't it be like that again?"[60]

Occupation

Unfortunately, things would not return as they were before in Lviv. The Germans immediately began making the city part of the Nazi sphere, organizationally, culturally, and even physically. Indeed, most citizens experienced this regime change most clearly in the physical spaces in which they lived, worked, and played. The Nazis began by changing the very name of the city itself, reverting back to the Germanized "Lemberg." The city's most fashionable streets, Legionów and Hetmańska—which enclosed a green space and circled the magisterial opera house—became Adolf Hitler Ring. German city planners demolished the 1898 equestrian statue to Jan Sobieski III who had defended Vienna from the Ottomans and replaced it with a brutalist eternal flame dedicated to the Führer.[61] The occupiers even changed the time, decreeing that Lviv's clocks be set to German time. A curfew banned inhabitants from the streets from 9:00 p.m. until 7:00 a.m.[62] German and Ukrainian replaced the Polish language in public spaces, and German was the only acceptable language for official business. Subtlety was not a Nazi strong suit.

Lviv became the capital of Distrikt Galizien, which was in turn added to the territory of the *Generalgouvernement* (General Government, GG) that had replaced most of Poland, under the control of Governor Hans Frank in Kraków. In the Nazi imagination, the city took on a new symbolic meaning as a "bulwark against the Bolshevik threat." It was to become part of Germany proper at some later date according to Hitler. This would, of course, require renovation and rebuilding to restore its "European look."

The new Nazi overlords seized businesses and buildings for both barracks and private housing. They systematically looted "museums, libraries, [and] factories containing objects of artistic, scientific or industrial value."[63] The Germans even stole whole neighborhoods of the city in their own sort of apartheid. They seized the most elegant and prestigious real estate for themselves. More than a few Janowska prisoners would work in this area as servants or other manual laborers. One survivor remembered signs at the entrance to this German enclave warning "For Ukrainians and Poles, entrance strictly forbidden." Any German wishing to live in this posh area need only find a Jewish-owned apartment, file the appropriate paperwork at the municipal housing office, and wait approximately three days for the unlucky residents to be evicted.[64]

Despite its location far to the East, Lviv was to still be a "city of the West," one that Governor Hans Frank claimed would link it to a "European cultural community."[65] The Nazis thus viewed their conquest of the City of Lions as a return rather than an invasion. In their minds, Germans had built the city and everything that was good in it. Their previous work just needed a good burnishing and cleaning. An internal German report on commercial planning called for Lviv to be the "easternmost great city of the German Reich, which is in the position to offer a western European appearance."[66] In short, the city was to be an outpost of civilization (German civilization) in a wild and dark land. Nazi administrators dispensed with civilization when it came to governing, however, as "unmediated coercion and naked murderous violence became the preferred method of governing."[67]

While combat troops pushed forward, longer term military occupants also arrived. The Luftwaffe took possession of the main airfield, Skniłów, former home of the Polish LOT airline and the Lviv Flying Club. It would become a major air hub for the entire Eastern Front and the Luftwaffe would eventually expand to twelve airfields in and around the city.[68] The Wehrmacht occupied the Habsburg citadel overlooking the city, turning it into prisoner of war camp STALAG 328, initially for Soviet POWs. This became the first Nazi camp in the city, where perhaps as many as a hundred forty thousand POWs died or were murdered.[69] Conditions there grew to be so horrendous that cannibalism became widespread—so much so, in fact, that the camp commandant had to issue an order declaring it "forbidden to carve up dead prisoners of war or cut off parts of them."[70] An Army motor pool and vehicle repair unit, Heereskraftfahrzeugpark (HKP) 547, occupied an open area on Janowska Street (now called Weststrasse).[71]

When Lviv and Distrikt Galizien officially became part of Frank's General Government on August 1, 1941, the full range of Nazi authority began to establish itself. The occupiers divided the district into sixteen administrative areas, with Lviv as the capital. Around fourteen thousand Germans had arrived by September 1942, with the largest group in Lviv itself, as befitting the district capital.[72] Karl Lasch, an avowed antisemite and ethnic German from Breslau (Wrocław), left his previous post as governor of the Radom district to take over the newly acquired Distrikt Galizien. "Lviv," he proclaimed, "is the last city with a proper culture far into the East."[73] A brutal thirty-five-year-old miner's son named Friedrich Katzmann, now risen to the rank of SS *Gruppenführer*, joined the administration as Lasch's SS and police leader (SSPF), stationed in Lviv. The SSPFs as well as their subordinates were critically important to the coming storm as they controlled all SS and police forces in their districts and Himmler placed "the whole executive responsibility for population policy in their hands."[74] Katzmann's progression through the ranks was "meteoric, because he fit an ideal profile almost perfectly." His former SS commander described him as "unusually ambitious . . . full of the fighting spirit . . . a fanatical political soldier."[75] If many of the newly arriving Nazis were less than stellar, Katzmann was a rising star with an impeccable resumé of anti-Jewish accomplishments. He would oversee the Holocaust in both Galicia and Lviv and become intimately connected to the Janowska camp. Indeed, he anticipated plans for total extermination of all Jews months before those plans became official policy.[76]

SS *Obersturmführer* Hans Kujath, having established a ghetto in Radom, assumed control of the administration of the city itself as Stadthauptmann (mayor). Along with SS officers also came a number of women who worked alongside them. Mara Edtmayer, thirty-two, from Bad Tölz operated the switchboard in Katzmann's office and Margarete Frech, thirty-four, from West Prussia was his receptionist. Ingebourg Krause typed up the daily orders of destruction that poured forth.[77]

Many of the Germans who volunteered to be stationed in the East (or were conveniently exiled there as dead weight by their previous agency) were not the best of the best. They yearned to salvage ruined careers and damaged reputations. According to one observer, once in the East these men "carried themselves like little kings."[78] A Nazi press officer was more eloquent, calling the stereotypical Nazi carpet-bagger "the idle and worthless type of... bureaucrat... the eternally hungry 'Organizer' with a swarm of like-minded Eastern hyenas."[79]

As a result, incompetence, corruption, and often downright criminality characterized many of those flocking to the city. Even the overlord of the General Government, Hans Frank, fit this profile. In the words of one historian, the General Government was "therefore predominantly staffed by people who for a variety of reasons—ideological commitment, hope of advancement, moral perversion—were inclined to racism and violence." Indeed, it "became a dumping ground not just for the Reich's racial undesirables but also its unwanted officials."[80] The late entry of Distrikt Galizien into the GG likely exacerbated this problem as the pickings for positions became even slimmer. Lasch's successor as district governor, Otto Wächter "railed against German bureaucracies unloading their worst on his Galizien."[81] Arnon Rubin's new neighbors on Marpacka Street, German civilians, spent their free time shooting stray dogs and cats from their apartment windows.[82] Regardless, for many of the officials, civilians, and those in uniform (particularly the SS), the East offered an elite status and standard of living utterly incommensurate with their actual rank or worth.

But neither the governing and control of the city nor this extravagant lifestyle would have been possible without the collaboration of local non-Germans. Indeed, they were pivotal. By the end of 1941, for example, the city administration employed 759 people, of whom only 20 were German, the remainder being Ukrainian (432) and Polish (307). By the end of German rule, at least 5,000 Ukrainians and 7,000 Poles were directly engaged in working for the Germans in some capacity.[83] As for local assistance, the German city commandant had appointed a Ukrainian geography professor, Jurij Poljans'kyj, as civilian mayor on June 30.[84] Nazi administrators established a Ukrainian auxiliary police force on August 31, 1941, with initially 425 officers, expanding to 874 by 1944 and including 420 cadets from the Lviv police academy.[85] Motivations for service to Nazi overlords varied widely: antisemitism, opportunism, hopes for an independent Ukraine, training and weapons to be carried to the partisans, to list a few. Some, like thirty-nine-year-old Artymon Szpaczynzky, a guard in the Jaktorów camp thirty miles from Lviv, may have been simply searching for a way to support their families.[86]

At the end of July 1941, the Commander of the Order Police in the General Government, Generalleutnant Riege, informed District Governor Lasch that he would receive 6.6 million zlotys for the establishment of a police force of initially 30 officers and 2,000 men.[87] By mid-August 1941, experienced Ukrainian policemen serving in Distrikt Lublin were transferred to Lviv to stand up several *kommissariate* (precincts) throughout the city.[88] A police academy was established in the city to train policemen. The Ukrainian police force was under the control of the German police commander (KdS, *Kommandeur der Schutzpolizei*). Many had previous experience in the OUN paramilitary militias and were diehard nationalists.[89] The Ukrainian police played a pivotal role in controlling the Jews of Lviv and in their destruction. These officers were the "major native Holocaust perpetrator in Soviet territory."[90] A postwar judicial opinion noted that the police "contributed to the public intimidation of the Jews of Lviv" and that Jews who saw them "were aware of their responsibilities and abuses they inflicted, [living] in fear of them."[91] Who were these men?

One of them was Ivan Kalymon, who arrived penniless as a stranger to Lviv in late 1941. He had been born in 1921 in the village of Komańcza, Poland (not far from the modern borders of Ukraine and Slovakia). It had little to recommend it beyond being the site of a bizarre and short-lived independent Ukrainian Republic at the end of 1918. Polish forces crushed this entity. Perhaps Kalymon's father died in the violence of the 1920s in the Galicia. In any case, Ivan grew up without a father, achieving only a seventh-grade education. In 1939 he moved to Bomlitz in northern Germany to work in a factory producing kielbasa for the Wehrmacht.[92] Perhaps he did this out of an affinity for the Germans or because he claimed to be an ethnic German. When he traveled to Lviv with one bag, Kalymon allegedly sought an education and a better job, not unreasonable hopes considering he was returning to a region where he spoke the language (Ukrainian). He did not have much initial success. Indeed, he lived in a homeless shelter before seeing a recruiting ad for the police, perhaps the one placed in the city's major Ukrainian-language newspaper on August 14.[93] He then signed up for the Ukrainian Auxiliary Police, ultimately serving in three separate precincts.[94] In a postwar court Kalymon claimed he joined "because of necessity to survive."[95] Regardless, he was simply one of many Ukrainians who walked through the doors of police precincts as volunteers in the late summer heat of 1941.

Living in the Opposite Direction: Beginnings of Anti-Jewish Policy in Lviv

After the intense and bloody violence of the July Days, the apparent stability of increasing German control may have seemed like a positive turn of events for the Jews of Lviv, now numbering around 160,000. On August 1, Lviv and its surrounding Distrikt Galizien became part of the General Government, the Nazis' premier colonial experiment. Here, they had the most Jews under their control and tested all manner of both anti-Jewish and anti-Polish policy, including failed attempts at massive demographic engineering to remove unwanted people in preparation for German settlers. As a result, anti-Jewish policy had become more or less standardized and would be accelerated in Distrikt Galizien.

A feeling of impending doom, an "atmosphere of fear," descended upon the city's Jewish community. Twenty-year-old Jack Ahrens recalled the mounting indignities forced upon the Jews of Lviv. German policy banned Jews from the sidewalks, consigning them to the wet and muddy gutters. It also required them to bow, doff their hats, and salute German soldiers. As Ahrens put it, "If there was any way how they could humiliate you, they found a way how to do it."[96] Nor were these attacks hidden. German civil engineer Georg Gilke testified that "anyone who walked through the streets of Lviv with their eyes open constantly came across atrocities."[97] Jews could still move freely but were always in danger of being abducted for labor by one German agency or another. The Nazis plucked Marian Rogowski off the street twice in the early days of the occupation.[98] In the first half-year of occupation, more vicious policies would dwarf these initial humiliations.

Following precedent elsewhere in the General Government, Nazi authorities in Lviv began setting up the framework that would eventually enable the Final Solution. With a template already in place, things proceeded quickly. A flurry of prohibitions such as those that Ahrens experienced flew from the offices of the Stadthauptmann Kujath. Already in July, Jews were consigned to the last car on the streetcar and later forbidden to use public transportation altogether.[99] They were required to wear a white armband with blue Star of David on it to identify themselves to all. This marking also helped to enforce other antisemitic policies like the two-hour window for shopping allowed for Jews, from 3:00 to 5:00 p.m., an indignity directed by the Ukrainian "mayor" Yuri Polanskyj.[100] The Jews of Lviv were forced to wear the star before those in Germany.

Badges, passes, and papers became central to Jewish life—simultaneously a life-saving currency and a death sentence. Documentation of employment could—for a time—also provide safety for a spouse or relative. At times, documentation from employers served as a kind of twisted "hall pass" enabling Jews to travel to their workplace unmolested. This paperwork also gives fragmentary glimpses into the lives of a community in crisis. On August 12, 1941, a desk officer for district governor Karl Lasch typed a short "certificate" for a Paula Günsberg requesting that she be allowed passage to work "unhindered." He noted that she worked in his office from 6:00 a.m. to 8:00 p.m.[101] A regional planner (*Baurat*) named Tripcke wrote a similar but temporary pass in October 1941 for "4 Jews" who worked in the "Furniture Transport Section," presumably tasked with moving looted furniture in the city. One of Tripcke's other responsibilities was laying out Lviv's ghetto.[102] The Ukrainian Fifth Police Precinct reported the arrest of thirty-six-year-old unemployed bookkeeper Frida Arnold for not wearing her armband. She had been denounced by a non-Jew. In her statement Arnold explained that she had lost her armband while returning home and had not noticed.[103] One of the police officers serving in the precinct at the time was none other than Ivan Kalymon.

Josef Parnas became the most identifiable Lviv Jew when the German administration appointed him head of the Jewish Council (Judenrat). Parnas had served as a captain in the Austrian cavalry before taking up the law. When placed in charge of the city's Jews, he was seventy years old. His deputy, Adolf Rothfeld, was also a lawyer and the former chairman of Galician Zionists. The Germans held the Judenrat responsible for, (1) performance of all orders and regulations of the German authorities with respect to the Jewish population; (2) regulation of internal relations among the Jews; and (3) establishment of social institutions, hospitals, an 'order police' *(Ordnungsdienst)*, and other entities."[104] By 1942 the Lviv Jewish Council had rapidly expanded to incorporate twenty-two divisions and six subdivisions. It employed around four thousand people, or roughly 4.5 percent of the city's Jews.[105]

One of Parnas's first duties as chairman of the Judenrat was scrambling to satisfy a massive extortion from Katzmann. The ss leader demanded 20 million zloty from the Jewish community, ostensibly for the cost of rebuilding parts of the city. On July 28, Parnas wrote an anguished plea for help in meeting the demands of the Nazis; otherwise, the Jews could "count on the most severe of reprisals."[106] For days the Jews of Lviv came and went at #2 Starotandetna Street, bringing whatever valuables they could contribute: currency, silver menorahs, jewelry, and other items of value. When the Judenrat paid its first installment on August 8, in addition to gold and jewelry, it handed over 1,400 kilograms (3,086 lbs) of silver. At current prices, that would be worth almost $1 million. The Nazis were following a tried-and-true tactic of extorting money from Jewish communities. This was all part of a larger plan to ensure that no wealth perished with the Jews. Almost every ghetto community experienced at least one (and often several) of these demands to raise funds or face reprisals. The extortion in Lviv did not go unnoticed around the world. The *Jewish Telegraphic Agency* warned that "Nazis Impose $4,000,000 Collective Fine on Jews in Lemberg" on August 13, 1941, while also noting that "both the Polish and Jewish populations there are being terrorised by the Ukrainian militia which the Nazis have organized, and which is supervised by the Gestapo."[107]

Nor did the expropriation stop with pure cash demands. In the winter of 1941–42, Nazi authorities forced the Jews to surrender warm clothing in what became known as the "Fur Aktion." The stalled and freezing Wehrmacht soldiers in front of Moscow now urgently required winter clothing. Rothfeld, who succeeded Parnas as chairman of the Jewish Council, issued the instructions on January 4, 1942. "All fur coats," he wrote, "must be handed over" at one of the Jewish police stations. Further, "the wearing and possession of furs and fur accessories is as of now strictly forbidden." The punishment for failure to comply was death. In addition, the city's

Jews were to hand over skis, ski boots, winter socks, scarves, and sweaters. Women and children's clothing was excluded, but women's ski boots from size 36 up were included.[108] House-to-house searches accompanied the Fur Aktion and also led to the removal and murder of many elderly Jews.[109] SSPF Katzmann proudly reported having delivered thirty-five train cars of fur and other cold-weather items.[110]

Confiscation of Jewish property often took on a very personal quality. As ghettoization progressed, a special department of the Judenrat, the *Besorgungsamt* or Procurement office, was established to catalog and warehouse Jewish property and then to fulfill German requests for household goods. Often, this procurement took place directly. David Kahane recalled that "all a Christian landlord had to do was to inform the Germans that rich Jews lived in his building" and "immediately a German with several carts would materialize at the door."[111] A group of German officers walked into Marek Redner's apartment and tossed it in search of money and valuables. They then left with "a leather suitcase, some wall hangings, two lamps, a coal loading shovel, and a soccer ball."[112] Perhaps a year later an infamous Janowska camp guard with a taste for music named Richard Rokita would procure a piano of "the best quality" from looted Jewish property.[113] On the outskirts of town, the Polish family that Jack Ahrens lived with informed a German officer of his presence. The German came in and took Jack's "beautiful Kodak camera" that this mother had brought from America. This was not theft, the officer insisted, pressing a worthless receipt into his hands. Fifty years after the war, Jack wistfully remarked that "I had that receipt for quite a while.... I wish I had it now."[114]

As mentioned, newly arrived Germans and their collaborators devoured real estate, a phenomenon that only accelerated with the creation of the ghetto. City officials began cataloging apartments and houses of Jews to be made available to Germans and other non-Jews. Stadthauptmann Kujath ordered on August 8, 1941, that all empty or new properties be reported to the city housing department. He also claimed full control over the confiscation of all housing assets.[115] Nazi police inspector Dr. Albert Ullrich arrived in Lviv in August 1941; shortly thereafter, the city housing department (in his words) "assigned" him a fully furnished two-bedroom apartment.[116] The furnishings remained almost assuredly because they had once belonged to Jews. Nor was German looting limited to private housing and effects. Jewish institutions fell victim as well. Redner watched in mid-1942 as the chief doctor of Distrikt Galizien, Wilhelm Dopheide, emptied a Jewish hospital with a "great deal of zeal, [stealing] all the expensive instruments left by the departing Jews, delighted with his looting."[117] Associated with the Nazi T-4 "euthanasia" program, Dopheide had already allowed twelve hundred mentally ill Jews and Poles to starve or freeze to death in his "care." He then turned that asylum into a military hospital.[118]

Ghettoization followed a course set out at least two years earlier. The architect of the coming Final Solution, Reinhard Heydrich, had sent out a communiqué in September 1939 directing the concentration of Jews in larger cities as "comprehensive measures" for an as yet unclarified "ultimate goal."[119] The removal of Jews from the public landscape and eventually from newly Germanized territories enabled, of course, the larger Nazi fantasy of attaining *Lebensraum* (living space), space preferably without "undesirable" populations—not just Jews but also Poles and Roma. The main theorist of Nazi colonial policy in the East, the Baltic-German Alfred Rosenberg, coldly described the ghetto as "living space in the opposite direction," that is, a path leading to death. Shortly after, Joseph Goebbels insisted that Jews "must be isolated completely, otherwise all of Europe will be poisoned."[120] Disease, particularly typhus, was also used as a justification, perpetuating antisemitic stereotypes of Jews as carriers of disease. Of course, the packing of tens of thousands of people in a small area with insufficient sanitation led to a self-fulfilling prophecy in which typhus did strike ghetto populations.

The ghettoization process began in Lviv relatively quickly thanks to the experience of occupation in Poland, and to the prior experience of Nazi administrators but unfolded slowly and incompletely in practice. Distrikt Galizien governor Karl Lasch had previously ordered the creation of ghettos in Kielce, Radom, and Częstochowa as governor of Distrikt Radom. These ghettos had been unfenced and simply marked by signage warning of danger of infection and forbidding entry.[121] His successor in Lviv, Otto Wächter, had organized the Kraków ghetto during his tenure there. SSPF Katzmann had served in a similar capacity under Lasch in Radom. Lviv's Stadthauptmann Kujath had also cut his teeth on ghetto creation working in Lasch's Radom administration. As a result, at least the idea of a ghetto formed relatively routinely. As in other cities in the east, the authorities chose an undesirable location for the Lviv ghetto. Here, the urban topography of the city played a critical role. An elevated railroad cut through the city in an east–west direction, just north of the opera house and the former citadel, now the atrocious STALAG 328 POW camp. The rail embankment not only provided a convenient and very visible demarcation line; it also offered limited access points via underpasses. Finally, and perhaps most importantly to the planners, the blighted neighborhoods north of the tracks consisted mainly of small buildings, often without basic amenities. Few Jews lived there, however, which required the transfer of larger number of Jews from other parts of the city. The Lviv ghetto area, even before the war, had been "especially dilapidated, with little or no city sewage, water, or electric service. Houses there were mostly shacks, and crime was high."[122] Some valued workers were tentatively granted a reprieve and allowed to live in areas south of the tracks. The Nazi authorities then divided the city into six zones to allow for an orderly clearing out of the Jewish population.

A final piece of the Nazi colonial plan that would greatly impact both the Jews of Lviv and the development of the Janowska camp was Himmler's desire for a grand highway through Distrikt Galizien and the Reichskommissariat Ukraine farther east. This was the Durchgangstrasse IV. While visiting the region in December 1941, Himmler quickly grew sick, perhaps literally, of the horrendous roads. He canceled meetings and chose to travel by air as much as possible.[123] In his attempt to become more and more of a military leader, Himmler lobbied Hitler for a massive building project to ease transportation problems in the East. Albert Speer, Hitler's architect and economic advisor, did as well but was only able to elicit a lukewarm approval from the Führer for a road "constructed in the most primitive way" and only built to last for two to three years.[124] This massive undertaking required vast numbers of laborers—to be supplied by the Jews of Galicia, particularly Lviv and its vicinity. The Janowska camp would serve as a clearinghouse for this slave labor as well as for a good portion of the SS overseers. The DG IV was a monstrous snake made of small, transient camps and aimed at connecting Lviv and Rostov, with a massive appetite for human lives. It also became, for Himmler, another opportunity to shine in the firmament of Hitler's subordinates vying for his favor. Over the course of 1942, over five thousand Germans would be involved in carving out this highway. Driven by the SS, approximately ten thousand Jews labored in the cold and the heat on empty stomachs to build this road. Many of these Jews had marched slowly under the Peltewna Trestle or through the concrete entrance of the Janowska camp. Most would never return. But all that lay in the future. For now, we return to the summer of 1941 when a series of SS officials visited Lviv and decided to build a labor camp at 134 Janowska Street.

The Devil's Workshop   3

> I don't know why Gebauer committed this crime. In general, nobody gave a thought to why a Jew would be killed. That was just an everyday thing. It was enough to be a Jew, that is, a creature excluded from the law.
>
> —Anna Cwirn, March 8, 1963

In early August 1941, as the brutal violence of the July days in the streets subsided, a small convoy of perhaps a staff car and a cargo truck stopped outside of a dusty lot that made up the addresses 122–138 Janowska Street (renamed Weststrasse by the occupiers).[1] The Nazi-appointed Ukrainian mayor Polanskyj had helpfully recommended the site.[2] Two ss officers stepped out of the car and walked around. A Jewish-owned factory once built mill machinery here, but the Soviets had nationalized the company in 1939 and the site was abandoned when the ss men arrived. A former arsenal building from Habsburg times was the most prominent building, but there was also a large construction hall where vehicles could be repaired and several auxiliary workshops including a metalworking shop, a turning shop, a carpentry shop, and a plumbing shop. An army motor pool unit Heereskraftfahrzeugpark 547 (HKP 547) had also taken up residence temporarily, making use of the facilities in a relationship that would continue for the next three years.[3]

The two ss men were *Untersturmführer* (Second Lieutenant) Wolfgang Mohwinkel and *Obersturmführer* (Lieutenant) Friedrich "Fritz" Gebauer. They had arrived from Lublin to set up a branch of the Deutsche Ausrüstungswerke (DAW) or German Equipment Works in Lviv. Mohwinkel was the old hand, coming to help Gebauer get his camp up and running. In

Lublin, Mohwinkel had served as the adjutant at a labor camp at 7 Lipowa Street since 1940; it had officially become a DAW camp in February 1941.[4] Described as "restless, arrogant, and tireless," he had "implemented a brutal regime of discipline, including beatings, hangings, and shootings" at that site.[5] He likely passed this "expertise" on to Gebauer as he helped him set up the DAW-Lemberg (DAW-L) on Janowska Street.

The DAW and the Business of Genocide

The DAW embodied SS efforts to control the economic exploitation attached to anti-Jewish policy. Himmler always sought ways to enhance his power and position in the Third Reich and inserting the SS firmly in the war economy served as yet another way to do this. Slave labor did not play a significant role in the early camps in Germany, however. Instead, it developed over time in complexity and scale. The first step toward the commercialization of incarceration came in many ways with the Deutsche Ausrüstungswerke GmbH, founded in Berlin on May 3, 1939. It would become one of the "largest and most important" economic enterprises of the SS. The DAW arose from relatively humble beginnings: a bakery to supply the Sachsenhausen concentration camp outside of Berlin, a mat-sewing operation in the Ravensbrück women's concentration camp, and an SS dress-sword works in the well-established Dachau camp.[6]

These workshops fell under the control of Oswald Pohl who became a member of Himmler's inner circle due in large part to his loyalty and dedication as a Nazi. He had written Himmler personally declaring his willingness to "serve him 'until I drop.'"[7] In his career, Pohl chose an economic track to power and success, eventually becoming head of the SS Wirtschafts-und Verwaltungshauptamt (WVHA) or Economic Administration Main Office. He later leveraged this important position to gain control of the entire camp system. Pohl himself certainly embraced the concept of prisoners as labor. He and his wife personally used both forced laborers from the East and concentration camp slave labor (including from the Ravensbrück camp) on their beautiful country estate at Comthurey.[8] Pohl preferred female Jehovah's witnesses as live-in servants just as Rudolf Höss did at Auschwitz, because they were supposedly trustworthy and unlikely to escape.[9]

The DAW empire would include at least twelve branches located in places like Auschwitz, Buchenwald, Stutthof, Neuengamme, Ravensbrück, Sachsenhausen, and Dachau—all notorious concentration camps.[10] By 1943, the DAW system employed 485 SS members and civilians and exploited approximately 15,500 forced and slave laborers. Each worker theoretically earned a wage, but in actuality it was paid directly to the DAWs, netting a 1943 income from "wages" of six million Reichsmarks (RM).[11] By the same year, the organization "sold" twenty-three million Reichsmarks worth of products for the SS.[12] These factory prisons produced a wide range of materials including furniture, clothing, and shoes; they responded to military needs by repairing frontline material and vehicles and building ammunition crates. By 1942, 90 percent of production was geared toward the military, with 45 percent in woodworking, 20 percent in metalworking, and 35 percent in other materials.[13]

As for Gebauer's DAW-L, it apparently sprang from the imagination of the thoroughly odious SS Gruppenführer Odilo Globocnik, who at the time controlled the DAW camps in Lublin and was the SS and police leader (SSPF) there. He was also, as one historian described him, "the vilest individual in the vilest organization ever known."[14] Globocnik craved power and he saw his route to that in the General Government at least in part through economic control. As a result, "through [his] initiative the Lublin district also became a center of SS economic enterprises and a base for future SS colonization plans in Eastern Europe."[15] "Globus," as his friends called him, would go on to organize and oversee the Final Solution but at this time he was content to terrorize only the population of Distrikt Lublin.

As the Wehrmacht thundered across the dusty expanses of the Soviet Union in the summer of 1941, Fritz Gebauer received a postcard from DAW headquarters in Berlin informing him that he would be taking over an SS economic operation. In July, he traveled with SS *Sturmbannführer* (Major) Gerhard Maurer (who ran the DAW for Pohl) to Lublin where he met with Globocnik in person.[16] Maurer was a committed Nazi and staunch advocate for SS participation in the armaments industry. The commandant of Auschwitz, Rudolf Höss, remembered him as "an energetic man [with] sharp eyes and ears" who was constantly on the move, inspecting camps and reporting conditions to his boss, Pohl.[17] At this meeting, Globocnik ordered Gebauer to "expand the so-called 'Economic Strongpoint Lemberg.'"[18] Given his experience as a deputy in the Lublin DAW camp, Wolfgang Mohwinkel was to accompany Gebauer to Lviv and help him establish the DAW-L. And so the two men arrived in Lviv in August 1941 at the site of the former Steinhaus company on Janowska Street.

The Janitor's Son

Gebauer may appear an odd choice for a position that seemed important to the SS. He was one of those men of middling ability hoping to make it big in the East. Gebauer was born in 1906 in Breslau, Silesia (now Wrocław, Poland). His father spent thirty-two years as a janitor and low-level employee for the Prussian board of weights and measures. Gebauer attended public school as required until he was fourteen. He then entered a trade school and trained to be a mechanic. After his father died when he was eighteen, Gebauer worked as an electrician at the Siemens and Halske factory in Breslau. In postwar statements, Gebauer claimed he was unemployed from 1930 to 1933 before working for airplane manufacturer Arado. After his certification as a master electrician he returned to Siemens, this time in Berlin. Gebauer was conscripted into the Luftwaffe shortly before the invasion of Poland, but Siemens exempted him from service by designating him as a skilled worker.[19]

Gebauer's early life may shed some light on his future. Germans on the periphery and borderlands of the country often tended to be *more* virulently nationalistic than those at the center precisely because national identity was often more fluid and contested where one nation ended and another began. The constant ethnic friction of the frontier "radicaliz[ed] German nationalism and anti-Semitism."[20] Russians, Slavs, and Jews came in for particular abuse in these regions. We can easily imagine that Gebauer may have been "radicalized" to some extent given his geographic proximity to these groups. One scholar has shown, for example, that Germans from border regions tended to be overrepresented in the brutal and ultranationalistic *Freikorps* during the interwar period.[21] Gebauer's employment history shows him to be a relatively uneducated but well-trained blue-collar worker. At first glance, he does not stand out as a future SS officer and camp commandant, but his background in factory work may have appeared useful.

Gebauer joined the Nazi Party and the *Allgemeine* (General) ss in 1932 (he had joined the sa in 1930).[22] He repeatedly emphasized after the war that his joining had been influenced by his period of unemployment.[23] According to him, he saw advertisements for the Nazis while collecting his welfare checks.[24] However, given that his unemployment began two years earlier and ended one year after his joining, one might suspect that he was masking other motivations. In addition, membership at that time brought no pay or benefits and was completely voluntary. He also met a girl. Unemployed and a new member of the ss, Fritz married Emmi Höfer, a seamstress, in 1932.

After the war, Gebauer tried to downplay his ss membership but his promotion to Untersturmführer (second lieutenant) may indicate more than a passing interest as well as some level of ideological commitment as well. At a minimum, he would have been exposed to an above average level of Nazi propaganda.[25] Gebauer insinuated that having only been promoted once indicated a minor role in the ss, but, as is always the case with Nazi criminals, the truth is a little more complicated and a lot more damning. The investigation into his past after the war revealed that, in fact, the future camp commandant had been banned from wearing the ss uniform and frequenting ss facilities due to charges in 1936 that there were "irregularities" in his expense accounts. In a further attempt to distance himself from his time in the ss, Gebauer claimed to never have received his promotion to *Hauptsturmführer* (captain), which the ss had duly recorded in its personnel files.[26]

After his short time in the Luftwaffe, Gebauer accepted an instructor position with the daw in Berlin training mechanics. However, as he himself admitted, "it became clear to me ... that the whole thing was a cover for a section of the ss Economic Office." "The actual task of the daw in Berlin," he freely admitted, "was supplying raw materials to the industrial operations of the concentration camps."[27] At no time in his postwar statements did he express any disapproval with this mission. Thus, when Gebauer joined the Waffen-ss (Armed ss) in 1941, he came as a man already experienced with both Nazi ideology and with the industrial exploitation of concentration camp labor for production.

What kind of a man was Fritz Gebauer? According to one former prisoner, he was "actually a good-looking man." Slender with brown hair and a "soft voice," Gebauer had "sad dark eyes" and "the face of a movie actor." The commandant was courteous and polite.[28] Yet, he also "quickly showed prisoners what kind of a man he was and what his proclivities were."[29] As we will explore later in greater depth, these "proclivities" included killing prisoners in various depraved manners. He also beat them with the ever-present SS man's riding crop or whip as well as slapping them with his gloves.[30] Importantly, however, the postwar court held that there was no evidence of any "abnormal personality."[31] Gebauer gained a position on the rising tide of the Nazi state that he likely never would have achieved on his own. For the son of a janitor, he reveled in his success and it fed his ambition. One survivor noted that Gebauer "strove for rapid advancement, taking after the example of Globocnik."[32] Perhaps he carried a need to excel driven by his humble upbringing and the less than prestigious position of his father. In this, he would not be alone in the SS where many men would be promoted beyond their qualifications or expertise and certainly beyond their social status in pre-Nazi society. Indeed, a postwar prosecuting attorney wrote that "Gebauer appears to be the prototype of the washed-up petty bourgeoisie, who came very early to the Nazi party and in this way achieved a position after 1933 that he was in no way equal to."[33] His ambition would drive him to both wanton brutality and a genuine desire to run his camp effectively.

Building the Devil's Workshop

When Mohwinkel and Gebauer stood in the autumn heat, the task ahead may have seemed monumental, though Gebauer as the future commandant never seemed to fully grasp his duties. Mohwinkel must bear a great deal of responsibility for the initial layout of the camp as he was clearly sent to mentor. The space was relatively modest, roughly 350 by 400 yards or approximately 40 acres. By comparison, the Majdanek concentration camp spread over 330 acres and the Auschwitz camp and its zone of interest covered over 15 square miles. In late summer 1941, Lviv teemed with Germans of all stripes energetically pursuing their own objectives with little regard for others and without much supervision. Gebauer himself recalled that he found no "regulated relationships" on his arrival in the city. Even after the war, he seemed proud of his achievement, taking care to point out that there was *no* DAW in Lemberg until *he* got there.[34]

Before his "factory" could produce a thing, however, Gebauer had to actually build it. It remains somewhat unclear precisely how much responsibility Mohwinkel shared with the future commandant. Not surprisingly, Gebauer tried to evade responsibility after the war by claiming that he was Mohwinkel's deputy until early 1942 when, in fact, Mohwinkel had already returned to command the Lipowa camp in Lublin by December 1941 at the latest.[35] Thus, it appears that Mohwinkel provided initial guidance but likely passed control quickly over to Gebauer. In any case, the two men struggled at the beginning to set up the camp.

They first needed laborers. Gebauer turned to the local *Arbeitsamt* (labor office). Before the addition of Distrikt Galizien, twenty-three labor offices had been established in the General Government with an additional seventy branch offices. These labor offices handled the transfer of industrial properties, social welfare for local workers, housing (and rehousing), and, last, the procurement of slave laborers (mainly Jews and POWs) and forced laborers (usually conscripted from the local population).[36] The head of this office in Lviv was Heinz Weber, a smirking, arrogant twenty-seven-year-old SS man who had previously worked in Arbeitsamts in Karlsruhe and Rzeszów in the General Government.[37] Survivors described him as "a degenerate and notorious drunkard," a "tyrant," and "brutal, uncouth, and unschooled."[38] Weber had one redeeming quality: he could be bribed. On this almost all survivors agree. Like many new colonizers of the East, he had an insatiable appetite for riches and he prospected for them among the wreckage left by Nazi anti-Jewish policy. Gebauer appeared in Weber's office and claimed to offer humane conditions and work cards signed by the SSPF Katzmann himself in exchange for volunteers.[39] Weber supplied him with around a hundred fifty laborers.[40]

Among these first laborers of the DAW-L were Helene Kaplan and Bernard Hirschhorn, both of whom had volunteered to avoid being dragged off to a worse fate. Hirschhorn had hoped that as an engineer he would be given better working conditions. Others had been forced. Itzchak Ferber had been plucked off the street and delivered to the camp in its early days.[41] The Gestapo arrested salesman Benjamin Schreiber in November and engineer Abraham Goldberg in early 1942 and delivered them to the camp as well.[42] Among other arrivals in October 1941 were the future Nazi hunter

Simon Wiesenthal and his wife, Cyla.[43] Twelve-year-old Arnold Kerner arrived with his father as a prisoner at the end of 1941.[44] The majority of this initial population consisted of Jews from Lviv; the rest were skilled Polish craftsmen.[45] Some of the Jewish skilled labor also arrived from Mohwinkel's Lipowa DAW camp in Lublin to provide some seasoned prisoners.[46] Their arrival is yet another strand of continuity with earlier forced labor operations in the General Government.

In the beginning, guards marched all workers to and from the camp from the Arbeitsamt in Lviv each day.[47] The first contingent of six to ten guards were not just any guards either; they were apparently men from the infamous Dirlewanger Battalion.[48] The arrival of this particular "special SS formation" added an additional element of horror to the opening act of the Janowska camp complex. The men of this unit consisted entirely (at first) of convicted poachers who occupied an oddly romantic place in Hitler's heart for their "daring" and apparently for their skill at shooting.[49] The leader of this motley group was Oskar Dirlewanger, a man who may well have been one of the minority of Nazis who was clinically a psychopath. One scholar described him as a "devotee of sadism and necrophilia."[50] Before coming to Lviv, the Dirlewanger men constructed fortifications and guarded camps in Distrikt Lublin, where they were under the direct command of Odilo Globocnik. In particular, they had worked in the Bełżec labor camps.[51] An SS investigation had already accused both Dirlewanger and his men of a dizzying variety of gruesome crimes. The deployment of these men to open the DAW-L may well indicate how important this effort was to Globocnik as his economic ambitions reached beyond Distrikt Lublin. In any case, he sent a group of brutal criminals experienced in camp operations along with an experienced administrator in Mohwinkel to establish the DAW in Lviv.

For the denizens of Gebauer's new principality, frenetic building activity filled the first days and weeks. Mohwinkel and Gebauer had the luxury of relative free rein in Lviv as they established the first major camp in the region. However, they seem to have arrived with little more than the clothes on their back. They found themselves tasked to build a camp without any materials. A survivor recalled that "the camp was not ready at all to receive the so-called *Häftlinge* [prisoners]." There was no kitchen to provide meals, no water, and no bathing facilities.[52] So, in typical SS fashion, the leadership resorted to theft. Gebauer was so desperate that he gathered his new laborers, gave them trucks, and ordered them to head into the city and "look around for raw materials and machines." The prisoners were then "forced into rapacious theft" in former government institutions. This improvised looting soon bore fruit, filling the camp with sheet metal, iron, paper, equipment, cement, and other materials.[53] Gebauer and Mohwinkel took full advantage of their powers as SS officers to be the first to loot the city, no doubt motivated by the knowledge that others would soon be doing the same. They were in good company with this technique; Rudolf Höss, commandant of Auschwitz, had done the same thing. "The urgently needed barbed wire just had to be pilfered," he wrote, "When I came across installations containing material I urgently needed, I simply had it taken away at once without worrying about the formalities. I had to help myself."[54]

Construction focused on building barracks, planting, and clearing footpaths, among other things.[55] In the first months of the camp, the labor force also grew to around five hundred.[56] Barracks construction was of paramount importance. This and the renovation of old workshops and creation of new ones dominated Mohwinkel and Gebauer's plans from August to October. As with many things in the camp, a sinister surprise lurked amid the bustle of labor and the staccato of hammers. Apparently, the workers had been told that the barracks under construction were to house Austrian and Czechoslovakian Jews who would soon be arriving.[57] However, this was all deception.

On Halloween 1941, Gebauer appeared before his assembled forced laborers with a startling revelation. "From today on," he announced, "you will stay here. You will not go home anymore. You will receive housing and meals here. Nothing will happen to you as long as you toe the line and obey. If not, you will get a thrashing. Whoever makes a run for it will be shot." If the prisoners had happened to turn around, they would have seen that the gates they had built were now closed. As a survivor present that day recalled ruefully, "They marched us into the barracks which we had built ourselves."[58]

This was also the moment of ascendance for Friedrich Gebauer, for Mohwinkel departed for Lublin the next day to take command of the Lipowa DAW camp. At that camp, day laborers had also been transformed into prisoners by being suddenly confined. Mohwinkel almost certainly passed this trick on to his pupil, Gebauer.[59]

"The Number Is Paramount": The Early Days of the DAW

In later years, Fritz Gebauer must have yearned for that cold winter of 1941. He did not know it at the time, but his career had already peaked. From November 1941 to May 1942, the DAW-L was perhaps the most important SS labor concern in the city. It was Gebauer's kingdom and he was its king. He had complete control and exploited his prisoners as much as possible. For example, in exchange for allowing packages from the ghetto into the camp, Gebauer extorted an expensive fur coat and all the furnishings for his residence from the Jewish community.[60]

The DAW was also a growing enterprise. In the months after his arrival, Gebauer added to his staff of guards, SS men, and foremen. Because very few German documents survived, one can only partially reconstruct this organization. This is complicated by the fact that both survivors and perpetrators sometimes mistake personnel from the ZAL with those of the DAW. However, we can arrive at a rough outline of the organization of the DAW-L. Gebauer, as commandant, was represented by a deputy commandant. He presided over a headquarters element that contained at least three female civilian secretaries, an accountant, and a number of purchasing and sales agents responsible for buying raw materials and selling the camp's products. There was a transport section of vehicle mechanics and drivers as well as a kitchen, likely for the German staff of the camp. The largest number of SS men (at least ten) made up the guard force. However, workshops made up the bulk of the camp. A factory manager presided over at least eleven identifiable workshops or departments, each of which had its own supervisor and foremen. For the prisoners, too, these shops represented the center of their daily misery in the camp and each often came with its own brutal tormentor.

Those arriving in the devil's workshops came from a variety of backgrounds which bear a bit of explanation here. Perhaps the most important was the arrival of thirty-one-year old SS Untersturmführer (second lieutenant) Gustav Willhaus. This smartly-attired man became Gebauer's deputy in November 1941. Willhaus had served in the Waffen-SS in Norway and arrived to Lviv from an administrative post in the ss Economic Main Office (WVHA).⁶¹ Gebauer also received a mixture of ss and civilians from Berlin in November 1942, each of whom had a background in a particular craft. These "colleagues," as he remembered them, made life in the camp "bearable."⁶² These included Willi Monz, tasked with heading the camp's construction office; Hugo Bleines, who oversaw the carpentry shop and later served as the deputy commandant; and Richard Kern, a fifty-something ethnic German from Ostrow, Poland. Kern apparently "knew his way around" lumber but not German, speaking better Polish. He had the habit of responding to all prisoners with the phrase "Man, you are insane!" Kern oversaw all the workshops, though this seemed beyond his abilities. Regardless, he stalked the camp in high boots, a sheepskin coat, and a fur hat, armed with a whip.⁶³ He was soon relieved by Karl Melchior, another German from a contested borderland (this time, the Saar along the French border).

Melchior had joined the French Foreign Legion in an attempt to escape his strict father, but lasted only six months before being discharged due to illness and returned home. He joined the Waffen-ss in 1939 and served in the Dachau concentration camp where an ear problem ended that stint of service after eight months. From 1940 to 1942, Melchior commanded a desk in the ss Economic Main Office in Berlin before seeking a position in the DAW-Dachau in order to be nearer to his family. He arrived in Lviv, according to him, as a punishment for friendship with a kapo (prisoner functionary) in Dachau.⁶⁴ Gebauer tasked him with finding the equipment and skilled workers to build a shoemaking shop in the camp.

Another important arrival, this time in January 1942 (five months after the camp opened), was Adolf Kolonko, a baby-faced ethnic German from the border region of Silesia. Born the second oldest of six children, Kolonko failed to complete an apprenticeship as a metalworker, which must have disappointed his foreman father. He joined the *Allgemeine-ss* in 1933, claiming after the war like others that he had done so in order to get a job. Yet he also was trained at the Security Service (SD) school in Bernau, which seems to suggest that young Adolf was more than a little committed; this was the same school used to groom potential leaders for the Einsatzgruppen.⁶⁵ During the war against Poland, he served in the military police in what would become the 2nd SS Panzer Division.⁶⁶ When Kolonko reported to Fritz Gebauer in the bitterly cold winter of 1941/42, he took command of the DAW-L's guard force. A guard force of Ukrainians arrived with him.⁶⁷ The Nazis called these non-German volunteers "Askaris," a term used by an earlier generation for local military contingents in German East Africa (now Tanzania). It is telling that the new German empire being roughly birthed in eastern Europe borrowed this term from the old one.

Some of these guards came from the Trawniki training camp near Lublin. Less than a month into the invasion of the Soviet Union, SS chief Heinrich Himmler realized that the scale of the planned decimation of the East had rapidly outpaced his resources. Simply put, he needed more men to solidify Nazi control on the ground. As a result, he made the ideologically hypocritical but pragmatically sound decision to recruit from the "racially inferior" local population. In order to avoid training brand new auxiliaries, Himmler turned first to the overflowing enclosures of human misery that the Nazis called prisoner of war camps. Heydrich told local commanders to select "persons who appear especially reliable and are therefore suitable for deployment in the reconstruction of the occupied [Soviet] territories."⁶⁸ Recruiters determined reliability primarily on ethnic grounds. Russian soldiers were considered hopelessly contaminated by Bolshevism, but ethnic Germans, Ukrainians, and other ethnic minorities were assumed to be relatively trustworthy. Of course, the recruiters relied on the atrocious conditions in the POW camps to make their argument for them.

It was a powerful argument. The Nazis intentionally made no provision for the feeding, lodging, or medical treatment of captured soldiers. These men had "lost all claim" to such care according to the general in charge of POWs (though they were allowed to eat horseflesh).⁶⁹ More than three million Red Army soldiers died in German hands and, of those, two million died in just the first eight months of the war.⁷⁰ That works out to over eighty-three hundred deaths a day. Given the opportunity to escape death in a muddy Russian field, many non-Russians volunteered to leave. Olkesandr Fedchenko was pulled from a POW camp in Rivne, one where five hundred men were dying each day. According to him, the Germans said he was going to be a policeman. Instead, he became a guard in the Janowska camp.⁷¹

The history and stories of these Ukrainian volunteer guards often remain in the shadows, due to a lack of sources, a focus on the Nazis, and/or the politically inconvenient nature of this collaboration. In any case, upon leaving POW camps, they arrived at a former sugar refinery on the outskirts of the village of Trawniki that the Nazis had repurposed as a training center. There, SS instructors taught them the rules of the Nazis' peculiar institution: the concentration camp. One recruit recalled that "that we were not to give the slightest quarter while guarding and escorting prisoners. We were not to have the slightest contact with prisoners; we were not to give them any water or food; and for the slightest 'infractions,' we were to shoot them without any warning." Conveniently, the SS established a labor camp for Jews next door where the new auxiliaries could practice their skills. For many, this included a gruesome final exam. "When we completed training," former Trawniki man Jakob Klimenko confessed, "the Germans ordered each of us to shoot a Jew. They apparently did this in order to be better able to rely on our loyalty to them." Their SS instructors called this "practical training."[72]

It is difficult to generalize regarding the volunteers' motivations. Certainly, the promise of escape from what must have seemed like certain death drove many. Trawniki veteran Fedor Tartynskij explained that "each one of us was ready to accept any terms if only to get out of this camp."[73] Yet, as one scholar rightly points out, the guards' "status and his benefits made it quite clear to him that he was neither a prisoner of war nor a forced laborer."[74] Many grew into their roles, enjoying the spoils they could accumulate, in addition to the better food, higher pay, and protection for their families. While the frequent (and relatively easy) desertion of Trawniki men remained a constant problem, many continued working in the extermination centers and labor camps. The fact that so many stayed suggests at a minimum a lack of concern for the plight of the Jews.

These, then, are the men who arrived with Adolf Kolonko in the DAW in January 1942. Some of these same men later served in the Sobibor extermination center where up to two hundred fifty thousand Jews were gassed.[75] A further ninety-two arrived as reinforcements in the spring of 1943.[76] However, not all the non-German guards came from as far afield. Many were natives of Lviv, just like their prisoners. We know this because

Gebauer arranged a meeting on December 15, 1941, with the commanders of the German *Schutzpolizei* (city police) and of the Ukrainian *Hilfspolizei* (auxiliary police). At this meeting, Gebauer described the "difficult conditions" in the camp and the German police commander approved the "necessity" of an additional guard force. Perhaps this urgency resulted from the departure of the Dirlewanger men. Perhaps it also resulted in Kolonko's arrival with Trawniki guards. In any case, the DAW commandant received only six men from the First Ukrainian Police Precinct for twenty-four-hour guard duty.[77] Of the sixty-five former Askaris arrested by the KGB after the war, the ethnic breakdown was: thirty Russians, twenty-nine Ukrainians, three Tatars, one Belarusian, one Bulgarian, and one German.[78]

Daily Life in the DAW-L, August 1941–May 1942

Gebauer ruled unilaterally on Janowska street until May 1942 when Willhaus's treachery resulted in the creation of the ZAL there. But that was a ways off, and the DAW operated as an independent entity for almost a year.[79] One cannot explore the nature of this place without examining the lives of those imprisoned and those who controlled them. The DAW-L fell into a routine not unlike that in many camps, but like all stars in that dark constellation, it also had its own particular quirks and anomalies.

Life in the first year revolved around work. Gebauer poured his energies into turning his fiefdom into a highly efficient production center for the SS. His ambition may have exceeded his expertise, but it drove him nonetheless. Even when questioned in custody in 1962, he could not conceal his pride in his achievements as he saw them. The brutal factory manager came out when he bragged that his DAW had made or repaired ten thousand uniforms for the Luftwaffe warehouse in Kiev; supplied nine hundred uniforms to the Ukrainian police; produced felt and leather boots for the Deutsche Reichsbank and Organisation Todt; and built wooden packing crates for a brandy distillery, brewery, slaughterhouse, and vegetable collection point—all in Lviv.[80] The woodworking shops represented perhaps the busiest parts of the operation, under the direction of Richard Kern and Richard Biedermann (both civilians, though Biedermann by his own admission wore an SS uniform).[81] Besides shipping crates, the DAW produced finished goods like furniture for offices and barracks. Individual Germans could also commission personal furnishings built by the prisoners. Gebauer noted that individuals would bring their own (likely looted) "raw materials" to the camp and that his workers would build them bespoke items.[82] This was a scheme no doubt rife with corruption, though the former commandant took pains to stress that "all goods produced were used in the Wehrmacht and civil sectors."[83] For Gebauer, the personal services he rendered represented a way to ingratiate himself with important people in Lviv. The workshops in the DAW also repaired vehicles for the army motor pool in Kiev. Here, the camp served in the role of a higher-level maintenance unit for military vehicles that could not be repaired closer to the front. Smaller workshops produced machined metal items, textiles, shoes, saddles, plumbing supplies, and leather goods.[84] Gebauer in a moment of pained honesty told investigators after the war that "it is important to me to explain that the DAW must be seen as a properly and precisely led production facility."[85] The operations manager, Karl Melchior, also attempted to highlight the productive qualities of the camp. He pointed out with some of Gebauer's pride that "his" section was purely an "SS economic operation" that "fabricated clothing and personal items for the fighting troops."[86] The extent to which the DAW-L was actually a vital enterprise for the war effort is, of course, highly debatable, but it was clearly so in the minds of the men who ran it.

Even after sealing of the camp on October 31, 1941, construction continued to be a staple of day-to-day operations of the DAW. With equipment pilfered from the city and brought in from Berlin, the camp's prisoners enlarged existing workshops and built new ones, all under Gebauer's self-described "technical leadership."[87] Construction must have been difficult on the rolling ground that Bernard Hirschhorn called a "string of mounds." He recalled the unusually frigid winter of 1941/42 in which he labored at breaking up the frozen ground with picks for twelve hours at a time.[88] No matter who was in charge, construction was constant in the Janowska camp.

Work dictated the rhythms of the day, beginning with a morning roll-call formation around five in the morning, which necessitated an abrupt wakeup from fitful sleep around four. Beyond "the count," this morning ritual also included an evaluation of fitness every few days, which involved running past Gebauer or another member of the camp staff. The SS pulled those who stumbled or seemed weak out of the ranks. One former prisoner recalled that Gebauer himself personally shot some of them.[89] The vast majority of those who faltered in the selection activities did not survive the day. This grim exercise became known as the "Death Run" among the prisoners, and Willhaus continued it when he got his own camp. It bears mentioning that it was not just the stereotypically brutal SS who carried out selections. Survivors identified civilians as those wielding the power of life and death as well. Karl Melchior took part, often beating prisoners to death.[90] Hugo Bleines discovered that workers in his carpentry shop had hidden a man named Loew who was weak with typhus. He and the metal shop supervisor (perhaps SS man Röhrich) beat the sick man before handing him over to Gebauer, who either shot him or ordered his execution.[91]

The camp leadership organized the prisoners into "columns" or brigades, each of which had a specific task. A Jewish foreman led each column and reported to a German supervisor. Some evidence suggests that a few Poles and Ukrainians also served as paid foremen. We know of at least one local man, Kasimir Boni, who acted as a purchasing agent for manufactured goods. He received four hundred zloty a month in salary. Boni was one of the many Ukrainians who simply shifted allegiances, having worked for the Soviet government before the arrival of the Germans.[92]

Gebauer's focus on production created divisions among the prisoners that had serious implications. The SS valued skilled craftsman (*Facharbeiters*) more highly than unskilled laborers (*Schwarzarbeiters*). Craftsmen often benefited from working indoors under less physically strenuous conditions while the Schwarzarbeiters like Bernard Hirschhorn toiled in the frigid air. Ukrainian Askaris drove these columns and beat prisoners with their rifle butts when they moved too slowly.[93] According to one witness, the concrete "literally froze in their fingers" in the unseasonably cold weather, and construction work ground to a halt. A furious Gebauer capriciously retaliated against his workers by forbidding them from bathing.[94]

Those with some expertise benefited significantly—apparently, even those who were not craftsmen. Helene Kaplan, who worked in the camp offices taking the names and occupations of arriving prisoners, recalled that if Gebauer "was in one of his more humane moods, he would talk with lawyers or teachers and inquire about their previous accomplishments. If they spoke German fluently, he would assign them to work in the office."[95]

One survivor remembered these were known by other prisoners as the "Prisoner Aristocracy" and those "Chosen by Fate."[96] Indeed, Jews constituted the majority of the architects, accountants, engineers, technicians, and administrative personnel who kept the camp from becoming more of a mess than it already was. Hugo Bleines put it rather more crudely, noting that "the more intelligent Jews were workshop and office supervisors."[97] Among new arrivals, the bold or savvy knew to claim that they had skills to avoid the crushing labor of the Schwarzarbeiters. The Nazis brought seventeen-year-old Leon (Weliczker) Wells to the camp in March 1942 after he unluckily took his father's place in a work detail. One of the Jewish secretaries registering new arrivals took mercy on him and told him to say he was a skilled worker, so he claimed to be a glassworker. When he arrived in his workshop, he was chagrined to learn he was the only glassworker in the camp. Regardless, he felt "lucky" because he "knew [he] could not have stayed with the outside work for more than a month." He reflected in his memoirs that he was glad to be in a workshop "where it at least would be warm and where constant beatings were not a fixed part of the day's work."[98] For Wells, warmth and protection were all the privilege he needed. Some prisoners reached positions of higher authority, such as foremen, though they still lived at the mercy of the ss.

While most remember their Jewish foremen as having sought to protect them or at least to navigate their "choiceless choices" with as much care as possible, two names remain infamous: a man named Zimmerman and Roman Kampf. Gebauer elevated these two Jews to positions of power in the camp. These men appear as little more than shadowy figures in the historical record, but they, or men like them, almost certainly existed. Nazis in most camps selected certain prisoners to help organize and supervise their comrades, usually in return for a more privileged existence in the camp. Zimmerman was from Warsaw and Roman Kampf was a former café musician from Lublin, perhaps originally from Tarnów.[99] It is unclear precisely what their relative ranks were but both appear to have been at the top of the prisoner functionary ladder. Hirschhorn identifies Kampf as the "commandant" designated by Gebauer.[100] Leon Richman provides much of the information about these two in his memoir, describing them as ambitious, selfish men who were "notorious characters among the dregs of their towns."[101] At least two other survivors also identify them by name. They all accuse Kampf and Zimmerman of corruption (trading with guards), toadyism, and general abuse of their fellow prisoners. The lack of familiarity with the men's origins by survivors suggests that they were strangers, likely brought in from other camps in the General Government. Perhaps that explains part of the animosity. We must, however, distinguish these men from those prisoners privileged due to their working ability, privileges that most likely stemmed from pragmatism and utilitarianism on the part of the SS.

Despite Gebauer's wishful thinking, his prisoners hardly received fair treatment. To the contrary, even when the horrific ZAL-L was well underway, survivor Irving Mandel recalled that "prisoners did not see working in the DAW to be beneficial due to the draconian supervision."[102] As always, the Schwarzarbeiters suffered more, being viewed as expendable beasts of burden. They carried out menial labor cleaning, moving earth, and carrying heavy materials from place to place, almost always while exposed to the harsh elements. Postwar trial estimates suggested that between two hundred and a thousand prisoners toiled in this way in the DAW on a daily basis.[103] Often, these prisoners suffered even more due to the proximity of the Kleparów train station. SS men and guards beat them and forced them to run back and forth to the camp while unloading building supplies from arriving trains. Schwarzarbeit often proved fatal. In the winter of 1941/42, Gebauer himself stood near the auto repair shop, watching prisoners running with lumber on their backs to the carpentry shop. Something about one prisoner's performance bothered him and he beat the man until he fell. Then, in full view of the camp, Gebauer stepped on his throat until the prisoner died. The court found that the commandant "willingly and intentionally killed the prisoner because the life of a Jewish Schwarzarbeiter meant less to him."[104] Stanisława Gogolowska, an astute observer of the camp, noted more directly that "the *Schwarzabeiters* worked without proper clothing in frost and rain, constantly tormented by hunger."[105]

At the end of the workday, which often stretched into the evening, the prisoners would file past the camp kitchen, perhaps noticing grimly the Jewish cemetery just outside the wire to the east. More likely, they focused on the meager items that landed in their metal bowls. They followed this routine at midday as well, receiving their meal in the open air, rain or snow, often in knee-deep mud. According to Richman, prisoners received "black, bitter coffee" in the morning, a watery soup for lunch (the main meal), and more coffee for dinner.[106] The German cook, Hösner, served up a putrid meal by all accounts. Gogolowska described the soup as made with "frozen, unwashed, unpeeled potatoes piled in the open near the SS toilet." Because the SS men relieved themselves on the potatoes, prisoners often could not eat the soup, which "stank of urine."[107] Bernard Hirschhorn gives a more specific account of food in the DAW, albeit dating from November 1942 after the ZAL was established. He testified that Gebauer turned to the Jewish Council because he could not feed the prisoners (likely due to Willhaus' interference). Prisoners received 140g (5 oz) of bread and 3/4 l (3 cups) of the watery soup with rotten potatoes and vegetables from the garbage. Hirschhorn went on to note that "at first, almost no one could eat the soup but after a short time, everyone was so starved that they would beg the kitchen for more."[108] It is perhaps a telling commentary that the only time the prisoners were full was when a horse died and was added to the soup. Gogolowska remembered that everyone got as much as they wanted . . . and more than ten prisoners died because their systems could not handle the sudden influx of nutrition. Gebauer was, naturally, incensed at the loss to his labor force, but the prisoner doctor concealed the cause of the deaths from him.[109] Prisoners attempted to supplement their meager allotment with food smuggled in, which they would sometimes warm on the stoves. This carried its own risk of beating by the supervisors.[110] A survivor who worked in the kitchen also remarked that skilled laborers got somewhat better meals than the others.[111]

With their bellies uncomfortably empty, the prisoners would head to the DAW barracks at the end of the day. Even here, the division between skilled labor, unskilled labor, and privileged prisoners reigned. Barracks for the Schwarzarbeiters more closely resembled barns than human dwellings. After an exhausting day of fearful work, these prisoners would find a place on the mud floor and attempt to hide from the wind whistling through the substantial gaps in the walls and from the rain that would drip through the roof. Many were simply unable to sleep in these conditions. The skilled workers "enjoyed" a somewhat more sturdy barracks that at least had gaps in the boards plugged with sawdust to keep in the warmth.¹¹² A select few prisoners of the privileged class did actually have relatively luxurious housing, at least for a while. The Jewish foremen, office workers, and engineers appear to have been allowed to live with their families in stone buildings within the DAW until 1943. This is confirmed by German and Jewish witnesses alike.¹¹³ In the early days of the DAW-L, it appears that women were not detained as actual prisoners, but allowed to remain in the camp while working or with their families. Such beneficent housing was definitely a rarity in the concentration camp system. A chain-link fence separated these buildings from the other prisoner barracks. Prisoners and their families lived here, often in bizarre proximity to their overlords. Helene Kaplan, who had once learned geometry from the former prime minister of Poland, Kasimierz Bartel, now lived with another university student in the DAW slave labor camp next door to volunteer Polish day laborers who sold them pierogi for thirty zloty each. Kaplan and her friend Alma shared a room with a cooking stove in the middle. Alma even had the temerity to ask Gebauer to bring them some of their furniture from the ghetto—to which he surprisingly agreed.¹¹⁴

All the Usual Weaknesses: SS Life in the Early DAW

For the SS men and Nazi civilians in the camp, life was good. While German soldiers marched and fought through the heat and choking dust in the autumn of 1941 and bled out during the Soviet counteroffensives of December in the record cold approaching -40°F, the men in Gebauer's theater of operations suffered very little. In fact, despite postwar claims of dedication to duty, most of them lived in fear of actually being deployed to the front to serve the Fatherland. They much preferred their existence as masters of life and death, with access to all the comforts they could extract from the Jews of Lviv. Many scholars have remarked before on the bizarre dissonance between the personal lives of SS men and their work.

Survivor Helene Kaplan observed of the SS in Janowska that "people who seemed to be endowed with all the usual weaknesses were transformed into cruel beasts who seemed at times not to be human beings at all."¹¹⁵ In the case of the employees of the DAW-L, photos likely taken between March and May 1942 go a long way toward illustrating this. In the first, members of the camp staff gaze at something out of the frame. They stand in front of a low one-story white building housing Gebauer's apartment and the DAW employee kitchen and dining room. A mix of men and women in uniform and in civilian clothes stand in a grassy courtyard with a light on a wire hanging above it. Hugo Bleines, dressed smartly in a sports coat and wearing knee-length leather boots, stands next to his wife, who is wearing a white dress to her knees, her hair nicely coiffed. Behind them, two women sit in rocking chairs lounging; one appears to be reading. An unidentified SS private stands with his hands behind his back. At his feet a black and white dog naps in the sun. This is Gebauer's dog, Bully. The scene could be mistaken for a garden party in peaceful times. But if one is aware of the physical surroundings, the picture becomes darker. Beyond the dark picket fence and brick wall in the background looms a ramshackle wooden structure that resembles a barn. This is a prisoner barracks, about a hundred fifty feet away. Perhaps it is the Schwarzarbeiter barracks where Leon Richman huddled on the cold mud floor trying to sleep. One wonders whether the proximity of this place of misery interrupted this lazy afternoon.

The second photograph is a group shot taken at the same time, this time with the Gebauer apartment and kitchen in the background. On the far left in a tartan pattern dress with a white collar, Karl Melchior's wife, Amalie, smiles at the camera. Next to her, turned toward the camera with his face shadowed by his cap, is Gebauer. A dark-haired woman stands behind them both in the background with her arms crossed beneath a flower box. According to SS guard Kolonko, this was a Jewish cook who worked in the kitchen whose name he forgot. The SS private and the Bleineses stand at the right, smiling.

These two images provide only one snapshot into the life of the Nazi staff in the early days of the DAW-L. However, it is a telling one: German civilians and SS men mingling in their leisure time, a tastefully landscaped and decorated German space in the midst of the terror of the concentration camp, a Jewish prisoner potentially included in a photograph without much notice. As others have written before, the camp staff had no concern about living, working, and relaxing while surrounded with suffering and death. This was not uncommon. The commandant of Auschwitz lived with his wife and children within sight and certainly sound of the first gas chamber and crematorium in that camp.

The wives of these men often actively engaged in the life of the camp. Emmi Gebauer oversaw the DAW kitchen for staff and was paid by Berlin for her work.[116] It is quite probable that she therefore supervised the prisoners who worked there, perhaps even the woman in the picture. Amalie Melchior brought her child with her to live in the camp in a building she shared with the Bleines, Bayer, and Willhaus families.[117] The German women in the camp all fiercely denied having any knowledge of what happened to prisoners there but they are most certainly lying. It would have been impossible to escape seeing, hearing, or smelling the assault on humanity that took place daily on Janowska Street. Indeed, Mrs. Gebauer took full advantage of her position in the DAW-L to enrich herself. One survivor recalls her demanding that he supply her with clothes and luxury items that he had to both find and pay for himself from a fund the prisoners had created specifically for that purpose.[118] Gebauer himself confirmed that his wife wore fur coats in the camp. Michał Borwicz specifically remembered the arrival of the "pretentious and corpulent" Emmi Gebauer with her peroxided "platinum blonde hair."[119]

Alma, Helene Kaplan's roommate, cleaned the Gebauers' apartment and described the commandant's wife as "polite." Yet Kaplan felt that Mrs. Gebauer's very presence in the camp made her feel like "we were being ruled by a complete royal court—a despotic king, a quiet queen, and all of us subject to their whims and aberrations."[120] It is an ironic choice of words. The wife of the infamous Amon Göth, commandant of the Płaszów camp, remarked in the 1970s on the "beautiful time" when she had lived in the camp. "My [husband] was the king," she said wistfully, "and I was the queen. Who wouldn't have traded places with us?" In Auschwitz, Mrs. Höss, too, enjoyed her home and chose to remain there even when her husband was stationed back in Germany.[121] For Emmi Gebauer, a life of fur coats and luxury items, even in a concentration camp, likely exceeded the life expectations of a seamstress married to a mechanic.

Beyond supervising prisoners in the DAW kitchen, Mrs. Gebauer, like many SS wives, took advantage of a free labor pool to live a bourgeois life beyond her means. She had at least two maids at her disposal, including Kaplan's friend, Alma. The other, Eugenia Maas, presented searingly accurate recollections at Gebauer's trial. She recalled, for example, that the commandant would complain to the whole staff that the cook served noodles with raisins far too often. She also distinctly remembered that the Gebauers' apartment was expansive with twelve rooms.[122] The commandant and his wife furnished their home no doubt with material looted from the Jews of Lviv (or made by them in the camp). Many camp staff and their wives lived nearby and SS men apparently entered the camp in the evenings, presumably for nonwork-related activities.[123] Gebauer seems to have had some extracurricular relationships as well. One survivor recalls taking the commandant and a "Polish girl" for a drive about which he was sworn to secrecy.[124] Leon Wells wrote that "Gebauer, for example, had amorous relations with a Jewess" and that as a result "Mrs. Gebauer found consolation in turning her attention to a Jewish chauffeur."[125] Despite potential awkwardness at home, Fritz Gebauer found cause to celebrate at the end of 1941. He "openly" admitted to authorities with false schoolboy innocence that he had celebrated the new year by firing a submachine gun into the air.[126]

Yet all was not well in the Deutsche Ausrüstungswerke-Lemberg. There was a traitor in its midst. Gustav Willhaus had bigger plans than being Fritz Gebauer's deputy in a Nazi imperial backwater. The two men appear to have initially gotten along, but the younger Willhaus clearly envisioned more. In a short period of time, their relationship deteriorated. Gebauer's bitterness at the palace coup that followed remained evident even two decades after the event. "Between Willhaus and me there arose serious differences," he complained to police, while claiming that disagreement concerned the treatment of prisoners . . . which it most certainly did *not*.[127] Gebauer lamented his treatment, griping that Willhaus was "supposed to help me in the office but he did not. He got in touch with the Police Leader Katzmann first thing upon his arrival."[128]

As prosecutors argued after the war, it seems more likely that Willhaus never really respected his superior officer. This much was clear even to the prisoners and likely worsened once Willhaus's power grab was complete. Leon Wells wrote that although the prisoners "could not know all the details of their private lives or of their relationship, some of it was thrust upon us." As a result, the two men seemed to him "at swords' points." Willhaus turned away when Gebauer approached, for example.[129] He also mocked his boss by naming his dachshund "Fritz" after Gebauer and enjoyed swearing at the dog in Gebauer's presence. Further, Willhaus enjoyed reminding *his* SS men of this joke and they all laughed about it.[130] The judges at a related postwar trial noted that "Willhaus made no bones about his rivalry and animosity toward Gebauer."[131] It is also possible that Willhaus, being an actual Waffen-SS officer, looked down on Gebauer, who never truly served in that formation.[132]

Whether Willhaus contacted Katzmann (as Gebauer claimed) or vice versa is unclear, but the two recognized a mutual opportunity. What played out at 134 Janowska Street was echoed throughout the Nazi world as officials plotted against each other for power. Katzmann sought to increase his status via anti-Jewish policy in Lviv. He likely saw the DAW-L as a threat to his power, controlled as it was by Pohl's regime in Berlin. Katzmann no doubt also recognized the financial benefits of controlling forced labor in the city and the accompanying prestige he would gain, particularly if supplied labor to Himmler's pet project of the DG IV highway. On a larger scale, a similar battle was taking place in the General Government, not within the SS but between the SS and Nazi civilians. On May 7, 1942, Himmler wrested full control of Jewish policy from Frank. This change perhaps not surprisingly coincided with a massive inflow of Jews to camps across the territory.[133] In any case, the SS general "pulled Willhaus to his side and built him up as an opponent to Gebauer."[134] Certainly Katzmann (and perhaps Willhaus too) envisioned greater things for Janowska.

This may have been something that Katzmann had plotted for a while. What we do know is that he appointed Willhaus as the commandant of a future Zwangsarbeitslager and authorized him to build it immediately adjacent to Gebauer's DAW. Further evidence of some plotting here may be a report compiled by Kurt May, the head of the lumber office (Amt W-IV) in Oswald Pohl's SS Economic Administration Main Office (WVHA). May had already enriched himself by buying distressed Jewish businesses, including a shady furniture enterprise he co-owned with Pohl himself.[135] In June 1942, shortly after SSPF Katzmann had tasked Willhaus with building a new camp, May undertook an inspection tour of various DAW facilities in eastern Europe including Auschwitz. He arrived in Lviv on June 5 and met with Katzmann's deputy before touring the DAW-L. His report includes several clues about Willhaus's ascendance. Katzmann, who was at a meeting in Kraków, expressed his desire that Willhaus be transferred out of the DAW and be responsible for the construction of a new camp. May agreed on the condition that Willhaus would not set up his own workshops. He then goes on to describe the camp that Gebauer constructed in a decidedly derisive manner. "The camp location [in the hills]," he reported, "made broad planning impossible." May went further, advising that "future investment be kept to a minimum" and that the SS "be on the lookout for another location with a railway siding." He concluded with the most damning of judgments. "Gebauer," he wrote, "lacks the necessary ability or he would have brought the most important lumber operation in Lviv [the Niesel and Kammer firm] into the hands of the DAW." This "sin of omission cannot be reprimanded strongly enough."[136] May all but directly called Gebauer incompetent. Was this determination influenced by Katzmann to facilitate the building of the new camp by Willhaus? It is unclear. However, May's critique certainly provided strong evidence of a need for change. That change resulted in the creation of the largest Nazi camp in Ukraine.

A Tragic Life 4

> The Jewish Council is to be instructed to register all Jews and Jewish families which are not productively employed and report them to the higher authorities. The resettlement should take place in rural towns which are away from the main highways and in unfertile areas.
> —Minutes of a meeting of Lviv Nazi administrators, January 10, 1942

Before we continue more deeply into Willhaus's ZAL Janowska, which began construction in the spring of 1942, we must turn to the storm building in Lviv from October 1941 (the sealing of the DAW) to August 1942 (the time of the "Great Aktion"). It is simply impossible to understand the place of Janowska camp and its evolution without exploring the unfolding of the Holocaust in the city. The history of this period demonstrates the ever-increasing severity of anti-Jewish policy in Lviv and the expanding place of the Janowska camps (DAW and ZAL) in the suffering of its Jews. We will return to the camp in more detail in the next chapter.

A Fence Unfinished: Ghettoization in Lviv

On October 7, 1941, as Gebauer was still struggling to set up the DAW, the German police commander in Lviv, Major Fritz Weise, wrote a memo to the Distrikt Galizien Order Police Commander, Paul Worm, regarding the "Construction of Jewish Residential District in Lviv." He laid out a plan for the Lviv ghetto in the northern section of the city, with the east–west rail line as a southern border. Despite acknowledging that most of the 111,000 Jews in the city (his estimate) did not live there, Weise plunged ahead with his argument. The rail line, he proposed, served as a "perfect and unmistakable border which considerably simplified the surveillance of the Jewish residential area through the few underpasses." The population of this area would, of course, triple, but "under the circumstances, the creation of the Jewish quarter would still be possible and manageable." Still, he recommended an incremental approach as a mass movement would require too many guards and offer Jews too much access to means of escape.[1]

The chief of the General Government, Hans Frank, had previously forbidden the creation of ghettos in Distrikt Galizien, though not for humanitarian reasons. He hoped to send "his" Jews further east, to the deepest parts of the Soviet hinterland. As a result, he sought to avoid creating *new*, more permanent concentrations of Jews.[2] This had two repercussions. First, any "Jewish residential districts" tended to be created where large numbers of Jews already resided, such as Lviv. Second, officials like Katzmann hoping to insert themselves in the growth industry of Jewish containment turned to the creation of forced labor camps . . . like the Janowska camp.[3] Still, Nazi administrators recognized that concentration of Jews was desirable, at least in the short term. Himmler's deputy, Heydrich, had already ordered this in September 1939, with the caveat that in the General Government "as few concentration centers as possible are to be set up, to facilitate the subsequent measures."[4] What those "subsequent measures" should be remained an open question in 1939, but all involved knew they would entail a further displacement of the Jews. By the fall of 1941, however, it became clear to many that those measures would be murder, not movement. The precise methods had not yet been identified but would be by the end of the year.

Frank appears to have relented on his ban by the end of October 1941, agreeing with the governor of Distrikt Galizien, Karl Lasch, and the German mayor of Lviv, Hans Kujath, on the creation of a ghetto there.[5] Police Commander Weise's memo proves this, and Governor Lasch pulled no punches regarding his attitude. "The Jews in Lviv," he said, "shall be gathered in Jewish quarters and vanish from the streetscape."[6] Behind the scenes, German administrators, contractors, and city planners devised a plan to remove Jews from the more desirable parts of the city in an incremental manner. They divided the city into seven sections not including the ghetto area.

Minutes and summaries of meetings of city planners illustrate the preparations for the ghettoization and forced relocation of at least eighty thousand Jews. On September 18, Governor Lasch reassured local businessmen that "Jews should be forced out of political and economic life. For this purpose, a special place for their isolation is being prepared. They will be transferred there within a short time."[7] At a meeting in Kraków on October 12, 1941, Lasch made clear his desire for a ghetto in Lviv, arguing that the city's Jews should be treated no differently than those in Warsaw or Kraków.[8] The commander of Schutzpolizei objected on October 7 that the area envisioned for the ghetto only included a population of forty thousand—of whom only 25 percent were Jews, while 80–90 percent of the city's Jews lived elsewhere. As a result, he considered the planned location "inadvisable."[9] He was apparently ignored. Regardless, he rightly insisted that the creation of a ghetto would require a massive movement of Jewish and non-Jewish populations. On November 6, Dr. Wiggers, head of the city health department, relayed the concerns of Dr. Dopheide, who strongly recommended the erection of a "simple crematorium building... of suitable size and fueled by gas." Dr. Wiggers coldly added that separate crematoria for individuals "would hardly be necessary" because multiple bodies would presumably be burned at once.[10] A meeting of all the important players (including *Baurat* [Building Officer] Tripcke responsible for the creation of the ghetto) took place on November 6. Among issues of timing and geography, the Nazi authorities decided that Jews would only be able to take bedroom and kitchen items and that they must be "clearly advised that anyone who destroyed remaining furniture or damaged an apartment would be severely punished."[11]

Governor Lasch told Katzmann on November 6: "I hereby delegate to you the execution of the entire operation. You are responsible for ensuring that it runs smoothly."[12] Two days later, large posters around Lviv proclaimed: "Notice: Creation of a Jewish Residential District in the City of Lviv." The text in German, Russian, and Polish, under Lasch's signature, informed Jewish citizens that they had until December 14 to move into the designated area. The poster included a map and a timeline of phased relocation.[13]

A frenzy of confusion, violence, and dislocation followed. As Jews in the affected areas struggled with heart-rending family decisions, the Jewish Council tried to intercede, though understandably from a position of zero influence. Apparently, the *Stadthauptmann* (German mayor) Kujath had only informed them of the plan on the day of the announcement (or perhaps only via the poster). Their anguish can be heard even eight decades later through the words on the yellow typewriter paper. "This decision [ghettoization plan] presents us with the enormous, almost insurmountable administrative task of the relocation of 120,000–130,000 souls. We obediently take notice of the Governor's decision and will apply all our strength toward carrying out this task. However, we take the liberty to mention the following difficulties which make the implementation of this extremely difficult if not in some ways impossible."[14] Writing for the Jewish Council, Vice President Adolf Rothfeld laid out for six pages the challenges facing the Lviv Jewish community in complying with the movement instructions. In closing, he asked Governor Lasch to extend the deadline and provide some reasonable material support to relieve the pressure.[15] In hindsight, the futility of these requests seems obvious, but they remain fully understandable in the context of the times and illustrate the practical challenges for the Jewish community. The Germans paid the Jewish Council's objections no mind; they *did*, however, supply some construction materials. On December 2, the construction chief in the mayor's office ordered 2,400 kg (2.4 tons) of barbed wire, 1,000 kg (1 ton) of wire nails, and 50kg (110lbs) of 50mm electrical wire.[16]

For most Jews, however, logistic decisions regarding ghettoization existed only at the domestic level, measured in suitcases, family heirlooms, food, and footsteps. Those in the targeted zones were allowed to bring "essential" personal possessions and furnishings. For very obvious reasons, the Nazis forbade any commercial inventory or merchandise from being brought into the ghetto. The civil administration promised collective punishment for any destruction of property or furnishings during the relocation and demanded a five-hundred-man contingent of Jewish police to supervise the operation.[17] Some companies exploiting Jewish labor sought to designate whole buildings to house their workforce. Indeed, when the full plan could not be accomplished, skilled workers were permitted to live in three "quarters" south of the tracks. Meanwhile, in Jewish homes throughout the city, families struggled with the ordeal of packing only what they could carry for a move to a run-down part of town and to an uncertain future.

The Jewish Council and its Housing Office scrambled against impossible odds to find accommodations for all the new arrivals. Nine-year-old Alex Kozlowski went into the ghetto with his mother, aunt, and uncle. "You took what you could carry," he said, "but I really don't remember anything about that part. Things were nothing. The only things that mattered were those that had value to trade for food. Like silver and gold, or maybe nice linen if you were trading with Polish people. Money had some value, but not much."[18] For the Jews of Lviv as elsewhere, ghettoization meant the great loss of all things normal, as well as uncertainty, fear, disease, discomfort, starvation, sickness, and, frequently, death. Abraham Goldberg had five minutes to gather his things along with his family and move out.[19] Architect Zeev Porath received a "sleeping spot" in a one-room apartment with one kitchen that he shared with three other families (six people).[20]

Great violence accompanied the move into the ghetto, particularly as those moving became easy targets at the only authorized entrance to the ghetto: the infamous Peltewna overpass. The same chokepoints identified by Major Weise, the railway underpasses, became terrifying gauntlets where Germans and Ukrainians victimized Jews lined up with their chosen possessions to enter the ghetto. These "so-called bridge guards" beat and robbed them at these five entry points until mid-December.[21] One Jewish witness lamented how "unheard of exploitation by the ... Ukrainian and, in exceptional cases, also the Polish population" marked the event, in addition to the Nazis' own killing and abuse.[22] The violence became so widespread and ferocious that the occupation of the ghetto in November and December 1941 became known as the "Trestle Aktion." SS men and Ukrainian police stopped and searched every cart entering the new ghetto, stealing any valuables they found. Meier Lewi was shocked by the regular beatings of elderly Jews by the police. Worse still, the Nazis had specifically targeted this group, separating them and shooting in them in the "Piaski" killing site behind the Janowska camp.[23] The movement into the ghetto was anything but ordinary and carried on well into 1942; the area was not officially sealed until late in its existence.

Non-Jews had to move as well to vacate space in the designated ghetto area. This meant that at least a third of the city was moving through the streets to new housing. In this process, Jews were further victimized financially, forced to cover rent increases for moving non-Jews.[24] At the same time, in the cruelly connected world of the Holocaust, another victim group, the Roma, sought refuge from the Nazis in the many now-abandoned Jewish homes.[25]

Under an Unlucky Star:
Life and Death in the Lviv Ghetto

The removal to the ghetto forced both new and old responsibilities on the Jewish community of Lviv. As Leon Wells's father suggested, it also challenged Jews at every level with unforeseeable dilemmas. Lviv had the third-largest ghetto in all of Europe. More Jews lived there than in all of the Netherlands.[26] Realizing, as they had elsewhere, that they could not manage such a large population alone, the Nazis forced the Jewish community to assist them. They appointed the first Jewish Council in July 1941 and named seventy-year-old lawyer Jozef Parnes as the first chairman. It was not an enviable position. Three out of four chairmen (including Parnes) and many members of subsequent councils would be murdered by the Nazis.[27] Eventually, the Lviv Jewish Council consisted of twenty-two divisions and six subdivisions and had a staff of 4,000, which represented around 4.5 percent of the ghetto population.[28] The breadth and subject areas of the departments covered every aspect of public life and emphasize both the crushing responsibility borne by the Jewish Council and the nature of the demands made upon the Jewish community by the Nazis.

The most pressing issue facing the Jewish Council in the beginning was housing. The new ghetto area in the undeveloped Zamarstynów area north of the city was not impossibly small, but the lack of accommodations posed a massive problem. People flooded in through the bloody underpass gauntlet with little more than they could carry, requiring not only a roof but also furniture, food, and basic necessities. The delay by non-Jews in vacating their homes exacerbated these problems. Between the first letter from the Jewish Council to the Nazi authorities on November 10 and the next on November 25, Dr. Adolf Rothfeld had become the president of the Judenrat. The Germans had shot his predecessor, Parnes, for refusing to hand over Jews for labor. Rothfeld protested in his letter that while they had successfully evacuated from two of the sectors, the "housing of [the new arrivals] thrust great difficulties [upon them] because the Aryan population had not moved out in the meantime." There was no room for them, he wrote. Jews were being temporarily housed in bathhouses and hallways of private homes.[29] Indeed, even in mid-May 1942, the Germans themselves counted 10,300 Aryans living in the ghetto and occupying 2,099 homes. In the same report, they noted that 16,425 Jews were living in 10,451 rooms on the Aryan side.[30] Rothfeld closed his letter with the canny mention of the first case of typhus in the ghetto . . . which had appeared in an Aryan home. He pointedly requested a pause in ghettoization out of "concern for an impending epidemic." Governor Lasch forwarded Rothfeld's letter to the city authorities.[31] The ghettoization of Lviv's Jews remained a spotty and incomplete affair, at least until summer 1942.

The lack of stereotypical German efficiency did little for the columns of the dispossessed streaming into the ghetto. Edmund Kessler remembered that "ungovernable crowds of people carried the remains of their miserable possessions." With nowhere else to go, they "filled the street and narrow alleys in front of the Housing Department." "Like camping gypsies," he wrote, "they clustered at nearby house doors and in courtyards."[32] The gathering storm also swept foreigners into the ghetto, including Jews from Palestine, Britain, and the United States.[33] The peculiar geography of the ghetto that was divided into a section for "artisans" south of the tracks made the work of the Housing Department even more complex.[34] One of the first victims of hunger, oppression, and crisis is perhaps decency, and Rabbi David Kahane remembered that some of the Jews already living in the designated area could be less than welcoming. According to him, the "poor and affluent alike refused to accept subtenants for free. They haggled for each square meter, each bed, each chair." Housing Department officials as well could be corrupt and susceptible to bribes for housing.[35] Of course, this does not characterize all experiences; in all catastrophes there are those who retreat into themselves and strive for their own benefit.

The Nazis themselves created most of the inequalities in the Jewish community, prizing skilled labor as they did. They adopted this leniency due to a lack of non-Jewish replacements, not from any desire to improve Jewish lives. German city administrators consciously compiled lists of those Jews and their families who were not "productively working" in January 1942 in preparation for the first major deportation to Bełżec in March. They also decided that working Jews and their immediate family would be excepted from deportation.[36] While the March deportation was ongoing, the new German mayor, Egon Höller, noted that "the wife and children under sixteen should suffice to care for the working Jews who remained."[37] In this way, some family units were able to stay together in the early days of the ghetto. Companies "employing" Jewish labor were also encouraged to consolidate their workers in the ghetto (which would become a source of friction between the Janowska camp and city authorities). The workers became known as the "barrack Jews" of a particular company and were supervised by other Jews working in those companies.[38]

A predictable food shortage accompanied the growing population and scarcity of housing. This, too, the Germans mostly created themselves. In addition to forced overcrowding and expropriation, Nazi policy curtailed the Jews' own ability to fend for themselves. In May 1942, Mayor Höller deemed it "advisable" that the Krakauerplatz market be cleared of "Jewish elements." In addition, occupation policy limited Jewish shopping hours to lunchtime or between two and four o'clock. Edmund Kessler noted that the Nazis often used this time to prey on Jews waiting in line at stores, snatching them up for forced labor.[39] The Germans saddled the Jewish Council with the responsibility of provisioning the ghetto, but provided no real aid. Within the ghetto, the actual task of finding food fell to the Economic Department, which managed an impressive forty-nine kitchens where Jews could receive food.[40] Unfortunately, the arithmetic would never work out. Recreating the actual allowances of food can be difficult as many survivors did not or could not precisely record their rations. However, table 2 gives at least a rough accounting of official food distribution.[41]

Table 2. Food allowances in the Lviv ghetto

ITEM	QUANTITY	FREQUENCY
Bread	700–1,400g (1.5–3lbs)	Weekly
Flour	400g (14oz)	Monthly
Sugar	100g (3.5oz)	Monthly
Turnip jam	100g (3.5oz)	Monthly
Fat	200g (7oz)	Monthly

Of course, this represents only the baseline and often the best-case scenario. The Jewish Council did what it could, sometimes successfully. In December 1941, it convinced the authorities to supply 25kg of potatoes to those "productively employed" workers, though their quality seems to be much contested.[42] Given that no eggs, milk, or meat were to be supplied, many ghetto inhabitants spent much of their time attempting to find food. In March 1942, the Jewish Council opened a kosher kitchen on Sonnenstrasse, not far from the city opera and the Brygidki prison. It also announced forty-eight locations where ghetto inhabitants could buy food.[43]

Hunger struck the weak, the old, and the very young particularly hard in Lviv as it did in other ghettos throughout Europe. A thriving black market arose, as it does in all situations of scarcity, and local non-Jews were only too happy to profit at exorbitant prices. For peasants from the countryside, ghettoization was "a great opportunity," worth defying an official Nazi ban on such behavior. They could supply simple foodstuffs and receive valuable items they never could have afforded before the war (and likely after). As Samuel Drix recalls, "We were giving away, piece by piece, what we still had at home in exchange for potatoes, flour, vegetables, and other foodstuffs to supplement the inadequate rations." He remembered victimization in very specific terms, as do many survivors. "I remember well," he later wrote, "how I gave a new, luxurious couch with a glass bookcase attached to the back for a not too great sack of potatoes."[44] Hunger also led to corruption by those with access to the food, including Jewish officials. The aching want drove others to even darker places. Alex Kozlowski used to watch the world of the ghetto from the window of the room he shared with more than fifteen people. One day, he watched as one man stabbed another in the back in a battle over food. "I saw a lot of things out that window," he later wrote.[45]

Hunger also weakened even the strong, making them more vulnerable to the diseases that thrive on overcrowding, filth, and poor sanitation. One of the greatest killers was typhus. An old saying notes that "plague follows the trade routes, typhus follows the wars."[46] Indeed, a scholar of epidemics noted tellingly that "typhus epidemics are manmade."[47] This was certainly the case in the Nazi war against the Jews. The disease decimated camps and ghettos throughout the territory of the Third Reich and it would also strike Janowska, likely transmitted from the ghetto.

For patients in the weakened condition of those in the ghetto, the disease was frequently deadly. Its symptoms (weakness and vomiting, for example) made its victims unable to eat and unable to take in food; this was a double curse in the ghetto environment. Without aggravating circumstances, the mortality rate can be up to 40 percent.[48] Jewish doctors in the ghetto fought tenaciously against this killer. Given the prevalence of Jews in the medical profession, there was a literal army at the ready. Samuel Drix, himself a physician, noted that according to the records of the Health Department there were at least five hundred twenty doctors in the ghetto.[49] Jewish physicians in the ghetto held a conference on January 31, 1942, to discuss issues relating to the typhus outbreak.[50] The Jewish Council also established three hospitals in the ghetto, including one specifically set aside for infectious diseases on Zamarstynówka Street run by a Dr. Elster.[51] However, the beautiful and well-equipped Rappaport Jewish Hospital, with its massive turn-of-the-century Moorish revival dome, was not available. Located well south of the rail line, it had been given to the Ukrainians along with any equipment not stolen by the Nazis.[52] An abundance of care and an appalling lack of supplies characterized medical treatment by Jewish healthcare professionals in the ghetto. The Jewish Council attempted to inform the ghetto of methods to combat lice and the disease in its newsletter, partly in response to letters in their "question box." Residents were told, for example, that they could make wood lye to bathe with by boiling 1.5 kilograms of ash. To remove lice from hair, a linen hood soaked in paraffin and oil was to be worn for twenty-four hours.[53] Jewish doctors were even sent by frightened authorities to battle the disease in the countryside.[54]

Ironically, the creator of the first successful typhus vaccine was living and working in Lviv on precisely that topic during the Holocaust. Rudolf Weigl was a Polish scientist and graduate of Lviv's Jan Kazimierz University. The Nazis forced him to continue his work for their benefit. Weigl resisted, however. He made his laboratory a haven for persecuted Poles and Jews. He went further and supplied the German Army with ineffective vaccines while funneling the more successful prototypes to the ghetto. Weigl also arranged hiding places for Jews in the botanical garden of the University of Lviv. Working on typhus was the perfect cover for him to smuggle the vaccine into the ghetto as the Nazis remained deathly afraid of a typhus outbreak on the Aryan side. Weigl was eventually named a Righteous Among the Nations by Yad Vashem for his rescue work.[55] His exploits even reached the West in February 1942 when the *Jewish Telegraphic Agency* reported that Jewish scientists from the ghettos had been sent to work for him.[56] Without a doubt, Weigl's experimental vaccines reached Dr. Elster's infectious disease hospital and saved lives. Meanwhile, the General Government seemed more concerned about a possible rabies outbreak, which it expressed in a "special order" in May 1942.[57]

Disease was not the only threat to the health of patients in the ghetto, however. Nazi administrators searched for the weak and the sick with the same vigor that Gebauer and Willhaus did in their camps. For the Nazis these were "useless eaters," incapable of working and thus worthless. Hospitals increasingly became dangerous places for both patients and staff. In January 1942, Ukrainian policemen under the command of the Germans surrounded a Jewish hospital for the incurably ill and removed all the patients. They were loaded onto trucks and taken away, most likely to the sands behind the Janowska camp where they were shot.[58] Doctors also died in large numbers; more than a few succumbed to the disease they were fighting. Perhaps that was the case for Dr. Joachim Reichler, who was eulogized in the March 1942 ghetto newsletter. He died in "the practice of his profession." In this "hard-working, capable, young doctor," the paper continued, "we have lost one of our best from the younger generation of doctors."[59] It could have been a eulogy for all the Jewish doctors in the city, if not the whole ghetto population. Samuel Drix estimated that of the five hundred twenty doctors registered in the ghetto, only seventeen survived until liberation.[60]

Elsewhere in Lviv, the Nazis murdered other patients, this time as a continuation of the "euthanasia" program that first took the lives of more than seventy thousand mentally and physically disabled German citizens. In a park south of the main train station sat the Kulparkow asylum, which had already gained notoriety in November 1941 when a Distrikt Galizien German doctor had requested that the twelve hundred patients be murdered; indeed, a gassing center had even been considered for Lviv.[61] By October 1942, all the patients in Kulparkow had been murdered through starvation, replaced by a German Army field hospital. By 1943, German patients were being transported from the Rhineland on the German border with France to starve to death in Lviv.[62] The crimes in Kulparkow followed the general pattern throughout occupied Poland where patients in mental hospitals were murdered to make room for either victims from elsewhere or for German military usage. There is also evidence that mental patients from Lviv including Poles and Ukrainians were murdered in Janowska.[63]

A critical department of the Jewish Council focused on Janowska itself. One of the somewhat unique aspects of the Lviv ghetto was its ability to support the Jewish community imprisoned elsewhere. The location of the camp in the city itself enabled a close relationship between ghetto and camp. The short distance was critical, but so too were the close connections between prisoners of the camp and prisoners of the ghetto. After all, families remained intact for some time and prewar relationships allowed for contacts lacking elsewhere. The Welfare Department directed by the social worker Dr. Joseph Cohen received only a small allowance from the Jewish Council, none from the Germans, and relied on donations from Jews in the ghetto to operate. Regardless, it established a Committee for Helping the Inmates of Camps in December 1941.[64] The Aid Committee operated from that time until roughly August 1942. Much of what we know about it comes in large part from the testimony of Stanisława Gogolowska, a Polish member of the underground who actively worked with the Aid Committee to deliver packages, in part to her son who was in the camp.

Both Gebauer and Willhaus allowed the committee to operate, likely because it relieved some of their burden of feeding and clothing their prisoners. Bernard Hirschhorn stated that the Aid Committee supplied DAW prisoners with blankets.[65] Willhaus refused to issue clean undergarments, demanding them instead from the Jewish community. They delivered these to the ZAL as ordered, but Willhaus put them into storage.[66] Accompanying the deliveries of packages into the camp, Stanisława Gogolowska had a unique opportunity to both observe the staff and interact with the prisoners. In the early days, she noted, the delivery of packages went relatively undisturbed, though this appears to have changed over time. The SS men clearly saw an opportunity to benefit. Gogolowska noted after the war that the proper delivery of the packages "could be 'bought' only with the greatest of gifts."[67] There are no doubts as to who the beneficiaries of these "gifts" must have been as any guard could disrupt the flow of supplies to a prisoner. At times, the SS even fired into crowds waiting for packages.[68] For Abraham Goldberg, the packages were "another means for Willhaus to torture them." He recalls standing in formation and watching two carts full of packages being intentionally turned away by the commandant, knowing it meant "another week of agonizing hunger."[69] Gogolowska hinted that a hidden delivery often accompanied the wagons. She notes that as typhus spread through the DAW, Gebauer could not be told for fear that he would immediately murder anyone who was sick. Instead, a camp doctor supplied a list of the medications required and the Aid Committee scrounged them for the camp.[70]

When the SS men herded prisoners from the camp to the city baths every few weeks, the Aid Committee was there. Abuse and humiliation accompanied these marches and the terror of arbitrary death haunted them, but still the committee set up a table at the exit of the baths "with baked rolls and bread that were distributed among the prisoners" as well as marmalade on bread.[71] Such compassion, generosity, and selfless risk-taking certainly speaks to the connection between the Jewish community and the camp.

Throughout the chaos of the early days of occupation, the Aid Committee even supplied packages to Lviv Jews imprisoned outside the city. Theodor Bialecki asked the Jewish Council to send packages to a camp near Złoczów

(Zolochiv). He remembered that "the families were agreeable and brought parcels to the synagogue for their relatives in the camp."[72]

Despite these efforts, the Jewish Council played a game rigged against them in every way. The reactions of ghetto leadership during the Holocaust to being thrust into command varied over time and space, from the arrogant and exploitative Chaim Rumkowski in Łódz to the pained and kindly Adam Czerniaków in Warsaw. Individuals drew their own conclusions about their own leadership according to their own experiences. Descriptions of the successive Jewish Councils in Lviv reveal a similar mixture of condemnation and praise. The first chairman Parnes was generally praised for his refusal to cooperate with the Nazis in handing over Jews for labor (for which he paid with his life). The ever-critical Rabbi Kahane wrote that his was "a shining example of the conduct of a representative of the Jewish community in times of crisis." Somewhat grimly, he saw Parnes's death as a "high point in the history of the ghetto."[73] Parnes's successor, Rotfeld, received more criticism, being seen as more compliant with German demands. Of course, one must view this in historical context. He had just seen his predecessor murdered for noncompliance and was in a hopeless situation. In any event, Rotfeld does not seem to have been eager or self-enriching. Adolf Folkmann generally concluded that the Jewish Council "made superhuman efforts to save as many victims as possible. They tried to help everybody, and they used every possible loophole and clause in the German regulations."[74] Ghetto inhabitants definitely recognized the difficult position of the council, even if they did not like their decisions. Jack Ahrens called the Judenrat "a necessary evil" but also recognized that they were "pawns" and that "if they didn't do it, they would have been killed and somebody else would have been in put in their place."[75] The Jewish police, on the other hand, seem to come in for general disdain from survivors. One described them as "merciless, beating other Jews" and another admitted that "I myself had a deep hatred for the Jewish police."[76] Kahane, too, criticized them, but with a bit more understanding. "People of conscience did not join the police," he wrote, but he "knew many policemen who risked their lives to save Jewish families from death." Even so, for him, the police were a "stain on the history of the Lvov ghetto."[77] Parsing the choices of those in the ghetto is always an incredibly complex matter as all operated in an environment of limited agency and crushing ethical dilemmas.

For a final example of this, we turn to the March 1942 deportation. In preparation, the Germans demanded that the Judenrat compose lists of "asocial elements" including those receiving welfare from the Jewish community. The task of providing those names fell to a Dr. Kahn, head of the Welfare Department. He was clearly uncomfortable with the task and an official meeting of the community's rabbis was called. They opposed the creation of the list and sent a delegation to Chairman Landsberg. What we know of this meeting comes from council member Rabbi Kahane. They greeted a "pallid and tired" chairman and informed him that according to rabbinical law he could not hand over fellow Jews to the Nazis, that "it is better for all to die than to hand one Jew to the enemy." Kahane remembered that "[Landsberg] was severely offended by these remarks and erupted in anger: 'You gentlemen must think we are still in the prewar era and that you are speaking to the chairman of the religious council. We are living in totally different times and our community administration is no longer a religious body but the Gestapo's executive tool, and anyone who opposes the Gestapo...' The chairman did not finish the sentence. We understood his trend of thought: he had no desire to run afoul of the Gestapo and risk his life."[78] And so the lists were (at least partially) made. And those selected disappeared as the rail lines bent in a slow crescent around the Janowska camp.

Aktion! Deportations Begin

Sometime in the late summer or early fall of 1941, Hitler made two critical, horrendous, and epoch-changing decisions. He decided that the only "solution" to the "Jewish Question" must be murder, first applying this to Soviet Jews and then to European Jews as a whole.[79] Subordinates presented Hitler with ever more extreme plans in hopes of divining his desires from rather vague pronouncements. This spared him the necessity of having specific plans and allowed to him to pick and choose as he saw fit. Hitler most appreciated subordinates who were "tough people of whom I know they take the steps I would take myself. The best man is for me the one who bothers me least by taking upon himself 95 out of 100 decisions."[80] Ian

Kershaw termed this "working toward the Führer." This is not to say that Hitler had to be talked into murdering Jews, but bureaucrats did explore real alternatives in earnest. The Nazis proposed a deportation of European Jews to a "reservation" in Poland in 1939, but Hans Frank opposed this vigorously, envisioning a much more ambitious future for his kingdom. In 1940, planners including Adolf Eichmann seriously examined the possibility of deporting Jews to the island of Madagascar. This plan was shelved as the Germans never could control the seas as required. The final and most ill-defined plan involved the future deportation of Jews to a "territory yet to be determined," pre-Barbarossa code for somewhere in the Soviet Union.[81]

Some scholars suggest that Hitler intended to begin these deportations after the defeat of the Soviet Union; therefore, the decision to proceed in 1941 may well indicate a confidence of an imminent victory and a desire to avoid unnecessary delays. Regardless of motivation, it is possible to narrow down a time frame. We do not have a document from Hitler specifically ordering this shift in anti-Jewish policy but it is impossible that such a path could have been taken without his approval. Moreover, a cluster of events throughout the Nazi universe align to indicate a marked turn toward murder in summer and late fall of 1941. Specifically, the move to annihilation can be seen in two decisions: the July 1941 decision to murder all Soviet Jews and a September/October 1941 decision to murder European Jews.[82]

In July 1941, Adolf Eichmann sought a "quick-acting agent" as a "humane solution to dispose" of nonworking Jews in the Łodz ghetto. The same month Göring signed and issued an ominous authorization (likely approved by Hitler) for Himmler's deputy, Reinhard Heydrich. "I hereby charge you," Göring wrote, "with making all necessary preparations in regard to organizational and financial matters for bringing about a complete solution of the Jewish question in the German sphere of influence in Europe."[83] In August, Himmler ordered SS Cavalry elements to kill Jewish women and children. Around the same time, the *Einsatzgruppen*, which had mainly limited themselves to killing military-aged Jewish men (as they had in Lviv), began to murder all Jews, irrespective of age or gender. On September 3, 1941, in the basement of a penal barracks in Auschwitz, Zyklon B was used for the first time to kill human beings. Three days later, the camp staff there gassed nine hundred Soviet prisoners of war in a makeshift gas chamber.

In addition, by October 1941 it becomes clear that a decision had been made to murder all European Jews, not just those in the Soviet Union. As Christopher Browning notes, by this time Nazi policy had shifted to "total and systematic extermination."[84]

While the intention to murder the Jews of Europe solidified in the late summer and early fall of 1941, the planning for this new operation needed coordination. The man in charge of the Final Solution, Reinhard Heydrich, scheduled a meeting for December 9, 1941, at an ornate mansion on a lake outside of Berlin. The Japanese attack on Pearl Harbor and a massive Soviet counterattack on the Eastern Front threw the Nazi regime into chaos and forced the meeting's postponement until January 20, 1942. When the Wannsee Conference convened, Heydrich began by reasserting his authority for carrying out the "overall solution" to the "Jewish question"; he left no doubt about that by including a copy of that July 31, 1941, memo in his invitations.[85] Attendees were mid-level bureaucrats from state agencies who would be central to the planning of the mass murder or had experience already, including Adolf Eichmann. In February 1942, Heydrich wrote that the conference "happily, has settled the basic outlines for the *practical implementation* of the final solution of the Jewish question."[86] To this end, he proposed that "in the course of the final solution, the Jews should be brought in an appropriate manner and under appropriate direction to work in the east." The "hardy" Jewish workers who survived their labor would have to be "treated accordingly."[87] There can be no doubt what that meant.

While the Wannsee Conference took place, construction on the first dedicated extermination camp in a small rural village called Bełżec about fifty miles northwest of Lviv was well underway.[88] It had begun on November 1, the first full day of the DAW-L's existence as a closed camp. On that day, Polish laborers began to build a camp on only around eighteen acres that would consume around half a million lives. Beside them, Trawniki men dug the mass graves that would hold the bodies.[89] SS *Obersturmführer* (First Lieutenant) Richard Wolfgang Thomalla from the SS Central Building Administration in Lublin personally supervised the construction (and may have drawn up the plans himself). Himmler had ordered Odilo Globocnik on October 13 to build an extermination camp, and he carefully considered the camp's location, choosing a site directly on the major Lviv-Lublin-Warsaw rail line. Globocnik earned the macabre distinction of responsibility for all the soon-to-be-built "Operation Reinhard" extermination centers (Bełżec, Sobibor, and Treblinka) in the General Government. The unfolding genocide there represented in some ways a grim continuity with earlier Nazi history. Many of the men selected for work in killing centers had begun by killing the mentally and physically disabled back in Germany.

The man in charge of the Ukrainian guard force and of overseeing the initial construction, SS *Oberscharführer* (Technical Sergeant) Josef Oberhauser, had previously burned bodies at three of the "euthanasia" killing centers.[90] When he arrived, a German foreman showed him the plans for the gas chamber. Oberhauser had no misconceptions about his purpose. In an attempt to maintain secrecy, Nazi builders replaced most of the Polish civilian workers with Jewish slave laborers for the final stage of construction.[91] One of those remaining Poles described the construction of a rectangular building 36 feet long and 24 feet wide. It was divided into three sections, with a hallway connecting them. Workers lined the interior walls with tar paper, filled the space between the boards with sand, and covered the floors with tin. They added rubber seals to the doors.[92] The whole wooden building was hastily disguised as a bathhouse. When completed, they had constructed the first gas chamber of the Operation Reinhard camps whose combined death toll would approach two million people. The number of SS men stationed at the camp never exceeded twenty with a guard force of a hundred thirty Trawniki auxiliaries at its height.[93]

Sometime around Christmas 1941, the commandant arrived. Globocnik chose Christian Wirth: a fifty-five-year-old World War I veteran and policeman, and the fourteenth of seventeen children.[94] He was also, like Oberhauser, a veteran of the T-4 "euthanasia" program. In fact, he was the highest-ranking member of the program assigned to Operation Reinhard, having overseen various nonmedical and security aspects including security, the falsification of death certificates, and the process of killing itself. He set up the gas chambers at the Hartheim asylum as well. By the official "end" of the program, Wirth had become the inspector of all the killing centers. Gathering his staff together in the December cold, he told them unambiguously that "in Bełżec, all the Jews would be knocked off."[95] Oberhauser, who served as his deputy, stated that Wirth's "special distinguishing characteristics were iron rigidity, unquestioning obedience, faith in the Führer, and a total lack of tenderness and empathy." Another subordinate described him simply as "malevolent."[96]

Soon the camp was ready to begin killing. Herman Höfle, the administrative chief of Operation Reinhard, told an administrator in Lublin that he could "receive four to five transports with 1,000 Jews each for the destination of Bełżec station. These Jews would cross the border [of the occupied territories of the Soviet Union] and never return to the General Government."[97] In Lviv, the ss and Ukrainian police stormed through the ghetto in the last two weeks of March, searching for "asocials" to deport. Local informants assisted them. A Ukrainian report from the Fifth Police Precinct from March 20, 1942, is especially revealing. In it, we learn that a woman in the Kleparów suburb reported the two Jews hiding in her home to avoid her own arrest. Someone denounced Albina Leschuk for "hiding a Jew called 'Shymko' who moves around without an arm band."[98] The Ukrainian police commander reported that his men had delivered 2,254 Jews to the Sobieski school collection site on March 25.[99] Two days later he reported another 1,648 rounded up.[100]

By the time these reports were filed, the "Asocial Aktion" in Lviv had been filling train cars at the Kleparów station for almost two weeks. The first trains arriving in Bełżec on that Tuesday in March, however, had not been fully filled, incensing Katzmann. A Polish railway worker who backed the trains into the camp estimated that usually the average train had 40–60 cars with an average of 100–120 people per car.[101] In the beginning, the rail spur in the camp could not accommodate that many cars, so full cars had to wait outside until space became available.

The train journey itself was a torment for the deportees; sometimes more than 1,000 died before arrival. Often, deportation trains had to wait for more important traffic to pass by. But that does not mean the event remained hidden from the public. A Polish railway worker in the Rawa Ruska (Rava-Ruska) station less than twenty miles from the camp recalled a train of Lviv Jews passing through during the March Aktion. "I knew perfectly well that they came from Lviv," he stated, "because I spoke personally with several of the people in that transport.... These people said that they were on their way to territory that had previously been occupied by Soviet Russia, that there were large collective farms and factories there, and they would work there." At the station in Bełżec within sight of the camp, deportees could buy water from the townspeople until the SS forbade it.[102] Likely, the Lviv Jews in the March Aktion sought to quench their thirst using whatever valuables they may have been able to take with them from the ghetto.

The first deportation from Lviv arrived in this small, dark place on the afternoon of March 17, 1942. We are able to reconstruct with disturbing accuracy the arrival of transports of Jews to the camp from both survivor and perpetrator testimony. Christian Wirth directed the performance and his routine would be adopted in the other Reinhard camps with few modifications. The SS men and guards opened the car doors in the beginning, but later the camp's "work Jews" were enlisted in this process. The SS met arriving victims with a deceitful introduction promising that they would work after disinfection. In the beginning, Wirth gave this speech personally so it is likely that the Lviv Jews heard from "Christian the Cruel" himself. Rudolf Reder, one of the two survivors of the half-million souls who entered Bełżec's gates, recalled that "delusional speech" and sadly noted that "people always drew comfort from that moment, and I saw the same spark of hope in people's eyes."[103] The remainder of the process must have been a bewildering and terrifying blur for the victims. Guards forced them to an undressing barracks, though the first arrivals in the Lviv transport probably had to undress on the platform as these barracks had not been completed. The Jews were quickly shorn of their hair, then driven down a narrow barbed-wire corridor called the "tube," which was camouflaged with fresh branches from the surrounding pine forest. The gas chambers waited at the other end.

The March and April transports of Lviv Jews ended in the first gas chamber. The Bełżec installation initially used bottled cyanide gas as had been used in the "euthanasia" centers but would later switch to carbon monoxide from a repurposed Soviet tank engine. The killing process took perhaps fifteen to twenty minutes, after which Jews of the Sonderkommando dragged the bodies out, searched them for valuables, and removed gold teeth. In the spring of 1942, the corpses would be dumped in the pits dug by the Trawniki men in November. The process, from opening the car doors to burying corpses in the pits, took between two and three hours for an entire transport of around five thousand people. Thus, when the train with "All Wheels Rolling for Victory" written on its side arrived on March 31, 1942, the night before Passover, everyone on board was murdered well before the Seder dinner would have started.[104] Bełżec only killed by day, so late-arriving trains stood full of victims until the next morning.[105] A month or so later, the camp ceased operations for six weeks while a larger concrete and brick building with six gas chambers was constructed.[106]

Between March 17 and April 1, fifteen thousand Jews from Lviv were murdered in the first gas chamber at Bełżec. Their clothes, however, returned to Janowska. The disappearance of family members caused great worry in the ghetto. While Jerzy Chyrowski successfully hid, other members of his family were not so lucky and ended up on the trains. With a kind of detachment present in many survivors' testimonies, Chyrowski simply said that "a part of my family lost their lives during the March Aktion."[107] Klara Szpilka found herself in the Janowska camp with her family during the roundup. She told authorities that there was a selection, and the rest of her testimony no longer mentions family.[108]

Those left in the ghetto were unsure at first about the meanings of the deportations. Abraham Goldberg testified that "at the time of the March action, it was generally not known what Bełżec was and it was a called a resettlement action. One did not have a lot of illusions, but we did not know anything about an extermination camp."[109] Samuel Drix wrote that "when the old people were taken I was truly perplexed and believed this was really a resettlement. When I heard rumors of what had happened to them, I simply couldn't believe it. I had not known or even heard rumors before this that the Germans were committing mass murders of people who could not possibly be a threat."[110] Rumors circulated in the ghetto. Rabbi Kahane heard that killing was done by electrocution, gas, or steam. Other rumors mentioned the creation of soap from the bodies.[111] As late as 1944 after liberation, David Manusevich told the Soviets with some conviction that the Germans had created a soap factory in Bełżec where they "processed human bodies into soap."[112] This confusion is, of course, understandable. Lviv's Jews had only an informal network of news to rely on, though it would become increasingly clear what Bełżec really was. Ironically, the outside world was better informed. The Polish underground government, the Delegatura, compiled a detailed report in April 1942 that correctly identified March 17 as the first date of gassing and stated that "between March 17 and April 13, about fifty-two transports (each of eighteen to thirty-five freight-cars with an average of 1,500 people) arrived in the camp."[113] The *Israelistisches Wochenblatt* paper in Switzerland told readers on May 22, 1942, that the Soviet news outlet *Pravda* "reports that in Lemberg about 13,000 Jews have lost their lives."[114]

At this point, the SS had decided that those capable of work would be used for labor and the rest murdered. This had important repercussions for the Janowska camp and the Jews of Lviv. Historian Thomas Sandkühler has concluded quite emphatically that "soon a direct connection became evident between the construction of Bełżec and the building of forced labor camps. It established itself as the basis of the National Socialist Jewish policy: Those who could work were used in road construction, those who could not were murdered in Bełżec."[115] Himmler himself had his eye on Distrikt Galizien. In February 1942, he ordered the construction of Durchgangstrasse IV, or Highway 4, which was to run through Lviv to Tarnopol and, with the greatest optimism, further east to Rostov. The supporting labor camps (and Janowska) allowed Katzmann to consolidate Jews despite Governor Frank's prohibitions.[116] Katzmann had already begun work on DG IV in the district; he himself proudly reported that the building of seven camps with 4,000 Jews had started on October 15, 1941, despite "significant difficulties."[117]

Nazi authorities in Lviv had, in fact, accurately predicted the labor element of the Final Solution before Wannsee. Because the SS had not succeeded yet in wresting control of all slave labor in the region from civil authorities, it instead claimed the power to determine who was capable of work and used Janowska as a means to physically control that workforce. It exercised this authority through the issuing and reissuing of work papers and authorizations.[118] Forcing Jews to obtain new work documents was a common tactic during Operation Reinhard and a "relatively simple and effective form of public confusion to prevent forgery of documents."[119] Globocnik "had instructions from Himmler to murder all the Jews from the district who were 'incapable of work.'"[120] On February 27, 1942, Major Weise, the head of Lviv Police, published guidelines establishing a Jewish police; this, too, was perhaps in anticipation of the need for their "assistance" in upcoming deportation operations.[121] Certainly, they performed significant work in the deportations. In the midst of this, the Jewish Council had to explain to Nazi authorities that it had been unable to collect a new residential tax because it had to dedicate 2,000 men including 500 Jewish policemen to the deportation operation. The irony of the Jewish community having to request an extension on its own economic exploitation due to being sent to its death is simply heartbreaking.[122]

Further preparations for the March Aktion appear in the records of the Jewish community. The circular published by the Jewish Council on March 1, 1942, informed readers that Distrikt Galizien was the only area in the General Government that had not completed a registration of workers and that this registration would begin soon with an emphasis on skilled workers. Indeed, much of the latest news concerned various aspects of labor and registration.[123] Local German initiatives and directives from Wannsee combined to make fitness the decisive element of the first deportation, which was cloaked in the camouflage of an aktion targeting "asocial elements."

While the March Aktion was the largest and most traumatic up to that point, it had not been the only one. As we have seen, in December 1941, there was a specific targeting of the elderly during the "Trestle Aktion" when Jews were moving into the ghetto area. According to several witnesses, Nazis sought out the elderly and shot them either in the sands behind the Janowska camp or in the Łyczaków (Lychakiv) suburb on the eastern edge of Lviv. Samuel Drix described older people rounded up for "resettlement" and trucked away. At the time, he observed that "nobody could understand this. Why . . . would the Germans . . . be resettling just these older people?" Later, he heard that they had been shot.[124] At the trial of Adolf Eichmann, Leon Wells testified that around two to three thousand elderly people—even those with work permits—had been caught on the streets and disappeared.[125] Tadeusz Tomaszewski wrote in his diary on December 9, 1941, that for three days Jews including elderly women were trucked to the Łyczaków Forest and shot.[126]

There no would be more deportations from Lviv until the cataclysmic "Great Aktion" in August 1942. Bełżec was building a new, larger gas chamber building in preparation for an escalation in killing, and so the camp was closed temporarily. The Nazis would have to do their own killings in-house (often at Janowska) until their extermination center reopened. Thus, the aktions tended to be shorter in duration and involve fewer victims. They also tended to be less likely to be remembered as discrete events. Survivor testimony indicates some higher intensity killing at the end of May and beginning of June 1942. Jerzy Chyrowski's uncle was caught up in this one, and Chyrowski went to the assembly point in the vain hope that he could save him. Chyrowski estimated four thousand victims during this "May Aktion."[127] Some of them were murdered in "the sands" behind the Janowska camp. Leon Wells told the Soviets in 1944 that "women, children, and old people were brough t[to the camp] for the first time from Lviv on 2 June 1942." They had to spend the night in one of the roll-call squares and were shot the next day. Wells estimated between eleven hundred and twelve hundred victims.[128]

Another assault occurred in late June 1942 and became known as the "Blitz Aktion" for its speed and severity. For two or three days between June 24 and 26, the SS and Ukrainian police conducted raids in the ghetto. Once again, the Germans targeted the elderly and those not deemed capable of work. They also apparently searched for Jews living illegally outside of the ghetto.[129] In their final report of arrests, the Ukrainian police distinguished between "Jews" and "beggars." Among those Ukrainian policemen rounding up Jews was perhaps the former sausage-maker Ivan Kalymon. At that time, he served in the Fifth Precinct along with twenty-five police cadets from the local police academy and thirty members of the National Socialist Motor Corps (NSKK). Kalymon's precinct delivered nine hundred Jews to the courtyard of the NSKK in Lviv. The Fifth Precinct arrested the most Jews out of all the Ukrainian police precincts in the city during the aktion. The policemen also dropped off a list of attempted briberies and "residence keys, money, and other items ... [including] four gold watches and one large chain" in the offices of the NSKK.[130] Some estimates of the total number of people shot during the aktion range between six thousand and eight thousand, though these may be high.[131] With Bełżec out of operation, the Janowska camp played an increasingly prominent role in aktions in and around Lviv. Leon Richman, who was already a prisoner, recalled that "in June thousands were brought to the camp" and that a hundred seventy-five children, young people, and elderly were shot.[132] It is not at all unlikely that smaller numbers of arrests brought more people to Janowska or the shooting pits in the Łyczaków Forest but did not register as distinct events.

The deportations of March 1942 introduced the ghetto population to the fear of involuntary relocation and, shortly thereafter, the terror of mass murder. They established a connection between fitness for labor and selection and a connection between the Janowska camp and the process of extermination. When Klara Szpilka and her family were separated during the March Aktion, it had been Willhaus and his deputy who had carried out the selections on the grounds of the camp. Having escaped from Janowska once, Leon Wells successfully broke *into* the ghetto to find his brother, only to be caught up in one of the ever more frequent actions. "I entered the ghetto," he wrote, "under an unlucky star."[133]

Cataclysm: The August Aktion

Dwarfing the March Aktion, the August Aktion in Lviv alone would claim more than forty thousand lives in a little more than two weeks. For the SS in the city, it would be a major effort. Almost everyone with a hand in Jewish policy was needed to ensure success. Deportations had stopped when Bełżec paused operations on April 1. The Jews of Lviv, however, were uneasy. Something was in the air and they knew it. Rudolf Reder recalled that "two weeks before the deportation, people everywhere were already talking about the coming misfortune. We despaired. We already knew what the word 'deportation' meant.... The legend of Belzec became a truth we knew about which made us quake in fear."[134] There was another bad omen. Governor General Hans Frank arrived on August 1 to commemorate the one-year anniversary of the incorporation of Lviv into his fiefdom. The Jews knew this because local Nazi authorities forced them to clean up the city in preparation. David Kahane observed that "all his previous visits came in advance of Aktionen against the Jews."[135] He was not wrong. That Sunday evening, Frank stood in the Lviv Opera House and told a gathering of Nazi leadership precisely what was before them. Referring to the Nazis of the General Government as "combat veterans in the reconstruction of a conquered land," he made it very clear what would soon take place. "We will be finished with these Jews." Frank continued: "After all, we Nazis are tackling this problem in accordance with our Party platform. It was particularly clear here. We are fortunate that we can deal with these Jews the same way they dealt with the German people.... Therefore, I only want to say this on the Jewish Question: we will solve this problem. No more Jews will come to Germany."[136]

There were other signs of the coming catastrophe. After Frank departed the city, officials shuttered the Labor Office, causing even more consternation among the Jewish population. The entire building was literally demolished. For Kahane, the meaning was clear: "we will no longer need Jewish labor."[137] Katzmann prepared the Ukrainian police for their role in the roundup, pairing them with German forces. Among them was Ivan Kalymon.

In the early hours of August 10, SS, Gestapo, and Ukrainian police crashed into the ghetto and the aktion began. The ghetto was supported by troops from a paramilitary organization, the NSKK, and the Sicherheitsdienst (SD). A German army unit of reserve infantrymen surrounded the ghetto.[138] Unlike previous roundups, little care was given about work cards; only those working in critical or war-related jobs had even a hope of being passed over. Christine Keren recalled the Germans going from apartment to apartment, sometimes shooting people on the spot or sending them to Janowska. She also remembered children being swung against walls and thrown into trucks.[139] The bodies of a woman and her child lay in the street by a Ukrainian police station, victims of Gestapo officer Carl Wöbke, from the office of Jewish affairs. He specialized in hunting down mothers with children, shooting the children "before their mothers' eyes" and sending the mother to Janowska. According to Kahane, Wöbke explained this macabre hobby by saying, "There is no point in sending children to Bełżec." The woman with the child in front of the precinct had attacked the Gestapo man and he had shot them both.[140] These deportations disproportionately affected women. Redner noted that "most of our female colleagues were annihilated during the August 1942 Action, when unlike the men, taken to the Janowski [sic] camp, they were liquidated on the spot." The epidemiologists who had worked with Dr. Weigl to combat typhus in the ghetto also were murdered during the Great Aktion.[141]

The Ukrainian police played a critical role in the roundups and not just by forming an outer cordon. They worked hand in hand with the SS and Gestapo rounding up Jews, preventing escapes, and marching prisoners to the Janowska camp and the Kleparów station. They appear to have carried out their work with zeal and a disturbing professionalism. Reports from Ukrainian police to their German superiors coldly relate attempts by the condemned to escape their fate:

> Berta Partel attempted to bribe policeman Johan Pocalujko (Fifth Precinct) with a diamond necklace on August 20, 1942.
> Jakob Holtmann attempted to bribe policeman Iwaschtschyn (Second Precinct) with 150 zloty and a pocket watch on August 20, 1942.[142]
> An unknown Jewish woman attempted to bribe policeman Wladimar Chorko (Second Precinct) with 234 zloty, a gold wristwatch, and a wedding band on August 21, 1942.[143]

These intimate snapshots of people frantically trying to save themselves (and their rejection by the policemen) give us a sense of the terror and desperation of August 1942 in the ghetto and of the complicity of local police.

We know that Ukrainian policemen were crucial to these roundups because Nazi police commanders required them to account for ammunition expended to ensure that they were not stealing it or handing it over to partisans. In the sterile language of police reporting, Kalymon reported that during the roundup, at 7:00 p.m. on August 14, he had fired four shots. He had wounded one person and killed another. These were undoubtedly Jews. His precinct alone reported having captured 2,128 Jews that day.[144] The Ukrainian police continued to hunt for Jews even after the aktion had officially ended.

Many local civilians openly cheered the deportation. David Kahane recalled seeing a crowd of spectators gathered to watch the roundup. He wrote, "among them were well-dressed men and women with mocking smiles on their faces, as if saying: 'This is how it should be. The Jews are getting what they deserve!'"[145] Some locals took a decidedly more active and despicable role. Older teenagers entered the ghetto from the city and helped by searching for Jewish hiding places. Kahane described these as well. One of the boys ran out of a house, shouting "Mister, mister, over here, over here, Jude!" Kahane recognized him as a student he had known, and bitterly wrote, "In the future he no doubt will be a prominent member of every national academic society."[146]

As the masses of those captured moved in a continual stream toward the Janowska camp and the Kleparów station, Lviv hosted an important visitor. Heinrich Himmler arrived in the city on August 17, at the height of the Great Aktion, along with Odilo Globocnik, the man overseeing the Reinhard extermination centers. Himmler toured SS offices and some of the DG IV slave labor camps. Given his presence during the largest deportation action in the city, it is quite possible that Himmler himself observed the proceedings. Katzmann was seen at the Sobieski school assembly point bizarrely wearing a leopardskin jacket.[147] Due to the massive numbers, it seems that Willhaus put a larger open area north of the camp into operation as a temporary holding area along with the outer precinct. Here, selections took place and a few workers were selected to remain in Janowska when the trains departed. Staff from the camp, including Richard Rokita, carried out these selections. Marian Rogowski recalled seeing Katzmann, Gebauer, Willhaus, and Weber present as well. Very few eluded death at this point. Rogowski estimated that 90 percent of them ended up on trains.[148]

These assembly areas in the camp witnessed families being torn apart. Samuel Drix arrived in Janowska during the August Aktion with his sister. The Nazis selected him to stay in the camp but pointed his sister to the group destined for Bełżec. He recorded the moment in his diary. "I said goodbye to my sister. I had tears in my eyes as I looked into her impoverished face for the last time. She had red spots on her cheeks. The veins on her forehead stood out. She looked at me and handed me four pieces of bread my aunt had given her on the way. I didn't want to take them, but at her pleading, I took one." Then the Nazis began driving her group to the trains. "Do not be afraid," she consoled him, "I can work. I'll figure it out." He later wrote, "My sister was driven in the direction of the train station. I watched her until her silhouette disappeared from my eyes. The long column of the unfortunates moved with their last strength toward the camp gates."[149]

Back in the city, the "Great Aktion" continued until the Nazis had murdered between forty thousand and fifty thousand Jews from Lviv alone.

Those with life-saving jobs still marched out of the ghetto every day to work. "We had to pass through S.S. cordons with raised hands," Adolf Folkmann wrote, "Not one of them knew when he returned whether he would find wife, father and mother, or children safe at home when he arrived."[150] Jews who could afford the exorbitant prices for cyanide committed suicide. David Kahane noted that "people offered their entire property for cyanide pills."[151] Others discovered they had been swindled or did not have a large enough dose and survived only to die in terrible agony.

The summer of 1942 was the bloodiest in the history of the Holocaust. It marked a period of escalation in the Nazi genocidal project and the peak of killing intensity. More than half the eventual Holocaust victims (overwhelmingly Polish Jews) were killed in this period. From late July to mid-September 1942, "daily death tolls were in the tens of thousands."[152] As Christopher Browning has noted, "In mid-March 1942, some 75 to 80 percent of all victims of the Holocaust were still alive, while 20 to 25 percent had perished. A mere 11 months later, in mid-February 1943, the percentages were exactly the reverse."[153] The Aktions in Lviv should be seen as part of this surge in killing, a surge that reflected the increasing clarity with which the Nazis themselves viewed their task. The wave of destruction would sweep away most of the Jews in the General Government. And in Distrikt Galizien, Janowska stood at the center of it all.

Map 1. Luftwaffe aerial photograph, June 6, 1944. 1 Gate to ZAL; 2 ZAL Headquarters building; 3 Workshops and warehouses; 4 Stables; 5 Women's Camp; 6 Entrance to inner precinct; 7 Roll-call square; 8 Prisoner barracks; 9 Willhaus Villa; 10 Camp kitchens; 11 Entrance to DAW; 12 DAW SS living area; 13 Kleparow freight station. The Jewish cemetery can be seen on the right. Courtesy National Archives and Records Administration.

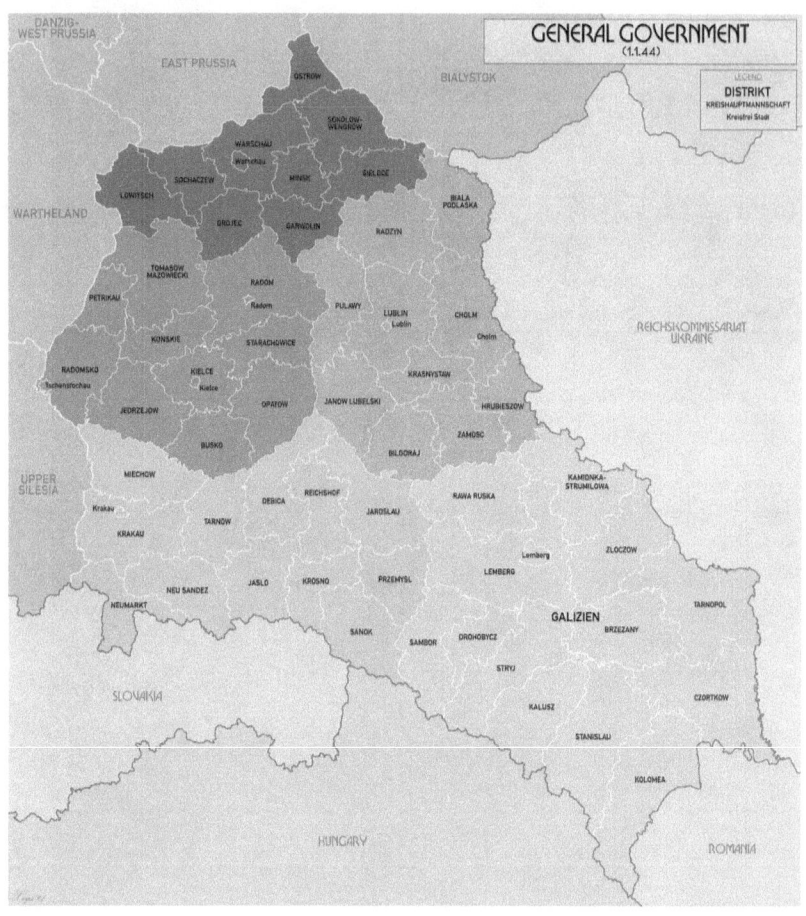

2. Map of German-occupied Poland (the General Government). Distrikt Galizien was added in August 1941. Map by XrysD, Wikimedia Commons.

3. A Jewish woman runs from her attackers during the July Days pogrom in Lviv in July 1941. Courtesy Stiftung Preußischer Kulturbesitz.

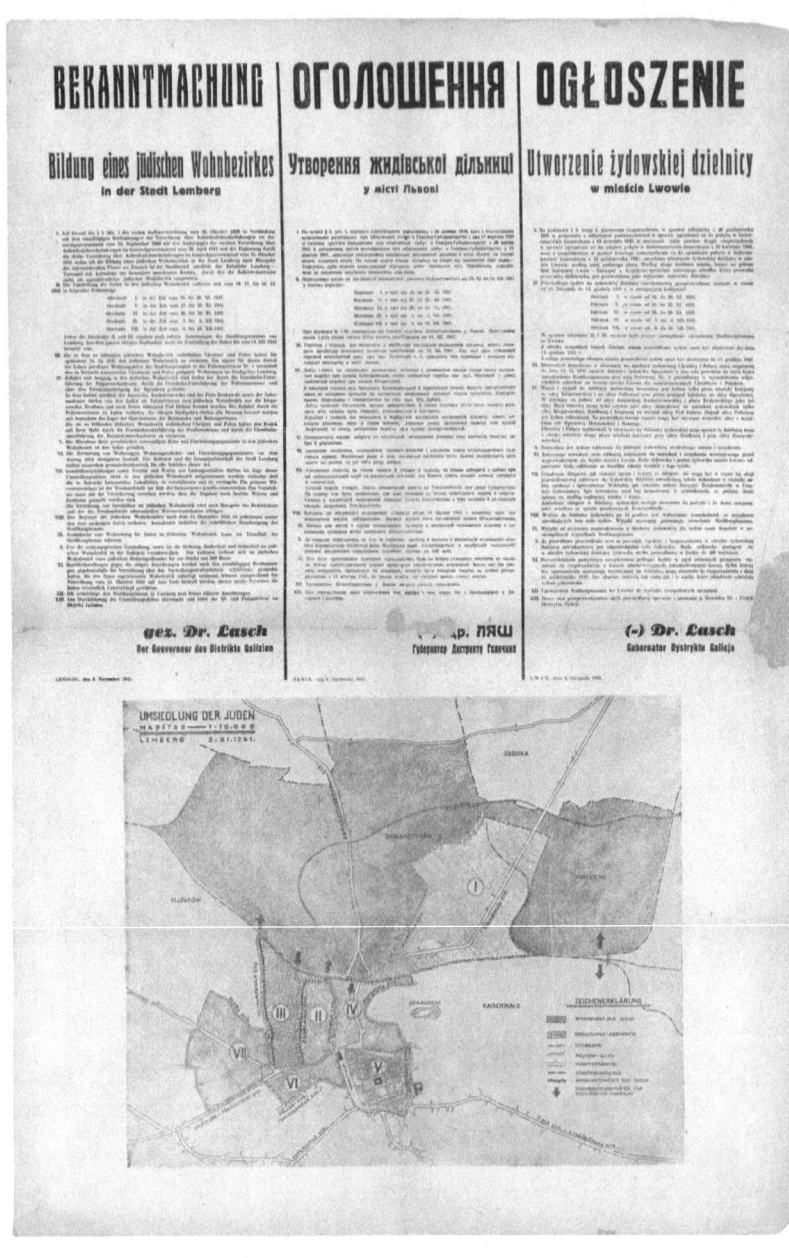

4. On November 8, 1941, the governor of Distrikt Galizien ordered the movement of Lviv's Jews into the ghetto area north of the railroad tracks in the Zamarstynow district, depicted here in the map attached to the public proclamation. Courtesy Leiden University Libraries, Collection Steegh-Teunissen.

5. Staff of the DAW-L, ca. 1941–42. *Left to right*: Amalie Melchior, Fritz Gebauer, SS man Vöske, SS man Preissler, Bleines's wife, and Hugo Bleines. The woman in the background under the window is variously identified as Gebauer's secretary (Elsa Röegner) or his Jewish cook. Courtesy Staatsarchiv Ludwigsburg.

6. Staff of the DAW in the SS living area, ca. 1941–42. The building in the background is a prisoner barracks. Courtesy Staatsarchiv Ludwigsburg.

7. (*opposite top*) Janowska camp SS with Ukrainian guards, some of whom were trained at the Trawniki camp. Courtesy Herman Lewinter Family Collection.

8. (*opposite bottom*) German troops enter downtown Lviv on June 29, 1941. Courtesy Narodowe Archiwum Cyfrowe.

9. (*above*) Lviv Jews being deported from the ghetto to the Janowska camp or Kleparów station by city streetcar. Courtesy Herman Lewinter Family Collection.

10. (*above*) Gustav Willhaus with wife, Liesel, and daugher, Heike, in the garden of his villa in the Janowska camp. Courtesy Staatsarchiv Ludwigsburg.

11. (*opposite top*) The camp headquarters building in an early postwar photograph. The windows on the third floor where the Technical Office was located are visible. Courtesy Herman Lewinter Family Collection.

12. (*opposite bottom*) Workers (likely from the Janowska camp) load destroyed tombstones from the Jewish cemetery onto a truck for use as building material. Courtesy Staatsarchiv Ludwigsburg.

13. Janowska prisoners doing paving work in the camp, likely with materials looted from the neighboring Jewish cemetery. Courtesy Herman Lewinter Family Collection.

14. Looted Jewish property in the camp, postliberation. Courtesy Herman Lewinter Family Collection.

15. SS men carry out an execution in the ravines behind the Janowska camp. This photo appears in the German investigation records. The original caption reads: "The Piaski [sands] shooting site behind the ZAL-Lemberg. The prisoners are already partly undressed for execution." Courtesy Staatsarchiv Ludwigsburg.

16. Photograph of the camp orchestra, by Herman Lewinter. Prisoner conductor Yakov Munt can be seen in the center of the circle. At right, in the light uniform, is Fritz Gebauer. To his left is Gustav Willhaus. At far right is Wilhaus's dachsund, Fritz, named after Gebauer. Courtesy United States Holocaust Memorial Museum.

17. Zeev Porath was a trained architect who was imprisoned at Janowska. He worked in the Technical Office and, along with others, participated in an active campaign of documenting Nazi crimes in Janowska. Porath escaped in 1943, taking his drawings with him. Courtesy Rachel (Porath) Popper.

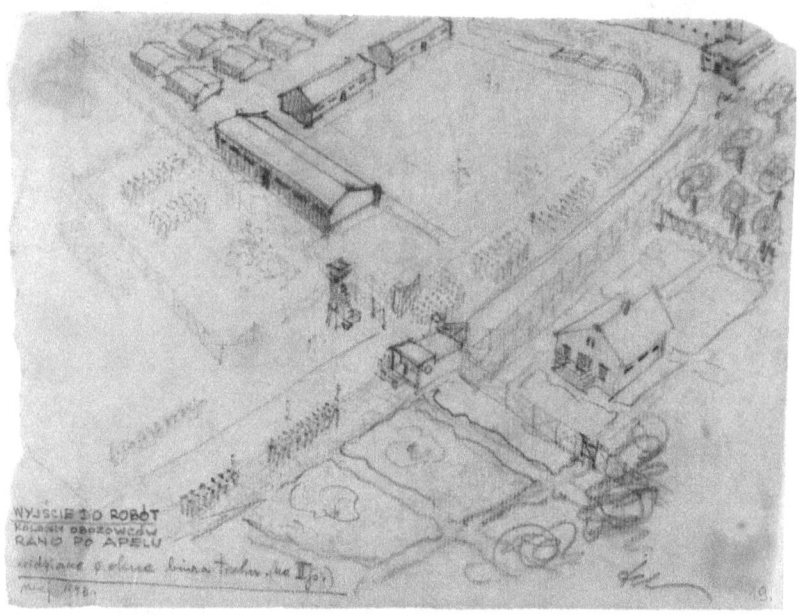

18. (*opposite top*) Zeev Porath drawing of SS man Adolf Kolonko, February 1943, showing Kolonko abusing prisoners. Original caption: "Preparing to demonstrate." Courtesy Ghetto Fighters' House Museum.

19. (*opposite bottom*) Zeev Porath captured the torture and humiliation of two rabbis from Jaworow, who were forced to dance at the entrance to the inner precinct of the camp for two weeks before being murdered. Courtesy Ghetto Fighters' House Museum.

20. (*above*) This drawing by Zeev Porath depicts the geography of the camp, showing prisoner brigades leaving the inner camp for work. Also visible is the "between-wire" to the left of the guard tower. Courtesy Ghetto Fighters' House Museum.

21. View of the commandant's house in Janowska. This photo depicts the balcony from which Gustav Willhaus and his wife shot prisoners in the camp. It is possible that the unidentified woman is Liesel Willhaus. Courtesy Herman Lewinter Family Collection.

22. Postwar mugshot of Peter Blum. Blum was the SS overseer of the tailor shop and remembered as a notorious rapist. Courtesy Staatsarchiv Ludwigsburg.

23. The first commandant of the Janowska camp, Gustav Willhaus, with his dog at the main gate of the camp. A small standing punishment cell was located in the gate behind him. Courtesy Staatsarchiv Ludwigsburg.

24. SS man Richard Rokita relaxing at his quarters in the camp. Courtesy Staatsarchiv Ludwigsburg.

25. Heinrich Himmler tours a camp along the Durchgangstrasse IV. At far right is the second Janowska commandant, Friedrich Warzok. The SS and police leader for Lviv, Friedrich Katzmann, is second from left with his hand on his belt. Courtesy United States Holocaust Memorial Museum.

26. SS man Adolf Kolonko. Kolonko brought a group of Trawniki men to Janowska and later commanded his own camp in Grodek-Jagiellonski. Courtesy Staatsarchiv Ludwigsburg.

27. This selection from a larger social network diagram of all Janowska perpetrators shows Adolf Kolonko's movements mainly from 1933 to 1945 as well as in the postwar period. The complete network diagram allows one to see the many patterns and overlaps among the SS men of the camp. Author creation.

28. Postwar photograph of Walter Schallock, who commanded the Lviv SK 1005, the so-called Death Brigade, at Janowska and the Lyczaków Forest sites. Courtesy Staatsarchiv Ludwigsburg.

29. Three former members of the Death Brigade pose with the bone grinder in Janowska after liberation. (*right to left*): Moishe Korn, David Manusevitz, and an unknown survivor. Courtesy Herman Lewinter Family Collection.

30. One of the many ravines in the hills behind the Janowska camp where thousands of Jews and others were shot to death. Courtesy Herman Lewinter Family Collection.

31. The Łyczaków Forest today, which was the site of the revolt by the Janowska Death Brigade in November 1943. Author photo.

32. Defendants in the dock during the Lviv Trial, 1966. *From left*: Paul Fox, Karl Ulmer, Ernst Heinisch, Ernst Inquart, and Adolf Kolonko. Courtesy Süddeutsche Zeitung.

33. A Jewish tombstone recently uncovered in Lviv, where it had been used as paving material. Courtesy Rohatyn Jewish Heritage.

34. The terrain of Janowska today, looking toward the Kleparów station from the hills surrounding the camp. It is still used a prison though almost none of the original buildings remain standing. Author photo.

Cerberus Awakens 5

> The camp on Janowska street was a university of bestiality, while Majdanek, Dachau, Auschwitz and Buchenwald were secondary schools of the same bestiality...
>
> —Michał Borwicz, *The University of Criminals*

The spring of 1942 must have been an incredibly awkward time for Gustav Willhaus and his former boss, Fritz Gebauer. Sometime in this period, Willhaus began to construct his own domain immediately next door to the DAW-L, separated by an east–west dirt road. Willhaus's star was on the rise: the SS and police leader of Distrikt Galizien had chosen him to build the "biggest labor and transit camp in Ukraine."[1] Intentionally or not, the Janowska camp under Willhaus would become a multifunctional space—of labor and detention, of transit and selection, and of murder. Yet, in late spring 1942, he still had to work at least somewhat with Gebauer who retained control over his labor force. Quite predictably, tensions rose rapidly between the two men as they competed for resources. It was a battle that Willhaus was destined to win. That much is clear from Gebauer's testimony even two decades later.

Though on trial for his own life after the war, Gebauer repeatedly expressed his resentment for the favor shown to his former subordinate. When Katzmann tasked Willhaus with the construction of the Zwangsarbeitslager (ZAL), Willhaus lost no time in asserting his authority. Gebauer bitterly recalled that Willhaus requested building materials and that he refused to hand them over. Willhaus soon also took the majority of Gebauer's skilled laborers, leaving him with only those unnecessary for the ZAL. Willhaus apparently appealed directly to Katzmann, an interesting relationship between a general and a second lieutenant. Gebauer complained to the DAW headquarters in Berlin and protested that he would not be able to meet his production demands, but the DAW had no more success against Katzmann than he had. In Gebauer's words, "with Katzmann behind him, Willhaus could get just about anything." After that, he, Willhaus, and Katzmann "had their differences."[2]

Having gained supremacy over his neighbor, Willhaus began building his camp, one that for many survivors came to represent the true Janowska. He had at his disposal a group of new SS men who had arrived likely specifically to serve under his command. But, like his predecessor, he stared out from the DAW wire at a more or less empty space that he would have to build from scratch. Next to Katzmann's support, he must have also felt the pressure of being entrusted with such an important operation. Like Gebauer, Willhaus began by looting (and not just from the DAW). SS man Richard Rokita recalled that he routinely took a truck to neighboring towns and villages, some as far away as two to three hours. There, Ukrainian mayors supplied him with Jewish labor to tear down wooden buildings and bring the materials to the local train station for transport to Janowska.[3] The almost constant construction reflected the commandant's grandiose plans. Miroslav Rycevski, a Ukrainian imprisoned in the camp for a month in August 1942, labored to construct more barracks. At that time, there were seven thousand prisoners in the camp, but he heard rumors that further expansion was planned to include twenty-five thousand prisoners.[4] Gebauer estimated that construction on the initial camp lasted three or four months.[5] However, building remained a part of life in the ZAL for the duration as it did in most of the Nazi concentration camps.

The grueling and torturous work done by prisoners cannot be subsumed under mere "construction," however. For prisoners, it was a fearful experience. Construction was one of the most perilous activities during the Holocaust. It required vast amounts of precious physical energy and exposed prisoners to the harshest of elements. Often it was accompanied by the impatience of the SS, which led to violence and death. The most horrific part was the "vitamin work" in which prisoners were forced to carry heavy building supplies from the Kleparów station to the camp, at a run, after a regular day's labor. Stanisława Gogolowska noted that a massive amount of "feverish work" began at the end of March 1942. The prisoners were "overworked in inhuman ways." A detail struggled to build barracks in the land adjacent to the DAW and a "Wire Brigade" enclosed the camp with a fence. Her testimony provides even more insight into the early days of the camp. Willhaus apparently was upset with the pace of construction. Until the ZAL was ready to house prisoners, he could not remove them from Gebauer's control. Construction work continued "day and night." Willhaus also evicted the local railway workers and their families living in small houses in his new realm and used these more solid buildings as workshops (in apparent disregard for the previous agreement that he would not challenge the DAW's jurisdiction as a factory).[6] Newly arrived SS man Adolf Kolonko noted that the "bulk of the prisoners were used for the construction of camp housing."[7]

As in the DAW, the prisoners themselves had to build their prison. They also had to design it. Willhaus "employed" expert Jewish engineers and architects to draft the plans for the ZAL. At their head was engineer Henryk Griffel who led the "Technical Office" in the camp headquarters. Griffel was a former professor from Lviv Polytechnic University and a "world-renowned scientist in the field of metallurgy."[8] Willhaus clearly lacked the skills for building his camp and he knew it. He needed these prisoners to be successful and hated them for it. Griffel suffered as a result. Willhaus treated him "according to his mood, sometimes with the greatest familiarity, almost friendly... or punched him in the face and swore at him with vulgar words." Griffel's "great knowledge sometimes impressed Willhaus but sometimes provoked him... [Willhaus] hated him and took it out on him."[9] Regardless, the commandant filled his headquarters with professionals. Griffel was often responsible for seeking out these experts among the new arrivals.[10] Architect Zeev Porath worked in Griffel's section along with other architects, electrical engineers, painters, watchmakers, and photographers.[11] He would often take a group of laborers under guard into the city to identify and remove necessary building materials.[12]

All evidence indicates that prisoners began to live in the ZAL-L permanently sometime in May or June 1942. By then, it was already demonstrating its flexibility as a multi-use complex. In this space, the young second lieutenant Willhaus reigned supreme.

The Saarland Swindler

Gustav Willhaus was born in 1910 in the town of Forbach on the French border, making him yet another SS man from a disputed borderland.[13] After World War I, France occupied this heavily industrialized area, the Saarland, in an attempt to recoup some of its economic losses. Not surprisingly, this caused great animosity among the overwhelmingly German population, which led to great support for the Nazis in the interwar period. One of these supporters was Gustav Willhaus. He joined the party early, in 1924, and occupied himself as a street thug at night, describing with pride his own beating in a street fight where he was "seriously wounded."[14] By day, he peddled a Nazi newspaper, *Westmark*.[15] This was particularly ironic given that he was functionally illiterate. He likely also met his future wife, Liesel Riedel, through their shared conviction for the Nazi cause as she was active in the nearby Nazi newspaper *Rheinfront*.[16] As a nineteen- and twenty-year-old, he worked for the Hitler Youth.[17] Like Gebauer, Willhaus came from humble stock. His father was a maître d' and he himself trained as a mechanic. Gustav joined the SS in 1932, becoming active in the violence that boiled over prior to the 1935 plebiscite on rejoining Germany. When 91 percent of the population chose a return to the Third *Reich*, Gustav and Liesel could congratulate themselves on their role in the violent political campaign preceding the vote.[18] Hitler himself appeared in Saarbrücken a few months later and made the ominous prediction that "what is written in ink will be blotted out by blood," referring to the Treaty of Versailles. The headline in the Nazi paper *Völkischer Beobachter* read: "Give your loyalty to the new *Reich*!"[19] Willhaus and Riedel had already done so.

The couple married shortly thereafter, though without SS approval. Willhaus had problems retrieving the proper ancestral evidence from France, but the couple flouted the rules.[20] The SS strongly reprimanded Willhaus for this.[21] The fact that both had abandoned religion in favor of the party speaks to the fervor of their belief in the Nazis. Like Gebauer, Willhaus (and his wife) could perhaps only have risen under the Nazis. Historian Wendy Lower suggests that "the fact that they came from the politically volatile region of Saarland may have helped them advance in the SS and the party, or at least to persuade Berlin examiners to overlook their shortcomings and dubious characters."[22] Both were petty, power hungry, and morally flexible.

The Wehrmacht drafted Willhaus in August 1939. Unlike Gebauer, he received no exemption but was posted to Infantry Regiment 32, which invaded Poland in September 1939, fighting all the way to Warsaw.²³ In 1940, he transferred to the Waffen-SS and participated in "security operations" in Norway from November 1940 to May 1941. He then moved to Oswald Pohl's SS Economic Administration Main Office.²⁴ This was Willhaus's last assignment before his arrival in Lviv. His career may well help explain his disdain for Gebauer, a man who certainly had never *actually* been a soldier let alone a combat veteran. Willhaus was both.

The first commandant of the ZAL-L was a frightening character. Standing around six feet tall and a hundred seventy pounds, Willhaus had a long, gaunt face punctuated by a sharp "hook nose" and blue eyes. His athletic frame hung on "narrow shoulders."²⁵ Leon Wells wrote that "the superficial appearance was uninteresting, not unlike that of a doll. His appearance was made all the more unsympathetic and even frightening by his persistent, cold, and ironic smile, as unchanging as that of a mask."²⁶ Another survivor remembered him as "a monster in human form."²⁷ Willhaus's exceptional cruelty and deviousness defined him for many survivors. He took a very active role in the supervision of the camp and seemed to be everywhere, which is probably why so many remembered him. The commandant stalked the camp, whip or club in one hand and a revolver in the other, according to one survivor. This is a man who once shot a prisoner for accidentally shutting his coat in a car door.²⁸ He "shot down anyone who loafed." He often "mauled his victims with his feet until they laid there covered with blood or died."²⁹ On April 20, 1942, Hitler's fifty-fourth birthday, Willhaus is said to have personally selected and shot fifty-four prisoners in celebration.³⁰

Willhaus was certainly ambitious, despite his obvious limitations. His relationship with Katzmann proves that, particularly if Willhaus approached him first. However, even if Katzmann initiated it (which is more likely), Willhaus seems to have taken full advantage of his position. It is not normal, then or now, for a lieutenant to have such a close working relationship with a general. Even among his own, he seems to have put on airs. He "distanced himself from his own SS colleagues and tolerated no disagreement. He gave the impression of a thoroughly tyrannical man."³¹ Willhaus clearly felt himself the lord and master of his domain. He had a stables built in the camp and was frequently seen on horseback, inspecting his realm. As one scholar of the camps has pointed out, "nowhere else in the SS could men with a modest education go further."[32]

Gustav and Liesel also took full advantage of their new power to enrich themselves and adopt the kind of upper-middle-class lifestyle that would have remained forever out of their reach in other times. Wendy Lower described the couple as "small-town swindlers out to exploit the system."[33] Indeed, they rapidly accumulated the trappings of wealth and power as they saw them. Willhaus would arrive in his limousine "like a deathly apparition," his arrival bringing a "wave of anxiety and fear."[34] The couple and their three-year-old daughter, Heike, moved into a large villa directly in the center of the Janowska camp complex, "eager to shed their working-class heritage for a new life of riches and power in the East."[35] Mrs. Willhaus took advantage of the free labor to avail herself of several housekeepers and servants chosen from the prisoners. SS man Adolf Kolonko stated that these women "often complained" about their "poor treatment" at the hands of the commandant's wife.[36] Michał Borwicz described Liesel as "in love with her *toilette*," noting that she "used to summon Jewish dressmakers to fulfill her orders, a matter she hid even from her own husband." He also characterized her as afraid of Gustav.[37]

In any case, the couple lived a comfortable and even luxurious life. Their house had six rooms as well as a winter garden and a second-floor terrace overlooking a garden.[38] Prisoners delivered fresh blocks of ice daily.[39] The house was bursting "with valuables plundered from the Jews of the ghetto."[40] Around a hundred feet away behind a fence and shrubs lay the Janowska camp Appellplatz where the prisoners gathered every morning and night. After the war, Liesel Willhaus tried to distance herself from her time in the camp, making the ludicrous claim that "I am hearing for the first time today about the actual conditions in the camp."[41] However, SS accounts state that she frequently visited her husband in the main headquarters building and so was certainly familiar with the camp.[42] A survivor went further, remembering that "she frequently walked around the camp." More ominously, he remarked that "the fact that she could stand the atmosphere in the camp proves that she was not a woman in the normal sense."[43] Of this, we will learn more later.

The Guards: A Collective Biography

The men who stalked the grounds of the Janowska camp also merit discussion. For all prisoners, they were the specific faces of Nazi terror that they saw every day. For many, they were also the last human faces they would ever see. Intriguing patterns and networks emerge from mapping the biographies and trajectories of these men. Almost all of the men came from border regions and of the forty-two whose origin can be identified, 70 percent were ethnic Germans (Volksdeutsche) from outside the borders of the Reich.[44] The average age was twenty-nine, but almost half the men were under twenty-four. Many of them followed similar routes, and it is helpful to examine some in detail. A significant cluster of the men came from ethnic German communities in what is now Hungary, the Balkans (former Yugoslavia), and Poland. Though all were SS, Volksdeutsche strongly outnumbered Reich Germans. This may signal a dearth of more "qualified" applicants. Some of the men's histories are representative of the group.

Peter Blum, for example, was a Volksdeutsche born in 1921 in Bácsalmás in modern-day Hungary, on the border with Serbia. Habsburg settlement programs meant that until the end of World War II, the majority of his village was ethnic German, "Danube Swabians." These ethnic Germans clustered in regions consisting of parts of southern Hungary, former Yugoslavia, and Romania called the Banat, Vjovodina, and Slavonia. They were among the seven million ethnic Germans living in eastern Europe after World War I.[45]

However, the Germanness of Blum and others like him required cultivation to move beyond a vague sense of ancestral connection.[46] Many Volksdeutsche integrated well into the local societies, but others increasingly identified with Germany. This separation worsened after the collapse of the multiethnic Habsburg empire when ethnic Germans found themselves stranded among energized majority populations that often did not want them there. For some, the "Swabian newcomers, together with the Jews, were the symbol of the evils of modernization with which the patriarchal ... society could not cope."[47] This rising animosity drove many ethnic Germans closer to Germany proper. The same year Blum was born, ethnic German elites began to publish a German-language newspaper hoping to "enhance the spiritual composure and depth of our people."[48] Perhaps he even saw some of the Wandervogel, German boy scouts, who took hiking trips to the region in the 1930s to "awaken some kind of support for Germany." They certainly outraged the Hungarian government when it became known that they were using maps including Hungarian territory that were labeled "the complete Germany." By the time Blum was six, over thirty-five thousand of these young propagandists had hiked through the region.[49]

Peter trained as a musician in Bácsalmás and played music there for several years before volunteering for service in the Hungarian army in 1940. With Infantry Regiment 3/20, he participated in the invasion of Romania before being released from service and rejoining the Steinfeld Orchestra back home. In March 1942, the Waffen-SS conscripted him along with other ethnic Germans from the region, according to him.[50] This chimes with some of the history. In his drive to build the SS as a rival to the Wehrmacht, Himmler had lobbied for some time for the right to recruit ethnic Germans into the Waffen-SS. On March 1, Himmler ordered the ethnic Germans in the Serbian portion of Banat to report for enlistment.[51] What was more problematic for Blum's story was that Hungary (where Blum was living) only authorized voluntary enlistment.[52]

Regardless of the circumstances, Blum became a member of the armed wing of the SS and reported to the Heidelager training center in Dębica sixty-five miles east of Kraków. The Nazis established the camp in a former factory (as they had at Dachau). Along with other ethnic German recruits, Blum arrived, received an SS blood tattoo, and began military training.[53] The Heidelager was one of the largest Waffen-SS training facilities outside of the Reich. It commenced operations on March 20, 1942, with the arrival of six thousand Hungarian volunteers.[54] In order to build and support this camp, the SS drew on an existing concentration camp nearby, the ZAL Pustków that had been in operation since 1940. In early March, Jews were brought in from Mielec and Kraków to perhaps help expand the Heidelager. They continued to support the training mission of the Waffen-SS, for example, by building shooting ranges.[55] An SS arrival recalled that "Jewish work details" worked on roads and barracks.[56]

The proximity of these camps was no coincidence either. The Waffen-SS commander of the training camp was also responsible for the ZAL and, therefore, for the guard force. It is quite possible that the recruits training there also performed guard duty for the concentration camp. Blum would have been among them. The Waffen-ss men abused and beat the Jews in the Pustków camp as well. The training apparently broke Blum. It was "exceptionally severe," he remembered, before dramatically claiming to have had "a few heart-attacks." He was sent to Kraków for examination, deemed unfit for field duty due to a heart defect, and returned to Dębica.[57] After perhaps two weeks, the hapless recruit was sent back to Kraków where he received orders to report to the ss and police leader in Lviv.[58] Katzmann assigned him to the Janowska camp where he took over the camp laundry.

Roman Schönbach took a different path to Janowska Street. He was born Roman Mucha in 1912 Eichendorffmühl (Brzeźnica), which was then part of Germany in Silesia, on the border with Poland, another border region in a traditionally Polish region. Schönbach was an ethnic German like Blum. He was the third of six children and completed vocational school as a furnace builder like his father. Schönbach began working for the Siemens factory in Ratibor (Racibórz). There, he met Adolf Kolonko, his future colleague at the Janowska camp. Schönbach's introduction to the Nazi Party began with his entry into the Hitler Youth in 1928. He then transferred directly to the Allgemeine-ss in 1937 and traveled to the other side of the Reich to work building the West Wall fortifications on the French border.[59]

When the Nazis invaded Poland in 1939, Schönbach was required to report for service back in Silesia. At this point, he felt that his real last name, Mucha, was perhaps not German enough and had it legally changed to Schönbach in Ratibor.[60] That he did so gives a strong indication of how much he identified with the Nazis and his ethnic German status. With his new name, Schönbach was assigned to the *Sonderdienst* in newly conquered Lublin. This shadowy organization sprung from a "bitter struggle over scarce manpower resources and policy control between the ss and police apparatus and the civilian authorities in the Government General."[61] Its predecessor was the so-called *Selbstschutz* (Self-Defense) force created from ethnic Germans in theory to help police the newly conquered Polish territory. In reality, it represented the first steps by Odilo Globocnik and Himmler to wrest full control of anti-Jewish and forced labor policy from Nazi administrators. This formation was also a "structure for 'recapturing' German blood" and deepening the loyalties of ethnic Germans.[62]

If Schönbach actually arrived in Lublin at the end of 1939 or the beginning of 1940, then he would have arrived as part of the Selbstschutz. Several other future SS men at Janowska had served in this same formation. This paramilitary group, made up almost entirely of Volksdeutsche, carried out widespread looting of Jewish property, murdered Polish civilians, and rounded up Jews for labor. In fact, Globocnik used this as his private army to man his Lipowa DAW camp, where Wolfgang Mohwinkel would work. One SS man referred to the Selbstschutz men as "like half-savages."[63] The Governor General, Hans Frank, managed to temporarily thwart Globocnik's further ambitions by bringing the Selbstschutz under civilian control through the creation of the Sonderdienst in May 1940. This new formation and the Waffen-SS absorbed the earlier Selbstschutz men, including perhaps Schönbach.[64] Frank intended the Sonderdienst to be his own police force and they often acted as such. They received significant political indoctrination including an identification of Jews as the enemy that "maliciously and destructively sought to annihilate the races, the nations, and the economy."[65] One scholar has pointed out that the Sonderdienst "represents an early effort of the National Socialist authorities to fashion an ethnically conscious and ideologically committed corps from young men of questionable, even dubious, German ancestry and heritage."[66] Schönbach assisted in this process as he served as an interpreter and driver for SS Sturmbannführer (major) Anton Binner.[67] His background as an ethnic German from a Polish region likely helped him in this job.

Schönbach's boss had earlier commanded a small forced labor camp in Zarzecze characterized by brutal conditions and many deaths.[68] Schönbach claimed after the war that Binner's task had been merely to find recruits and that Binner had nothing to do with the "larger tasks" of the Sonderdienst.[69] This is curious, not least because Binner was a battalion commander in the Selbstschutz who was connected with the massacre of a hundred fifty Polish civilians in Józefów. While it is unclear when Schönbach joined Binner and therefore what the extent of his involvement in these earlier atrocities was, one can imagine the conversations he may have had with the major as they drove through the Polish countryside. By the end of 1940, Schönbach had been transferred to the Chełm region where he oversaw roadbuilding operations.

Unfortunately for Schönbach, his career took a turn for the worse here. An SS court convicted him of drunkenness in uniform, reduced him in rank to private, and sentenced him to three months in the Danzig-Matzkau SS prison camp. This was not easy time, either, for this camp was brutal. Perhaps his experience as a prisoner himself would inform his later behavior in the Janowska camp. Rudolf Höss, the commandant of Auschwitz, was himself the veteran of a five-year prewar prison term. In his memoirs, Höss ironically reflected often on the lessons he learned during this time, writing at one point that "the place was a regular school for criminals" where the newcomers "were enthusiastically initiated into the secrets of their craft."[70] Schönbach was released from prison and sent directly to Krzezowice outside Kraków where he served as a guard at Hans Frank's summer residence. In March 1942, the SS transferred him to the office of the SSPF in Lviv, where he was forwarded on to Janowska. Schönbach assisted with managing the "Askaris."[71]

The trajectories of Blum and Schönbach tell us a good deal about a large number of the guards in the camp. The SS men actually seem to have had a great deal in common. A large proportion were ethnic Germans, some barely able to speak German. Seven came from within an eighty-mile radius of Blum in Hungary and Yugoslavia. Eight guards came from within a fifty-mile radius of Schönbach in Silesia. Some, perhaps many, knew each other. Most of the guards had some previous experience with Nazi paramilitary or auxiliary formations before coming to Lviv. The majority were of relatively low quality, either medically unfit for strenuous service like Blum or with poor service records like Schönbach. One guard was missing an arm.

How does this perhaps explain their later behavior? Roots in contested border regions could mean stronger identification with "Germanness" and/or a desire to prove themselves. This could lead to increased violence. Many from these regions might have already had strong preexisting antisemitic beliefs. On the other hand, few seem to have been particularly ambitious or even particularly capable of great ambition. They were poorly educated and from the backwaters of the Nazi empire. These SS men had not been wildly successful economically or socially prior to Janowska. Certainly, most were motivated to avoid actual combat if they had not already secured that privilege for themselves. As a group they seem to have been characterized by coarseness and brutality. They were an undisciplined bunch who frequently abused alcohol and took advantage of their posting to an out-of-the-way camp (and its relative lack of supervision) to indulge their own brutal inclinations. This is not to say that they were psychologically abnormal; for the most part, they were not. With some exceptions, these were the kind of men who patrolled the inner sanctum of the Janowska camp that we will enter now.

The Inferno: Landscape and Its Uses

The Holocaust was an experience eternally tied to place. Places to live, places to die, places to escape from, places to escape to, places of safety, places of fear. One cannot truly understand the history of a camp or the experience there without also knowing the built environment and how the landscape impacted the lives of those who walked across it.

Prisoners arrived at the camp in various ways: on foot, by truck, by streetcar, or by train from someplace outside the city. If it was the latter, they hurriedly leaped from cattle cars at the Kleparów freight station and then had to run around a quarter of a mile to the camp gate. The main gate was an imposing but simple concrete structure. Iron gates swung open under a long concrete slab between two rectangular pillars. Two eagles clutching swastikas perched above each. At night, these would be illuminated. Hidden within each pillar were two standing cells called "the Bunker," which one prisoner called "vestibules of death."[72] On the right, a guard occupied a small wooden guardhouse. One was now in the outer precinct of the camp. The pavement beneath newly arriving prisoners' feet disappeared, replaced with shattered tombstones looted from the adjacent cemetery. The prisoners stood in a large open space. Ahead on the right was the camp headquarters building where they would be shaved, registered, and assigned work. To the left was a long row of low buildings that housed the garage and various workshops. Further in the distance stood the stables that housed the commandant's horses. New arrivals could possibly have glimpsed the five smaller barracks of the women's camp beyond that, but likely they were too afraid. Ahead was the inner gate to the camp itself.

Here, the stone walls from the exterior disappeared and were replaced by a double barbed wire fence with perhaps five feet of space in the middle.

Teardrop-shaped lights lit this area in hours of darkness. Approaching the gate, prisoners could see a small guardhouse on the right with an open covered porch. SS men would shelter here before counting the numbers of each work detail as it left the camp. Across from it was one of several crude guard towers, small, square open shelters on four vertical beams supported by cross-ties. At its feet lay the dreaded "behind-wire" or "between-wire," a small makeshift enclosure of wire where the soon-to-be-dead languished in misery and humiliation.

Once past this wire, the prisoners had entered the inner sanctum. They now arrived at the dusty Appellplatz, the 1.5-acre roll-call square where prisoners stood for hours, in heat and in cold, witnessing the executions of friend and stranger alike. A green hedge lined the fence along the southern edge. A daring prisoner could just glimpse the Willhaus villa's second-floor terrace overlooking the camp. The residence was one of several buildings for the SS and their families situated among greenery and landscaping in a grim oasis separating the ZAL and DAW. Further ahead inside the wire lay the old and new camp kitchens, though they hardly met that definition in even the most generous sense. Behind them, a set of macabre makeshift gallows shaped like soccer goals cast long shadows. Across the Appellplatz from the Willhaus residence stood the barracks, and behind them the latrines. Looming over it all, in the ravines and winding paths in the hills behind the camp lay "the Sands," the execution sites where thousands were murdered.

This landscape hosted a variety of functions and the almost simultaneous execution of this hybrid role makes the Janowska camp a rare, though not entirely unique, phenomenon. Specifically, it served as a slave labor camp, a transit camp, and an extermination site for almost all of its existence. This hybrid character sets it apart and is also a consequence of its own location both on the map and in the Nazi genocidal project. Despite its haphazard and amateurish nature, the Janowska complex gained an oversized importance precisely because of its ability to remain relevant in varied spheres of importance for the Nazis. Its location in the midst of the third largest Jewish population in Poland meant that the camp would always be closely tied to Nazi anti-Jewish policy, from labor to extermination. The local, regional, and national circumstances dictated a more ad hoc approach. Of course, the camp itself made no decisions, navigated no political landscape, and insinuated itself into no policies. People did this. The stakeholders of Janowska—the guards, the commandants, Katzmann, and higher Nazi authorities—consciously ensured that the camp could claim importance. As one scholar has written, "the main constant of the [concentration camp] was change" with each following "an unsteady route, with many twists and turns."[73] Necessity may be the mother of invention, but she is also the mistress of oppression.

An Eastern Plantation: Janowska as Slave Labor Camp

Labor and confinement have historically been intertwined. Whenever a government classifies one group of people as inferior and imprisons them, forced labor usually follows. The Holocaust was no exception. Ideology may have ultimately won out in favor of extermination, but pragmatism demanded that those Jews fit to toil for the Reich did so, at least for a time. Indeed, up until at least the summer of 1942, the Nazis targeted mainly Jews "incapable of work."[74] The world of economic exploitation also offered opportunities for power, prestige, and, not infrequently, personal enrichment to those Nazis who could force their way in. Oswald Pohl and Friedrich Katzmann are just two examples of men who saw the potential of controlling the pool of Jewish workers. Jurisdiction over the construction force for prestigious projects like the DG IV highway and work for war industry attracted many in the SS. Even though he predicted the destruction of his Jewish labor force carving a road out of the Ukrainian steppe, Katzmann still fixated on the successful completion of the project.[75] His power grab from the DAW thus ensured that he would be a key player in the economy of Distrikt Galizien. The Janowska camp became the largest Nazi camp in Ukraine, a position due in no small part to its geographic location in the capital city and its access to a massive population of potential labor. Willhaus and Gebauer both used slave labor to power their own camps, produce products for sale, and, particularly in the ZAL-L, as a profitable workforce to be contracted out to third parties.

Before we examine the Janowska camp as a slave labor camp, we must address the term "slave labor" itself. For some, the terms "forced labor" and "slave labor" are interchangeable. Others argue that Jews in the camps were not slaves, that is, chattel slaves, and so that term is inappropriate. I will, however, join with other scholars in using the term "slave labor." It is the most correct with all its historical connotations. The Nazis did employ forced labor as well when they impressed civilians (including Jews) to do temporary work or forcibly moved them to Germany to work. As Christopher Browning rightly notes, Jews in camps were "slaves in the literal sense of the word: property owned by the SS who were 'rented out' on a contractual basis."[76] A Dachau prisoner described war work by inmates in 1943 as "modern slave rental." Even more convincingly, the Nazis themselves saw their Jewish prisoners as slaves. Around the time of the March deportation from Lviv, Heinrich Himmler referred to camp inmates as like "slaves in Egypt" and later described them as "work slaves."[77] If the comparison to chattel slavery is jarring to us, it is perhaps our own pasts that make us uncomfortable. After all, one of the largest work details at the flagship Dachau camp consumed labor for agricultural work on what the Nazis called the "plantation."[78]

All the prisoners in the camp worked. The SS organized them into a number of brigades categorized by the job or location. Each brigade was led by a prisoner functionary who was responsible above all for ensuring that none of his workers escaped. Slave labor at Janowska took several forms. The first most closely approached the "extermination through labor" method of solving the "Jewish Question." More than a few prisoners recalled crude "work details" whose only purpose seemed to be to destroy prisoners. Leon Wells described a "compulsion" brigade. Assignment to this group meant "certain death." He wrote that "members of the compulsion brigade were forced to pick up huge stones far too great for an ordinary man to lift, much less to carry." On another occasion, he witnessed a group of prisoners forced to carry a truck chassis on their shoulders as they walked in endless circles. "The sole object of the work," he wrote, "was to make the men suffer."[79] Abraham Goldberg survived time in one of these punishment brigades. It was clear to him that this was "unproductive work." In the winter, guards forced him and others to throw tree stumps into a pit and then pull them out the next day. "The point of this work," he stated, "was apparently to weaken the people. I can't imagine another point. It had no point."[80] Samuel Drix recalled that the guards would make work for the prisoners on Sundays when they did not work outside the camp. They forced prisoners to carry heavy building supplies back and forth for two hundred meters "just to prevent us from resting and relaxing."[81] Another former prisoner recalled that when they did not leave the camp for work, the ss men would scatter shredded paper across the camp and make the prisoners pick it up.[82] Perhaps unaware of the irony, Rudolf Höss, commandant of Auschwitz, wrote that "work plays a very large part in a prisoner's life. It can serve to make his existence more bearable, but it can also lead to his destruction."[83] This kind of torturous and destructive labor left indelible marks on the memory landscape of Janowska survivors, but it seems to have been more ad hoc than systematic. The majority of work had productive goals, if still completed under appalling conditions.

Like many other camps, Janowska lived in a constant state of construction. For the men of the construction brigades, this work frequently was a death sentence. Those toiling to build and improve the camp lost the luxury of leaving it and escaping the guards, if only for the working day. Prisoners built barracks and dug latrines. Leon Wells recalled a work party hacking at the frozen ground to expand the Appellplatz.[84] David Manusevitch narrowly escaped death when he was spared from meaningless labor because he was a mason. He worked building barracks.[85] Even those prisoners not formally assigned to camp construction work often found themselves entrapped in it.

A ubiquitous memory is that of "vitamin work" (*Vitaminarbeit*). Willhaus forced prisoners returning from an already exhausting day of work outside the camp to unload building supplies from trains arriving at the Kleparów station. The prisoners called it "vitamin work" (B, C, D) after the Polish words for beams (*belki*), bricks (*cegly*), and planks (*deski*). ss guards mercilessly forced prisoners to run the quarter mile from the station to the camp carrying their heavy loads. Adolf Folkmann described the attitudes of the guards as "the same as one reads in history about the way in which slave-drivers treated their slaves. Their only method was violence and intimidation."[86] The physical and mental torture of this work must have been excruciating. Camp inhabitants feared it in particular as it always resulted in "tragic events."[87] Prisoners had to run to the railroad platform to receive their burdens and then up an embankment while "ss-men stood ready to shoot, whips swinging to and fro."[88] And the work attracted the worst of the ss, those with a "fondness for violence" according to survivor

Moses Osterweil. He had reason to remember SS Scharführer Paul Fox in particular. Fox beat him "mercilessly on the head with his club," detaching Osterweil's retina and leaving him blind in one eye. Fox also shot between ten and twenty prisoners in his presence.[89] Bernard Nestler was attempting to help two fellow prisoners with a long board when Roman Schönbach beat him to ground with his crop, causing permanent vision loss.[90] Peter Blum beat a youth suffering from typhus until he fell, stomped on him, and then shot him to death. Prisoners had to carry the body back to the camp so that the count would be correct.[91]

Willhaus himself took a personal interest in this work. He particularly enjoyed ordering this work late at night. One survivor recalled that "under the light of search lights, thousands of prisoners were carrying bricks and wood, beaten mercilessly by the Ukrainian Guards and the SS men."[92] The commandant himself shot prisoners he thought moved too slowly. For many, these nights of additional slave labor were their last nights on earth. Michał Borwicz described the outcome of one of these periods of "vitamin work": "Those who proved unable to manage the loads were dragged from the columns of five and placed 'behind the wire', that is between the two rows of barbed wire entanglements encircling the camp, with sections differing in diameter. Here the victims passed the whole night. In the morning, half-frozen, they were loaded onto automobiles and carried away for execution to the 'Sands'. After one episode of 'vitamins' lasting from six in the evening until midnight, one hundred and thirty people were taken to their deaths."[93] This forced unloading of trains proved to be an awful equalizer. Even those prisoners who enjoyed better working conditions and chances of survival in jobs outside the camp could be killed in an evening of "vitamin work." The Nazis took advantage of the proximity of slave labor to also unload other types of cargo from the trains at Kleparów. Adolf Folkmann recalled that "a never-ending stream of trains carrying men and munitions passed through Lwow to the east in those days. Trains had to be unloaded and reloaded."[94] Leon Wells described a Sunday morning spent unloading artillery at the railhead. Lacking proper tools, all the work had to be done by hand by human effort. As a result, many prisoners "were crushed under the wheels of these artillery guns."[95] While accomplishing a necessary task, this crushing work perhaps most blurs the line between slave labor and annihilation through labor. The mental and physical toll of brutal exertion, mortal fear, and uncertainty on already exhausted, malnourished, and often severely ill prisoners can scarcely be imagined.

For those prisoners tasked with building Janowska, a variety of jobs needed to be done. The cemetery brigade figures prominently in the memories of survivors. For Willhaus, the proximity to the Jewish cemetery provided easy access to building supplies, specifically the flat Jewish *matzevot* (tombstones). Emil Kruszewski was the prisoner leader for the cemetery brigade until 1943. The work detail contained around thirty men and some Ukrainians. Kruszewski stated that slave laborers knocked down tombstones, which Germans then trucked away for use elsewhere.[96] Prisoners from the camp labored year-round knocking these down and harvesting the material. Some of them were used to pave the roads in the camp. The occupiers often repurposed valuable stone like marble. A Polish prisoner in the camp explained that he was forced to crush tombstones into gravel that was used on the driveway of "the Governor of Lviv's house."[97] Slabs of "prime marble" were supposedly sent back to Germany.[98] Some of these gravestones may have even been transported out to the DG IV highway for use as paving stones.[99] A photograph freezes this moment in time. Three laborers throw shoebox-sized chunks of tombstones into a flatbed truck with the German company name on the door: Schuchardt.[100] A block of stone hangs in midair. Behind the truck, a forest of gravestones stands, awaiting its destruction. Prisoners even had to dig up corpses of Jews buried in the cemetery to search for gold teeth; as a result, many members of the cemetery brigade were dentists.[101]

Prisoners not only built the camp; they also designed it. On the third floor of the camp headquarters building, in the technical office, a number of prisoners drew up plans for the buildings their comrades would construct. Professor and metallurgist Henryk Griffel led a staff of engineers, architects, and draftsmen, including Zeev Porath and Bernard Hirschhorn. While camp staff often forced prisoner functionaries to assist in architectural work, it seems that at Janowska the prisoners did not simply do the basic tasks of drafting under an SS architect, but instead were responsible for the entire task of designing the camp. This speaks to the improvised nature of Janowska that Willhaus was forced to entrust its expansion to his inmates, lacking a German expert to plan it. A prisoner named Herman Lewinter was the official camp photographer, allowed to wander Janowska and document its "successes" for the SS.

Beyond construction, there was plenty of labor required to maintain the camp in operation. As a carpenter, Leopold Zimmerman repaired bunks and beds and could move around relatively freely.[102] Lidia Eichenholz did kitchen work and cleaning. To her, even that relatively good job was "very hopeless, because we knew that it would not last."[103] Other prisoners worked as maids and housekeepers. Many worked in the various workshops located in the outer precinct of the camp. Leon Wells installed glass. Others worked in the cobbler shop, making and repairing shoes. Moische Korn and his brother and nephews were among those who cared for the twenty-three horses in the camp stables; Moische cared for Mischka and Minka, two horses he had once owned.[104] Others worked in the warehouses, managing the flood of looted Jewish property that inundated the camp.

Particularly important in this area was the laundry and tailor shop under the command of Peter Blum. The operation consisted of washing machines, a drying room, ironing facilities, and a warehouse. The short, freckle-faced SS man had assembled his own workforce of around forty women and eight men who sorted, washed, and mended clothes before storing them in warehouses.[105] He held his own separate roll call every morning after marching his workers into the outer precinct of the camp. In his broken German, Blum would lay out the day's tasks. Klara Szpilka, who had arrived with her family during the March Aktion, was only feet away when Blum shot a Mrs. Wolisz from the ironing group in the head and then told the prisoners to "take that crap away."[106]

Besides serving the needs of the camp for uniforms and presumably laundering the clothes of the Germans, Blum's shop also sorted and mended the belongings of murdered Jews. In their desire to strip Jews of everything of value, the Nazis also sought to resell, recycle, or reuse even the clothes off their backs and the sheets off their beds. Prisoners sorted these items, washed them, and repaired them. They also searched them for valuables in pockets or hidden within the clothes themselves. Blum told investigators that "during the searching of the clothing millions worth of valuables were found. In particular, gold coins and diamonds." Certainly protesting too much, he added that he was required to account for these riches and constantly turn them over to Willhaus.[107]

Mountains of garments came from several sources that varied over the course of the camp's life. While Bełżec was in operation, some of the clothes removed at that small clearing in the woods made their way back to Lviv, only fifty miles or so away on the train. Prisoners in the laundry detail recalled seeing clothing with labels or other evidence from Czechoslovakia, Yugoslavia, Hungary, France, Belgium, and the Netherlands.[108] David Kahane wrote that "suits were found with tags from nearly every European country." Judging from identifying material, the prisoners could "tell which townships in eastern Galicia had become *Judenrein*."[109] After the Great Aktion in August 1942, Rachel Weniger was struck by the 5 two-story buildings filled with clothing.[110] Other items came from the in-house killing space behind the camp. During mass executions, victims disrobed in or near the main camp before disappearing into the sands. Their clothes were loaded onto trucks and taken to Blum's warehouse.[111] Some Jews arrived in the killing ravines clothed and their garments returned to the camp with bloodstains that the prisoners had to wash out.[112] Blum himself openly admitted that he processed clothes from murdered Jews.[113] Prisoners in his commando suffered the additional horror of recognizing the clothes of loved ones and finding family photos among the things they received.[114] Other things arrived from the ghetto after each aktion. "Post-Jewish things" like rugs, bedclothes, and hand towels were deposited in Blum's warehouses.[115]

The second lives of Jewish clothing took different forms. Janowska staff used their proximity to the material to enrich themselves first. One survivor stated that one of the reasons for stripping Jews to their undergarments before deportation was that "he [Willhaus] didn't want the . . . commandants in Belzec . . . to get this stuff because, still, they find diamonds, a $20 piece."[116] "The Germans divided this clothing among themselves," Rachel Weniger recalled. "The better part went to the SS men and their women, who dressed quite nicely."[117] Another prisoner stated that Willhaus's parents visited the camp and took a great deal of clothing back with them.[118] Much of the currency and other valuables was likely sent back to Germany, but Blum and others with early access enriched themselves as well. The best remaining clothing was sent back to the Fatherland to be worn by citizens of the Reich. Clothing that could be repaired to be wearable was stored for prisoner use. German officials from Lviv also visited the camp to pilfer clothing, rugs, and other textiles for themselves.[119] In this way, the journey of Jewish clothing arcing across the European continent binds Janowska with the Final Solution, the relentless larceny of the Nazi state, the individual greed of the ss, and the torturous slave labor of the camp.

Prisoners working outside the camp felt themselves the most fortunate. External labor offered the opportunity to escape the restless cruelty of the guards, to perhaps work under better conditions, to barter for food and other items, and, surprisingly often, to escape. Plenty of employers in Lviv clamored for Jewish labor. But it did not come free. Katzmann's office informed businesses that they must pay the ss 5 zloty per man per day and 4 zloty per woman. Even in the world of the camps, the glass ceiling existed. Employers could deduct no more than 1.60 zloty per day for feeding of prisoners and administrative costs. Users of slave labor paid their rental fees to the Emissionsbank in Lviv, the Nazis' central bank of the General Government created specifically to extract wealth from the territory.[120] By the third of every month, business owners deposited their checks in the bank building across from the city's botanical park at Siegfriedstrasse 102.[121] Hugo Bleines of the DAW remembered that even the DAW had to pay the ss for laborers from Janowska.[122] Failure to pay would result in the loss of the labor force as the #1 Clothing Factory learned in a threatening letter from the Katzmann's headquarters in January 1943.[123]

The surprising diversity of employers of camp labor underscores the breadth of complicity in the Holocaust, outside the ss sphere. One brigade worked for the Ostbahn, the eastern subsidiary of the German national railway, Deutsche Bahn. Leon Wells remembered these workers "always look[ed] black from the soot, and they are very lean."[124] In the Ostbahn rail yard, future Nazi hunter Simon Wiesenthal painted insignia on trains after he bribed a foreman for the job with one of his wife's dresses; his wife also was assigned to the rail company.[125] By early 1942, as many as a thousand prisoners worked on the railway. Some of these worked laying track, punishing work that was "non-mechanized and backbreaking."[126]

Three hundred prisoners worked for the Lueg auto company.[127] This civilian company from the Ruhr valley acted as a contractor for the Wehrmacht. Its director, Hans Pickert, was friends with Willhaus and sent the mother of one of his workers to Janowska to be shot.[128] The Lueg company still exists and was the seventh-largest auto-seller in Germany in 2017.[129] In Lviv, Lueg's workshops were located with a German Army motor pool unit, Heereskraftfahrzeugspark 547 (HKP 547), where they supported the repair of military vehicles sent back from the front. HKP 547 also directly used a large number of slave laborers from the camp. Karel Orenstein worked there cleaning and polishing parts.[130] Other branches of the German military also relied on slave labor. Physician Samuel Drix found himself assigned to the Hannebeck firm where he worked digging sand for the Luftwaffe airfield at Skniłów, on the outskirts of the city.[131] Prisoner brigades also performed various duties at military quarters throughout the city. Others worked in factories making uniforms, in a canning factory, digging potatoes, and in the local brewery making beer for the Wehrmacht.

Labor constantly occupied both prisoners and guards alike. Slave labor built the camp. It maintained the camp. It generated income for the SS. It killed and saved prisoners. It led to both imprisonment and escape. Indeed, despite the sheer brutality and magnitude of the killings in the camp, for many prisoners, the routine of work dominated their daily life. Work was the clock that tolled the passing of time from the hours of the day to the days of the week. Prisoners expended much mental energy on the negotiations and bribes that would secure for them a place in a "better" labor brigade. Of course, not all prisoners were local, and here the camp's second face as transit camp comes into focus.

Hell's Last Waystation: Janowska as Transit Camp

One of the unique roles that Janowska played in the Holocaust was as a transit camp. This space consolidated Jews from a larger area in preparation for deportation, usually but not always to a killing center. Some functioned to also divert workers to places that needed labor. The "pure" transit camp was largely a western European phenomenon, epitomized by places like Drancy and Rivesaltes in France; Westerbork in the Netherlands, which received Anne Frank; and Fossoli in Italy, from which Primo Levi was deported. Others like Žilina in Slovakia are even more forgotten than Janowska. Moreover, unlike Janowska, these places had relatively short lives and were then closed owing to their singular purpose. Transit camps rarely appeared in the East because ghettos usually served this function of consolidation. Janowska, however, clearly played this role almost from its start. It sat at the center of a web of misery and death that stretched across Distrikt Galizien. When Gebauer chose the location for the DAW in the summer of 1941, he was surely thinking of the convenience of Kleparów for the loading and unloading of goods. However, when the murder of the Jews of Europe became the goal of the Nazi state, the proximity of an out-of-the-way freight station within several hundred yards of the camp took on a more sinister utility. Flexibility characterized Janowska as transit camp for it also became a clearinghouse for slave labor and looted property.

While the extermination center at Bełżec was in operation, the camp became a waystation for those unfortunate souls marked for death. Janowska first fulfilled this purpose during the "Asocial Aktion" of March 1942 during which the SS organized the actual transports in the camp itself. The March Aktion became the model for deportations. Jews from the ghetto entered the outer precinct of the camp where a selection took place. This is where Klara Szpilka lost her family. After sometimes waiting overnight within the camp, the guards then forced deportees to Kleparów where they were crowded into cattle cars bound for the gas chambers. Beginning in spring 1942, Jews also began arriving from elsewhere. In February 1942, a transport of a hundred ninety-five men, women, and children arrived from the town of Stanislau (Ivano-Frankivsk) seventy miles to the southeast. These, however, were not sent to Bełżec, but taken to the sands behind the camp and shot instead.[132] During the March Aktion, "asocials" from Tarnopol (Ternopil), too, arrived in Janowska to be added to the death trains. Six hundred elderly and sick people as well as the children from the orphanage "were thrown on freight cars like cargo and taken off to Janowska."[133] Jews from a myriad of towns across Galicia arrived in the Janowska camp during its operations.

The Great Aktion of August 1942 saw the largest influx of people passing through the camp as around 50,000 Jews from the city were deported to Bełżec and murdered. However, as long as the gas chambers remained open, trains with Jews bound for death passed through the rail hub in Lviv and often exchanged passengers in Janowska. The tracks from Janowska led not only to the Bełżec extermination camp but also to another Operation

Reinhard camp, Sobibor. In the winter of 1942/43 and into the summer of 1943, trains carried Jews from Lviv and the surrounding area to the gas chambers there, where between 15,000 and 20,000 Jews from the region were murdered.[134]

A German police report on a September 1942 transport provides us a glimpse into this constantly moving stream of humanity. On September 10, Josef Jäcklein, a railway police officer, took command of a train in Kolomea (Kolomyia), a hundred miles south of Lviv. He and his nine men were responsible for delivering 8,200 Jews to Bełzec. Shortly before nine in the evening, the locomotive pulled out of the station pulling fifty-one train cars full of Jews. Each car held around 160 people. Fourteen-year-old Tomasz Mieszieński had boarded the train in Kolomea with his brother, Dziunek, after having been deported from his village of Horodenka earlier in August. He recalled "Dantesque" scenes at the lumber yard where the Jews were assembled before being "crammed" into the train cars. From the beginning of the journey, the situation inside the wagons seemed to him like hell "or worse."[135]

Jäcklein had problems almost immediately. So many Jews broke out of the cattle cars and jumped from the train that he had to stop the train in Stanislau after only thirty miles. Miedziński was one who escaped. Fellow passengers lifted him up and pushed him out a window. Unfortunately, the train was already in Stanislau and he was recaptured.[136] Here, railway workers boarded up windows and escape holes and covered them with barbed wire. "All of this was of very little help," Jäcklein complained in his report, as more Jews escaped and he even found deportees using hammers and pliers to break holes in the train. He was then forced to stop at each station to repair damage from escape attempts.

The Kolomea train arrived at the Kleparów station at eleven fifteen the next morning. It had taken fourteen hours, which meant that the train had averaged seven miles per hour. Jäcklein, too, was upset by the speed of the train and in Lviv the engine was replaced, but with an older one. At the station, the policeman handed over nine cars of prisoners marked as laborers for the ZAL to the head of camp administration. He then loaded around 1,000 prisoners from Janowska to the already desperately overcrowded cars. Three hours after arriving, the train set out for Bełzec. Jäcklein's troubles mounted as the "train driver never managed to reach top speed with his engine so that the train, particularly when traveling uphill, moved so slowly that the Jews could jump off without any risk of injury." His escort policemen used up all their ammunition shooting at escaping Jews and eventually resorted to bayonets when guarding the train during stops. Jäcklein coldly notes in his report the "ever-increasing panic among the Jews, caused by the intense heat, the overcrowding of the wagons" and the "stink of the dead bodies." The Jews of Kolomea arrived at Bełżec just before seven in the evening where the train sat for three hours before being unloaded. The unloading revealed that 2,000 people had died during the journey.[137] Tomasz Miedzieński, however, was not one of them. He and his brother had pried open a door and leaped from the train into the frozen darkness.[138] Over three days, September 7–10, the Nazis deported and murdered 17,300 Jews from Kolomea and vicinity.[139]

As the Final Solution started to become reality in 1942 and 1943, Nazi authorities began clearing ghettos, sending the majority of the Jewish population to killing centers and maintaining only a small force of laborers (or none at all). In Distrikt Galizien, ghetto clearing often meant transportation to Janowska, both for those intended to die and for those designated for work such as the 1,000 Jews from Kolomea in Jäcklein's train. However, the terrible unpredictability of the Nazi system often intervened. Zeev Porath recalled that "it happened that prisoners who had been already selected in another town as capable of work were labeled as incapable of work in Janowska and killed in one way or another."[140] The list of those workers sent to Janowska as the Nazis liquidated ghettos in 1942 and 1943 is long: several hundred from Móściska (Mostyska) in May 1942; 400 from Borszczów (Borschsciv) in March 1943; 159 able-bodied Jews from Bobrka (Bibrka) in April 1943 who had to make the journey sitting on piles of bloody clothes from those selected for death; survivors of the ghetto liquidation in Borysław (Boryslav) in June 1943.[141] But not all transports brought workers. Many of those brought to the Janowska camp—by truck, train, or tram—were meant to die there immediately, and not through labor. When the Jewish Council in the lake town of Janow-Lwowski (Ivano-Frankoye) could no longer satisfy Nazi demands for loot, the Security Police arrested the entire council and sent them to Janowska where they were presumably killed.[142]

Into the Sands: Janowska as Killing Center

The role of Janowska as a killing center more than any other elevates the space in the dark hierarchy of Nazi camps. Almost no Nazi documents regarding the camp survived the war, but a crude reconstruction of the camp's potential death toll can be created. A very conservative estimate suggests that the Germans murdered at least 40,000 Jews in or around the camp.[143] The actual number is almost certainly much higher. Thomas Sandkühler estimates that the death toll exceeded that of Majdanek (approximately 78,000, of whom 59,000 were Jews).[144] Martin Winstone similarly writes that "although there were no gas chambers in Janowska, it is likely that more people were murdered there, mostly by shooting, than at Majdanek."[145] This comparison is important because some scholars have previously listed Majdanek among the Nazi extermination camps. Likewise, Janowska and Majdanek generally held about the same number of prisoners.[146] Regardless, even at the lower end of the death toll, more Jews died in Janowska than in Dachau, Bergen-Belsen, Buchenwald, and Mauthausen.[147] If one adds the killings done by Janowska's staff elsewhere and its role as central facilitator in the delivery of Jews to the gas chambers, the camp's lethal status becomes even more pronounced. One prominent early historian of the camp argued that Janowska "relieved the burden on the gas chambers of Bełżec caused by chronic transport shortages."[148] In any case, the scale and frequency of the killing on-site have still remained shrouded in the mists of time for many.

But if Janowska's murderous function is perhaps a new "discovery" for historians, it was no secret for the wartime population of Distrikt Galizien and Lviv. Samuel Drix described himself as a former inmate of the "Janowska extermination camp."[149] The *Washington Post* wrote in 1945 that the camp had perfected "a savage system of extermination."[150] Rudolf Dantsches called the camp an "extermination camp" in 1947.[151] Another survivor defined it as a source of "free labor" and "simultaneously a place of destruction."[152] Marcel Lubash was even more nuanced. "The official name at this camp was Forced Labor Camp," he wrote, "but in reality it was an extermination camp."[153] In 2003, a scholar described Janowska as a "labor/ extermination camp."[154] Of course, for Holocaust historians, an extermination camp or center has a more precise definition, usually including the specific mission of the Reinhard camps and the purpose-built facilities at Auschwitz and Chełmno to murder Jews in large numbers. Janowska does not meet all those requirements, but neither was organized mass murder an occasional phenomenon; rather, it was a central purpose of the camp from its birth.

The killing described here occurred above and beyond the frequent murders stemming from the "death runs" and selections of unfit prisoners. It also differs from the daily, capricious killings of individual prisoners carried out by guards. Both of these contributed large numbers of people to the camp's death toll. In this, Janowska was not unlike other concentration camps. Almost all Nazi camps were the sites of this kind of bloodshed. What makes Janowska unusual is that it became the designated killing ground for the region and fulfilled a very intentional role in the extermination of the Jews of Distrikt Galicia. One survivor stated that people (Jews and non-Jews) were brought into the camp and shot in the sands "almost every day."[155]

From almost the very beginning, the Janowska camp and the "Piaski" or sandy ravines behind it witnessed organized executions. The site was designated for the murder of those the administration wanted dead, not just from the city but also from the surrounding region. Unlike Majdanek and some of the other concentration camps that carried out periodic mass executions, Janowska did so over its entire existence, potentially even before it was established in the case of killings during the July 1941 pogrom. Nazi authorities sent specific groups of people designated for destruction to the camp. Leopold Zimmermann testified that at least two hundred mental patients from Lviv, for example, were brought to the camp and shot in the "Valley of Death." Further, he described how people from the city and surrounding towns were "systematically" brought to the camp and shot by the SS and Ukrainian guards.[156] Even before the Great Aktion, which serves as a decisive turning point in the history of the camp and the Holocaust in Lviv, Janowska played host to frequent organized mass killings. One of these was the transport from Stanislau who were murdered in February 1942. Leon Wells remembered a mass shooting of between eleven hundred and twelve hundred Jews from Lviv on June 2, 1942.[157]

The mass shootings behind the camp contained all the horror of the "Holocaust by Bullets" taking place across the East. Stanisław Solarewicz was brought to Janowksa in 1942 as a sixteen-year-old. He described the first stage of a mass shooting.

> The place where the Jews were penned up was about 100 meters from the headquarters building. [This was in the outer precinct of the camp.] It was divided into a few separate spaces surrounded by barbed-wire. The first transports arrived during the day, the next at dusk and into the night. . . . In the twilight, lamps and searchlights illuminated the area. This enabled me to see what was taking place and how the Germans acted. Everyone brought to the camp came to the first area. Here, they left their outer garments, luggage, and the things they brought with them behind. Through screaming and beating with crops, the SS men forced the unfortunate souls through two gates into the next area. Here they had to strip naked and without concern for age or sex were led into the third area. . . . Baskets were placed here in which the Jews had to throw their rings, wedding rings, earrings, watches, etc. that they had with them. From, here they went out through a small door and, after SS men carried out a strict inspection of hands, ears, and mouth, went to the next place. There, the naked people were formed into columns for the sand hills. First went children, then women, and then men at the end. The extermination action ended around 4 in the morning. A few hundred people were murdered.[158]

This description of a large killing action demonstrates just how systematic the process of mass murder at Janowska was and how it mirrored the processes at extermination centers, minus the gas chambers. The SS not only established a carefully orchestrated routine but also physically altered the geography of the camp to support this mission. Certain areas of the camp were designated with distinct roles in the killing process, not unlike the extermination centers of Auschwitz and Bełżec. We can learn something of these killings from SS men and prisoners alike who witnessed the killings or their aftermaths. Janowska SS guard Hans Sobotta described a mass shooting that he took part in. He had been responsible for confiscating Jewish valuables at the rear entrance of the camp. Denying any involvement in the actual killings, he admitted to investigators that he had simply been "interested" and followed the condemned into the hills. There he saw a large trench, six to eight meters wide and ten meters long, that had been dug in the sandy soil. As he arrived, the shooting was "already in full swing." Groups of naked Jews stood a short distance away from the grave awaiting execution. Sobotta stood within twenty feet of the pit and watched as "mothers took their children to the trench, leading them by the hand or carrying them in their arms" and how "the children were shot first and then the mothers."[159] Leon Wells, a prisoner who barely escaped his own execution, recalled:

> When we got to the sand we found there was no grave prepared for us. We got undressed, again registered every name so to know for sure that no one disappeared on the marching road. Everybody got a shovel and we started to dig our own grave. When the grave was finished they started to read from these registration lists and by two walked down the grave, had to lay down side by side with their faces down and were shot.
>
> The next two had to cover a little sand over the first two and lie down in the other direction, line by line, and were shot again, and so it went ahead.[160]

The rhythm and routine of mass shootings in the ravines behind the camp could vary depending on the number of prisoners to be killed, the season, and the time available. However, throughout the existence of the camp, these systematic murders remained intimate, traumatic events.

As we have already seen, the summer and fall of 1942 was the deadliest period in the execution of the Final Solution, and Janowska's role here was central. This was partly due to changes at the higher levels of Nazi leadership. In June, Governor Hans Frank lost control over the "Jewish Question" and the SS took charge of the Final Solution in the General Government.[161] By this point, the Nazis had committed fully to answering their self-imposed question via the wholesale slaughter of every Jew they could capture. For many of the Jews of Distrikt Galizien, this slaughter took place in the gas chambers of Bełżec. We have seen how Janowska played its own significant role even in this process. Deportations increased. At the end of September, SS transportation experts from Eichmann's IVb4 section in the Reich Security Main Office allocated a train each day to take Jews from Lviv to Bełżec.[162] However, it appears that despite the increased traffic to the extermination camps, authorities in Lviv also leaned on the Janowska camp to increase the death toll. Executions by shooting increased in the Sands as the Jewish population was continually reduced.

December 1942 marked a decisive turning point. On the eleventh of that month, the last transport arrived in Bełżec. Himmler had decided that the Jewish populations remaining in the General Government simply no longer justified the dedicated extermination camps. This decision reverberated in Lviv. Now, with no other option for mass killing, Janowska became the biggest centralized killing site in Distrikt Galizien. The same deportation procedures functioned with the important difference that onward movement ended at the camp and the lives of the victims ended not in the gas chambers but in Janowska's ravines. Even work for the military no longer provided safety. In March 1943, for example, Anton Löhnert, Katzmann's chief of Jewish employment, rounded up eight hundred Jews from the Schwarz Uniform Factory. Guards from the Janowska camp escorted them from the ghetto to the sands where they murdered them.[163]

The partial liquidation of the Lviv ghetto over the summer of 1943 saw perhaps as many as twelve thousand people shot to death behind the camp. Almost all of the SS and Ukrainian guards not necessary for securing the camp participated in this massacre. A survivor identified Blum and Heinisch as participants and stated that "as the SS men came back, their clothes were splattered with blood and we had to wash them."[164] As the net tightened in the city, Jews caught hiding and workers who had been spared were consolidated in the prisons and then transported to Janowska to be executed.

Jews were not the only ones murdered in the sands. Non-Jews also died there. Janowska SS men forced a group of political prisoners evacuated from Poltawa (Poltava) to run back and forth pushing wheelbarrows of sand for three days before shooting them all.[165] Perhaps the most unlikely people to be shot in sands were Italian soldiers. After Italy overthrew Benito Mussolini and surrendered to the Allies in 1943, Nazi authorities in Lviv arrested the Italian soldiers stationed there. Around two thousand apparently refused to swear allegiance to Hitler. They were trucked to the camp, forced to surrender their weapons, and shot. The dead allegedly included five generals and forty-five officers.¹⁶⁶ Mass killing both in the camp and elsewhere by camp staff would continue almost until liberation in July 1944.

Janowska stands out as a Nazi camp not simply because it fulfilled many functions but because it did so continually and with such single-mindedness. The ZAL-L in all its guises gives us the opportunity to examine how one hybrid installation on the edge of the Nazi empire managed to perform so many of the central roles to be played in the Holocaust. It functioned as a dedicated pool of slave labor for the war effort (and for profiteers) while also annihilating Jews through labor. It served as a critical engine in the machinery of deportation and industrialized mass murder as a transit camp. Indeed, the camp leadership not only facilitated deportations but intertwined the needs of the camp with them by replenishing a depleted labor force with new arrivals and by getting rid of unwanted prisoners by adding them to the death trains. Simultaneously, Janowska operated as a dedicated killing center from its earliest days. It was not a camp that *could* serve as a place of execution as many were. Rather, it was the destination of choice, and the camp staff emulated the advanced routines of the extermination centers to handle larger and larger killings when the primary apparatus of the Reinhard camps ceased operation. In all these roles, Janowska also connected the Holocaust in Janowska to the Holocaust at the regional and even European scale.

Behind the Wires   6

> For a long-term camp inmate, the awareness of the approach of fate rarely takes a straight road. Logic uses premises or human associations. In the lager such reasoning failed; the course of events was usually inhuman. Experience did not help because human experience, even the bloodiest, gave one knowledge only of wrongs already seen and of deviance already experienced.
> —Michał Borwicz, *The University of Criminals*

What was life like in Janowska? We have explored in a somewhat chronological fashion the development of the camp and its roles. But this ignores the human element, the experience of residing in this space. For, as incomprehensible as it may be, the daily ebb and flow of camp life, its personalities, and its routines provide an unflinching and detailed glimpse into human behavior during the Holocaust, of perpetrators and victims alike. In the muddy microcosm of the Janowska camp, we witness the Nazi genocidal project in all its power and horror.

Prisoners negotiated their tenuous existence in ways both similar and locally differentiated from prisoners in other camps. They developed relationships with each other, the guards, the ss men, and the outside world in attempts to survive. At the same time, the guards and ss men lived transgressive but "normal" lives as custodians of this particular little hell. Yet, here in Janowska, the violence and brutality seem to exceed that of other places and to demand some kind of additional explanation. In the torture and humiliation inflicted on the prisoners, there may be some insights into the worst of human behavior. Survivor testimony from Janowska also sheds light on a particularly uncomfortable aspect of the Holocaust: sexual violence and assault, and sexualized violence. Until very recently, Holocaust scholarship often found these to be taboo subjects, yet they must be explored. Of course, even in the depths of this dark existence, prisoners found ways to resist and to escape with surprising frequency. None of these elements of camp life, of course, took place in a vacuum, but were all associated with locations, lending meaning and significance to very tangible parts of the camp. We must therefore consider how the micro-geography of the camp, its spaces and places, played crucial roles in daily life. And so, we once again enter the gates of Janowska.

Together in the Fog: Janowska Prisoner Society

For most of those imprisoned in Janowska, their experience must have seemed exceptionally discordant; they lived minutes from their familiar surroundings, friends, and family, yet the several acres they inhabited could not have been a more alien landscape. Prisoners existed in a deadly world of arbitrary violence, confusing rules, and unrelenting hardship; at Auschwitz, Primo Levi called them "our comrades, out in the fog."[1] They did not, in the face of suffering, cohere into the community that some might imagine. Life in the camp was often far too short for that. Few prisoners survived more than a year. As a result, the population of the camp functioned more like a society, small groups of people connected by past relationships or by specific elements of camp life such as work assignments.

Prisoner society can often be characterized just as much by division as by comradeship. The SS forced a "taxonomy of social classes" upon prisoners by categorizing them as "skilled" or "unskilled" labor as we have seen.[2] This was, of course, based on the Nazis' own warped definitions of utility. Those like Leon Wells, who claimed a trade, could perform useful work. As he himself recognized, "that I had put myself down as a glazier was very satisfactory.... I had good prospects of being allocated to a workshop where it at least would be warm and where constant beatings were not a fixed part of the day's work."[3] Zeev Porath and the other members of the Technical Office had similar perks. Yehuda Eismann's life was saved because he was an engineer. He had been caught with a secret report, bound to a stake in the camp and destined for the gallows when spared due to his expertise.[4] For some, like Leopold Zimmerman who repaired bunks, the ability to move around allowed opportunities for barter critical to survival.[5] Musicians, too, received special treatment owing to the existence of a camp orchestra and SS man's Rokita personal interest in it.[6]

Poets, lawyers, professors, and doctors served, however, no purpose in the Nazi worldview and therefore were classified as unskilled workers, a determination that sentenced many of them to death, not least because they often were not accustomed to physical labor. Samuel Drix, a doctor himself, remembered that "we were the subject of general pity among the inmates." According to him, Willhaus's attitude was "doctors or not doctors, all Jews are trash and dung."[7] Some medical personnel served as such but most did not. The non-Jewish prisoners in the camp represented another division. One survivor estimated that there were around fifteen hundred Poles and Ukrainians imprisoned in the camp alongside the Jews.[8] These non-Jewish prisoners were often serving fixed sentences for criminal or political offenses. Michail Javorskiij, for example, told the Soviets that he had been imprisoned for two months and fifteen days for "allegedly" storing Jewish property for safekeeping.[9] One prisoner noted that he received a "P" to identify him as a Pole.[10] Those in the construction brigade could get extra food from relatives; according to a Jewish prisoner, this "carried us through."[11]

As prisoners spent most of their time at labor, work brigades and the associated relationships could often be critical. Yet these relationships were often also the most morally fraught. As in other camps, the Janowska SS managed the massive numbers of prisoners by recruiting assistance from other prisoners and elevating them to varying levels of privilege and authority. This topic immediately raises a variety of difficult moral and ethical challenges, complicated not least by survivors themselves who often make vastly different judgments about these people. The SS employed the *kapo* system of prisoner functionaries and overseers that had been developed almost at the same time that they created concentration camps. Like many elements of camp life, it was not a Nazi invention. The commandant of Auschwitz Rudolf Höss had himself been a prisoner functionary while serving his murder sentence in the prewar years.[12] Himmler referred to the system as a way of "holding down subhumans."[13] Early camp administrators turned to veterans of the penal system to carry out this role in exchange for power and favor. The SS expected these prisoners to enforce camp rules, punish fellow prisoners, and generally ensure that the whole operation ran smoothly. Most camps followed a roughly similar hierarchy of privilege beginning with a block leader in charge of a barracks and ending with a camp elder or head kapo who oversaw all functionaries for the SS. In almost all camps, the Germans placed prisoners in charge of workshops and labor brigades.

Though not under the jurisdiction of the Inspectorate of Camps like Auschwitz, Janowska, too, adopted this system. One difference seems to have been that the majority of these functionaries were Jewish due to the camp's location on the fringes of the Reich (without access to the usual cadre of non-Jewish repeat offenders) and also its almost purely Jewish population. The camp "aristocracy" did enjoy very real luxuries and were sometimes allowed to live with their families, sometimes even outside of the wire.[14] Some lived in the attics of the barracks with blankets and electric burners.[15] Privileged prisoners could even visit the separate women's camp.[16] It is unclear precisely how many kapos there were in Janowska. By way of crude comparison, when Buchenwald held about the same number of prisoners in 1939 (around eleven thousand), there were five hundred kapos; there were probably fewer in Janowska.[17]

By far the most numerous of these functionaries were the so-called brigadiers who managed the work details. Every morning at the inner gatehouse, these men reported their numbers to the SS and managed the group throughout the day. At night, they ensured that the same number returned to the camp, dead or alive. For even the most well-intentioned kapo, the camp environment presented challenging ethical dilemmas. The guards expected kapos to control their workers with the same ruthlessness and zeal that they did. That also often meant beating one's fellow prisoners to avoid punishment. Few men could perfectly negotiate this obstacle course. Heinrich Griffel appears to have been one. He was the overseer of the Technical Office and an engineer himself. According to Zeev Porath, Griffel helped form the staff of the office into a "community."[18] During the liquidation of the ghetto, he boldly approached Willhaus in an attempt to save lives, asking permission to find more engineers among those marked for death.[19] This was not the first time. He also managed to get Aron Spinner's future wife removed from a group destined for the shooting pits.[20] Others were less benevolent. The brigadier of the concrete brigade, for example, demanded a bribe in exchange for taking Samuel Drix on.[21] Sometimes prisoner characterizations of the same person contradict each other. Drix recalled that Henryk Schleicher, a brigadier in the laundry brigade, intervened at considerable personal risk to prevent SS man Büttner from shooting his brother.[22] Stanislawa Gogolowska, on the other hand, called him a "malicious and unaccommodating man" who "never gave any help to his fellow prisoners." Indeed, she described him as Peter Blum's "right-hand man."[23] The complexity of the Holocaust makes it thoroughly possible that both were right. The fact that Blum recalled him by name and said they had a "good personal relationship" probably does not help Schleicher's case.[24] Nor does David Kahane. He stated that Schleicher had "lost all human dignity" and devoted himself "wholeheartedly to worshipping the golden calf and finding a 'fat suit' with diamonds or gold dollars sewn into it by its dead owner."[25]

Survivors praised Richard "Rysiek" Axer who was promoted to a position of some authority. He served as a kind of chief labor overseer. He was in his midtwenties and the son of a prominent Lviv lawyer murdered in Bełżec during the August Aktion.[26] Axer worked closely with Adolf Kolonko in assigning prisoners to work details. Kolonko remembered him well and said he was a "great guy."[27] Like other privileged prisoners, Axer lived in a separate house with some of the staff from the Technical Office and he had his own workspace in the headquarters building.[28] Axer often stood with Kolonko in the control house by the gate as the brigades left in the morning and returned at night.[29] His fellow prisoners greatly respected him, however, for by all accounts he actively worked to help them. Simon Wiesenthal wrote that the prisoners "idolized" him and that Axer was "always there with heart and soul to help" them. Perhaps equally importantly, he "enjoyed great popularity with the SS," which often made them reverse orders for punishment.[30] Samuel Drix recalled that Axer would frequently pull prisoners out of groups selected for death, cursing under his breath, "You are a specialist. I should smack you, you idiot."[31]

Survivors reserved the most scorn for two men: Zimmerman and Roman Kampf, who occupied the highest positions in the camp, though their dates and ranks are not exactly clear. Primo Levi wrote that "if one offers a position of privilege to a few individuals in a state of slavery, exacting in exchange the betrayal of a natural solidarity with their comrades, there will certainly be someone who will accept."[32] Kampf and Zimmerman distinguished themselves as particularly unsavory characters. It seems likely that both had functionary positions under Gebauer in the DAW and then perhaps moved to the ZAL-L. In any case, they stand out in survivor memories. Zimmerman was from Warsaw where Leon Richman claimed that he had been a criminal. As one of the highest camp functionaries, he "terrorized his co-religionists in a manner no less murderous than the SS men."[33] Roman Kampf was a jazz musician from Tarnów. It is worth noting that both men were not from Lviv. Perhaps the SS intentionally elevated strangers who would be less likely to have connections with their fellow citizens. Richman described both men as "notorious characters among the dregs of their town."[34] They earned that description in Janowska.

Both men took advantage of their position for personal profit. Zimmerman presided over the packages supplied from the ghetto, and after the SS and Ukrainians had stolen what they wanted, he, too, robbed his fellow prisoners.[35] Kampf took bribery money from prisoners' families to get them into better work brigades and kept it for himself.[36] Both men used their theft to ingratiate themselves with the SS. Gogolowska reported that Zimmerman and Kampf would drink and play cards with the SS at night.[37] Kampf had an even stranger connection to the SS. It seems that SS man Richard Rokita had known him from the jazz club scene in Katowice before the war. Recognizing him in the camp, Rokita elevated him to be his prisoner deputy, a position Kampf reveled in.[38] Kampf lived in the camp with his child and wife who also enjoyed a position of authority in the camp office where she routinely bullied and spied on a fellow female prisoner, once reporting her to Willhaus. She was a "worthy partner" for her husband.[39] Certainly, the two of them seemed to be fully capable of all manner of misdeeds.

Perhaps this explains why Kampf outlasted Zimmerman to become to sole prisoner functionary at the top. During an evening formation, perhaps in early 1942, a group of SS men dragged a prisoner onto the Appellplatz. He had been beaten almost to a pulp, but eventually the prisoners recognized this poor figure as Zimmerman. Interestingly, Roman Kampf moved back and forth, inspecting the prisoners as if he had no idea what was taking place. SS *Scharführer* Schlippe, however, made a point to call Kampf over. The functionary came to attention and attempted to give a report, but Schlippe told him to shut up. Instead, he pointed at Zimmerman with his crop and said to Kampf, "There's your friend. Do you want to give him a few?" Kampf appeared reluctant. At this moment, Zimmerman painfully dragged himself to his feet, stood in front of Kampf, and spit in his face. As Kampf stood in shock, the SS resumed beating Zimmerman until Gebauer arrived and shot him. Chuckling as he returned his pistol to his holster, Gebauer said, "And that's how the best escape plans should end." As Gogolowska reports, the whole camp knew that Kampf had informed Gebauer that Zimmerman planned to escape. Even more sinister is the revelation that many prisoners suspected that Zimmerman had no such plans and that Kampf had simply invented the accusation to remove a rival.[40]

For this and countless other reasons, prisoner society in Janowska loathed Kampf. He enjoyed his position and was not averse to beating prisoners himself, even taking over for SS men at more public spectacles. Leon Richman recalled a moment when a prisoner, a former boxer, fought back. After the prisoners were separated, Kampf "got out his poisoned weapon." He threatened to report his opponent, saying, "I've been able to find out that you, you dirty dog ... have ideas about making a getaway." Richman called this "a crushing blow, which constituted a moral knockdown of his opponent."[41] It also lends a good deal of credence to the claim that Kampf had framed Zimmerman. On another occasion, Kampf suspected that prisoners had stolen some of his butter and promptly informed Rokita. The SS man then simply assembled all the prisoners who had been working there and without a thought shot one. As he was aiming at the next, Kampf familiarly gestured to Rokita and said, "That's enough for today." Addressing the prisoners, he said, "That should be a lesson for you. Keep in mind that my things are sacred."[42] Leopold Szor remembered Kampf as a "horrible fellow" and an "animal." He went on to relate that the sister of a Janowska prisoner went to see Kampf seeking his release. And Kampf raped her.[43]

Eventually, an accordion killed Kampf ... in a manner of speaking. In addition to valuables, he had a taste for intrigue and turned on Rokita.

According to Gogolowska, who seems knowledgeable as always, sometime after the August Aktion, Kampf informed Willhaus that Rokita had sent an accordion packed with looted valuables home to Germany. Perhaps he thought he could sow discord between Willhaus and Rokita? In any case, Kampf had fatally overplayed his hand. Willhaus may have disapproved of Rokita's side activities, but he was not about to remove him. Rokita and Kampf both knew too much about the corruption going on in the camp. And Kampf was expendable. So Kampf disappeared. One day Rokita and Kampf left his apartment together, but the camp elder never returned. That evening, Rokita summoned the prisoner in charge of burials to bury an "accident" victim. At the time, it was clear to the camp that Rokita had executed his erstwhile minion.[44] Rokita spread a rumor that he had fled to Hungary, cursing Kampf's "black ungratefulness." Of course, this lie became less believable when SS man Peter Grieshaber appeared wearing Kampf's gabardine pants and boots. That day, Willhaus and Rokita stormed into the Kampf family's apartment and conducted a search. The two SS men found "a real treasure trove: gold, diamonds, foreign currency, countless vouchers for the best materials, shoes, and the most expensive delicacies and sweets." Two days later, when a train bound for Bełżec stopped at Kleparów, Willhaus made sure that Mrs. Kampf and her child were on it.[45] Officially, the camp "elder" had disappeared without a trace, but the camp knew the truth and no doubt the lesson behind it.

One should not, however, take away from this discussion the idea that all of prisoner society lived in the "state of nature." Kampf was a despicable human and likely rose to his position precisely because that was the kind of prisoner most valued by the SS. Many more prisoners strove to help one another survive. Helping behavior falls into the category of resistance as well, which we will discuss later in this chapter. Perhaps we should close this section on prisoner society by contemplating what it meant to prisoners to be confined in the space called Janowska.

The prisoner demographics changed over time with the addition of more non-Lviv residents arriving and the establishment of a women's camp, but the camp population must have usually consisted of locals. Thus, they lived in a parallel universe adjacent to their familiar one providing some comfort but also intensifying the pain of camp life. Family and friends could and did lend support, even at times being able to exchange words or at least glances. On other hand, it was abundantly obvious that prisoners were cut off from their prewar lives. Every day reminded them of the dangerously alien environment in which they found themselves. More to the point, in addition to personal suffering, many prisoners must have been doubly tortured knowing that their family and friends were going through their own intense torment a short distance away and simultaneously completely alone. It drove some mad. One survivor recalled a prisoner running up to the camp gate. When the SS guard asked where he was going, the man replied, "I have to go to my wife in the ghetto. She is sick and I have to take care of her." The SS man knocked him to the ground with a fist and shot him twice. The ghetto had already been liquidated by that time.[46]

Knowledge of the fates of loved ones had a very clear psychological effect on the Janowska prisoners. Leon Wells told the court at the Eichmann Trial that "in the beginning one always had somebody to lose, a family to worry about. By 1943 nobody cared. Torture was more real to these people than death."[47] Leopold Zimmerman [no relation to the kapo] spoke for many when he said that "human understanding cannot grasp the breadth of these crimes. I lost the most precious thing I had, my family. These innocent people died before my eyes."[48] The extreme violence and unpredictability of camp life drained prisoners of will. Samuel Drix observed that "it was no easy feat to survive for thousands paid with their lives for their inability or mistakes in navigating" the rules of the camp.[49] Ever the student of the prisoner condition, Auschwitz commandant Rudolf Höss noted that concentration camp prisoners were "oppressed and tormented and brought to the verge of despair, far, far more by the psychological than by the physical effects and impressions of the life."[50] The combination of the psychological and the physical broke many. Edmund Kessler watched his fellow inmates marching like "passive machine-like mannequins, deprived of will . . . For these were no longer people but ghosts, to whom death appeared as a benevolent liberator."[51] Indeed, suicide was not uncommon. Drix revealed matter-of-factly that "sudden unexpected death without torture was what we were wishing for ourselves." He also observed how, "at such a time of distress and struggle for life," people behaved "in a manner quite hard to predict from their education and social status. They showed themselves as they really were, beneath this veneer."⁵² Another survivor recalled that "we were so accustomed to the place that at night we often sat upon the corpses of Jews shot by Rokita and ate our bread."⁵³ Chaim Segal saw that "my comrades changed. They got weaker and weaker and only thought about food. Many started to steal from their fellow prisoners."⁵⁴ Felix Ash adopted a more compassionate view, saying, "You cannot judge someone else [who] is hungry. Hunger is a destroying element in most of human natures. You do a lot to be treated a bit better, to get one more piece of bread, to try to get some cigarettes, to make yourself just going through."⁵⁵ Primo Levi summarized this descent, writing, "To destroy a man is difficult, almost as difficult as to create one: it has not been easy, nor quick, but you Germans have succeeded."⁵⁶

In this society of shattered souls, some managed to survive. Often, this was thanks to small groups formed among the prisoners themselves. As in most camps, distinctions developed between the veterans and new arrivals. When Drix arrived, he was examined with "pity and curiosity" by the "locals" who looked at him like cattle and estimated how long he would last.⁵⁷ If one survived long enough, comradeship could develop and friends could be found. Friendships could make all the difference. Though she had escaped the camp and was living in hiding in the city, Helene Kaplan described feeling "forlornly alone," noting that "at Janowska I was with friends."⁵⁸ Drix, too, was comforted by having a group of friends in his labor brigade.⁵⁹ Aba Beer and two friends "formed a gang." "We helped each other," he said, "we three acted like one."⁶⁰ Given the scale of the atrocities in this place, even a small circle of friends was critical. And, even in this degrading, brutal, and all-too-often fatal environment, Jews found a myriad of ways to resist.

Paths to Salvation: The Diversity of Resistance

For all the daily horror and relentless oppression of the camp, prisoners resisted their persecution in surprisingly varied and courageous ways. Scholars of the Holocaust have debated the meaning and definition of "resistance" ever since 1945. Jews themselves pondered their own reactions to the Nazi genocidal assault in the moment. Writing from the Warsaw ghetto, historian Emanuel Ringelblum lamented, "Why didn't we resist when they began to resettle 300,000 Jews from Warsaw? Why did we allow ourselves to be led like sheep to the slaughter? Why did everything come so easy to the hangman?"[61] Indeed, some people privilege only armed resistance as worthy of the term. However, this overlooks the very real challenges to this most extreme form of resistance and to opposing the Nazis in general. The concept of *amidah* (standing against) represents a more inclusive and nuanced approach. One scholar describes amidah as "'all expressions of Jewish "non-conformism" and for all the forms of resistance and all acts by Jews aimed at thwarting the evil design of the Nazis,' a design that included not only physical destruction, but also to 'deprive them of their humanity, and to reduce them to dregs before snuffing out their lives.'"[62] Primo Levi summed up survival in Auschwitz by saying, "If the drowned have no story, and single and broad is the path to perdition, the paths to salvation are many, difficult and improbable."[63]

Janowska prisoners fought against their imprisonment, dehumanization, and even murder in a variety of ways. Sometimes they achieved physical salvation. Sometimes they succeeded only in achieving a moral victory. Werner Rings has proposed a helpful categorization of resistance:

1) Symbolic Resistance (*I remain what I was*)
2) Polemic Resistance, (*I tell the truth*)
3) Defensive Resistance, (*I aid and protect*)
4) Offensive Resistance, (*I fight to the death*)
5) Resistance Enchained, (*freedom fighters in camp and ghetto*).[64]

This framework helps us better place the many ways in which the Jews refused to accept the fate set out for them by the ss. Prisoners used all these approaches up to and including two mass revolts (which will be discussed separately). Holocaust survivor turned psychologist Hilde Bluhm argued in 1948 that "death in a Nazi concentration camp requires no explanation. Survival does."[65] And so, we must explore the arsenal that prisoners employed in their daily battle against their oppressors.

For many of those caught in the conflagration of the Holocaust, maintaining some sense of normality and human dignity itself constituted a rejection of Nazi power. With each tighter circle of physical confinement, from city to ghetto to camp, the options for a "normal" life became more constrained, but not impossible, even in a place of constant surveillance and assault like Janowska. This symbolic resistance, remaining who they were, took several forms. One was religious. Judaism for Nazis and many Jews alike became synonymous with what it meant to be Jewish. For those who remained observant, practicing their faith was not only spiritually important but also a way to foster community and to maintain a connection with tradition. As Leon Richman observed, perhaps cynically, "It is a known fact that during times of material dearth mankind embraces beliefs in miracles. . . . Disbelievers become believers. People without religion transform into religious people and impious men become pious."[66] Jews who were not observant or had lost their faith still sometimes participated in religious activity as way to feel Jewish and to resist.

Samuel Drix recalled Rosh Hashanah 1942 in the camp. "We all tried to keep our faith," he wrote. Someone had found a prayer book and "we were taking turns hiding in the barrack and praying, while the others took care not to let those praying be caught committing this crime."[67] Passover 1943 brought painful longings for Drix and the others who remembered their own family celebrations from before the war. The barracks leader, Nuchim, however, was a pious man and his "sad eyes shone with the radiance of the holiday."[68] Religious commemorations showed the prisoners that the Nazis had not completely won and did not have complete power. Leon Richman recalled a small act of resistance in which he and his comrades quietly recited the Kaddish prayer for the dead after they had been forced to bury a prisoner.[69] Leon Wells and others fasted for Yom Kippur, even as they were forced to excavate and burn corpses. In the Death Brigade itself, a Hasidic rabbi served as a "moral compass" for the group.[70]

David Kahane, a survivor and rabbi himself, gives us personal accounts of the power of religion as resistance. A friendly Polish factory manager allowed him to make a Seder dinner while at work away from the camp. On another occasion, Kahane and a Hasidic scholar friend, David Shapiro, enjoyed an engaging study of two charred Talmud chapters one night in the barracks. At Hanukkah, fellow prisoners asked him to say the blessings. The men of barracks 5 appeared to be "all ears" as his words "fell like a cool, enlivening rain on scorched, arid soil." Some of his message was incendiary as he reminded his congregation that God had "delivered mighty warriors into the hands of the weak, and the many into the hands of the few."[71] Even the indomitable Kahane could be humbled by the power of the spirit. He recalled a meeting under the gallows beside the kitchen with Rabbi Feibisch, one of the holy men from Jaworow who Willhaus forced to dance at the main gate. Five decades later, David Kahane recalled the power of the moment. He approached Feibisch and stood next to this man who was enduring the worst moments of his life. "I didn't have the guts to ask him anything," Kahane said. "For a few minutes we were both quiet until he took my hand and said 'How will we sing God's song in a foreign land?'"[72]

For other travelers in that foreign land, secular culture provided some respite and sense of humanity. Because the prisoner population came predominantly from Lviv, a number of renowned local intellectuals arrived in Janowska. Emanuel Schlechter had founded the Golden Mole Theater where he wrote cabaret numbers and was also a successful lyricist and screenwriter.[73] Other luminaries like literary couple Yerachmiel and Helena Grin arrived in the camp and contributed to its surreptitious cultural life. On New Year's Eve 1941, Schlechter organized a "literary evening" where authors shared their work with their fellow inmates. Other prisoners who worked in the headquarters mimeographed compositions by the camp literati for dissemination.[74] David Kahane remembered that "nighttime conversations among the occupants of the sleeping boards often resembled the symposia from the good old days before the war."[75] Even in the darkness of Janowska, people continued to create. Lviv poet Yankel Schudrich expressed the value of artistic work as resistance in a 1942 letter: "I am leaving these poems unpolished, in raw state, without improvement [or] embellishment. I see that the extermination of my people is an accomplished fact. So, let these songs remain as a testimony that I lived and I created even at a time when the sword was hanging over my neck."[76]

Just as the elite of Lviv's Jewish writers passed through 134 Janowska Street, so too did the city's musical finest. Former jazz club musician turned ruthless SS man Richard Rokita was on the lookout for these men and assembled them into a camp orchestra of immense talent. He gave the violin virtuoso Leonid Striks the opportunity to see his son, Maximilian, himself a talented pianist and prisoner, if he agreed to lead the orchestra. Striks helped assemble the group, which he led along with famed conductor

Jozef Mund.[77] Around sixty men played in the Janowska camp orchestra, which included former members of the Lviv Philharmonic, instrumentalists like cellist Leon Eber, and music professors like pianist Leopold Münzer.[78] Another famed musician was Artur Hermelin who studied under the same teacher as Gideon Klein and Rafael Schachter, Jewish musicians who performed in Theresienstadt. Hermelin had played all across Europe and in the United States and joined the Warsaw Philharmonic. His fellow prisoners may well have heard him on Polish Radio.[79]

The SS forced the camp orchestra to "accompany" the prisoners leaving and returning from work. Possibly Janowska's overlords were emulating their comrades at Auschwitz, which had had a camp orchestra since December 1940. The camp SS also enjoyed recreational concerts from "their" musicians. They also required the musicians to perform during major killing operations, perhaps to mask the sound of shooting or, as one scholar suggests, to allow the SS to "maintain a self-image of refined German culture and civilization, not apart from, but precisely in the context of, the activities in which they were involved."[80] Indeed, Rokita forced composer Schatz to arrange a special "Death Tango" to the popular tune "To Ostatnia niedziela" (The Last Sunday).[81] The sorrowful melody lamented a final goodbye from two lovers, but one can see from the lyrics why the SS found it appropriate:

> ... I ask for one thing only, perhaps it's my last demand
> The first since many years
> Give me this Sunday
> The last Sunday
> And may the world collapse after that.
> This is the last Sunday.
> Today we will part,
> Today we will part forever.

It was often played during executions in the sands, sometimes as the musicians' relatives marched to their deaths.[82] Simon Wiesenthal remarked that "executions with musical accompaniment are often carried out on the operatic stage, but at Lwow they fired real bullets while the music played."[83] It is hard to say whether the musicians themselves found some small comfort in being able to at least play music. One prisoner observed that conductor Mund "put all of his skill into the melody of the music."[84] Perhaps they were able to enjoy their music when they were alone. In other camps, they did so.

For some of the prisoners, music actually contributed to their suffering. Samuel Drix remembered that "the violin wept tenderly. Only when facing death, it seems, can one play so sadly and so straight from the heart."[85] David Kahane found the music a reminder that "you will never enjoy real music in a concert hall; perhaps you are hearing Jewish musicians playing for the last time in your life."[86] Others, however, likely felt like Auschwitz prisoner Franz Danimann who found that "the music warned us not to despair and lose hope."[87] The lyrics of the camp songs themselves constituted a form of resistance. The SS forced prisoners to sing but often the words they sung were subversive. Some were satirical and poked fun at the suffering they endured.

> And we boys good enough,
> Working at Janowska camp
> They make us toil, give no food
> And at us they daily shoot.

> As for dinner hurly-burly
> Mostly water with some barley.
> Then on Sunday we get grits,
> You want to puke before you eat.

Another, more vulgar version proclaimed:

> When they get out line
> You won't get a box of pine
> In the sand you'll go to sleep
> Fuck off, man, suck my dick.[88]

Samuel Drix remembered a slightly different verse, similarly rebellious:

> Are we this or are we that,
> From Janowska labor camp
> The world will someday hear of us,
> Sonofabitch, fuck your ass.[89]

Such marching songs illustrate the delicate dance of perception where the SS felt that they were forcing the prisoners into humiliation while the prisoners took grim satisfaction in subverting that very humiliation, often to poke fun at those same SS men. For some, musicians and ordinary prisoners alike, it became a "collective strategy of cultural and moral survival, and self-assertion."[90]

Some prisoners fought the Janowska regime of terror by seeking to "tell the truth," to document their existence and the crimes they witnessed or endured. The poet Yankel Schudrich expressed this desire for the history to be told in his 1942 letter. Gustawa Jarecka was a writer involved in historian Emanuel Ringelblum's project documenting life in the Warsaw ghetto. Shortly before she and her children were deported to Treblinka, she wrote that "these documents and notes are a remnant resembling a clue in a detective story ... we are noting the evidence of a crime" and that "record must be hurled like a stone under history's wheel in order to stop it."[91] Likewise, several prisoners in Janowska made a conscious effort to document the crimes they witnessed, not in testimony afterward but while they were in the midst of that hell. Henryk Gryffel directed an aggressive witnessing project from the Technical Office. He was "particularly interested in everything that went on in the camp" and established "a kind of observation post in the Technical Office."[92] Gryffel ensured that someone was usually at the window watching the camp below. Architect Zeev Porath was one of those working in the office, drafting architectural plans. He remembered "a feeling of community" among the specialists there that "under the influence of Gryffel made it our goal to remember as many events as possible so that if someone succeeded in surviving they could reveal these things to posterity."[93] As a result, Porath drew almost sixty drawings, maps, and plans that remain critical sources of information about the camp. Indeed, his sketches of the camp are incredibly accurate. Another courageous engineer was caught by the authorities with a hundred paintings of the camp. He attempted to commit suicide but survived and was instead thrown in prison.[94] Herman Lewinter was another Technical Office worker who was able to document Janowska; as the camp photographer, he took clandestine photos in addition to his official work and then escaped with the negatives. Others like Wells and Kahane wrote diaries during the war, capturing their experiences. Like Ringelblum's group, these prisoners sought to resist their destruction with the knowledge that they hoped would reveal the crimes of their oppressors.

Other prisoners found more active measures to thwart the Nazi genocidal plan. Prisoners sought to help and protect each other, particularly through medical care. A surprising number also managed to escape the camp. While not directly targeting the guards, such actions enabled some to resist the Nazi attempt to murder them, simply by remaining alive. Ordinary prisoners and those in positions of authority made efforts to save the lives of their fellow sufferers.

Some defensive resistance could be very individual. Leon Richman noted that he and fellow prisoners padded their hats because SS man Michalski "specializes in the head, always aims for the head."[95] However, some of the most effective defenses came from other prisoners looking out for one another. A Janowska survivor wrote that "if another person had not always had sympathy for me and gave me a piece of bread, I would have starved to death."[96] An artist in the camp gained the confidence of Willhaus by painting his portrait, and this "daredevil" used his influence to intercede for his fellow prisoners.[97]

Men like Rysiek Axer in privileged positions often leveraged their authority to help prisoners in need. Axer, as camp elder, had his own room in the camp and was allowed to go into town alone. He once used this opportunity to escape but returned of his own volition. According to Leon Wells, "he felt guilty for trying to save his own life when we in the concentration camp were clearly doomed."[98] Moty Stromer approached Axer after three weeks in the camp and pleaded to be moved to a work detail in town, fearing he would not survive camp labor. Axer got him reassigned. Stromer later wrote that Axer "always helped the Jews who were in trouble and saved them."[99] Henryk Gryffel, from the Technical Office, also actively intervened. He got Aron Spinner removed from a truck destined for the sands, for example. Aron himself found a survivor hiding in the ghetto and successfully snuck her into the camp and got her assigned to the women's camp.[100] Gryffel also convinced Willhaus to let him select "skilled workers" from new arrivals to save them from execution.[101] Even the act of providing rest or covering for another's labor could mean the difference between life or death. Another prisoner managed to rescue a woman who had been imprisoned in the bunker at the main gate. She was his best friend's wife, but "she was not normal anymore." Even though she could not work, the female prisoners took her from place to place and did her work for her.[102]

For the sick, the camp was truly a monumental struggle. A survivor observed that "sickness was treated as the greatest of crimes."[103] It was quite literally a death sentence. If the sick were not immediately shot, they were placed in the "between-wire" where they "suffered terribly and knew that they were being delivered to their death."[104] Prisoners would try to hide the sick in the middle of the marching formations. The urbane nature of Lviv society and the function of the Janowska camp as a transit facility meant that many of the city's large number of physicians passed through the camp. Unfortunately for many, Gustav Willhaus did not value their expertise. Unlike other camps where authorities used hospitals at least somewhat as vehicles to treat prisoners and combat disease (though usually for the benefit of the SS), the existence of a dedicated killing site at Janowska meant that most often the treatment for the slightest malady was death. As Gogolowska wryly noted, "it was forbidden to be sick in the Janowska camp."[105]

For this reason, perhaps, Gebauer actually allowed patients to be transported to the hospitals in the ghettos initially. Renowned doctor Maximilian Kurzrock directed the ghetto hospital before he, too, was sent to Janowska. While still in the ghetto, he successfully had prisoners transferred to his hospital. If they survived, they often could avoid returning to the camp.[106] Some meager medical facilities did exist. Gebauer claimed to have had a surgeon, internist, ear-nose-and-throat specialist, and a dentist installed in a stone building in the DAW.[107] If this was the case, the almost total lack of medication and equipment made them only slightly capable of any real healing. The official camp hospital lay just behind the camp, still surrounded by barbed wire. In reality, it was little more than an infirmary or sick bay with almost zero capabilities, even when staffed by competent Jewish doctors and nurses. Still, the doctors battled to keep their fellow prisoners alive. Physician Samuel Drix received caffeine and strychnine to keep him going when stricken with typhus.[108] When typhus broke out in the camp, "no attempt was made to treat any of the men and women who fell sick. As soon as the symptoms showed themselves, they were loaded on to trucks and taken off to 'Piaski' for execution."[109] Doctors worked hard to hide sick prisoners from SS men like Brumbauer and Biermann who would empty the hospital twice a month by shooting the patients.[110] David Kahane noted that "fellow prisoners showed great devotion in caring for their sick comrades. . . . Comrades of sick prisoners, the entire work crew, went to great lengths to shield them from the eyes of the S.S. man at the checkpoint."[111] Even at the last moment, some doctors saved lives. Dr. Rapaport was called to pronounce execution victims dead, and in at least one case the prisoner was still alive. Rapaport declared him dead, nursed him back to health, and helped him escape the camp.[112]

In fact, a surprising number of prisoners managed to escape Janowska, including during a mass revolt in November 1943 (which will be discussed in chapter 9). The proximity of the camp to the city and the prisoner connections to it offered some refuge for those who managed to get through the wire. On the other hand, that same proximity meant that the Nazis could (and did) retaliate against escapees' families. Regardless, many risked everything to escape the clutches of Willhaus and Janowska SS in what certainly represent acts of resistance. Ironically, because many testimonies occurred in legal settings, survivors often just casually mention that they escaped at such and such a time without explaining how they managed this monumental task. However, we do have the details of some of these incredible achievements.

Those prisoners with time outside the camp had the best chance of escaping and quite a few did. One chose a dismal rainy day in November 1942 to flee his work detail at the train station.[113] Ida Wiesen dropped to the back of a column marching to the baths and slipped away.[114] Proximity to home may have aided escape, but it also brought agonizing decisions. Aba Beer successfully walked away from a work detail. However, the SS arrested his mother and made it known that if he returned she would be released. As he hid in an abandoned factory, a friend in Lviv brought him a message from his imprisoned mother: do not return to the camp. He did not and she was murdered.[115] Others escaped from within the camp itself. Leon Wells walked out of the camp with a pane of glass as if he were going to a job. Marian Rogowski fled from his workshop in the DAW during the bustle of the lunch hour.¹¹⁶ Pawik Garmada found a part of the wall under construction that had not yet been topped with broken glass. One night, after the searchlight played over the spot, Rysiek Axer boosted him over the wall to freedom.¹¹⁷ Heinrich Chamaides pried a board loose in the fence and escaped temporarily; however, Ukrainian police recaptured him.¹¹⁸

Some prisoners successfully escaped death at the eleventh hour. Marcel Lubasz leaped from a truck destined for the sands. He timed his jump so that he landed under the trailer being towed, which gave him a few seconds' head start. He sprinted away under ss fire before disappearing into a Lviv city streetcar. All but one of the other prisoners on the truck went to their deaths.¹¹⁹ Alexander Schwarz escaped death when he crawled out of a shooting pit and managed to hide himself in a truck of victims' clothing and then in the clothing warehouse. He changed clothes and mixed back in with the prisoner population. He survived the war.¹²⁰ While the ghetto existed, escaping prisoners in the Janowska camp probably benefited from the proximity of a slightly safer and welcoming place to go. Most other concentration camp inmates found themselves far from home and surrounded by an unfriendly populace. Regardless, resisting by escape still remained a terrifying prospect with altogether different risks to families.

While the most difficult form of resistance, physical violence against Nazi overseers seems to have been not infrequent in Janowska. This is the offensive form Rings discusses: I fight to the death. Some prisoners seem to have chosen the moment to fight back as a way of writing their own ending. Two such events that make their way into several testimonies involve the former jazz musician turned camp guard Richard Rokita. In one, Rokita targeted a young prisoner for a beating, allegedly "unsatisfied" with the prisoner's carrying of bricks. Enraged, the prisoner hurled a brick at the ss man, shouting, "Carry them yourself!" According to Gogolowska, Rokita stood there "stunned and speechless only coming to his sense when the next brick hit him in the face." He then shot the prisoner, but "the evidence of this incident could be seen on Rokita's face for a long time, much to the delight of the prisoners."¹²¹ In another such episode, a prisoner flew into a "fit of rage" when Rokita prepared to kill his sick and exhausted brother. He grabbed at sand and stones on the ground and threw them at the guard before all the surrounding ss men pounced on him.¹²²

Stanislawa Gogolowska's own son, Janek, a Pole, attacked no less than the commandant Willhaus himself. After some insult, Janek spat back, "You can torment and kill us but you will not defeat us." The commandant became enraged and lunged at the young man, but Janek was faster and managed to strike Willhaus in the face. Willhaus froze for a moment before brutally shooting Janek to death.[123] A prisoner being led to his death in the sands beat the young Adolf Kolonko so badly that he took to his bed for several days. After he recovered somewhat, he lamented, "Look at what that Jew did to me! And how can I be good to the Jews?"[124] After the liquidation of the Janowska camp in 1943, a Ukrainian militiaman wrote to his mother that during the executions "some of the Jewish men had revolvers in their pockets, and they shot seven comrades."[125]

Another attack on an SS man took place in the women's camp. It seems that the female prisoners there targeted the self-appointed "commandant" of the Frauenlager, Karl Brumbauer, likely for his sexual assaults. He was well known for leering at women in the bathhouse and for forcing himself on them in their barracks. One night, members of the camp resistance snuck into the women's camp using camp police armbands and laid a trap of some kind. When Brumbauer next visited the women's barracks at night, drunk and singing an obscene song, he stumbled through the door and "discovered iron spikes in his legs. Frightened and gripped with pain, he began screaming as if he were being skinned alive." He appears to have suffered for a while because he was not heard in the rest of the camp and the Ukrainian guards (who disliked him) remained in their towers. Gogolowska noted with some satisfaction that after the attack, Brumbauer was seldom seen in the women's camp and never watched the women in the bathhouse again.[126]

Finally, Janowska had its own organized resistance group within the camp. Its members included the writers Yerachmiel and Helena Grin, camp chronicler Stanislawa Gogolowska, and architect Zeev Porath. Much of what we know about the underground in the camp comes from Michał Borwicz, himself a member of Zegota, the official Polish government Council to Aid Jews.[127] Two of the influential leaders were camp elder Henryk Axer and a man named Bienenstock. Axer communicated with the Home Army via a camp doctor and was likely a commander of one of the fighting units that eventually revolted.[128] The camp underground was particularly well organized and connected. For example, Axer arranged a job for Yehuda Eisman in the camp headquarters where he "got calls from Krakow about messengers bringing . . . Aryan papers to get certain people out."[129]

The camp's clandestine organization directly attacked the camp by setting fire to the DAW while Gebauer was absent in May 1943. Wailing sirens awakened the prisoners. As they stumbled from the barracks, they saw flames "blazing from the DAW," making the camp "light as day." SS men dashed about in various stages of undress and Willhaus "roared like a madman."[130] Ukrainian guards fired wildly from the towers, assuming an escape was underway. Karl Melchior, who Gebauer probably left in charge, ran around beating and shooting prisoners, killing around fifty.[131] Eventually the fire was contained, but the carpentry shop was completely destroyed. Gogolowska revealed that a resistance group under the engineer Frey from the Technical Office had set the fire.[132] Even Willhaus recognized this resistance, though spinning it into a positive. "This is not Warsaw," he told an army captain, "these are my Jews."[133] Though not Warsaw, Lviv did witness armed resistance to the liquidation of its ghetto. The survivors of this revolt ended up in Janowska, no doubt bolstering the camp underground.[134]

The Ukrainian testimony of Jews shooting at their would-be executioners in the sands sheds some light on what seems to have been a concerted effort to smuggle weapons into the camp in preparation for a mass revolt. Michał Borwicz wrote that Bienenstock tirelessly worked to build an "arsenal" in the camp. By raising funds from the prisoners and working through work details moving about the city, he succeeded in supplying the underground with quite a few revolvers. Despite the incessant risk, frequent scams, and setbacks he endured, Bienenstock continued his work. Showing a photograph of his murdered wife and child, he told the assembled resisters, "It is the truth for which one lives and dies."[135] His sacrifice would pay dividends in the uprising that followed.

Adjudicating what was or was not resistance during the Holocaust becomes, in the end, a useless endeavor. For the oppressed, the fight against their oppressors could be symbolic, intellectual, emotional, or physical. Or any combination of those. It is not for posterity to weigh the merits of these responses, but perhaps they help us understand the ways in which human beings react to great injustice, torture, and death. Moreover, the only true arbiters of what constituted resistance are those who were there. Remaining human or spitting in the face of certain death may have been the only way some saw to claw some degree of agency back from the subjugation they endured. During an argument in the camp about resistance, one prisoner recalled a group of women who had gone to the shooting pits singing. "That is also dignity," he told his comrades, "the dignity of contempt for a world disappearing into darkness, which had cheated them."[136]

Here Be Monsters 7

> Monsters exist, but they are too few in number to be truly dangerous. More dangerous are the common men.
> —Primo Levi, *The Reawakening*

Janowska's sixty acres bore witness to some of the most depraved acts of violence and abuse rivaling any in the Nazi portfolio. After sorting through the mountains of testimony, one might be forgiven for thinking it one of the most brutal places of confinement in the Holocaust. Engaging in competitive suffering is not a useful endeavor; torture and abuse were obviously awful for all who endured them. There is, however, something peculiarly horrible about Willhaus's domain. Stanisława Gogolowska told a Lublin court in 1947 that "of all the concentration camps I was in, Janowska in Lviv was the worst." She testified, "I was in many camps. But I never experienced anywhere else the things that happened in the Janowska camp. I have never encountered such conditions elsewhere."[1] Besides Janowska, she had been imprisoned in Buchenwald, Ravensbrück, and Auschwitz.[2] The horrors visited upon inmates of the camp can seem especially grotesque, even in the already dreadful universe of Holocaust experience. The SS men of the camp excelled in torture, humiliation, and senseless violence in ways that are difficult to imagine. There is also significant evidence of systematic rape and sexual assault in the camp that demands explanation. What is it about Janowska and its personnel that enabled such transgressive violence? A wealth of testimony helps us approach this issue. Survivors recalled with great detail the specifics of suffering inflicted, but also began to analyze the dynamics of this torture, even while still imprisoned.

The following discussion is graphic, difficult, and disturbing. It is undertaken not as a prurient form of historical voyeurism, but because it must be addressed. Prisoners themselves observed the outlines of twisted meaning in the physical and mental assaults. Historians cannot flinch from also examining this experience, for it is another relationship. It is an intimate physical relationship between oppressed and oppressor founded on violence. But these interactions can help us understand the perpetrators, their motivations, and the role the camp itself played in the victimization of those who walked its grounds.

Jean Améry, an Austrian philosophy student and Nazi victim, understood this better than most. Before being sent to Auschwitz, Buchenwald, and Bergen-Belsen, he was tortured by the Gestapo in Belgium. In his postwar writing, Améry contemplates the meaning of torture. It was, he writes, "the most horrible event a human being can retain within himself." He continues, "The first blow brings home to the prisoner that he is helpless, and thus it already contains in the bud everything that is to come." Améry makes the painful observation that beyond physical pain, the greatest loss is our "trust in the world." The abuser violates our most basic boundary—our own skin. Thus, for Améry torture is like a rape; the torturer "forces his own corporeality on me with the first blow. He is on me and thereby destroys me." The victim also feels the torture of being helpless, beyond aid, and in a world whose social contract no longer applies. "If no help can be expected," Améry writes, "this physical overwhelming by the other then becomes an existential consummation of destruction altogether." After the first blow, he concludes, "a part of our life ends and it can never again be revived."[3] This was the world of the Janowska camp and its prisoners. How the SS created this world is of critical importance as is how the prisoners navigated its treacherous ground.

A Taxonomy of Violence: Assault, Abuse, and Torture

Most prisoners in the camp likely experienced their first moment of abuse in much the same way as Améry. SS and Ukrainian guards continuously lashed out at those around them with physical abuse and beating. The unpredictability of response and uncertainty as to the rules of this new world added mental anguish, particularly for newcomers. The brutality of the prisoner "welcome" was "an elaborate routine of humiliation and violence" that had been a feature of the concentration camp system from its first days. Meanwhile, the potential to be murdered for practically nothing beyond bad luck terrified even the most veteran of prisoners. On the warped scale of abuse, beating may *seem* oddly bearable compared to other assaults, but it not only caused immense psychic damage at the first blow; it could often be fatal. One survivor testified that SS man Martin Büttner in the DAW "beat three people to death with his bare hands, quite slowly, blow after blow, until they died."[4] Karl Melchior beat Meier Entenberg so badly that he lost four teeth. He then ordered Entenberg to report to him after work and then beat him with a leather-covered steel bar.[5] Beatings, even severe or fatal ones, were incredibly common. One survivor testified that Michael Hügel had "beaten hundreds of inmates" including him and his father.[6]

These beatings combined with other "punishments" often took on the characteristics of public performance. In spring 1942, a prisoner was caught trying to escape. At the evening roll call, Gebauer and Willhaus together put on a "show." First, Willhaus whipped him twenty-five times, "aiming at the kidneys." Then Gebauer lashed him twenty-five more times. Somehow, the prisoner was still alive when dragged off the whipping block. Gebauer then kicked him in the chest until he "breathed his last breath."[7] This brutal demonstration clearly aimed at punishing an offender but also, more importantly, at deterring future escapes. The impunity with which SS men could publicly commit murder also reinforced feelings of hopelessness among the prisoners. Public performances frequently showcased violence for a prisoner audience, but the SS also disseminated messages of intimidation in less organized but equally public ways. For some unknown offense, the SS men gave an eighteen-year old boy twenty-five lashes and then hung him "spread-eagled" on the side of the guardhouse at the inner gate. Leon Wells noted matter-of-factly that "this is his end; as a result of his punishment he will be unable to work; he will be kaput, shot."[8] Prisoners marched past this scene twice a day on their way to work. The SS even modified the environment of the camp itself to accommodate their abuse. Michał Borwicz observed that "pillars, sunk into the corners of the pleasant square, are used to tie the condemned in the air with their hands attached behind them in such a way that their feet cannot touch the ground. After vain and futile requests for execution, they perish after several days from hunger and emaciation."[9] In this way, torture literally became part of the landscape. These posts appeared both on the roll-call square as well as by the kitchens where makeshift gallows were also constructed. Sometimes, Willhaus brought violence home. When a former brigadier named Landau was recaptured after escaping, the commandant had him tied to a post "fifteen to twenty steps" in front of his house. Willhaus and Rokita sat on a bench and took turns aiming shots just above his head, seeing who could come closest without hitting Landau. After fifteen minutes of this, other SS men beat him with clubs. Landau stayed tied to the pole for a day and was then shot.[10]

This kind of target practice became a routine part of camp life but also a particularly unique aspect of Janowska. Perhaps it evolved from SS men like Heinen shooting at empty bottles by the camp kitchen.[11] But evolve it did. Rokita dealt with a prisoner who had resisted by turning him into a target. He had the prisoner tied to a post and then shot him, aiming specifically at first for nonlethal shots in the legs and arms. Marian Rogowski described it as reminiscent of "Indians" torturing a victim at the stake.[12] Another SS man would frequently select prisoners from the "between-wire" holding area and practice shooting them in the nostrils with an air rifle. He became proficient enough to show off his "art" to fellow SS men.[13] SS man Fox forced prisoners to hold a coin between two fingers as he tried to shoot it. Not surprisingly, he often shot the prisoner instead.[14] Willhaus, Heine, Siller, and Blum would practice their aim in a similar exercise with a living target holding a glass of water.[15] Werner Hahn, an amputee assigned as an SS guard, also shot prisoners, telling people that it was training for his "good hand."[16] At other times, this "target practice" was less organized. Sometimes, SS men simply took aim at prisoners going about their daily tasks.[17] Blum, Heinen, and Schönbach took advantage of incoming prisoners to add an "artistic" element to their murderous activities. They would approach the crowds of waiting people and "phlegmatically choose this one and that one, assembling them in inventive poses, as if molding their postures in clay, before taking aim: a shot in the womb, a shot from the side, from behind."[18] Some mornings after roll call, Richard Rokita forced sick prisoners to run around him in a circle and on the count of three would shoot one of these moving targets with his pistol.[19] Martin Büttner would often borrow a rifle from Roman Schönbach and beckon three or four women over before "jovially" shooting them; it was, as a survivor recalled, "sport."[20] One prisoner told a court that "Blum just went around the camp shooting people. I believe that was his sole purpose!"[21] Another Janowska survivor said that "around Blum, our lives were never safe."[22]

Gustav Willhaus unquestionably set the example in this particular "game." One of the most striking and ubiquitous memories of survivors is his proclivity for sniping at prisoners from his office and villa balcony. Twenty-one survivors testified to this behavior. The geography of the camp was critical to these crimes. The commandant's house stood between the ZAL-L and the DAW. It was only about three hundred feet to the barracks on the opposite side of the Appellplatz. From the balcony to the far side of the outer precinct was only around five hundred feet. This put the most trafficked areas of the camp well within the range of even a casual marksman. As a result, the occasional gunshot often punctuated the interminable days in Janowska.

Much as his counterpart at the Płaszów camp, Amon Goeth, did, Willhaus entertained himself by shooting prisoners with a rifle from his balcony. His targets varied. Sometimes he picked out individual prisoners. Other times he shot into work brigades as they marched in or out of the camp. Henry Chamaides recalled walking with his work brigade while bullets whistled through the ranks.[23] According to one survivor, this was a daily occurrence.[24] Prisoners learned quickly how to negotiate the dangerous terrain that fell within range of Willhaus's shooting eye. Leon Wells recalled that "I used to be able to walk by every day any place I wanted because I took a piece of glass in front of me ... they wouldn't break glass."[25] Others chose routes that would keep them out of the line of fire by keeping buildings between them and Willhaus's shooting positions. To survive, they had to be able to react quickly. Chaim Rosen saw Willhaus appear on the balcony with his rifle and ran away from his group, ducking into a barracks. Several shots followed.[26] Stanisława Gogolowska observed that because "he had a sure hand and rarely missed; the prisoners avoided as much as possible the pretty white villa with the wonderful garden."[27] Dorothy Haffner hid herself in a crowd of men when Willhaus opened fire. When she dared to look up, she saw Mrs. Willhaus on the balcony as well ... with a gun in her hand.[28]

Indeed, one of the most surprising participants in this human target practice was in fact Willhaus's wife, Liesel. At least ten survivors were eyewitnesses to her crimes, and many more had heard of them. According to one prisoner, "the devil himself must have been the matchmaker of this couple."[29] Liesel would appear on the villa balcony with a small-caliber rifle and, like her husband, shoot prisoners. Both the weapon and the killer had a shorter range and she would sometimes shoot prisoners working in her garden or near the house.[30] Miroslav Rycevskii offered a very detailed description. Liesel "appeared on the balcony every morning, sometimes alone, sometimes with her husband. She either wore a dressing gown or riding pants and boots. From the balcony of the house, she shot prisoners who were working in the area. Sometimes she killed two or three. Sometimes she only wounded them and the SS had to then kill them. During my time in the camp, the wife of the commandant executed up to twenty people this way."[31] During a Sunday punishment work session where prisoners were forced to pick up litter on the Appellplatz, she wounded a prisoner in the shoulder. On another occasion, Liesel Willhaus rested her rifle on the railing and shot a prisoner working in her yard in the neck, killing him.[32] Worse still, the Willhaus's five-year-old daughter, Heike, was often present and entertained by her parents' shooting, though surely not fully understanding it. David Kahane recalled that Heike clapped her hands as Gustav picked off members of the "cripples brigade," people unable to work.[33]

Liesel Willhaus's cold-blooded killing transgressed the traditional boundaries of both gender and status. Women are frequently thought to not be capable of the same atrocities as men and perpetrator wives were often absolved from guilt on the grounds that they did not actually contribute to the killing. Yet Liesel did both. How do we explain this? Another SS wife and murderer, Erna Petri, explained, "I seldom came into contact with other women, so that in the course of this time I became more hardened, desensitized. I did not want to stand behind the SS men. I wanted to show them that I, as a woman, could conduct myself like a man."[34] Liesel Willhaus certainly had a community of SS women to socialize with, including Katzmann's wife. Liesel denied everything, to include ever having set foot in the camp proper and that she could even see the camp from her balcony. Instead, she said that "despite being the wife of an SS officer, I always conducted myself as a normal woman and mother."[35] Despite these lies, it seems clear that she was an antisemite and a convinced Nazi, and potentially shared Petri's desire to prove herself in the male world of her husband. Survivors stated they had personally witnessed Liesel laughing during these shooting parties.[36] In her book on female perpetrators, Wendy Lower suggests that female perpetrators used violence "to achieve a mastery that was not otherwise available, to lord it over victims of the regime rendered powerless."[37] Liesel Willhaus certainly sought this. Even Améry, the torture victim, admitted "a kind of wretched admiration for the agonizing sovereignty they exercised over me. For is not the one who can reduce a person so entirely to a body and a whimpering prey of death at least a demigod?"[38] Lower goes on to warn that "minimizing the violent behavior of women creates a false shield against a more direct confrontation with genocide and its disconcerting realities. . . . Genocide is also women's business. . . . Minimizing women's culpability to a few thousand brainwashed and misguided camp guards does not accurately represent the reality of the Holocaust."[39]

Genocide also is a communal activity. The balcony of the Willhaus residence often became the site of parties involving this same target practice. Michał Borwicz described "elegant women," the wives and fiancées of SS men gathering on the balcony with their men for shooting fun. An SS Schärführer Steiner would draw a white circle in chalk on a prisoner's chest and partygoers would take aim. In this instance, pediatrician Professor Progulski was shot, apparently by a female guest. His son also died in this competition.[40] On a separate occasion, Willhaus invited the camp SS to his house on his birthday and shot at prisoners along with Karl Melchior and Fritz Gebauer. This caused "a great panic in the camp as no one knew where to run."[41] Sometimes, the games became even more perverse if that is possible. One survivor testified that Willhaus ordered "a strong Jew named Schleicher to throw a one to two year old child in the air" for him to shoot while his daughter Heike looked on.[42]

Target practice as torture and murder was not unique to Janowska, but it does seem to have been particularly prominent there. There are perhaps several interconnected explanations for their frequency. Thanks to the patronage of Katzmann, Willhaus perhaps enjoyed a freedom of action that other commandants did not. The ss and police leader was "not interested in issuing explicit guidelines for the behavior of camp staff. He preferred to just give them guidelines."[43] As a result, Willhaus presided over an important but obscure camp and could easily get away with unauthorized firing of weapons, and he allowed his men the same freedom. By comparison, each ss man serving at Auschwitz had to sign "a statement affirming his understanding that 'the Führer alone decides over the life and death of an enemy of the state' and that he therefore had no authority 'to physically mistreat' inmates."[44] Of course, in reality, any thin veneer of civility required of ss men was never truly upheld, despite Himmler's idealistic visions of "professional" camp staff. One of Himmler's own aides described "unnecessary torture" as that which "breached decorum or caused disorder."[45] But this order does suggest that firing a weapon haphazardly would not be permitted. And the level of supervision in Janowska was lower than elsewhere combined with a commandant who enjoyed unnecessary torture. Indeed, Janowska (and the other camps that Janowska men commanded) lacked any real senior oversight.

There is likely another element, a kind of ss-specific feeling of inadequacy, particularly for the men in Janowska who were relatively to close to the actual fighting. Endless convoys of troops headed to the front (and wounded men returning) would have been constant reminders in Lviv of the war on the Eastern Front. Perhaps the ss men wished to connect with that most basic of combat tasks, shooting, in an attempt to reinforce to themselves that they, too, were soldiers. Willhaus's proficiency at shooting certainly played to this. While Himmler could tell his men all he liked that they were fighting a battle just as important as the combat troops, that must have rung hollow for some. Perhaps demonstrations of martial prowess soothed the bruised egos of those men fighting on "make-believe battlefields inside camps."[46] One must also add the banal but equally important element of boredom that probably underlies some of the abuse at the camp. The routine itself of camp life was no less monotonous to the guards than it was for the prisoners, though obviously with different effects. Making sport of victimization thus provided some variety and entertainment for the ss.

It also provided some an opportunity to prove themselves. Such was certainly the case of SS Scharführer Friedrich Heinen. Heinen was young at twenty-one in 1941. Coming from a sailing family, he had tried to join the navy in 1940 but had a vision defect that kept him out. Instead, he worked in an armaments factory. This must not have satisfied him, however. In November 1941, he volunteered (or was called up) for the Waffen-SS; given that his father was an SS man, the former is more likely. After a series of illnesses (and a honeymoon), Heinen arrived in Janowska in spring 1943, where he immediately made an impression on the prisoners.[47] Heinen desperately wanted to be a soldier. With his usual impeccable insight, Michał Borwicz took his measure. "He is tortured," Borwicz wrote, "by a boyish ambition to pass for a mature man." Moreover, it seems his fellow SS men teased him relentlessly about his age. Heinen sought to demonstrate his manhood by creating his own particular mode of shooting prowess: lining up prisoners head to head and trying to kill as many as possible with one bullet. Borwicz noted sardonically that "Heinen wanted to stand out or be recognized for something, but in the camp it was not easy to distinguish oneself."[48] In the end, the prisoners of the camp suffered for Heinen's insecurities. He seems to have escalated his abuse. The *Washington Post* reported in 1945 that he would pull out women's fingernails, strip them naked, and hang them by their hair. After pushing them so they swung back and forth, he would then shoot at the "moving targets."[49]

Heinen was not alone, however, in gravitating toward a particular form of killing and abuse. Survivors often grouped perpetrators by their preferred method of murder. Gebauer preferred strangling and sometimes drowning victims. When he caught someone resting, Gebauer would "throw them to the ground and stand on their throat until there were no more signs of life while two other SS men beat the unfortunate with clubs."[50] According to one survivor, Gebauer had a "passion for strangling people with his own scarf."[51] In the summer of 1943, Irving Mandel stood in the carpentry shop while Gebauer strangled Moishe Mehr for having roasted a potato on the stove.[52] In the DAW tailor shop, the commandant sat down across from a seamstress before strangling her with his scarf until she dropped to the ground dead.[53] Through a barracks window, Chaim Rosen watched Gebauer kick a prisoner until he fell. The DAW commandant then kneeled on the hapless man's chest and "pressed his thumbs into the prisoner's throat until he died." Gebauer then stood up, wiped his hands with his white handkerchief, and ordered the body taken away.[54] Abraham Goldberg described the murder of a sick friend by Gebauer. "Gebauer saw him and asked him 'Don't you want to work or can't you work?' He didn't know how to answer and Gebauer simply strangled him to death and walked away."[55]

Prisoners certainly viewed this behavior as sadism and they may well be right. Such an intensely personal form of murder very often fits a sadistic profile, even in the normalized violence of the Holocaust. In the ordinary world, these kinds of murderers often target family members or relatives, frequently targeting weaker victims like woman and children. Strangulation has "been firmly associated with sexual and sadistic murders" as well. Profilers often link methods like Gebauer's with "expressive rage" and a need for "greater intimacy" with the victim.[56] This connection is meaningful because, while many survivors understandably describe their tormentors as "sadists," in reality, most were not psychologically abnormal. Perhaps, in this case, Gebauer *was* actually a sadist.

Willhaus's preferred method was shooting, as we have seen. Human target practice functioned for him both as a social entertainment and a personal act of torture. Unlike Gebauer's brutish and intimate killing, Willhaus could use the precision of a firearm to both perform his military prowess (and his masculinity) and to prolong the suffering of his victims. In March 1943, three rabbis arrived in the camp from the countryside. Willhaus had them march with outstretched hands across a plank while the orchestra played. He then shot all three at the same time.[57] His behavior clearly influenced others, such as the young Heinen, to also use Janowska prisoners as their own private targets. During mass shootings in the Sands, Peter Blum sometimes intentionally shot victims in the gut for a change of pace.[58] The distance afforded by a firearm allowed a dehumanization that Gebauer's murders seemed to deny.

Throughout the camp, guards became known for their proclivities. Some were known by their preference for blades.[59] Martin Büttner was "known as a specialist with a knife."[60] Others like Kolonko and Schönbach excelled at beating prisoners to death.[61] Interestingly, Simon Wiesenthal testified that Kolonko was *not* a sadist. Schönbach, on the other hand, he credited with the "most abominable acts" heard during the postwar trial. Wiesenthal stated that Schönbach had shot a nine-year-old child in the German railway subcamp in Lviv.[62] Another survivor described how Schönbach once murdered a row of children with a hammer.[63]

For all of these men, the camp geography itself provided venues for specific cruelty and humiliation: a gallows behind the kitchen, a whipping post near the stables, Willhaus's balcony shooting platform. The special hell of the "between-wire" provided an almost endless source of "useless" prisoners for the enjoyment of the SS men. Indeed, the small size of the camp itself meant that these horrific scenes could not remain hidden, and, indeed, the SS men often intended it that way. Openly transgressive violence served only to heighten the sense of helplessness felt by the prisoners and to emphasize the complete impunity enjoyed by the SS.

The SS frequently staged public humiliations and executions. Peter Blum enjoyed forcing two prisoners to fight each other.[64] The posts installed throughout the camp often displayed grim warnings to prisoners. In October 1943, Schönbach and Heinen hung a prisoner upside down and cut him with a knife for not taking his hat off when he passed them.[65] A cook caught with stolen food was beaten and then thrown into a cauldron of boiling soup.[66] When two rabbis from Jaworow arrived in Janowska, Willhaus made a spectacle of them on a platform beside the entrance to the inner precinct. Rather than giving them prisoner uniforms, he kept them in their traditional Orthodox clothing and forced them to dance with each other while holding a torn red umbrella. The camp orchestra provided the accompaniment. Every day when marching to or from work, prisoners would pass this humiliating scene, and it made an impression on many survivors. David Kahane recalled Willhaus saying, "'Look, I know you work hard and I've decided to add entertainment to the camps. Before going to work, I'll bring you some dancers, some entertainment for you. And, of course, you will be happy.' As they were being beaten, the rabbis sang 'Ana hashem Hoshiana Na! (God save us).'"[67] Kahane wrote that this was one way the Nazis "added humiliations, trampling underfoot and spitting on Jewish dignity and human values."[68] This macabre drama lasted for two weeks until the SS grew tired of it and executed both men behind the camp kitchen.[69]

The environment itself became a weapon for the SS. Willhaus's successor, Friedrich Warzok, had five escapees tied to telephone posts during the heat of the day and then soaked in water in the bunker overnight. They were later moved near the kitchen where all the prisoners had to pass by and hear them crying, "shoot us! Shoot us!"[70] Many survivors recall a cold Sunday evening roll call where Gebauer chose several of the "dirtiest" prisoners, forced them to strip naked, and then threw them bound into barrels of water. "Since you swine won't wash yourselves otherwise," he joked. The other SS men laughed. Leon Wells wrote that "after two hours, chunks of ice could be broken off the corpses of these unfortunate youngsters."[71] On another occasion, Gebauer forced fourteen prisoners to remain on the Appellplatz overnight. They could not move without being shot by the Ukrainian guards and so they all froze to death.[72] The "behind-wire" itself, with its unfortunate inhabitants awaiting certain death in full view of the camp, tolled a continuous warning to the prisoners.

Why is this uncomfortable discussion necessary? Janowska offers the opportunity to plumb the depths of atrocity in a place that at least anecdotally seems have been exceptionally violent. Every camp had its resident villains even among already cruel men, and each camp witnessed its infamous acts of cruelty. In attempting to reconstruct daily life in Janowska, however, it seems that torture and abuse were incredibly frequent, visible, and often of high intensity. It is telling that, while survivors elsewhere often frequently note incredible violence from Ukrainian guards, this criticism is muted in the Janowska testimony. One might argue that even exploring such a distinction is irrelevant at best and engaging in competitive suffering at worst. Yet, if the Germans in this small place did, in fact, appear to routinely transgress even the already inhumane norms of the SS, there must be value in seeking to understand why. Such an inquiry might well help explain the relationship between geography, individual personalities, and disparate power structures.

Why might it appear that this camp was exceptionally violent? There are several potential explanations. The first is the nature of the personnel. Of course, the most "refined" of individuals could become murderers during the Holocaust; after all, three of the four Einsatzgruppen commanders held doctorates and many of their subordinates did as well.[73] As we have seen, though, the camp personnel in the ZAL-L and the DAW certainly did not come from a well-educated or elevated social status. Nor did they seem to profess even the cold, driven SS form of professionalism that could somewhat govern the behavior of staff in other places. An example of this odd code appears in Himmler's 1943 Posen speech where he waxes eloquent on the "moral right and duty" to murder the Jews while praising the SS for demonstrating their "character" by not stealing from their victims.[74] Another indicator of the lack of professionalism and oversight is the relatively low rank the Janowska men held compared to their levels of responsibility. Gustav Willhaus was a second lieutenant at the beginning. The first commandant of the Majdanek camp, on the other hand, was a colonel. Franz Stangl of Treblinka was a captain, but the commandants of Dachau, Buchenwald, Sachsenhausen, Mauthausen ranged from major to colonel.[75] Having a lowly lieutenant as the final authority meant very little hierarchy and thus very little oversight, even from a military discipline perspective. The commandant of the small Szebnie concentration camp about a hundred miles west of Janowska, for example, wrote to his wife in May 1943 that there he "would be his own boss and God on earth. That would be my favorite thing of all, far off the beaten track."[76] The combination of low rank, fewer social graces, and generally more vulgar men certainly contributed to an excessively brutal environment.

Willhaus and Gebauer also bear responsibility for creating this environment based on their own personal proclivities and tendencies for violence. As in any organization, subordinates take their cues from leaders. Particularly for a place like a concentration camp, whose daily standards already break most taboos of civilized society, any inclination toward excess can become a powerful engine for escalating violence. The commandants of the two sections of the camp signaled their endorsement of excessive brutality with their actions. Examples like that of Heinen also suggest that Willhaus inculcated a culture of competitive brutality as a way of proving oneself in his eyes. At a minimum, his own killing gave carte blanche for his subordinates to do likewise. Further, the frequency of abuse by the SS men certainly normalized the behavior and perhaps professionally benefited them. Nikolaus Wachsmann has argued that "violence not only united camp SS hard-liners, it propelled their careers. In a community based on the veneration of the political soldier, brutality brought valuable social capital."[77] All peer pressure steered the ss men to more violence, not less, as did notions of toxic masculinity.[78] In addition, even the prisoners recognized that Janowska was important enough to ss and Police Leader Katzmann that he more or less allowed Willhaus free rein there.

While there seem to have been few displays of disapproval from the Janowska ss men, at least one instance shows that the violent culture created there was not all-encompassing. Johann Prinner, a nineteen-year-old ethnic German from Hungary, was assigned to the camp in June 1942. Employed as a courier between the camp and Katzmann's office, he "did not like his association" with the camp or "the whole way of life there." He appealed directly to Katzmann to be sent instead to the front. A colleague in the camp chided him, saying, "Stay here. Out there you will only get shot." Nevertheless, Prinner persisted and received his transfer to combat in February 1943.[79]

Certainly, antisemitism, both latent and fervently held, drove many of the perpetrators. The specifically antisemitic choices to humiliate rabbis clearly indicate this, for example. Peter Blum appears to have believed in the Judeo-Bolshevist myth that Jews were behind communism. According to one survivor, Peter Blum fired into a crowd of prisoners at Christmastime while shouting, "Now we are going to deal with you as Stalin dealt with us!"[80]

The place of the camp in the Nazi universe at a variety of scales also contributed to its potential for above average brutality. At a transnational level, unlike the majority of concentration camps, Janowska simultaneously sat on the periphery of the Nazi empire yet at the center of much of the Holocaust. Frontiers have always been wild and lawless places. Perhaps that applies to camps as well. Unlike Buchenwald, Janowska did not overlook the home of Goethe and Schiller. After all, in the Nazi worldview the East was a wild, savage place. Nazis committed atrocities in public against eastern European Jews that would have been unthinkable in Germany proper. Planners unflinchingly envisioned a massive extinction of thirty to forty million people in eastern Europe, not including the Jews. Of course, German camps were not without their horrors. It is worth considering, however, whether the proximity of German society in which camp staff lived had some impact on their behavior. Perhaps Janowska's relative isolation allowed for greater freedom of expression for brutality.

The hybrid nature of the camp itself also contributed to extreme violence. For a long period, the majority of prisoners in German camps were actually non-Jews. Even when Jews began flooding into the camp universe, large groups of non-Jews remained, perhaps somewhat mediating the general level of abuse, though Jews always received the worst treatment. In Janowska, Jews always made up the overwhelming majority of the population. Combining a large labor pool on-site with a continuous (and escalating) process of murder could have very well signaled to SS men that their charges were more or less dead already and could be abused with impunity. The Reinhard camps had similar environments, but the vast majority of Jews only lived a few hours, leaving little time for torture, while those few Jews who remained alive to work fulfilled specific skilled tasks and could not necessarily have been killed as easily without causing inconveniences to SS daily life. Perhaps Jean Améry had it right when he reflected that the SS men "placed torture in their service. But even more fervently they were its servants."[81]

The Territory of Forbidden Knowledge: Sexual and Sexualized Violence

Writing about rape during the Holocaust, an oral historian noted astutely that "there are memories that remain private, iconic incidents during the Holocaust that are banished into the territory of forbidden knowledge."[82] Violence of a sexual nature, usually perpetrated against women (as well that against men), has indeed remained a taboo topic for both survivors and historians for a long time. Survivors were often ashamed to be victims of these assaults, and scholars seemed unwilling to follow paths leading to discussions of rape and sexual violence. As a result, Nechama Tec has observed that "judging by the hesitation I encountered among interviewees to recount these coercive sexual experiences, I have to assume that most of these stories will die with the victims."[83] However, the passing of time and willingness of researchers to explore this painful history have revealed the widespread nature of this specific kind of victimization. Indeed, none of the testimony from female Janowska survivors includes firsthand experiences of rape; there is, however, a great deal of testimony from survivors about rape and sexualized violence taking place in the camp. For many women this most intimate of violations transcended all other forms of suffering. A survivor of the Ravensbrück camp described her rape as "the most horrible of my experiences."[84]

The Janowska camp witnessed frequent abuse of a sexual nature. These assaults can best be characterized as "sexual violence" or "sexualized violence." The former involves a nonconsensual sexual act while the latter is an assault that has a clear sexual component not leading to intercourse. Brigitte Halbmayr expands on sexualized violence, pointing out that such assault "is not about sexuality but is a show of power on the part of the perpetrator and includes many forms of violence with sexual connotations, including humiliation, intimidation, and destruction."[85] Further, it is important to distinguish what I call "instrumental sex" from rape, which I see as a violent assault. As I have written elsewhere, I "must preface this important distinction with the recognition that in almost all instances, the victim was powerless to grant consent; specifically, if they could not refuse consent, then they also could not give consent." Yet even in the throes of the Holocaust, "some victims may have had the ability to dictate in some way the manner of their own subjugation such that they were able to derive material benefits" from what were unquestionably "choiceless choices."[86] Scholars of slavery have struggled similarly and have noted that while "no law or moral scruple prevented white men from forcing themselves on black females ... some women negotiated this predicament by subjecting themselves to patrons, yielding to some white men who could protect them from the rest."[87] Even such grim opportunities were, however, more limited in Janowska than elsewhere. Women arrived in larger numbers in August 1942 with the construction of a camp laundry; female prisoners worked predominantly here and in the clothing warehouses in typically gendered roles. They may only have numbered around a hundred.[88] A specific women's section was not established in the camp until the spring of 1943 as the ghetto was being reduced.[89]

Sexualized violence in the camp seems to have been both commonplace and public. It ranged from humiliation to outright physical assault and murder. Sometimes, assaults combined both. In a halfhearted attempt to improve hygiene, Willhaus instituted torturous weekly or biweekly trips to a bathing facility downtown. During these trips and at various times in the camp, SS men leered at naked prisoners and abused them. For women in particular, "forced nakedness was a repeated assault."[90] Karl Melchior, for example, preferred to enter the women's baths, pull out naked women, and beat them.[91] The baths also became sites of rape as well, as the guards could easily select their victims.[92] SS men often demanded that prisoners lower their trousers before being beaten on their bare buttocks, as children often were. Enforced nudity accompanied much of the abuse in the camp for both men and women. Beyond increasing pain, this practice added the humiliation of both nudity and infantilization. Paula Spinner recalled being stripped naked and beaten by Melchior until she fainted.[93] Melchior, the failed Legionnaire, seemed to have a gender preference for his victims. A survivor recognized this, stating that "what is interesting is that he beat women even more than men."[94] Melchior once beat a woman for wearing lipstick and smeared grease on her face as a punishment.[95]

Friedrich Heinen, the ambitious youth, carried out one of the more notorious examples of sexualized violence corroborated by multiple witnesses. Sometime in late 1942 or early spring 1943, a group of men, women, and children were brought to the camp. They had potentially jumped from the death trains or been caught hiding. After the SS men had set a dog upon a young boy and shot others, only a married couple remained. Sergeant Heinen decided to hang them on the gallows behind the kitchen. However, the rope broke ... twice. At this point, Heinen had another idea. He ordered the couple to have sex. The terrified couple attempted this while the gathered SS men "held their sides laughing." When the SS men became bored with this, they executed the pair. It took three tries to hang them properly. They then laughed their way to the SS canteen.[96] It seems that Heinen did this more than once. Survivors recall a similar incident in which he bound a young girl and an old man together with wire while forcing them to have sex. Heinen then hung them upside down from the gallows while he, Köller, and Brumbauer took turns shooting at them.[97]

The Janowska SS men carried sexualized violence to the point of death and beyond. Martin Büttner forced a woman named Lera to lay on top of a male prisoner and then shot her. He pulled her dress off afterward. SS man Biermann likewise forced a "well-dressed girl" to strip naked on the Appellplatz and executed her.[98] The one-armed Hahn did likewise in the summer of 1943.[99] The men frequently targeted genitals in their physical abuse. In September 1942, Richard Rokita, Adolf Kolonko, and Martin Büttner brutally beat a prisoner and hung him alive and upside down on a post near the camp entrance. Every SS man that passed by delivered several blows to his groin.[100] Heinen, too, frequently chose this form of sexualized violence. Zeev Porath wrote that one of Heinen's "specialties" was beating naked young men and women, particularly targeting the men's genitals.[101] Samuel Drix witnessed another of Heinen's crimes in May 1943. The guard led two young women to a grassy area, forced them to undress, and telling them to lie down. He then slowly aimed at different parts of their body before ordering the taller one to spread her legs. He then shot her in the vagina and "for a moment enjoyed the sight of the victim writhing in pain" before he shot her in the mouth.[102]

Encapsulating the trauma of camp life, Terrence Des Pres wrote that "the death of the soul was aimed at. It was to be accomplished by terror and privation, but first of all by relentless assault on the survivors' sense of purity and worth ... the physical inducement of disgust and self-loathing, was a principal weapon."[103] It is difficult to describe better the sexualization of torture in Janowska. It truly represented what Primo Levi called "the demolition of a man [and a woman]." "It is not possible to sink lower than this," the Auschwitz survivor wrote, "no human condition is more miserable than this, nor could it conceivably be so. Nothing belongs to us anymore."[104] Some of this violence is probably more easily explained than others. Sexualized assaults always contain an element of humiliation, the perversion of the intimate in the service of the despicable. Certainly, the forced coupling of prisoners and forced nudity falls into the category. The SS men targeted genitals as both a more painful form of torture and as a way of reasserting their own manhood and masculine dominance. Perhaps this, too, was an element of the abusive culture of the Janowska guards, given how widespread it seems. In addition, if reproductive organs represent us at our most private and protective, then violence directed toward them is the ultimate show of unbridled power short of taking life—a figurative or literal neutering of the victim.

One final explanation could be the (relatively) forbidden nature of Jewish women in particular. The Nazi state's position on sex with Jews was clear to all, a prohibition honored more in the breach than the observance. Still, physical assaults of a sexual nature are often seen as proxies for sex itself. Helene Kaplan wrote in her memoir of a bizarre encounter with Fritz Gebauer. She stood at the window watching a group of male prisoners being beaten outside when Gebauer ran over, furious. "Do not look at those men!" he screamed. "You do not have anything in common with them. I don't ever want to see you looking this way." He then said, "You will never in your life be as well off as you are here."[105] What the commandant meant is unclear, but one can detect an odd note of attraction. The scene is eerily reminiscent of that in the 1993 film *Schindler's List* where Amon Goeth, the commandant of the Płaszów camp, beats his Jewish maid to whom he is attracted.

Many of the SS staff felt no compunction about sexually assaulting female prisoners. Indeed, the evidence for sexual violence and rape in the camp is quite extensive. It also maps strongly onto certain places in the camp. The camp laundry, the clothing warehouses, and the tailor shops were mostly female spaces but all under the control of Private First Class Peter Blum, the ethnic German musician from Hungary. These buildings were located in the outer precinct of the camp, about two hundred yards south of the inner gate. Blum testified that he supervised a group of around forty women and a smaller group of men. Henryk Schleicher served as his prisoner brigadier. A Mrs. Jakubowicz appears to have also been a foreman for the women.[106] Klara Winter, who survived a year in the camp from October 1942 to October 1943, stated that between a hundred fifty and two hundred women worked in the laundry. They worked from approximately four in the morning to seven at night. She recalled that Blum would "verbally harass them with foul language."[107] Blum, who the women nicknamed "the Squirrel" because of his red hair, was a violent man.[108] In 1943, a female prisoner ran from a formation, and as he shot her the SS man called her a "whore."[109]

His abuse went much further than words, however, as survivors roundly condemn Blum as a sexual predator. One testified matter-of-factly that "the Gestapo [sic] kept the pretty Jewish women as washerwomen in the camp. They were raped and later shot."[110] Maria Halbkram, who worked in the laundry, stated that Blum "raped and violated the women."¹¹¹ Zeev Porath concurred, writing that "it was generally known that Blum sexually abused the women in spite of the Nuremberg Laws."¹¹² Porath himself confronted Blum in custody and reminded him that he had "employed" two "particularly pretty" women named Hella and Anuschka. Blum replied that "there were lots of pretty women. I never made a distinction." Porath asked him if he remembered what happened to them. Blum refused to answer.¹¹³ Porath, who had an insightful understanding of the camp, also testified that Blum had a "special room" in the clothing warehouse where he lived.¹¹⁴ No doubt this space served him well as a private location for his assaults.

The women's section of the camp, the *Frauenlager*, created in spring 1943, also became a fearful space for SS men seeking to torment women. This cluster of five smaller barracks was set off from the rest of the ZAL-L in the outer precinct, backing up on the large field used to hold victims prior to mass shootings. According to Stanisława Gogolowska, Karl Brumbauer, another Hungarian ethnic German, appointed himself the commandant of the women's camp. He was "good-natured" toward the female prisoners, looking after their rations and clothing. However, at night he "appeared in a completely different form." Brumbauer would arrive in the barracks drunk and for fun rip the covers off the women and then lie down with them and "behave obscenely."¹¹⁵ She does not elaborate but the implications are clear. Another survivor implies similar activities, stating that Brumbauer "operated" in the women's section of the camp.¹¹⁶ Other predators included Paul Rösnitz. It was an "open secret" in the camp that he would "seek out pretty young Jewish women to seduce by promising to save them from destruction."¹¹⁷

Evidence of other rapes including mass rape appears in sources from the camp as well. One survivor recalled that a transport of young Jewish women arrived in the camp after dark. Younger SS men "took a few of them into their quarters . . . Their fate was known only to the SS."¹¹⁸ Leon Wells and other prisoners from the "Death Brigade" body disposal group recalled a similar episode where SS men had taken approximately twenty-five Jewish girls between the ages of sixteen and nineteen for a drunken party lasting all night. After they had almost certainly raped the girls, the SS man in charge, Schallock, apparently sought to offer them to the prisoners, ostensibly as housekeepers. The young women, upon realizing this, refused and were taken away to be shot. Wells recalled that the ss man "now saw quite clearly that the girls were not willing to live here, indeed, that they preferred death."[119]

Some Jewish women found themselves faced with the "choiceless choice" of potentially leveraging sex in exchange for survival. Reconstructing these "relationships" is a complex and highly fraught endeavor that rarely results in black-and-white answers. Gisela Urbach vocalized this painful process herself. Her sister, Käthe Haber, worked as Gebauer's secretary, but Gisela further explains that "in order to save herself, she had to live with Gebauer." Even when speaking to the police in 1971, Gisela said, "I will not talk about my sister for painful personal reasons."[120] These instrumental relationships took a variety of forms in the camp. A prisoner in a work camp in Germany tried to explain how she survived nightly rapes by an ss man. "As the months went by, I got used to him," she said. "He kept me out of the gas chamber. He gave me food. I didn't think of the future then. I lived one day at a time. Whatever I did was my way of surviving."[121] It is hard to imagine the trauma of such a bleak existence. Leon Wells perhaps confirmed Gisela's suspicions about her sister when he wrote that "Gebauer, for example, had amorous relations with a Jewess. Thus, the girl succeeded, at least for some time, in making her future secure." He went on to suggest that Emmi Gebauer in turn had a relationship with her Jewish chauffeur.[122]

The Jewish prisoner cook, Weinbaum, apparently trafficked in female prisoners with Richard Rokita, procuring women to satisfy his lust. Weinbaum "realized how he could capitalize on this weakness of Rokita's."[123] Rokita may have inadvertently confirmed his assaults on women many years later in a particularly cringeworthy moment when confronted while in German custody by Leon Wells in person. Wells had worked on Rokita's house and had noted that he "some knowledge of this private life." Rokita nodded his head at the former prisoner and, to Wells, "his smile seemed to say: 'Women. A charming and likable weakness. I know you will agree.'"[124]

Few of these instrumental arrangements ended well for the prisoners involved. As one scholar has noted, "in parts of Galicia in Poland and elsewhere, Jewish women were kept as sex slaves, and sometimes the most beautiful women from deportations to the camps were chosen to work in the homes of camp officers. Most were murdered later, and some were pregnant when they were sent to their deaths."[125] This was also the case in Janowska. Wells remember watching two SS men walking with a beautiful Jewish prisoner from Vienna named Hilda. She was "known to have affairs with SS men." This may well have been Hilda Goldberg, an accountant in the camp office.[126] Leon later found her in the ravines, naked and dead with her clothing in a pile nearby. As he saw it, "there is one law here: the more one gets involved with the Germans, the quicker the death. It is forbidden for the SS men to have anything to do with Jews; therefore, Hilda has something on them, and because of it she must be silenced."[127] Rosa Kohn testified that Karl Melchior had a "special relationship" with a seventeen-to-eighteen-year-old girl. She watched at one selection as Melchior himself designated this girl for execution.[128] Throughout the Holocaust, the proximity of the killing machine allowed German rapists to destroy the evidence of their crime.

And a crime it was, according to the Nazis. In 1928, Hitler himself had railed against the "pollution of the racial body through blood poisoning" by Jews.[129] The Third Reich had defined sexual relationships with Jews to be *Rassenschande* (race defilement) in 1935 in the Nuremberg Laws. Theoretically, the consequences of such a transgression, particularly for an SS man, could be severe, including potentially the death penalty. Yet despite the protestations of former Nazis and the convictions of history buffs, a great many Germans ignored the Führer in this area. An SS judge in 1943 estimated that at least half of the SS in the East had violated the Führer's prohibition on race-mixing.[130] It happened so frequently that a female in the Ravensbrück camp assumed that "raping Jewish women wasn't considered *Rassenschande* (race defilement); therefore, it was allowed."[131] It is instructive for those who see all Nazis as ideological zealots that so many simply did not believe that sexual contact carried any risk. Leon Wells concluded wryly that "the SS were loath to put the principles of the Nazi racial theory into practice when their private lives were involved.... Murder was one thing, lust another."[132]

The widespread disregard for Rassenschande did not, however, mean that it had no impact on the SS. While authorities did not usually go out of their way to uncover these kinds of sexual crimes, they represented a potentially fatal liability in the politics of the SS. Authorities would be hard-pressed to look away from a report that one of Himmler's elite had "defiled" himself. Denunciations of this sort in the hands of a sympathetic party could quickly remove a rival. In this way, Nazi race laws did not prevent sexual assault of Jews, but they *did* almost guarantee the subsequent murder of the victims.

Dismissing the simplistic fig leaf of Rassenschande, then, requires a deeper examination of sexual violence in the Holocaust. Moving beyond a clear "flexibility" with the rules, some insights into the meaning of this behavior are in order. First, rape has always accompanied war and mass violence. Once one social norm (murder) is destroyed, others quickly follow. Even in the most "righteous" of conflicts, morality becomes distorted, tendentious, situational. State-sanctioned mass violence opens the door for conquests of another sort. In the context of the Holocaust and genocide, this perversion of basic human dignity becomes ever more pervasive. Second, as Steven Katz astutely points out, "rape is a language." In the Holocaust, it was a "a political declaration as to the degenerate status of the Jewish victims in accordance with Nazi ideology."[133] It must be placed alongside the physical violence and torture in the camp as another way the SS signaled to themselves and others that the prisoners had no control, no value, no future. Katz goes further, suggesting that rape "could be understood [by perpetrators] as legitimate retribution" for the racial crime of being Jewish.[134] In the eyes of these SS rapists, therefore, Jewish women could be seen to truly "deserve it." The constantly murderous environment of Janowska served to reinforce the "disposability" of these victims. For a time, the constant flow of new arrivals also offered the SS predators the opportunity to replace those they murdered. The contagion of death permeated this as it did everything else in the camp.

Rape is fundamentally about power, not sexual gratification. In its most basic form, it demonstrates the power of the rapist and the powerlessness of the victim. In the context of genocide, it demonstrates the power of the regime, the ideology, and the perpetrator. In this sense, Christopher Browning has termed it "a ritual of humiliation aimed at degrading the entire camp population."[135] It is interesting that while public rapes took place in some camps like Starachowice, which Browning worked on, survivors do not mention them in Janowska. Yet the effect might well have been the same. The SS men's rampant sexual assaults did not remain secrets in any sense. For the prisoners, particularly the men, the frequency of rape may well have reinforced a sense of helplessness, an inability to serve as the stereotypically male protector figure. For the women of the camp, however, the threat was in no way an abstraction. It was a clear and present danger. Given the relatively small female community in Janowska and the prevalence of rape, the fear of this most personal of tortures must have been acute in a way that the men could never understand—while we know that men experienced sexual violence in camps as well, there is no testimony about it from Janowska.

While historians are well warned to avoid arguing that one camp was "worse" than another, it does seem that Janowska exhibited levels and extremes that at least merit investigation. It seems that its location on the periphery of Nazi empire as well the relatively lowly positions of its perpetrators combined with some more familiar violent elements to spawn some exceptional and frequent violence there. This is particularly noteworthy given the influence of the camp's personnel throughout Distrikt Galizien.

The Spider's Web 8

> I read somewhere that everybody on this planet is separated by only six other people. Six degrees of separation. I am bound to everyone on this planet by a trail of six people. It's a profound thought. . . . How every person is a new door opening up into other worlds.
>
> —John Guare, *Six Degrees of Separation*

When Adolf Kolonko arrived in Janowska at the head of a group of Trawniki men on January 27, 1942, he carried with him a surprising collection of prior experience and relationships in that strange fraternity of Holocaust perpetrators. An ethnic German, he joined the SS in 1933 and in August 1939 was called to Berlin. In an exemplary Bauhaus complex in the Bernau suburbs, he attended a two-week course of "military" training at the SD school there.[1] While it is not clear precisely what his training entailed, the SD school at Bernau could count as its graduates the leaders of the Einsatzgruppen killing squads (shortly before Kolonko's arrival) and Klaus Barbie, the "Butcher of Lyon."[2] While multiple courses for a variety of officials were offered, the whole place served as a pedagogical initiation into the Nazi war against the Jews. Many "murderers of Jews" passed through its doors "as instructor or student."[3] Among those there that August was Jozef Grzimek. Grzimek was the son of a slaughterhouse worker who grew up only twenty miles away from Kolonko in Silesia. His training prepared him for the false-flag attacks on Polish sites that provided the pretext for the start of the war. Grzimek would go on to command multiple concentration camps in Distrikt Galizien including the Lviv ghetto remnant known as the JULAG. He would later march survivors from the Płaszów camp to Auschwitz.[4]

Kolonko left Berlin for Częstochowa, Poland, where he served as a paramilitary. In the home of the Black Madonna shrine, he overlapped with two future Janowska men: Paul Fox and Hans Sobotta. Leaving Częstochowa, Kolonko headed for the city of Radom where he guarded the SS and police leader, the man who established the Radom ghetto and would go on to create the Lviv ghetto: Friedrich Katzmann.[5] Before training Volksdeutsche paramilitaries in Lublin in late early 1940, Kolonko helped establish a slave labor camp in Biała-Podlaska along with four other future Janowska SS men.[6]

His next major assignment saw him stationed at the Trawniki camp as a trainer. Kolonko arrived in Lviv with new guards for Janowska from that camp. Once in the ZAL, he reunited with an acquaintance from his prewar job in a Siemens factory, none other than Roman Schönbach. Finally, Kolonko graduated from his supervisor duty in Janowska to command his own camp in Gródek-Jagielloński before returning to the ZAL after his command's liquidation. A close examination of the staff of the ZAL/DAW reveals that a surprising number of Janowska SS men also walked similar paths and encountered future colleagues as Kolonko did. We can retrace his footsteps so well because he survived the war and was tried for his crimes. There may be many more connections that have been lost to the vagaries of time and war.

The Janowska camp lay at the center of a web of violence and control and also provided an education in those areas. Indeed, survivor Michał Borwicz titled his book about the camp *The University of Criminals*. Compared to it, he wrote that "Majdanek, Dachau, Auschwitz, and Buchenwald were secondary schools."[7] This may be a bit hyperbolic, but he reveals an important truth: the camp *did* provide an education of sorts. Throughout its history, perpetrators passed through its gates (sometimes more than once) carrying norms, personal relationships, and profane wisdom brutally acquired. They brought their experiences with them and carried them away when they left. Through this network of SS men, Janowska cast a much larger shadow over the Holocaust outside of the camp in Distrikt Galizien.

What a Tangled Web: A Genocidal Network

The SS men of the camp formed a social network that helps us better understand the history of the place itself. They were men bonded by the violence of which they were a part. It helps us answer some of the questions raised earlier in this book, such as why the SS men in the camp appear to have been particularly brutal. It also tells us much about their interpersonal relationships over time and what their common experiences were. A pioneering mathematician wrote of such networks that "the greatest value of a picture is when it forces us to notice what we never expected to see."[8] Picturing these perpetrators as part of a network allows us to "see" data in a way that we have never done before.

It is perhaps surprising that most historians "have so far been reluctant to explore social webs as a means of making sense of life in the camps."[9] Thinking of the men of the camp as a cohort (or multiple cohorts) proposes connections important to our understanding of them as individuals, but also of the camp as the center of a web of oppression. A social network approach views people as connected in a variety of ways: they exchange ideas, they share experiences, they give and receive orders, they disseminate practices.[10] Indeed, this is what a society is. If the Holocaust is a "division-of-labor-based crime," then understanding these structures becomes critical at all scales.[11] If we can map these structures, we can better analyze them.

Almost a hundred fifty years ago, a German sociologist wisely said, "Tell me who you deal with and I will tell you who you are."[12] Looking at a group of seventy-eight perpetrators with over four hundred identifiable geographic locations, we can learn a lot about who the Janowska camp staff were. This discussion is more than a collective biography, however. It is a sketch of a group of men with a surprising number of common overlapping experiences and connections that illustrate who they were, who they became, and how the camp "played a central role in the Holocaust."[13] Shared training and initiation in the business of genocide shaped many of them before they arrived at the camp. Once there, the experience behind its walls imbued them with a shared sense of norms that they then carried out into the surrounding area.

Before ever arriving in Lviv, many of the men had served in common locations and even knew each other. Peter Blum belonged to a sizable cohort of ethnic Germans from the Banat in what is now northern Serbia, and he provided a good deal of information about this group. Blum claimed to have been conscripted into the Waffen-SS and trained in the Dębica camp with its adjacent concentration camp. Philipp Federmann, another future Janowska man, also was trained at Dębica.[14] A group of ten to fifteen of these "Hungarian and Yugoslavian" ethnic Germans from the Dębica camp arrived in Janowska in the summer of 1942 and were assigned first to guard duty under Adolf Kolonko and later to supervising work details. Kolonko himself had already known future fellow ss man Roman Schönbach since 1933 when they had both worked in the Siemens plant in what is now Racibórz, Poland.[15]

Other Janowska perpetrators also first met in training. Hans Sobotta and Paul Fox had both been called to Beuthen (now Bytom, Poland) from neighboring towns in Silesia to begin their ss service.[16] Four guards overlapped in Biała-Podlaska where they helped build work camps for the Jews there. Adolf Kolonko was assigned to the Trawniki camp in the summer of 1941. There he trained the former Soviet prisoners of war who had volunteered to serve the Nazis.[17] Richard Rokita, deputy commandant of the ZAL, also served in Trawniki. Kolonko testified that they had been there together and that Rokita had provided seventeen "Askaris" who went with Kolonko to the Janowska camp.[18] It is perhaps telling that Kolonko himself described these men as "very trigger-happy" and always wanting to participate in the shooting of the Jews.[19] After all, he had trained some of them personally.

Quite a few of the ss men in Janowska had also served together already as part of the Nazi genocidal project in occupied Poland. Many identified themselves as having been part of the *Selbstschutz* or *Sonderdienst* paramilitary formations. These violent groups of Volksdeutsche volunteers carried out the murders of Poles as well as Jews across the territory and brought "chaotic terror" to newly conquered Polish lands, operating with relative impunity before more formal occupation structures were created. Indeed, one SD leader noted cynically that "the liquidation will be able to be carried out for only a short time. Then the German administration as well as other factors outside the NSDAP will make direct action impossible."[20] Eight men at Janowska including Kolonko, Schönbach, Sobotta, and Fox carried out various *Selbstschutz* duties in Lublin.[21] Himmler chose Odilo Globocnik, the same man who would go on to oversee the Reinhard extermination camps, to preside over the Lublin district. The experience of the *Selbstschutz* there "foreshadow[ed] the murderous methods that would be employed

to destroy racial enemies after the invasion of the Soviet Union in 1941."²²
This, for many Janowska SS men, was their preparatory schooling.

Some, like SS Scharführer Paul Fox, came to Janowska with prior experience in concentration camps and ghettos. Prior to arriving in Lviv in 1942, the thirty-year-old Fox had already served as a paramilitary in Częstochowa, Radom, Lublin, and Zamósc. In that latter place, he had been the commandant of his own camp. The guard force was made of *Selbstschutz* ethnic Germans. Future Janowska guard SS Rottenführer Hans Sobotta worked at the neighboring Białobrzegi camp.²³ Fox recalled that "the condition of the prisoners was alarming. They were starved almost into skeletons." He was then transferred to the town of Ławrykowce (Lavrykivtsi) where he oversaw a hundred fifty to two hundred Jews working in a quarry for a German company building roads. The camp commandant was a Dirlewanger Brigade veteran.²⁴ The quarry was a subcamp of Zborów (Zboriv), which Fox's Janowska colleague Sobotta would go on to command.²⁵ In early 1942, Fox left Ławrykowce to serve as deputy commandant of the Jaktorów labor camp. His replacement, SS Unterscharführer Karl Kempka, would later find his way to the Janowska camp as well.²⁶ Fox's new boss in Jaktorów (Yaktoriv) was SS Haupsturmführer Jozef Grzimek, the man who would command the remnant of the Lviv ghetto and preside over its liquidation.²⁷

Of the fifteen labor camps set up in the region to build military highways, Fox's ZAL Jaktorow had one of the highest mortality rates. One prisoner wrote in his diary that "of all these camps, I know Jaktorów the best, and in the literal meaning, as torture. I was kept there only two weeks and each day was true hell."²⁸ Fox also developed the habit here of shooting prisoners from his balcony, as Willhaus did.²⁹ Survivors remember that Fox liked to try to shoot bottles off Jaktorow prisoners' heads; in Janowska, he would graduate to aiming at coins in hands.³⁰ SS Scharführer Paul Fox, therefore, arrived in the ZAL-L in the spring of 1942 with a wealth of experience in the Nazi system of oppression... and with a surprising number of contacts with future colleagues. Indeed, compared to other guards, his experience is not atypical, if better documented.

While Fox and those like him may have brought with them prior camp experience, the Janowska camp served as a two-way channel into the sea of violence that flooded Distrikt Galizien. This is where Borwicz's "university of criminals" description may be most apt. Even for young perpetrators like Kolonko, the camp provided an education, an internship of sorts for a large number of men who would leave Lviv to command their own camps and ghettos in the surrounding area. In addition, the connections made in the camp greased the machinery of death by building on established working relationships and even friendships.

After distinguishing himself for a year in Janowska, Kolonko was placed in charge of the labor camp in Gródek-Jagielloński (Horodok) 30 kilometers west of Lviv in March 1943.[31] This small moment during the destruction of Galician Jews merits a longer discussion as it illustrates an important larger phenomenon that repeated itself throughout the region. Willhaus informed Kolonko of his new command as they were actually disassembling barracks in a nearby town that they then brought back to Janowska and rebuilt. Even in 1943, Willhaus's construction continued apace.[32]

By the time Kolonko arrived, there were not many Jews remaining in Gródek-Jagielloński. Multiple aktions had decimated the population and the ghetto had been liquidated in January 1943. In fact, according to Soviet investigations in 1944, Gustav Willhaus and his fellow Janowska SS man Richard Rokita had led that very ghetto liquidation, resulting in the murder of fifteen hundred.[33] A month or so later, Kolonko organized around fifty or so Jews into a small labor detail in what he called a "branch" of the Janowska camp. He naturally claimed after the war that he had treated them well, stating that seventeen Jews had volunteered to join his camp. Jews voluntarily entering camps (or buying their way in) was not unheard of, but they were most certainly seeking protection from both the closing Nazi net and from the local population if they were in hiding.[34] His camp consisted of a stone building that had formerly been a butcher shop. It was surrounded by a simple chain-link fence and guarded by Ukrainians. Kolonko's Jews worked for the German Philipp Holzmann construction company continuing to build Himmler's Durchgangstrasse IV highway.[35] Until the end, the chief of the SS dreamed of accomplishing this feat of military engineering. The thirty-five-year-old private settled into his little kingdom. Kolonko, of course, did not live in the camp itself. His wife, Ottilie, who lived in their Lviv home, visited him with their two toddlers on the weekends and holidays.[36] No doubt he enjoyed the sense of independence and importance he felt as the commander of his own camp, however small.

That all came crashing to an end on June 27, 1943. The gruesome scene that played out in the former butcher shop in Gródek began in Lviv with Katzmann. He told Anton Löhnert that the last Jews there should be liquidated. Löhnert's official title was Chief of Jewish and Forced Labor Camp Affairs. According to him, Willhaus had called Katzmann to request the liquidation of Kolonko's camp. Willhaus had even suggested that the bodies should be burned in the house. Katzmann had already agreed and now tasked Löhnert (according to him) with ensuring that it had been done and that the fire had been kept under control. Katzmann then called Willhaus to inform him.[37] There are some curious dynamics here, starting with Willhaus directly requesting the liquidation from the most senior SS officer in Lviv. Perhaps this speaks to their special relationship dating back to the establishment of the ZAL. Löhnert's role is also interesting. According to some, he and Willhaus were good friends. Löhnert certainly visited the camp frequently and had personally shot three Jews in the camp during the Great Aktion of August 1942.[38] This makes it more likely that Löhnert was tasked with aiding in supervising the killing, rather than simply observing.

In any case, Löhnert's first stop was not Gródek-Jagielloński, but Janowska. There he secured a staff car or jeep and a driver (likely Philipp Federmann). Willhaus had informed a group of his men that they would not have Sunday afternoon off but would be going on an operation outside the camp. They put on their helmets, grabbed their rifles, and climbed into a military truck and drove off with Löhnert. At a minimum, it seems that, from the Janowska guard force, the following men took part in the liquidation of the Gródek-Jagielloński camp to some extent: Martin Büttner, Philipp Federmann, Peter Grumbach, Werner Hahn, Roman Schönbach, and Hans Sobotta. The truth of what happened when they arrived at Kolonko's camp that Sunday is shot through with recriminations, but it is possible to reconstruct the most likely sequence of events.

Willhaus met briefly with his subordinate. Kolonko claimed to have been shocked to learn his camp was to be liquidated, but this is difficult to believe. Willhaus informed Kolonko that he was to ensure that the action went "smoothly" and that it didn't result in a "mess."[39] Between fifty and sixty Jews were rounded up by a combination of the Janowska SS and the local Ukrainian militia. The SS men placed themselves at key locations in the building; Sobotta stood watch in the kitchen. Kolonko screamed at the Ukrainians to drive the Jews into the house.[40] From his vantage point, he watched as the Jews mounted the stairs, each carrying a piece of firewood.[41] Kolonko claimed the Jews went "submissively" to their deaths; this self-serving statement ignores that most likely saw no chance of escape given the presence of the SS men and Ukrainian militia.[42] Yet, on the stand, he admitted that one man had cried that he did not want to die and begged the SS man for help, causing a few women in the packed courtroom to audibly "sob."[43]

When the killing began, it revealed a special kind of horror. The SS forced the Jews one by one to a dim second-floor room where Kolonko shot them with a pistol. Others also took part, included the one-armed Werner Hahn and Roman Schönbach.[44] Katzmann's Chief of Jewish Affairs, Anton Löhnert, denied participating, but watched Kolonko shoot. He further observed that it seemed like "an amusement" for Kolonko. He called them to their deaths by their first names, saying, for example, "Come on Abraham, lie down over here."[45] The aftermath was no less gruesome. While Löhnert looked in on the shooting room, Willhaus and the Ukrainian mayor stood outside watching. Then, the SS and the Ukrainian militia prepared to destroy the evidence. They entered the house with spray cans of gasoline and set it aflame. Unbeknownst to them, however, there was another witness who suggests an even darker version of events. Ptachia Hochberg, a Jew who recognized Kolonko from his time in Janowska, was hiding across the street. As he watched the house catch fire, he heard "monstrous, heartrending screams" from inside the building followed by gunshots. He insisted that at least some of the prisoners had still been alive when they were set on fire.[46] Despite Willhaus's desires, the liquidation of Kolonko's camp truly had devolved into a "mess."

After the building was set on fire, Löhnert returned to Lviv to report to Katzmann and Willhaus and his men returned to the camp. Kolonko was left literally standing in the ashes of his command. He had invoices to settle with the Philipp Holzmann firm. The next morning, he investigated the results of his action and found that "the fire hadn't developed properly... only the top layer of corpses had been charred." He told investigators that "I couldn't stay in the room very long because it stank terribly of burnt flesh." His colleague Peter Grumbach arrived from Janowska with ten Jews to clean up the building.[47] After a short stint in another camp, Adolf Kolonko returned to Janowska where he served until its final liquidation in July 1944.

Gródek-Jagielloński provides a telling illustration of the interconnections between the men of Janowska and their impact on the wider Holocaust in Galicia. It is important because it is not an isolated event. Janowska men fanned out from the camp to work in various camps and ghettos throughout the region before and after service in the ZAL-L (see table 3). For example, Richard Rokita oversaw the large forced labor camp in Tarnopol. Other SS men were part of the camp administration in Drohobycz (Drohobych). Willhaus's successor in Janowska, Friedrich Warzok, commanded a multitude of camps throughout Galicia before arriving in Lviv. As is always the case in history, the minutiae also tell us much truth. In April 1943, Jakob Kraus, a forty-two-year-old Janowska truck driver, drove in a convoy of six or seven trucks (and Janowska SS men) to the town of Bóbrka twenty miles from Lviv. Once there, he shuttled the Jews from the ghetto to the Woluwe Forest, watched as they were murdered, and then returned to Janowska with his trucks loaded with their clothing.[48] A survivor of the town recalled hearing of the ghetto liquidation, writing, "Our hearts were so heavy that if you stuck us, blood would not flow."[49]

Ties that Bind: The Importance of the Janowska Perpetrator Network

Table 3. Janowska DAW and ZAL SS staff deployed to other camps and ghettos

NAME	RANK	CAMP OR GHETTO LOCATION	DATES (IF KNOWN)
Benke	n/a	Tempory camp near Polonica	Aug–Oct 1942
Büttner, Martin	PFC	KZ Buchenwald	Sep 1937–Mar 1940
Büttner, Martin	PFC	KZ Dachau	Mar–May 1940
Dyga, Richard	SSG	Jezierna (Ozerna)	1942–1943

NAME	RANK	CAMP OR GHETTO LOCATION	DATES (IF KNOWN)
Dyga, Richard	SSG	Jaktorów (Yaktoriv)	Feb–Apr 1942
Epple, Ernst	SGT	ZAL Kurowice—commandant	1942
Fox, Paul	SSG	Jaktorów (Yaktoriv)—staff	1942
Fox, Paul	SSG	Zamoś—commandant	1940
Fox, Paul	SSG	Zborów (Zboriv)—commandant	1941
Fox, Paul	SSG	Steinbruchlager Ławrykowce (Lavrykivtsi)	n/a
Gebauer, Fritz	CPT	KZ Dachau	Jun–Aug 1942
Heinisch, Ernst	PVT	Tyszowce—commandant	Jun–Oct 1941
Heinisch, Ernst	PVT	Hermanów—commandant	Oct 1941–Summer 1942
Heinisch, Ernst	PVT	Winniki (Vynnyky)—acting commandant	April 1943
Kauke, Friedrich	n/a	KZ Stutthof	1943–1944
Kempka, Karl	CPL	Ławrykowce (Lavrykivtsi)—staff	1942
Kempka, Karl	SGT	Przemyślany (Peremyshliany)—staff	1942
Kolonko, Adolf	SSG	ZAL Gródek-Jagielloński (Horodok)	Mar–Jun 1943
Kolonko, Adolf	SSG	ZAL Złoczow (Zolochiv)—staff	n/a
Kolonko, Adolf	SSG	Biała-Podlaska—staff	1939
Kolonko, Adolf	SSG	Trawniki	May–Jul 1942
Lisson, Heinrich	n/a	Winniki (Vynnyky)—commandant	n/a
Mellar, Paul	PVT	Stupki—staff	Spring–Summer 1942
Mellar, Paul	PVT	Kamionki	Summer 1942–Jul 1943

Minkus, Erich	CPL	Jezierna (Ozerna)—commandant	Fall 1941–Apr 1942
Minkus, Erich	CPL	Borki-Wielkie—commandant	1942
Minkus, Erich	CPL	Drohobycz (Drohobych)	1943
Pramor, Ernst	PFC	Biała-Podlaska—staff	1939–1940
Pramor, Ernst	PFC	Hluboczek (Hlyboczok)	Jan 1942–Jun 1943
Rokita, Richard	2LT	Tarnopol (Ternopil) Forced Labor Camp	Nov 1942–1943
Rokita, Richard	2LT	Trawniki	n/a
Salzborn, Johann	PVT	Biała-Podlaska—staff	Sep 1939–Jan 1942
Schönbach, Roman	SSG	ZAL Drohobycz (Drohobych)—staff	Summer 1943
Schönbach, Roman	SSG	Boryslaw (Boryslav)	1943
Schulz, Willi	1LT	Mosty Wielkie (Velyki Mosty)	1942–1943
Siller, Anton	SGT	Rawa Ruska (Rava-Ruska)—staff	n/a
Siller, Anton	CPL	ZAL-Winniki (Vynnyky)	Fall 1941–Mar 1942
Sobotta, Hans	CPL	Zborów (Zboriv)—commandant	Aug–Nov 1942
Sobotta, Hans	CPL	Białobrzegi—commandant	n/a
Sobotta, Hans	CPL	Beskiden Oil Camp Boryslaw—commandant	1943
Sobotta, Hans	CPL	Drohobycz (Drohobych)	Nov 1942–Jan 1943
Warzok, Friedrich	CPT	Złoczow (Zolochiv) region camps—commandant	1943
Warzok, Friedrich	CPT	KZ Neuengamme	1945

Note: Many of the dates listed are rough approximations based on survivor and perpetrator memory, incomplete documentation, and the often relatively short duration of stay before these sites were liquidated.

What does reconstructing the Janowska network tell us about the camp and the Holocaust in Lviv? Quite a lot. Paul Jaskot has argued that "a true integrated history of the Holocaust that works towards a total understanding of the event must by definition be a relational one. It is only by thinking relationally that we do not lose the survivor's story in the vast abstraction of a systemic analysis of the concentration camp network. Each records its side of the history, each remains distinct, and each is necessary to explaining the Holocaust."[50] Examining the social (and professional) networks of the Janowska SS men is a critical component of this as well; it takes the abstraction of assignments and personnel moves and inextricably links them to individual experience and history. This includes survivors as well for many were able to identify perpetrators in their outlying communities because they encountered them later in Janowska.

One can always best explain perpetrator behavior and choices as the complex interplay between belief and situation: they inform each other in an infinite feedback loop. All the interactions of the Janowska SS before, during, and after their time in the camp itself worked to mold them into the men that the Jews of Galicia encountered. Co-location cannot always definitively prove relationships, but this research yields tantalizing possibilities. Did Adolf Kolonko know Friedrich Katzmann when he guarded his headquarters in Radom? Did Willhaus pick up his penchant for target practice from Paul Fox (who had done this in his prior assignment), or did these two proclivities coincidentally complement each other? Regardless, men like Kolonko, Fox, and future Janowska commandant Warzok came to the camp not as shocked acolytes but as men with years of experience dealing in the persecution of Jews. The experience of many in the *Selbstschutz* paramilitaries perhaps left them with a taste for the ad hoc, unsupervised freedom for violence that they had previously enjoyed. The common ethnic background of many of the men as discussed earlier also provided connective tissue. The many Volksdeutsche among the guard force created instant bonds of commonality, with perhaps an extra dose of racial awareness.

Simple familiarity certainly developed from the multitude of overlapping assignments and service periods. A surprising number of these men knew each other—some, like Kolonko and Schönbach, from before the war. The Banat Germans probably knew each other as well. Familiarity does not, of course, ensure friendship but could certainly have accelerated the kind of bonding through transgression that Thomas Kühne has described as "comradeship [that] lived off collective breaches of the norm."[51] For perpetrators, "interpersonal relationships that developed 'on the spot' forming informal networks were another form of integration. They seem to have been of importance especially in instances in which institutional structures were rather weak, as was the case in the remote outposts in the East or in areas that had only recently been occupied."[52] If this is true, the cohort of Janowska guards may represent the perfect storm.

The experience of camp life and the leadership of Gustav Willhaus added another layer of influence on newly arrived SS men. The culture of cruelty that he cultivated in Janowska had a profound effect on the guard force. Recall young Friedrich Heinen who strove to distinguish himself through his escalating violence. The prior associations of the guard force could have acted as a powerful catalyst for brutality, particularly among a small group of men isolated on the Nazi frontier. If Janowska was a "university of criminals," its students certainly graduated to a multitude of follow-on assignments, most with even less supervision, where they could put their violent lessons into practice on their own. In addition, the seemingly constant flow of SS men in and out of the camp on their way to other assignments in Distrikt Galizien must have spread Janowska's organizational climate.

We find perhaps some of the most important conclusions in the larger shadow cast by the Janowska camp over the surrounding region. It appears that often informal relationships bypassed official channels. Consider the curious relationship between Willhaus and Katzmann, a lieutenant and a general. If he could arrange the liquidation of another camp by simply calling Katzmann, it seems that Willhaus played an outsized role in the Holocaust in Galicia, likely beginning with his early alliance with the high-ranking officer when he was Gebauer's deputy in the DAW. Indeed, the frequent excursions from the camp by Willhaus and his men to carry out executions and liquidations indicates that they stepped into this role traditionally held by the SD. The promotion of Janowska men to other commands suggests either that they distinguished themselves in the eyes of the SS authorities or that personnel were limited on the edge of the Reich (or both). Indeed, it appears that Katzmann frequently drew new leaders from his existing force. This also would explain why such low-ranking men were given such authority and independence.

Exploring Janowska networks also provides insight into the unfolding of the Holocaust in the East. This surprisingly cohesive group likely enabled both the implementation of anti-Jewish policy and the rise of Janowska as a central player in the Final Solution in the region. We have already seen that the camp itself maintained a variety of connections with other locations in the area. It drew prisoners from the surrounding region. It transferred building materials. It provided trucks and personnel for aktions. It received the property of Jews murdered throughout Distrikt Galizien. What is critical to remember is that all of these connections required people and relationships. As this chapter has shown, many of the Janowska men (and other officials in Lviv) had met or worked together before. This familiarity bore fruit both when they were dispersed and when they were concentrated in the Janowska camp. Given the often ad hoc and improvised process of destruction in the East, how much easier was it to coordinate the working relationships required to consolidate, rob, and, ultimately, murder the Jews of Galicia when the killers could rely on an informal but strong network of fellow travelers? Social network research has revealed that "the trust generated through repeated interactions between networked individuals facilitates collective action."[53] If such a network of intersecting paths can be reconstructed for a place like Janowska, there must surely be value in doing so for other organizations. Ideology may drive intentions, bureaucracies may craft policies, but individuals must, in the end, do the work—and they do not work in isolation. The social networks of the Janowska camp strongly suggest that we may be overlooking these individual relationships to our detriment when seeking to understand how the Holocaust took place on the ground.

Holokaustos 9

holocaust. from Greek *holokauston,*
from *holos* "whole" and *kaustos* "burnt"

The beginning of 1943 marked the beginning of a steep descent into oblivion for the Jewish community of Lviv. This year saw the beginning of a third wave of killing that swept through the occupied East as the Nazis tried to complete their Final Solution.[1] In the midst of military catastrophes on the Eastern Front and increasingly destructive bombing of Germany, the ss continued to wage the Nazi war against the Jews. In July 1942, Himmler had ordered the "resettlement of the whole Jewish population of the General Government" by the end of the year.[2] This had profound repercussions in Distrikt Galizien as well. Local ss including members of the Janowska camp exterminated remaining camps and ghettos throughout the region as they had Kolonko's in Gródek-Jagielloński.

In Lviv, the ghetto would be decimated, leaving only a small remnant. The history of Janowska as a physical reality also ended for all intents and purposes in 1943. Throughout its final days, though, the camp and its staff remained central to the Holocaust in Galicia. Its men killed Jews throughout the region and during the liquidation of the ghetto. The ZAL-L intensified its role as a killing center, murdering thousands. It also played a leading part in the denouement of the Holocaust—the massive and gruesome attempt to destroy all traces of one of the worst crimes in history. But, to the end, the camp remained a complex place, for it also witnessed a daring and massive escape of prisoners from death's antechamber, allowing in some small measure the prisoners themselves to have the last word.

The End of Jewish Lviv

As it had been in the creation of its ghetto, Lviv lagged in its destruction. The Jewish population in the capital and the region had been winnowed through maltreatment and the mass killings of the summer of 1942. But, despite Himmler's exhortations, Katzmann's realm was decidedly *not* free of Jews by the end of 1942. Perhaps as many as sixty-five thousand Jews remained in the Lviv ghetto at the start of the new year when a new wave of killing swept through. On January 5, SS and police surrounded the ghetto and began rounding up the residents, ostensibly based on whether they possessed the proper work identity card. Only those with the "R" or "W" denoting work for the armaments industry or the military were to be spared. Their family members, however, who had been previously protected were ruthlessly rounded up.[3] Returning to the ghetto, David Kahane encountered "a scene of confusion" where "large crowds of ghetto residents were milling about, awaiting their fate."[4] Some houses were set on fire and children thrown into the flames.[5] Leon Wells and his two younger brothers hid for two days in a cellar with a dozen others, eating only turnips in complete darkness. When they emerged, they saw "bodies everywhere" and the ghetto looked "as if a whirlwind had raged there."[6] Around fifteen thousand people found themselves on trucks and trams headed for Janowska. Some survivors believed incorrectly that some of these deportees ended up in the gas chambers at Bełżec, which had received its last transport in December 1942—it is possible that some of these Lviv Jews were transported to the Sobibor extermination camp.[7] The Nazis murdered many of them much closer to home in the sandhills behind the camp.

If it was not already clear that the end was near, the Nazis executed the last Jewish Council at the end of the January 1943 . . . in Janowska.[8] A reorganization of the remnants of the ghetto followed. Katzmann renamed it the *Judenlager* (literally "Jewish camp") or JULAG. Himmler had ordered the creation of a similar camp in Warsaw for essential workers. For his JULAG, Katzmann chose SS *Hauptsturmführer* Jozef Grzimek as its commandant. The thirty-eight-year-old Sudeten German ushered in a brief period of greater torment for the Jews remaining in the city. Grzimek had participated in the false-flag attack that had served as the provocation for the invasion of Poland in 1939 and had then gone on to a long career in a series of Galician camps, including having served with several SS men from the ZAL-L. Adolf Folkmann described him as "a born sadist without parallel in all my terrible experience."⁹

The JULAG comprised a small section of the former ghetto. The Jews that survived the January roundups lived in specific buildings according to their many employers such as the brush factory; the bicycle factory; the Schwarz clothing company; and the Behring Institute, which was still working on its smallpox vaccine.¹⁰ This arrangement also allowed Katzmann to bypass the city administration and collect payments directly from the companies using Jewish labor.¹¹ Grzimek brought a pathological obsession with cleanliness to the JULAG. He inspected housing and killed those whose dwellings he found unclean, he forced the Jewish police to hand over six "illegal" Jews each day for execution, and he spent his days drunkenly stalking his domain carrying a submachine gun.¹²

The SS struck again in March 1943 in what was known as the "Schwarz Aktion" as it targeted a number of Jews from that textile factory. Schwarz & Co. was originally based in Lublin before opening a branch occupying 5–9 Marcinastrasse in the Lviv ghetto. It took advantage of three thousand Jewish laborers, mainly women.¹³ There was a particular cruelty to this aktion even in a universe of cruelty. The Nazis drove the women out of the JULAG and then rounded up the children remaining behind and hiding inside. As a result, three hundred fifty children were among the thousand others murdered behind Janowska.

Just three months after the Schwarz Aktion, Katzmann ordered the final battle against the Jews of Lviv: the liquidation of the JULAG and any remnants of the ghetto. The City of Lions was to become *judenfrei* (free of Jews). As it always had, Janowska played a critical role in this last chapter of the Holocaust here, but Katzmann almost lost his opportunity to oversee the destruction of the ghetto. His replacement, SS Brigadeführer Jürgen Stroop, had arrived in Lviv between February and April 1943. In his time there as "Higher SS and Police Leader without staff," he visited the Lviv and Tarnopol ghettos as well as the DG IV camps.¹⁴ As he awaited his new command, however, Stroop received word that he was needed to oversee the liquidation of another ghetto: Warsaw. On April 17, 1943, he traveled to Warsaw to direct the "grand operation" set up by his predecessor that would make him infamous.[15]

Stroop's destruction of the Warsaw ghetto had important consequences for the Jews of Lviv. Warsaw's liquidation had begun in January but an organized and ferocious resistance by the Jewish underground had stunned the overconfident Germans. The ss officer in charge bungled the German response and was relieved. Jürgen Stroop then received the call to take over in Warsaw. As the fighting intensified in April, the Nazis became ever more concerned. Six days after Stroop's arrival, Heinrich Himmler personally ordered the burning of the ghetto and Stroop escalated the violence. On May 10, Himmler ordered the murder of all Jews remaining in the General Government.[16] Others in charge of ghettos were paying attention, including Friedrich Katzmann. Stroop eliminated the last resistance on May 16, 1943, and that same month Katzmann ordered the liquidation of the JULAG. Nazi fears of Jewish resistance were contagious.

Katzmann's ghetto-clearing operation began in late May and early June 1943 and would, in his words, be "energetically prosecuted."[17] Throughout the region, camp commanders received a phone call with the code "pick up rations tomorrow," telling them to prepare for liquidation.[18] The impending cataclysm must have been apparent to some as the prices being charged by Christians to hide Jews outside the ghetto skyrocketed into the thousands of zlotys.[19] ss men and Ukrainian police surrounded and stormed into the ghetto. Among those Ukrainian police was Ivan Kalymon, now a seasoned veteran of previous aktions.[20] Willhaus placed Janowska on lockdown because 70 percent of the ss men were participating in the ghetto clearing.[21] Katzmann also called upon Police Regiment 23, which had recently arrived to liquidate other ghettos in Distrikt Galizien. The Nazis conducted this roundup with increased brutality because the last Jews in Lviv fought back. The Jewish resistance in the ghetto had been preparing for this day and met the Germans with gunfire, grenades, and Molotov cocktails.[22] They had been particularly successful in purchasing weapons from disillusioned Italian soldiers.[23] Adolf Folkmann heard "shootings and explosions."[24] Bodies littered the streets. Thousands of Jews committed suicide rather than be dragged off to Janowska. Katzmann himself reported that the Nazis encountered "enormous difficulties in the aktions as the Jews attempted to elude the resettlement in every instance."[25] Perhaps taking their cues from Stroop in Warsaw, the Germans quickly escalated to simply burning down houses where they found resistance. Katzmann reported eight killed and twelve wounded during the ghetto clearing, but that number was likely higher.[26] Of the local population, Samuel Drix observed that they "watched the death throes of the ghetto with either stoic calm and indifference or they showed unbridled joy and satisfaction. Many had enriched themselves with the money and property of Jews they were holding for safekeeping and whose owners were now being killed."[27]

The vast majority of the killing, however, took place not in the ghetto and not in gas chambers, but in the Janowska camp. This serves as just another recognition of the camp's ongoing role as a killing site. The SS killed perhaps as many as 12,000 men, women, and children in the sands behind the camp in June 1943. Though he had avoided the March Aktion, Leon Wells was swept up along with his two brothers in the ghetto liquidation and found himself in the camp again. He recalled a father telling his young daughter "that in the very near future she would be in Heaven together with her mother and all her friends that she used to have and not be lonely anymore."[28]

The Janowska men followed the tried-and-true execution methods they had already perfected. Thousands of people flowed into the camp as deportation was no longer an option; Bełżec was already being erased. Prisoners in the camp watched in horror as the SS corralled the ghetto Jews in the women's camp (or the open area directly behind). In the early morning, Leopold Zimmerman arrived in Janowska by streetcar along with his twelve-year-old brother, Jozef. As they awaited their fate in the camp, Paul Fox—previously deputy commandant under Grzimek in Jaktorów—began selecting laborers. A mass of people volunteered, including Leopold and his brother, Jozef. Fox accepted both, but another SS man, Siller, shot young Jozef anyway.[29]

SS men drove their victims in groups of 100 from the assembly area into the hills where they were shot. Victims sat or laid on the ground, sometimes for a day, before they were forcibly undressed and forced to run to their deaths in the ravines. The SS of the camp played an active role. Roman

Schönbach stationed himself at one of the shooting trenches where he killed between sixty and seventy children under ten years old with a hammer.[30] The shooting and the screams coming from the Sands could not be masked by the truck engines left running by the Germans. At least 10,000 people were likely killed in the Janowska camp when the ghetto was liquidated; Katzmann claimed that 20,000 Jews had remained in the JULAG. Altogether, over 80,000 Jews were shot in Distrikt Galizien in June 1943.[31]

Emulating his would-be successor Stroop, Friedrich Katzmann also compiled a triumphant closing report in June 1943 in which he proclaimed that his district was now *Judenrein*, "free of Jews." Katzmann's narrative reads as both after-action report and self-aggrandizing résumé; like Stroop, he "begins by describing the difficulties created by the civil administration in relation to the plans to establish a ghetto."[32] In the end Katzmann boasted that he had "resettled" 434,329 Jews so far on his watch. The Katzmann Report also contained a grim accounting of the violence done to the Jews of Galicia, expressed in property stolen: 180 pounds of silver necklaces, 46 pounds of wedding rings, 25 pounds of gold fillings, 756 pounds of cigarette cases, 68 cameras, 98 pairs of binoculars, 7 "complete" stamp collections, and on and on.[33] Even in the aftermath of the liquidation of the ghetto, Janowska remained linked to the city. A "cleaning brigade" made of camp prisoners marched into the partially burned-out ghetto area to salvage whatever remained of value. This included searching walls and floors for hidden items. Any valuables were sent to Germany as "spoils of war."[34] Aron Spinner went with a group of plumbers, electricians, and mechanics to the ghetto to search for tools that could be used in the camp. In addition, he also found a Jewish girl hiding in the ruins. He managed to dress her in men's clothing and to sneak her into the camp with his brigade.[35]

In the summer of 1943, Katzmann and Willhaus both exited the stage. Katzmann was promoted to become the higher SS and police leader for the Danzig and West Prussia region. He had stayed on in Lviv to oversee the liquidation of the ghetto but now left to take up his new post. Surprisingly, Gustav Willhaus left Lviv as well. The circumstances of his departure are curious to say the least. On January 18, 1943, he had apparently written directly to Himmler himself requesting a transfer to a combat unit. It is not at all clear why a man like Willhaus, with a powerful (and comfortable) position with influential patrons, would voluntarily give that all up. But he appears to have done so, with the temerity to write directly to the head of the SS, Heinrich Himmler. The Reichsführer's personal secretary, Rudolf Brandt, informed Willhaus in April that "your presence in your current position is necessary for a little longer."[36] Indeed, Katzmann himself had declared that Willhaus was critical for the construction and expansion of the ZAL-L. Willhaus must also have been disappointed to learn that he was not classified as "fit for combat" (kv), merely as "fit for garrison duty on the home front" (g.v.H.).[37]

Ever the grifter, Willhaus appears to have continued to pester the SS and Himmler himself for a transfer, ever more recklessly. In an attempt to show that things were in hand, he sent a "performance report" directly to the Reichsführer SS. Brandt intercepted the report and wrote back coldly that he had not passed it on to Himmler "for your own good" because he "would have no sympathy for the way in which you put yourself in the forefront."[38] We do not have a copy of Willhaus's report, but evidently he, too, recognized that he erred and wrote to Brandt: "I wrote the entire report incorrectly and it had no factual basis."[39] While almost certainly apocryphal or wishful thinking, a Polish underground member claimed that the resistance wrote a counterfeit letter on Willhaus's letterhead to the SS requesting a transfer.[40] Whatever the explanation, by the end of June, Gustav Willhaus and his family left Lviv for vacation. The former commandant then reported to the 13th Waffen-SS Mountain Division made up of Balkan volunteers and desperately short of German officers.[41] After training, this unit took part in the anti-partisan war in Bosnia in 1944. Not surprisingly, the 13th Division committed a series of atrocities against civilians.

Willhaus's successor in the Janowska camp was forty-year-old SS *Hauptsturmführer* Friedrich Warzok, another product of German borderlands, born in Rogowo, Pomerania (now Poland). Like many of the Janowska SS, he had served in SS paramilitary units in Lublin before joining Katzmann's staff in Lviv. Warzok went on to command a series of camps in the Złoczow district forty miles to the east. From Złoczów, he gained a great deal of experience in Nazi anti-Jewish policy. While some survivors described him as "more sociable and less arbitrary" than Willhaus, he came to Janowska fully qualified to serve in such a brutal place.[42] A short, chubby alcoholic with graying hair, Warzok "humiliated people in the most degrading ways." While commandant of the Złoczów camp, he "lived in splendour, in the lap of luxury [and] enriched himself with money, gold, jewels, and gems which he extorted from the Złoczów Jewish council."[43] Warzok's grift appears to have been very advanced. He brought with him to Janowska "a band of 'his' prisoners" who were "unscrupulous scoundrels" who served as informants for the commandant.[44] His greed served him well in the end, ultimately financing his flight from justice. Warzok's tenure would also see the attempt to eradicate the evidence of mass murder and the final mass killing: the liquidation of the camp itself.

The Death Brigade

In November 1942, Himmler wrote a somewhat odd letter to the head of the Gestapo, Heinrich Müller. The Reichsführer SS was concerned about reports in the British and American press concerning the mass murder of European Jews. Confronted in February 1942 with an anonymous German earlier report of publicly visible Jewish corpses, Gestapo chief Heinrich Müller had responded lackadaisically, "in a place where wood is chopped splinters must fall, and there is no avoiding this."[45] Nine months later, more and more detailed reports emerged about the fate of the Jews. American rabbi Stephen Wise was attempting to raise awareness for the Holocaust as it happened.[46] Himmler actually enclosed a copy of one of Wise's speeches and then sharply instructed Müller that "your responsibility is to see that the dead Jewish bodies are buried or cremated. It is forbidden to do anything else with the bodies."[47] In contrast to the subterfuge often used in the West, killings in eastern Europe remained little better than open secrets. The killers themselves made few attempts to hide their crimes; the vast majority of the people there, Jews and non-Jews, were not expected to survive Nazi colonization anyway. One scholar has suggested that "the prime target of the cover-up was in fact the Nazis themselves."[48] Of course, no matter what the killers thought about their actions, the reality of the rapidly approaching Red Army brought a new urgency to the task of hiding what they knew were crimes.

The response of the Nazis to the evidence of their crimes remains a perplexing issue. The SS were proud of solving the "Jewish Question," but also felt the need to hide their achievements from both their own population and the Allies in what could only be recognition that the Final Solution would be seen as criminal. Whatever the motivation, Heydrich had already decided in the early 1942 on a more systematic plan for the permanent disposal of the victims, but it would not get off the ground for several months. He tapped SS Standartenführer Paul Blobel to lead the effort, code-named Sonderkommando 1005 (SK 1005). Blobel, an architect by training, had led one of the Einsatzgruppen killing squads and participated in the largest open-air shooting of the Holocaust at Babi Yar in Kiev. He now turned to the grim task of exhuming and burning as many Holocaust victims as he could find. One historian has called him "the ideal author of the practical methods" of corpse disposal.[49]

Blobel applied a gruesomely scientific approach to his new mission. He first traveled to the first of the extermination centers, Chełmno. An SS unit supplied a flamethrower; explosives were also tested but they succeeded only in setting the forest on fire. He eventually settled at Chełmno on "field furnaces" described by the last commandant as "holes in the earth."[50] Blobel also experimented with methods to grind up bones which were often more difficult to destroy.[51] Later, he traveled to Kiev to employ his skills at his Babi Yar killing site. As the Operation Reinhard camps began closing, Blobel's SK 1005 focused on removing the traces of the extermination centers. Excavation and burning of bodies started in autumn 1942 in Belzec and Sobibor and in Treblinka in February 1943. Blobel visited Auschwitz shortly after Heinrich Himmler in the summer of 1942 in order to brief the commandant, Rudolf Höss, on body disposal methods. Höss, in turn, visited Chełmno in September 1942 to watch Blobel's men in action.[52] By March 1943, SK 1005 had completed the second destruction of the Jews of Lviv buried in Bełżec along with the hundreds of thousands of other Jews from Galicia and had excavated at least thirty-three burial pits.[53]

In May or June 1943, Blobel arrived in Lviv where he met with Katzmann to coordinate the destruction of bodies in the area, specifically at Janowska and the Lyczaków Forest.[54] Distrikt Galizien had priority because it lay farthest to the east in the General Government meaning that its graves would be the first discovered by the advancing Soviets. Katzmann assigned command of the Lviv SK 1005 unit to a gaunt SS *Untersturmführer* Walter Schallock, the "Resistance Expert" in the Jewish Affairs office of the Gestapo in Lviv. Blobel himself appears to have suggested basing the Lviv SK 1005 in Janowska, noting the high number of graves and the ease of excavation in the sands. Once again, the camp played an outsized role in the Nazi universe, this time in its twilight. Before leaving Schallock in command, Blobel arranged an exhibition of the techniques he had developed—which he himself demonstrated, according to Schallock. Katzmann himself as well as his boss, Friedrich Krüger, the higher SS and police leader for all of the General Government, attended the show. After a week, Blobel departed the city.[55]

The task he left Schallock was a large one: in 1944, Soviet investigators discovered sixty separate mass graves at Janowska alone.[56] The SS man in charge of the Death Brigade seems to have been up the task. Walter Friedrich Karl Schallock was born into a farming family in 1903 in Stettin, about ninety miles north of Berlin. Schallock's mother raised him and his five siblings alone after his father was killed in 1914 in World War I. In 1920, he joined the fledgling interwar German Army as a radioman but was released due to a respiratory illness five years later. Still, he was a "man of the first hour," an early acolyte of the Nazis; he joined not only the Nazi Party but also the SA and SS in 1930. By 1934, he was serving in the *Sicherheitsdienst* (SD). With the outbreak of war in 1939, Schallock served with the Gestapo and early Einsatzgruppen in Kattowitz and Rszeszów in occupied Poland, where he almost certainly participated in massacres. His career seems to have been progressing nicely until February 1941 when he made some serious mistake in his counter-resistance job. Like so many others, he was sent east as a chance to redeem himself, arriving in Lviv where he was assigned to an Einsatzgruppe in July and likely took part in the mass executions of that summer. He then moved into his role in Katzmann's offices.[57]

Walter Schallock was forty years old when he took command of the Janowska SK 1005. He was "a stocky . . . broad-shouldered" man with a "Goering-style pompadour."[58] Leon Wells noted that he was "always drunk but never rowdy" with "glassy, shifty eyes." Still, the Death Brigade veteran conceded that Schallock was a "shrewd and an excellent administrator." He joined in the killing himself and joked to his prisoners that the work of the Death Brigade will go on for a thousand years.[59] Despite his "fatherly" demeanor and pandering to his workers, Schallock was a cruel man. Intimate family memories reveal his dark and violent side. In front of his young son, he shot the family dog to death because it had disturbed him, and he also beat his wife for giving a Jewish woman some food. According to relatives, he "loyally served the Fatherland but left his family to their own devices."[60] He was, in short, the perfect man for the job.

Schallock chose as his deputy SS *Oberscharführer* Johann Rauch of the SD. A small group of other SS men drawn from Katzmann's office rounded out the leadership. Anton Löhnert, Katzmann's Chief of Jewish Affairs who had brought Kolonko the order to eliminate his camp, held administrative responsibility.[61] Schallock's manpower was a platoon of policemen out of Tarnopol from Police Regiment 23. When formed in 1942 in Krakow, it was built around Police Battalion 307, which became the 1st Battalion in the new unit.[62] Pol. Bn. 307 had its own dark history. It was made up not of "randomly selected 'ordinary Germans' . . . but a well-trained group of young men who were self-selected for a police career in a police state."[63] Its long résumé included open-air mass shootings of thousands of Jews during the "Holocaust by Bullets" and the liquidation of multiple ghettos. These were dedicated men assigned to a task that certainly required dedication to carry out.

Forty-five Janowska camp prisoners provided the manpower for that first demonstration and became the kernel of the Janowska SK 1005 or Death Brigade. They were initially told they were being selected for "road-building."[64] Eventually, over a hundred twenty camp prisoners labored in the graves. Pathways to Schallock's unit varied. Henry Chamaides was on his way to be shot when an SD man pulled him out of line.[65] Abraham Feinsilber survived the ghetto liquidation by hiding in a truck full of goods headed for Janowska . . . where he found himself assigned to the Death Brigade.[66] There is also some evidence that the SS chose troublemakers for this work. Leon Wells stated that "the SS found out that I had often escaped and handed me over to the SD."[67] David Thürhaus was called out by name and accused of smuggling weapons into the camp. When he refused to reveal their location, he was assigned to the Death Brigade.[68]

Like those working in the gas chambers and crematoriums in the Auschwitz Sonderkommando, the Janowska SK 1005 prisoners were to be kept isolated from the rest of the camp population. Shortly after their work began, the Death Brigade moved into a temporary camp in the sand hills behind the camp, keeping them closer to their work and away from the rest of the prisoners. Wells referred to it as "an island . . . completely cut off from the rest of the world." He continued, "here where we work, except for the bodies, our murderers, fires, hills, and sand, nothing exists. There is no connection with the community which exists in the concentration camp."[69] Certainly, at some level, they were as "desperately and ferociously alone" as the prisoners Primo Levi observed in Auschwitz.[70]

The Death Brigade operated at two sites in Lviv. The first was the temporary camp in the Janowska ravines, where prisoners built their own barracks.[71] Their meals were trucked in from the camp kitchen. ss man Martin Büttner admitted that he sometimes delivered food to the ravine camp, but said that sd men took the vehicle to the outer perimeter and drove it to the prisoner barracks. They would return the truck with the empty food containers, and sometimes with clothing in it.[72] After the Death Brigade completed its work in the camp, it moved to the Lyzcakow forest on the eastern outskirts of the city, which had served as an additional execution site throughout the Nazi occupation. The new site lay five miles across the city from the camp and so required the building of its own infrastructure. A guardhouse marked a forest track leading off the Gliniankska road. The sd and policemen converted an existing villa into a kitchen and mess hall while the prisoners lived in tents under guard. Policemen occupied requisitioned houses just outside the forest.[73]

The daily operations of the Death Brigade remained generally the same in both locations, and it is difficult to overstate the horror of this work. Based on Blöbel's experiments and refinements, a distinct division of labor existed in this macabre industry. Leon Wells describes it in detail, listing eight work groups.[74] The ss were meticulous. They arrived with lists of graves and quite often the precise numbers of bodies to be excavated from each. When unsure, they forced the prisoners to bore into the ground, as David Manusevich recalled. When the bore holes yielded "the strong smell of decay," body parts, and pieces of clothing, the work could begin.[75] Leon Wells himself recalled a long day searching for one missing skull . . . which was his; when he had escaped from Janowska in 1942, Ukrainian guards had reported him dead.

The first group began the heavy labor of excavating the pits. The second group, the body carriers, then began to pull corpses out of the graves with iron hooks. Prisoners from the third group carried the remains to the burning site. Often in this process, they learned about the victims. In the Lyczakow Forest, prisoners identified the corpse of Professor Bartel, former president of Poland, from his identity papers. Moische Korn found the body of medical professor Ostrowski. Both men had been shot in July 1941 during the Professor Aktion.[76] They also discovered the bodies of prisoners of war and Italian soldiers.[77] As pits were emptied of corpses, the fourth group of "cleaning people" spread lime or chlorine to help eliminate the stench and to dissolve blood and remnants of clothing. Sometimes the blood itself had to be set on fire. Once this was complete, the excavating group backfilled the grave with earth and seeded it with grass. Schallock's deputy, Johann Rauch, oversaw this portion of the operation.

The heart of the Death Brigade's work occurred at the burning site. Here, forty-five-year-old policeman Willi König oversaw the destruction of corpses. Prisoners like Henry Chamaides laid the corpses in a crisscross pattern, alternating with layers of wood, to build gruesome pyramids. The stack of bodies measured as much as sixteen by sixteen meters.[78] A nearby machine pumped a mixture of recycled oil and gasoline that flowed from metal drums through a primitive pipe system. A detachment from the camp orchestra played while the pyre burned.[79] Though König was in command of this task, he placed two prisoners in charge of ensuring that the fires kept burning. The SS called these men the *Brandmeister* (fire master). They chose Abraham Feinsilber as one. They placed a cap with two horns on his head and mockingly called him "Head Devil." He was outfitted with a hook or pitchfork and led processions of singing brigade members as the SS demanded.[80] Feinsilber "escaped into madness," pretending to be insane with the benefit that the SS tended to dismiss him as nothing but amusement.[81] Beside the Brandmeister stood a prisoner who recorded each body as it was added to the flames. Wells recalled the importance of this, as he himself served as the counter while the grave he had escaped from in 1942 was opened. He stood there while the SS counted and recounted the skulls because Wells had been erroneously marked down as dead. This count was regarded as top secret and only could be given to Schallock himself. Wells wrote, "We were looking sometimes for hours for one body or more because it was buried on the side." At the end of each day, Schallock would ask the counter how many bodies were burned. Every day, the counter responded with the required answer: "I don't know."[82]

The process continued after the fires died out. ss *Oberscharführer* Friedrich Lelittko oversaw the final stage of erasure. He was a builder by trade from Berlin who "[beat] the inmates less than the others" and who pretended to yell at the prisoners whenever a colleague was around.[83] A "bone carrier" detail transported ashes and any remaining bones that often were not easily destroyed to the "Ash Brigade." This group worked on a solid platform built of tombstones from the Jewish cemetery cemented together. They used sieves to literally sift through the ashes and bone searching for gold or jewelry that may have escaped pre-execution searches by the ss.[84] It was a lucrative measure with an estimated eight to ten kilograms of gold and platinum harvested per day.[85] Schallock jokingly referred to this group as the "Alaskan Gold Prospectors."[86] The Ash Brigade delivered the remaining bones to a bone-grinding machine.

Prisoner Moische Korn operated the grinder. He described it as built on a four-by-two-meter platform with diesel motor that rotated a barrel in which the bones were placed. The "bone meal" was captured under the rotating barrel.[87] Others compared it to a cement machine and said it also contained heavy steel balls to accelerate the grinding process.[88] Death Brigade prisoners appear to have built the jury-rigged contraption themselves.[89] Mounted on a flatbed so that it could be transported, it would be taken with them when the sk 1005 detachment relocated to the Lyczaków forest site. Four hundred bodies created about a ton of dust.[90] Similar machines were used elsewhere as part of the Nazi attempt to hide the evidence of their crimes, and Janowska would serve as an example to other operations. The final act in the Death Brigade's daily routine was done by the spreaders. These prisoners scattered the finely ground ash and bone meal "as a farmer sows his seeds." However, unlike seeds planted in the ground, the ash and dust disappeared in the wind after a few days.[91] The number of bodies burned passed from the prisoner counter to Schallock to ss *Obersturmbannführer* Josef Witiska, the commander of the sd in Distrikt Galizien. Each week, the Death Brigade's tally joined those of sk 1005 units operating throughout the occupied east. The reports were submitted to Gestapo chief Heinrich Müller under the heading "Weather Report 1005." The numbers of graves destroyed were reported as "rainfalls" and the numbers of bodies burned disguised as "incidents."[92]

The work of destroying the dead did not signal an end to the destruction of the living. Leon Wells observed that "now the inmates are transported alive. They undress, and are shot in front of the fireplace."[93] In the ravines of Janowska and particularly at the Lyzcakow forest site, the SK 1005 workplace served as the only remaining execution site in Lviv as well as a convenient place for the disposal of the bodies. Shootings were "routine."[94] Numbers varied. Sometimes there were only a handful of victims, sometimes thousands. They arrived from the Janowska camp and from the city itself. Many of them were Jews who had been caught in hiding. Sometime in the fall of 1943, at least two thousand Italian soldiers were also murdered. Their deaths were part of Hitler's vengeance for the betrayal of the Italian surrender.[95] The SD and SS men carried out the executions themselves. Death Brigade member Feliks Ash described executions in the forest. Transports from the camp would arrive two or three times a week with hundreds of men and women. They were ordered to climb out and undress on the edge of the camp. Guards quarantined the Death Brigade prisoners in their barracks or tents while the heavily intoxicated SD personnel shot them.[96] Leon Wells recalled watching the SD prepare for a mass killing, handing out ammunition. Then the prisoners were marched into their tents.[97]

Like all mass murders, these killings were horrendous, but they had the added horror of often taking place during the burnings themselves. Women who had lost all hope "[threw] children into the fire and jump[ed] in after them, even before it was time to shoot."[98] Rauch ordered victims into the fires himself.[99] In addition to their daily suffering, Death Brigade prisoners bore the experience of throwing newly shot victims into the flames only to discover that they were still alive.[100] The SS and police then forced the prisoners to clean the blood off their uniforms for them.[101] We know a great deal about these killings as the prisoners poked holes in their tents to witness them. Thousands of Jews were murdered at both SK 1005 worksites through 1943, brought from the Janowska camp, from German jails, from hiding places throughout Lviv, and from places that will remain unknown forever. Tens of thousands of bodies disappeared in the foul smoke. A policeman noted that a "vile stench spread across the city so that the people soon knew that we were burning the bodies of the executed."[102] A survivor noted that "one could not go down Janowska Street in the summer of 1943 because it stank of the fire here."[103] The flames climbed so high into the sky at one point that the Lviv fire department rushed to the scene, fearing a great conflagration. Policemen guarding the site dismissed the firemen, explaining that everything was well in hand.[104]

Leon Wells recalled of his fellow prisoners in the Death Brigade that "one has a feeling that except for one another, and our assassins, we shall never see another living soul again."[105] For some, this was certainly the case. Despite this sense of isolation, a community did develop in the Death Brigade. Paradoxically, the conditions for prisoners improved in some ways compared to life in the camp. Like their colleagues in the extermination centers working in the gas chambers and crematoriums, the SK 1005 prisoners were compensated with better food and material possessions. Even the Nazis recognized the terrible nature of this work and saw some concessions and "luxuries" as a way to keep the work going. One survivor described the food as "pretty good."[106] Schallock himself would visit the Janowska camp kitchen to ensure that his detail received better food and larger rations.[107] He was also paranoid of disease to the extent that he took the unusual step of providing a temporary shower facility and disinfectant for the men.[108] After a detail working at the Luftwaffe airfield at Sknilow was murdered and disposed of, the Death Brigade men discovered "bundles of clothing and shoes . . . packages of bread, butter, sardines, chocolate and so on, 'everything' one could desire; even a roasted duck." Walter Schallock even procured a violinist to entertain the prisoners after work hours.[109] Some of the entertainment, however, was much more problematic. Schallock seems to have attempted to supply the men with Jewish women. When he delivered a dozen women from the camp to the SK 1005 site, however, they fled in terror at the sight of the Death Brigade and its quarters. They were all shot.[110]

Schallock himself had a very peculiar relationship with the Death Brigade. He seemed at some level to believe that they were partners with him. He portrayed himself as a "kindly father" to the men. He would visit them as they worked and ask, "have you any complaints? . . . Is there anything that you would like changed? Just ask me. I want you to be happy." He would visit them at night and tell the terrorized men, "I want you to think of me as your father. You are my children and I am your father. I will do anything for you."[111] Feliks Ash remembered Schallock telling them, "My fellow workers, you have been freed from concentration camp, from all the misery what you have done before. You are going to start a life where you will never be hungry, where you will get first-class shoes, shirts, two change of suits, and if you would work together with me, without any questions, you will live a thousand years." Tellingly, Ash recalled that the response from the men was "unbelievable silence."[112] While the prisoners believed this to be a ruse, Schallock did, in an odd way, rescue his wards from immediate death. At Auschwitz and the other extermination centers, the SS killed the Sonderkommandos en masse periodically. As the ultimate witnesses to the Nazis' crimes, they represented a massive liability and the only way to destroy their knowledge was to kill them. In Janowska, these were Schallock's orders as well. The men of the Death Brigade had become skilled workers in their own terrible way, and men who could withstand the daily revulsion of the work were not common. Therefore, out of pragmatism or laziness, Schallock ignored his orders to purge the prisoners every few weeks, saving himself the time and trouble of retraining and reorganizing his underlings. He brought the prisoners themselves conspiratorially in on his scheme; they were told to lie to any visitors when asked how long they had worked in the Death Brigade. Naturally, realizing that this would keep them alive, the prisoners played along.[113]

Regardless of Schallock's attempts to provide for his "children," life in the Death Brigade was horrendous. The work itself was physically demanding, even with a better diet. Wells described the prisoners with "faces blackened . . . clothes bloodstained, the odor of death in our every pore."[114] The men labored for long hours surrounded by the most horrific of sights, smells, and experiences. Somehow, Schallock and his men managed to torment their prisoners still more. Moische Korn recognized his own wife among the bodies he was to burn. Distraught, he begged Schallock to shoot him to which the SS man responded that he would stay alive as long as he was capable of working. Schallock then forced Korn to throw the body of his wife into the fire.[115] The SS made another unfortunate prisoner burn his two daughters who had just been shot; he, on the other hand, had been selected to live as part of the Death Brigade.[116] The SS men also knew the Jewish calendar well enough to mock their prisoners. They ensured that on Yom Kippur 1943 there were over a thousand bodies to burn in a celebratory pyre.[117]

The violence of the SK 1005 Germans extended beyond the psychological. Both Schallock and Karl Ullmer executed any prisoner who "deviated from his orders in even the smallest way" or who became sick. The SS men simply said, "Turn around. You must pay with your life" or "you will not infect the others." Then the offenders were shot and thrown into the fire by their colleagues in the Death Brigade.[118] Johann Rauch discovered that one of his prisoners named Lufko had been secretly trading with a policeman. The SD men beat him senseless before reviving him with a bucket of cold water. The Germans then took turns shooting at his "hands, fingers, nose, ears, feet." After a bit of this target practice, Lufko was shot and his comrades carried him over to the fires.[119] Along with the constant threat of death, the men of the Death Brigade endured constant beatings and abuse on a daily basis.

The SK 1005 prisoners lived in one of the darkest corners of an already horrendous world. Feliks Ash described the work as "so inhuman that it could only be done for a few weeks."[120] One historian has argued that the "vast majority of prisoners behaved like 'zombies,' reduced to the physical functions of the body."[121] Some were "men in decay," Primo Levi's "drowned."[122] Some committed suicide. Yet others managed some kind of functional numbness that allowed them to continue. Leon Wells recalled that during lunch breaks the prisoners would eat their meals sitting on corpses awaiting burning.[123] A kind of fragmented camaraderie did develop. A surviving song from the Death Brigade exhibits the gallows humor that dominated: "Hey old whore, / Why did you have even have me? / What a life this is, what a life this is! / Better to have lost me!"[124] Togetherness took many forms. For example, even the "antireligious" prisoners stood guard outside the tents while their observant comrades worshipped.[125] These connections would serve them well in the months to follow.

If the prisoners felt themselves isolated from the rest of the world, the perpetrators intentionally plugged themselves into a wider network. Blöbel designated Janowska (and later the Lyczaków Forest) as the official training site for the men who would staff the SK 1005 units that would spread out across occupied Poland and the rest of the Nazi empire. Officers and sergeants assigned to Blöbel's operation filtered through Lviv for ten-day training courses, arriving from Warsaw, Krakow, Lublin, and other places to learn the "best practices" in the eradication of human bodies. Schallock served as the professor, giving "practical instruction" on-site at the mass graves. He explained how to exhume the bodies, how the bone grinder worked, the ins and outs of his cremation methods, and concluded with the processes of planting trees on the site. One survivor recalled at least ten iterations of the course.[126] SK 1005 units appeared across the East, from Lithuania to Ukraine, some educated at Schallock's Lviv training center. They scrambled to identify all the grave locations and eradicate the evidence. Yet, while various units of the SK 1005 reported burning over a hundred thousand corpses in eastern Galicia, Blöbel's task was never a realistic one.[127] "O, earth, cover not my blood," Job cried out in the Old Testament, "and let my cry find no resting place." The work of the SK 1005 could never cover that blood—not even in Janowska, where the Soviets would quickly discover evidence of mass murder on their arrival in 1944.

"Paying for Our Deaths": Liquidation and Revolt

The fall of 1943 marked the end of both the Janowska camp and the Death Brigade. Both the looming catastrophe of the war (for the Germans) and the successful destruction of large Jewish communities triggered not only the eradication of evidence but also the dismantling of the killing apparatus and, finally, the murder of surviving Jews in Nazi hands. The surprising ferocity of Jewish resistance during the Warsaw ghetto uprising (and in Lviv) rattled Himmler and other senior leaders during the summer of 1943. In June, the Reichsführer SS ordered the camps in the eastern part of Galicia destroyed. Only the camps of the Carpathian Oil company, the Czortków tobacco farms, and Janowska remained after that summer. Approximately twenty-five thousand people were murdered.[128]

After Katzmann finished clearing the ghetto in July 1943, a new SS and police leader, SS Brigadeführer Theobald Thier, arrived in Lviv.[129] Thier was a forty-six-year-old career SS officer and World War I veteran as well as a "convinced Nazi" from Stuttgart who had most recently served as an SSPF in the Crimea where he had overseen "pacification" operations.[130] Thier quickly began to implement Himmler's orders. The Inspector of Camps, Friedrich Hildebrand, recalled that Thier ordered the elimination of remaining DG IV camps; the order "simply came across my desk and so it went very quickly." By the end of July, the camps in Lacki Wielkie (Chervone), Jaktorów, Pluhow (Pluhiv) und Zloczów, Hluboczek, Jezierna (Ozerna), Kurowice (Kurovychi), Sasów (Sasiv), and Tarnopol had been closed or liquidated.[131] In August, Thier "suddenly" recalled all Jewish forced laborers from the military and armaments productions in the district.[132] The noose was tightening.

Events a few hundred miles north of the city would add urgency to Thier's mission. On August 2, 1943, prisoners in the Treblinka extermination center attacked the SS and staged a mass revolt. Then, in the late afternoon of October 14, the last prisoners in the extermination camp of Sobibor violently turned on their captors, luring fourteen SS men into ambushes and killing them. Himmler, already nervous about the remaining Jews, now believed there may be a network of conspirators in Distrikt Lublin. He explained that "the Jewish problem in Lublin Distrikt has grown to extremely dangerous proportions. This matter must be solved once and for all."[133] And so, after a fifteen-minute meeting on November 7, 1943, Himmler ordered SS and Police Leader Wilhelm Koppe to "clear" the remaining camps in the General Government.[134] This set in motion a wave of mass killing known as Operation Harvest Festival (Erntefest).

Thus, two weeks after the Sobibor uprising, Thier ordered the liquidation of most of the Janowska camp. Warzok apparently prepared the ground for this action by leaking rumors of a planned evacuation of the prisoners to Majdanek; Wells called the operation "a study in deception and cruelty."[135] On the morning of October 25, prisoners assembled in the Appellplatz but noticed few guards or SS men around besides Warzok. The commandant even handed out new shoes to the work brigades leaving the camp. But, as Michał Borwicz observed, "nothing good was to be expected of any variation to the normal camp routine."[136]

SD, Gestapo, and police surrounded the camp. Selections were carried out and some prisoners were murdered in the sands. Warzok and his men also liquidated the women's camp.¹³⁷ The DAW stood more or less empty after this. It appears that most of the killing took place in the Lyczakow forest. This makes sense as the SK 1005 had already completed its cleanup work in Janowska. Marcel Lubasz watched as trucks with trailers carrying a hundred people at a time drove back and forth from the ZAL-L to the forest site. A kapo took poison and died. Lubasz leaped from the truck and managed to jump on a passing streetcar.¹³⁸ Thousands of others were not so lucky. The work brigades that had marched out to work with new clothes arrived instead at the Death Brigade's Lyczakow forest camp. There, the SK 1005 prisoners were confined to their tents while drunken SS men spent the day shooting. When the shooting died down, the prisoners emerged to begin burning the thousands of bodies of Janowska camp inmates. Estimates of the number of prisoners murdered range from two thousand to seventy-five hundred.¹³⁹ The stunned prisoners remaining in the Janowska camp then received "new" clothing from their former comrades.¹⁴⁰

After this partial liquidation in October 1943 or perhaps much earlier, a group of Janowska prisoners began planning a revolt. It became starkly clear to many that the end was in sight. Yehuda Eismann in the Technical Bureau "began to sense that the entire camp was going to be annihilated."¹⁴¹ Most of what we know about the camp resistance comes from Michał Borwicz, a member who continued to fight the Nazis even after his escape from the camp. The conspirators planned an armed uprising and there had been considerable discussion among the prisoners about the prospects and manner of that resistance. Borwicz records some of these conversations in his memoirs. One man named only as Artur probably expressed the thoughts of many of the camp underground, saying: "What I want to do is fight. And I, you must understand, want to kill those bastards. I don't want to only shoot at them, but to shoot them down. That is the difference. So although our prospects are crappy, it is unacceptable to let even one occasion slip away. We must do our best to obtain the guns and to organise ourselves. So that this shooting fight is not only for your own vanity—excuse me—your own dignity, but also in order to ensure those bastards pay for our deaths as dearly as possible."¹⁴²

To that end, they attempted to smuggle firearms into the camp. It was a constant struggle as the SS discovered hidden guns or as outside contacts swindled the camp underground. Despite these obstacles, the resistance appears to have been successful in acquiring several revolvers and handguns. The underground leaders recognized that they would not have enough firepower to support a firefight with the guards. Instead, Borwicz proposed provoking "a massacre [of the prisoners by the guards] out in the street" in view of civilians, something even he admitted was a "minimalist response."[143] On the other hand, many of the prisoners were armed with small knives that they carried for daily use. They were "part of the private equipment of the prisoners, and although the authorities did their best to eliminate them, they were in fact the most common possession."[144] There was another connection between city and camp that was decisive for the uprising. After the liquidation of the Lviv ghetto, Thier and his security personnel continued to search for and arrest Jews who had escaped the conflagration or were in hiding. Those they found often ended up in the ZAL-L. In so doing, the Nazis had added to the prisoner population a group of prisoners who had already resisted and fought against their oppressors. The introduction of these people added strength and motivation to the camp underground.

The moment of cataclysm for Janowska coincided with broader regional policies. Due to the revolts elsewhere, a massive regional mass killing operation kicked off at the beginning of November 1943. During Operation Harvest Festival, the Nazis began to murder thousands of prisoners from the remaining camps in the General Government. The Majdanek camp served as in many ways as the epicenter, as it had its own dedicated gas chambers. Eighteen thousand Jews were killed there on November 3, 1943.[145] The Trawniki and Poniatowa camps also served as centralized killing sites. But the liquidation action also reached Lviv. SS and Police Leader Thier ordered that the Janowska camp be finally liquidated on November 19.

Warzok attempted his deception again, informing the remaining prisoners that they were to be transferred out of the camp for "agricultural work." One must assume that most did not believe this subterfuge. A survivor recalled that the rumor of a coming liquidation began circulating a week earlier.[146] On that Friday morning, a line of trucks full of SS and militia parked on the street in front of the DAW, and morning roll call found the camp clearly surrounded.[147] It is unclear precisely how the revolt began or even whether there was a signal, but as the SS moved into the camp, the last prisoners of Janowska rose up. Some attacked the guards with their knives and the few guns they had. One account says that a Jewish woman stabbed a guard, signaling the beginning of the attack.[148] Others sought to break out in the melee. Michał Borwicz wrote that "with bare hands they grabbed the barbed wire fence and in the hail of bullets, over the corpses of their comrades struck down in the escape."[149] Some took poison and died on the spot. Aron Katz and his brother tried to break through an electric fence. Aron made it, but his brother's body was left hanging on the wire.[150] Zbigniew Bitsch managed to find a drainage pipe and crawled out of the camp. He and many others fled for the forests.[151]

Warzok watched with binoculars from a safe distance as the SS and police fired into the panicked crowd of prisoners.[152] The Germans tossed hand grenades into the camp, some of which the prisoners picked up and threw back at their attackers.[153] Guards in the watchtowers fired machine guns down at the scattering prisoners as well. Adolf Kolonko, who ludicrously claimed that the camp staff was "completely surprised" by the liquidation, noted that there were "terrible scenes" and "heartbreaking cries" from the prisoners as the killers moved in.[154] At some point, the uprising was overwhelmed and some level of order restored. The SS and police forced the surviving prisoners to strip naked. While waiting, some sang spiritual songs or prayed. They were then led out of the back gate of the camp through a cordon of Germans. The Nazis (including most likely the camp SS) then shot them all to death in the sands behind the camp. The killers left the bodies unburied.[155] At least two thousand were killed. Perhaps ten guards died at the hands of the prisoners.[156]

Numbered among the dead were the members of the camp orchestra. It seems that once an uneasy calm had been restored, the orchestra was assembled. They stood by the gate to the inner precinct, on the appelplatz, as they had many times before. The musicians played or sang the popular German wartime song "Es geht alles vorüber" (Everything passes).[157] As they played, SS man Richard Rokita, who had formed the musical group in the first place, shot them one by one. He left their bodies on the roll-call square where they were later picked up by trucks and taken to the sands.[158]

The shooting in the hills lasted most of the day. Afterward, Kolonko and others searched the grounds and discovered a few Jews who had been hiding. These people were "taken away."¹⁵⁹ As the Death Brigade had already cleaned up the Janowska killing sites, the liquidation of the camp added a new mass of corpses. Kolonko recalled that "already after a few days, one could not bear to be in the camp. The terrible smell of corpses crept over the camp day by day... the smell stuck in the nose." Sometime later, an SD detail supervised the final cremation of the bodies.¹⁶⁰

Whoever that body-burning detail was, they did not come from Schallock's group, for they, too, had revolted. On the night of November 19, the men of the Death Brigade staged their own uprising. They knew more clearly than most that they truly lived on borrowed time and had no illusions that they would survive; indeed, they recognized that they only owed their lives to Schallock's laziness. By the middle of October, the brigade burned the last of the bodies in the forest. It then began to excavate and destroy sites in the immediate vicinity. As Henry Chamaides recalled, "We knew that we would be shot in the next few days, so we decided to escape."¹⁶¹ The absence of a threat of reprisal against loved ones also encouraged the prisoners to act. Leon Wells recalled that they said, "We have freedom [to act]."¹⁶² So, they planned. Much of what we know about the revolt comes from the testimony of Wells and Feliks Ash, who both survived; Wells, in fact, kept a diary during the time he was in the Death Brigade.

A committee formed to explore their options. The men lived in two tents surrounded by two barbed-wire fences. Outside the fence were two "guardhouses" used by the policemen. Spotlights at each corner of the camp illuminated the enclosure at night. Policemen manned two bunkers on the ridge above, equipped with a field telephone. Another group patrolled the outside of the camp during the night. The members of the brigade themselves were divided in the tents by status. Eighty prisoners lived in one tent and a group of "elite" prisoners, including Wells, occupied the second. These included the foreman Herches, camp workers, and some craftsmen. As Leon recalled, "We are the ones who don't smell, who don't have direct contact with the bodies."¹⁶³ The conspirators met in the leaders' tent and determined that there would be no individual escapes; the entire Death Brigade would have to break out as one. Songs from the prisoner musicians provided cover for these nightly meetings.

The bone-grinder operator Moische Korn received a tip that the Sonderkommando would be liquidated on November 19, 1943.[164] No doubt this was to coincide with the end of the Janowska camp. The leaders had planned the escape for the night before. However, Herches discovered that some of the more unsavory members of the detail had stolen the valuables set aside for the prisoners to use after they had escaped. He demanded that they be returned, which they were, but at the cost of a day. The next night, as the musicians played, Herches laid out the plan to the conspirators. "Tomorrow," he said, "we will be in the fire or free."

The plan, however, must be reconstructed from fragments of imperfect memory. One group of prisoners would approach the gate guards under the guise of ongoing black-market trading. They would then kill the guards to release the prisoners. A second group had gained the confidence of the guards and was allowed to leave the camp to cut firewood in the forest, some of which went into the guards' fire to keep them warm. On the night of the escape, these men were to kill two more guards and then turn their weapons on the policemen sleeping in their tents. Music from the musicians and six prisoners singing was meant to mask the sound of shooting, allowing the remainder of the Death Brigade to don the uniforms of the policemen, take their weapons, and march out of the camp. The majority of the prisoners would learn about the escape only as it unfolded. Some had decided not to even try. Yehuda Goldberg, who had lost his whole family, simply said, "Why would I even want to survive or escape? What for?"[165] For him, there was no plan. In any case, little went according to plan.

Around seven o'clock in the evening, Feliks Ash and another comrade left the camp as part of the firewood detail. It was "a cold wintery day with dry snow falling." Somewhere in the forest near the camp, Ash killed one of the Germans with an axe and likely his comrade killed the other. Ash took the guard's gun and two grenades and approached the police tent. He tossed the two grenades into the tent, killing several men. When the startled policemen staggered out, Ash emptied the magazine of the machine gun into the crowd, killing even more. He then fled into the forest.[166] Meanwhile, at the gate, something went wrong from the start. One of the guards managed to cry out, or perhaps there was a timing issue with the attack on the tents. In any case, the action at the gate turned into a mad rush. A prisoner bashed the policeman in the face with a shovel. Leon Wells was one of the first out and knocked down a guard, stomping on his face with his heel. The following prisoners trampled him to death as he pled for his life.[167] The remaining Germans opened fire, sweeping the little camp with bullets. As Yehuda Goldberg quietly awaited his fate in the tent, the rest of the Death Brigade scattered into the dark woods.

Leon Wells headed for the hills after fighting his way through rolls of barbed wire. Others just ran. Joseph Wind recalled, "We all ran out, just nobody knew where to go. You couldn't see from here to the bushes."[168] Muzzle flashes filled the night as the remaining policemen fired at the shadows. The Germans in Lviv went on full alert. Parachute flares illuminated the woods as around a hundred twenty men, alone or in small groups, fought to escape the growing manhunt. Only a few would be successful and fewer still would survive the war. Most of those who survived the revolt, however, would testify against their oppressors in court.

Warzok's Shield: The Unraveling of Janowska
After the smoke of the burning bodies had cleared from the hills behind Janowska, the camp ceased to function in any real sense—but it remained in operation. In fact, on paper, Warzok's command moved up in the world. On January 13, 1944, it officially became a subcamp of the Majdanek camp in Lublin.[169] In reality, the camp must have seemed as if it had gone back in time to its ignominious beginnings in 1941. The prisoner population increasingly featured Poles and Ukrainians. Despite the complete annihilation of Jewish inmates in November, more Jews trickled into the camp as the Nazis continued to discover them hiding in the city. The Nazis sent Rebeka Kuryniec from the Gestapo prison on Łąckiego Street. Warzok locked her in the gatehouse "bunker" with four other Jews and two children. Executions continued in the hills; they were smaller, less frequent, but no less terrifying. Kuryniec remembered that "every day there were new people brought in from the Aryan quarter, the elderly were put to death, the young were taken to work. We counted the days and hours that divided us from death."[170] Work details no longer left the camp for no work remained for

them in the city. Instead, they confined themselves to the required tasks necessary for the camp's operation.[171]

Everyone but the most delusional Nazis saw that the end was near in the spring of 1944. Increasingly effective partisans ripped holes in German logistics and turned whole swaths of ostensibly German territory into no-go terrain. Already in January, the *Palestine Post* could report that the Nazis were preparing a "new defence zone" along the San River, west of Lviv; reportedly, they were already evacuating heavy machinery and railroad infrastructure.[172] The Red Army landed devastating body blows on Erich von Manstein's Army Group South. By the end of February, it had killed or wounded fifty-five thousand German soldiers in Ukraine.[173] Soviet bombers hit Lviv repeatedly. After one bombing in May, the guards mocked the prisoners who had been left in the open by asking "Did you shit your pants?," but the Germans could not have forgotten that they had been forced to cower in a bomb shelter.[174]

Then, in June, shortly after over a hundred fifty thousand Allied soldiers stormed ashore in France, Stalin unleashed Operation Bagration in the East. Named after the famous Russian general who had defeated Napoleon, this Soviet offensive swept all before it. Friedrich Warzok began preparations for an evacuation of the camp. Killings stopped on the orders of his superiors. One survivor recalled him saying, "You're lucky that we aren't allowed to shoot Jews anymore." Prisoners hastily burned and buried the bodies of those who had been killed after the November liquidation.[175]

On the morning of July 19, 1944, Warzok assembled the remaining fifty or so Janowska prisoners and marched them the short distance to the Kleparów station. According to Simon Wiesenthal, the commandant told the future Nazi hunter, "You are coming with us, and together we'll get through the war."[176] There, they climbed into one freight car. The flight from Lviv became more and more bizarre. The rapist Peter Blum shoved a dog and a caged canary in with the prisoners, warning them he would kill them if anything happened to the animals.[177] Blum himself escaped the train ride himself by bringing along his seventeen-year-old bride, Alina, in an old civilian car.[178] Two Soviet tank armies bore down on the city from the north and the south. Eight days after the last denizens of Janowska fled, the Germans abandoned Lviv. One of the units essentially destroyed defending the nearby town of Brody was the 14th Waffen-SS Grenadier Division, otherwise known as the SS Galizien Division, composed mostly of Ukrainian volunteers.

The first destination of Warzok and the Janowska remnants was the Polish fortress town of Przemyśl. Due to the deteriorating military situation and the low priority of the train, the normally forty-five-minute journey extended to an excruciating two-day ordeal for the prisoners. In Przemyśl, they discovered they were now part of *Baustab Venus* (Construction Staff Venus), a fictitious organization that Warzok had made up. It was an important-sounding name for an SS scam. It is unclear how exactly it developed, but Warzok managed to turn the remaining Janowska prisoners into an "essential" part of the war effort digging anti-tank trenches and other defenses as the Nazis sought to hold back the Soviets. As the leader of Baustab Venus, Warzok created a safe haven for himself and his SS men. They would not be sent to the front or impressed into service by the military police roaming the rear areas looking for deserters. It must have struck someone as odd that there were almost as many prisoners as guards, but Warzok managed to move frequently and avoid too much suspicion. Wiesenthal worked as a painter, creating impressive-looking signs reading "Camp Venus" and "Camp Mercury." The other prisoners labored moving earth, and slept in the open, guarded by the remaining SS men.

This band moved across slowly westward, "slept in abandoned work camps" and, in Wiesenthal's words, they "became one big party of war tramps."[179] At least some of the hundred-mile trek to the town of Grybów was made on foot. Along the way, the killing continued. The SS executed prisoners who fell ill or were unable to continue.[180] Peter Blum murdered a diabetic prisoner who had dropped from exhaustion.[181] Guards shot three Jewish tailors along the way as well.[182] It seems that Warzok's group disintegrated in Grybów in September 1944. SS man Richard Dyga then took a group of the survivors to the Płaszów concentration camp in Kraków, made infamous in *Schindler's List* (1993). They arrived on September 15; among them was Simon Wiesenthal.[183] There they experienced new horrors under some old hands, like the former commandant of the JULAG in Lviv, Josef Grzymek, who was now stationed at Płaszów. He remained as brutal and committed as he had always been; when the Plaszów camp was evacuated, Grzymek supervised the execution of fifty prisoners from the Montelupich prison in Krakow.[184] At least two prisoners from Janowska (and certainly more) did not survive Plaszów.[185] For others, the end of their suffering lay farther in the future. Helene Lehmann was further deported to Auschwitz, then Bergen-Belsen, before being liberated in the Mauthausen camp in Austria in May 1945.[186] Along with the other men of the camp, Simon Wiesenthal was evacuated by cattle car to the Gross-Rosen camp and eventually also ended up in Mauthausen.[187]

Thus closed the operational chapter of the life of Janowska as it passed from history to memory. The perpetrators became the hunted and, in some cases like that of Wiesenthal, the survivors became the hunters. As those who had endured the concentration camp at 134 Janowskastrasse began to search for families and piece together their lives, the perpetrators began to flee their past and to settle into an unobtrusive peacetime existence.

Testify for Us All 10

> I hope that I will survive long enough to see my remaining family. Then I will laugh at life, because on more than one occasion I have looked death in the eye.
> —Diary note, Mordechai Stromer, June 6, 1944

In the early morning darkness of July 27, 1944, Leon Wells furtively emerged from a cellar hidden beneath a barn. A Pole named Wojciech Kalwiński had saved him and twenty-three other Jews, telling them when the SS executed a neighboring family for hiding Jews, "Whatever happens, my children, we shall share in your fate."[1] Because he was afraid of his own neighbors, Kalwiński asked the survivors to leave in small groups before daylight. After surviving Janowska twice, the revolt of the Death Brigade, and seven months of hiding in darkness, Leon Wells walked into Lviv a free man.

But it bears remembering that many lost their lives, even as the end was within sight. One of these was Max Ringer. The twenty-one-year-old had managed to survive outside the ghetto, living in warehouses and vacant buildings. He successfully passed himself off as a Pole fleeing ethnic violence and had secured false papers under the name Piotr Rogosz. He even worked for a German construction firm. Ringer met a young Polish woman, Irena Barylak, in the city center, and it appears she took a liking to him, meeting him on Sundays. On their third meeting, she invited him to her apartment. At ten o'clock at night on May 21, 1944, an informant denounced them both to the German military police. Barylak was released after the investigator was satisfied with her protestations that she had not known Ringer was Jewish; Ringer had "misled Barylak" for his own "Jewish" reasons. As a result, Max was delivered to Janowska on June 19, a little more than a month before liberation. He did not survive. The Gestapo dutifully logged receipt of his only possessions: a briefcase, a notebook, two glasscutters, photographs, a gold watch, a telescope, and 1,056 zloty.²

Even for those who survived to liberation, the postwar years brought continued struggles for the former prisoners of Janowska. They would seek to find family and rebuild their lives as best they could in the wake of measureless loss. For most, liberation did not remove the lingering damage of their time in the camp. Others found meaning in the fight for justice against their tormentors. The end of the war turned the SS "supermen" into the hunted. Those who had stalked the roll-call square now sought to make themselves scarce and to blend into domestic life amid the chaos of a defeated Germany. Simon Wiesenthal started on a lifelong quest to bring these men to justice, though the justice delivered must, in the light of history, be seen as unsatisfying at best. Many survivors found themselves trying to live up to Elie Wiesel's charge for those who would go forward: "The one among us who would survive would testify for all of us. He would speak and demand justice on our behalf; as our spokesman, he would make certain that our memory would penetrate that of humanity."³

Liberation and Loss, Evasion and Escape

Leon Wells was not alone when he walked, half-dazed, into downtown Lviv as a free man for the first time in four years. But very few survivors joined him at the temporary registration center for Jews. Perhaps 700 presented themselves, representing one half of 1 percent of the prewar population; eventually 2,571 Jews arrived in Lviv, though many were from the surrounding area.⁴ In the region, Katzmann himself had reported "resettling" 434,329 Jews as of June 1943. Survivors emerged as strangers in their own city. There was little sympathy for them, even from their liberators. Leon walked for hours until he could not walk anymore. He simply sat down as passersby walked around him. Jack Ahrens recalled meeting Red Army soldiers who demanded to know, "So why weren't you fighting actively? Why—what did you do in hiding?"⁵ They called the survivors "nothing but a bunch of cowards." The Russians "didn't want to understand that [hiding] was the only way how to survive, because the population was against us."⁶ The NKVD interrogated Samuel Drix, who felt as if he "was accused of being alive."⁷

Lost in a city no longer their own, survivors of the camp looked for relatives and many returned to their prewar homes. Edmund Kessler and his wife (who had survived with Wells in the basement hiding place) found a Red Army officer living in their apartment, but fortunately he allowed them to stay with him.[8] Joseph Wind returned home but found a Polish neighbor living there; she brought him "a nice soup" but did not let him in.[9] Wells forced himself back into his parents' apartment where neighbors were now living. His family's furniture was all still there and the new owners tried to tell him that "we didn't have it too easy either." He stayed a few days and then left for good.[10] Most, however, felt as Isaac Wolf did when told by the Russians he could go back to Lviv. "I can't go back to Lviv," he replied, "because Lviv is a Jewish cemetery."[11]

With the Red Army still driving the Nazis back toward Berlin and local Jews trying to pick up the pieces, the Soviets began the earliest investigations into the Holocaust. In November 1942, Stalin personally founded the awkwardly named Extraordinary State Commission for the Establishment and Investigation of the Crimes of the Fascist German Invaders and Their Accomplices, and of the Damage They Caused to Citizens, Collective Farms, Public Organizations, State Enterprises, and Institutions of the USSR (hereafter the Extraordinary State Commission or ESC). The top-level leadership represented an eclectic mix of aspiring bureaucrats and academics, including a relative of the great Russian writer Tolstoy. Stalin clearly intended the ESC at least partly to create a documentary basis for external propaganda. As often happens, the higher the reports went, the more politicized they became. ESC documents can still be quite insightful, though, particularly initial reports. The investigation into Nazi crimes across the Soviet Union generated over 54,000 statements, 250,000 witness interrogations, and 4,000,000 documents.[12]

And so, toward the end of 1944, two Soviet officials named Gontscharenko and Kornil from the commission arrived to inspect the abandoned Janowska camp. Moische Korn, the bone-grinder operator in the Death Brigade, accompanied them. Together, they documented the layout and buildings of the camp in precise detail. The officials noted among other things the bone grinder, the mountains of household goods, and an estimated 11,000 pairs of shoes in an abandoned warehouse. The ESC identified sixty burial pits of ash and bones as well as three graves of prisoners executed at the end of June 1944. The investigators also discovered that the soil around some of the graves was "bloodsoaked to a considerable depth."[13] Having surveyed and documented the Nazi site, the Soviets then turned it into a prison for their own use.[14]

Most Janowska survivors realized that little remained for them in the East (or in Europe). Poles made it clear that if they had not supported the Nazi removal of the Jews, they were not unappreciative of the results; they murdered 150 Jews in liberated Poland in the first four months of 1945 alone.[15] In Kielce, a hasty lie told by a child led to the murder of 42 Jewish Holocaust survivors in retaliation for an imagined ritual murder. Many Jews traveled west into Germany en route to new homes. There, they found themselves categorized as "displaced persons" and often confined in a new set of camps as the occupation authorities struggled to deal with their numbers. As a journalist wrote in 1948, they "are willing to go anywhere on earth except home."[16] Many Janowska survivors spent years in the land of their oppressors before they could emigrate. Leon Wells had time to earn an engineering degree in Munich before he finally could leave for the United States in 1949.

The perpetrators also followed a myriad of trajectories after their time in the camp. Many (unlike Warzok) found themselves eventually fighting enemies who shot back. First among these was Gustav Willhaus. The SS had granted his request for assignment to a combat unit, the 13th Croatian Waffen-SS Division. He fought partisans in Yugoslavia before joining the 6th SS Mountain Division in January 1945. In the last week of March, American soldiers killed the former commandant of Janowska as he defended the small village of Steinfischbach near Frankfurt. He was hit in the back by a machine gun burst and was buried with four other SS men in the cemetery there. According to his wife, he died "protecting the people from reprisals by the invading Americans." The mayor returned Willhaus's bullet-holed leather coat, wedding ring, and briefcase to Liesel.[17]

The other commandant of the ZAL, Friedrich Warzok, successfully avoided frontline duty, was transferred to the Neuengamme camp outside Hamburg, and slipped back into postwar society for the moment.[18] Fritz Gebauer, the longest-serving of the Janowska commandants, returned to his wife and settled down, first as a mechanic building bridges in Torgau, East Germany.[19] During the retreat of Baustab Venus, Peter Blum had crashed into a towed anti-tank gun while driving without headlights at night. He and his bride-to-be ended up in a hospital in Slovakia. He was then returned to the fighting forces where he was trained as a tank crewman. Blum's unit dissolved toward the end of the war in Czechoslovakia, keeping one step ahead of the Russians and reaching Austria. By 1953, he had settled with his family in Germany where he worked as the handyman in the Werneck Palace, a former psychiatric hospital involved in the Nazi "euthanasia" program.[20]

Most Janowska SS men ended up in Germany, through various routes. The Americans captured Friedrich Heinen, but later released him from a POW camp in 1946.[21] They also interned and released Roman Schönbach.[22] The US Army actually hired the boyish killer Adolf Kolonko as a night watchman in Bavaria.[23] With the exception of some of the most prominent Nazis, most Germans who had carried out the Holocaust were able to reenter civil society with little difficulty. The Nuremburg Trial, while sensational and important, targeted mainly the highest-profile Nazis that could be found. The surviving high-ranking perpetrators in the dock were absolutely responsible for the genocide of millions, but few had actually killed any with their own hands. Hans Frank, the chief of the General Government, who was responsible for the administration of occupied Poland, met the hangman in Nuremberg. Twelve subsequent trials reached farther down, targeting actual killers such as Einsatzgruppen leaders. A US court convicted Paul Blobel, the innovator of Sonderkommando 1005, of crimes against humanity and sentenced him to death.

But, for the moment, the SS men from the out-of-the-way camp at the end of Janowska Street seemed to have escaped their past. They settled into the relative obscurity and postwar chaos of a shattered society. This was what Germans called *Stunde Null* (Zero Hour)—a term that expressed the absolute destruction of the Nazi state and the need to rebuild from scratch. The turmoil of a defeated Germany can seem hard to believe today. One US official described the situation as "complete economic, social and political collapse ... the extent of which is unparalleled in history unless one goes back to the collapse of the Roman Empire." In 1945, 20 million people were homeless, 53,000 lost or orphaned children sought refuge in Berlin alone, and an average of 10 people were dying each day from exhaustion, malnutrition, and illness at the main Berlin train station. The American occupiers authorized only 860 calories per day for Germans.[24] In many ways, though, it was an opportune time to be a fleeing Nazi. Millions of Germans flooded into Germany from the East, pushed like a great wave before the advancing (and much less conciliatory) Soviets. Some Lviv perpetrators were fortunate enough to be released from Soviet captivity due to illness. Those who did not leave voluntarily were driven out by newly created national governments, a policy that Czech president Edvard Beneš coldly summarized by saying, "We have decided to eliminate the German problem in our republic once and for all."[25] In addition, by September 1944, almost 7.5 million non-Germans lived in Nazi Germany, most of them not by choice.[26] Hundreds of thousands of ethnic Germans and eastern Europeans flooded west during and after the collapse, fleeing repression by the Soviets, their soiled past with the Nazis, or both. Perpetrators could blend in amid this river of humanity—one of the largest population transfers in European history—while seeking safety and new lives. At first, the Allies tried to forcibly return them to the East, but by 1947 ended these efforts, recognizing that many of those refugees were repatriated to gulags. For perpetrators particularly anxious about their past catching up with them, Germany was not far enough.

The last Janowska commandant, Warzok, made it to Berlin with twelve of his SS men. In 1946, former guard Martin Büttner visited Warzok's wife asking about her husband ... and then conning her out of money. The ex-commandant, however, had been missing since March 1945 when he had sent his wife a message from the Neuengamme camp.[27] Frau Warzok had her husband declared dead in 1950.[28] In 1949, Peter Blum tried to emigrate to Argentina with his wife and two-year-old son. He applied to the International Refugee Organization for assistance and presented himself as a Hungarian and reported that he had served in the Hungarian Army from 1940 to 1944, stating that he did not want to return to Hungary "because of the political situation." The interviewer seems to have had doubts, noting on the application that "the applicant claims to be a Hungarian but in my opinion he is a *Volksdeutsche*." He further observed that Blum had a scar on his left upper arm; this was quite likely Blum's attempt to remove an SS tattoo. In any case, the interviewer concluded that "the applicant has voluntarily assisted the enemy forces," making him ineligible for assistance.[29] The Blum family remained in Germany where Peter again became a musician in a local band. Richard Rokita changed his name to "Domagala" and took a job as a night watchman in Hamburg because he knew it would allow him to avoid much notice.[30]

Ivan Kalymon, the Ukrainian volunteer policeman who helped round up Lviv's Jews, was more successful. He had made his way to Munich by 1949 where he applied for displaced person status and emigration to the United States. He conveniently left out his service in the Ukrainian Police on his application and the United Ukrainian American Relief Committee (which still exists today) vouched for his character. As a result of his omissions, the US counterintelligence corps determined that he had not participated in any hostile activities. The United States issued Kalymon and his family visas and permitted them to enter.[31]

While some sought to immerse themselves in an entirely new population, many former Nazis remained connected to their wartime comrades in the shadows of the postwar miracle recovery of Germany. These continuing connections, overlapping social circles, and even friendships of Nazi war criminals after Hitler's defeat remain a difficult and understudied history of the Holocaust, but, uncovered or not, these relationships existed. Links forged in the concentration camps persisted after the fall of Germany. The "masters of life and death" became men with a very particular set of vulnerabilities. Groups of SS men formed to help "one another, mostly to start over at home but also to emigrate overseas."[32] Peter Blum admitted that he and Adolf Kolonko visited each other.[33] Philipp Federmann ran into Peter Grumbach in a POW camp and also had contact with Roman Schönbach after the war.[34] The nature and depth of these relationships remain unclear, but a surprising number of the Janowska perpetrators inadvertently revealed that they knew at least what cities each other lived in, which means they must have been in some contact. Sometimes these contacts had a direct bearing on the search for justice, however. In early 1962, Fritz Gebauer, accompanied by his wife, dropped in on his former DAW construction foreman Willi Monz, who lived nearby. During the visit, Gebauer related to Monz that he would soon be arrested and they discussed the investigation.[35] These contacts remain a crucial area for further historical study.

While some former Nazis might have enjoyed a sense of community, for many others the country must have seemed too small a place, for they kept bumping into survivors who recognized them. The Americans had interned Karl Melchior in 1945, but two years later he escaped. Shortly thereafter, Janowska survivor Rudolf Dantsches recognized him in a suburb of Munich attempting to buy black-market goods with gold.[36] The Military Police was unable to initially catch him but he was arrested a year later on Christmas day.[37] A similar scenario played out in June 1947. Survivor Max Hoening recognized Johann Rauch of the Death Brigade in Munich. Hoening grabbed the former Nazi by the collar and flagged down a passing American MP who brought them both to the local police station. Rauch denied everything but the Americans agreed to keep him in custody if he could be identified. Hoening rushed to the apartment of Leon Wells, who was studying in Munich. Hoening then traveled to a nearby displaced persons camp to fetch another Death Brigade survivor, David Manusevich. The next morning, the three appeared in the police station and instantly recognized their tormentor from Sonderkommando 1005. On seeing Rauch, Manusevich kicked him in the head before he could be dragged out of the room. The three men convinced the American officer of Rauch's identity. The lieutenant offered Wells an iron bar and privacy to exact some revenge, provided he did not kill the former Nazi. Wells punched Rauch "a few times" until he fell to the floor. He then shook hands with the American officer, who turned out to have been born in Poland, and left.

The beating did not stop Rauch and his family from later reaching out to Wells. The Rauch family apparently had gotten Wells's address and visited him *eight* times pressuring him to retract his statement that Rauch had participated in executions.[38] Rauch's sister described their interactions with Wells in disturbingly antisemitic tones. She wrote to her brother in 1948 telling him that a relative had visited "one of the Jews who denounced you. He found out what kind of people they are." She went on to question why "these people are allowed to come to Germany when they have so much dirt on their hands that they are afraid of their own courts back home. And yet they can cruelly and falsely denounce innocent people."[39] The family efforts failed, however. The Poles executed Johann Rauch in 1949.[40] Justice in Germany, however, would be less swift and often less severe.

The Murderers Are among Us: Janowska on Trial

The first feature film produced in Germany after World War II debuted in Berlin one day before the Nazis condemned at Nuremburg were executed. *The Murderers Are among Us* (1946) confronted the return of Nazi perpetrators to German society with a critical eye far ahead of its time. But, as much as it attempted to remind people of an uncomfortable truth, the film itself reflected the problem. The leading actress, Hildegard Knef, had put on a German uniform and joined her lover in fighting the Red Army in a Berlin suburb in the last days of the war. The Soviets captured her but she escaped.[41] Her costar, Ernst Wilhelm Borchert, had to be removed from promotional materials after accusations surfaced that he had lied about his Nazi Party membership on his denazification forms.[42] Even the director of this stridently anti-Nazi film himself was a *Mitläufer* (fellow traveler) with the Nazis, having helped in the production of *Jüd Suss* (1940), one of the most successful Nazi antisemitic propaganda films.[43]

Perhaps some of the Janowska men encountered the film in a German theater. Most likely, however, they did not. One German writer recalled the reactions of his countrymen when forced to watch documentary films on Dachau and Buchenwald before they could receive their ration cards. "In the half-light of the projector," he wrote, "I could see that most people turned their faces away after the beginning of the film and stayed that way until the film was over. Today I think that that turned-away face was indeed the attitude of many millions.... The unfortunate people to which I belonged was both sentimental and callous."[44]

This is not to say that postwar authorities did not attempt to "denazify" Germany. Between 1945 and 1949, the Allies interned two hundred thousand former Nazi officials and collected sixteen million questionnaires interrogating individuals about their Nazi past.[45] Local "denazification" courts (*Spruchkammern*) under Allied supervision attempted (often halfheartedly) to determine the relative depth of participation by Germans in the Nazi state. In reality, these courts usually just laundered the pasts of their subjects. Germans nicknamed them *Persilscheine*, after a popular laundry detergent, as they were seen to cleanse one's history. Many perpetrators slipped through this net. Anton Löhnert, the Jewish and Forced Labor Camp expert in Lviv, appeared before one such court without revealing much of his past and was classified as a "minimally implicated" person. He faced no negative repercussions from his classification.[46]

Walter Schallock, the commander of the Janowska Sonderkommando 1005, also stood before a denazification court. He filled out his questionnaire from a refugee camp where he was receiving a welfare check from the German government. Schallock massaged his Nazi history by stating he was a member of the "German Police" and denied any connection with the SD or Gestapo. He stated that he had never been employed in a concentration camp (which was technically true) and that he knew of no other perpetrators (which was decidedly not).

The court classified the commander of the Death Brigade only as a Mitläufer. He suffered no further penalties and, in 1955, applied for reparations payments to compensate him for his imprisonment in Denmark.[47] The Janowska men, like many others, benefited from these "spectacles of hypocrisy," as one scholar termed the denazification courts, which "lost [their] impact at the lower levels."[48]

Former members of the Waffen-SS (to which many of the Janowska men belonged) could also rely on their own lobbying organization. The Mutual Aid Organization for Former Waffen-SS Members (HIAG) was formed in 1951 and advocated for the rights and particular needs of this constituency, which numbered around two hundred fifty thousand. SS veterans had been disenfranchised in a way that other veterans had not. The Nuremburg tribunal judged the Waffen-SS to be a criminal organization. Therefore, membership alone indicated, for the court, "a political understanding of National Socialism and at a minimum a tacit agreement with its crimes."[49] Ostensibly, HIAG lobbied for Waffen-SS veterans to receive the same pensions and benefits as Wehrmacht veterans. However, HIAG also functioned as an underground support community. Some of the more publicly visible leaders attempted to distance themselves from those SS involved in the concentration camps. In reality, however, these men also benefited from the resources of HIAG. Within the organization, "members of the Death's Head units [the camp SS] were well-regarded as members . . . and generally did not have to worry about any unpleasant questions."[50] Perhaps the men of Janowska were also well received by comrades in the HIAG.

Large swaths of the German population also showed little support for legal reckonings. German popular opinion polls revealed a substantial remnant of Nazi believers: 37 percent of respondents to a 1952 poll agreed that "it was better for Germany to have no Jews on its territory."[51] In addition, the policy of many postwar German politicians was to "integrate rather than alienate ex-Nazis" in the interests of a unified society.[52] Many Germans placed full responsibility for the crimes of the Third Reich with the main Nazi leaders such as Hitler, Himmler, and Göring. After Nuremburg, they preferred to consider the judicial prosecution of Nazi crimes as completed. Moreover, many Germans saw lower-level Nazis (as well as themselves) as also victims of Hitler's regime. All these challenges led to very uneven judicial outcomes.

Germans were not the only ones who found zealous pursuit of former Nazis problematic. The Allies, faced with the very real challenges of rebuilding a functioning society, often struggled to separate the most criminal Nazis from those who had joined the party out of practicality. The general in charge of the American occupation, Lucius Clay, related that "our major administrative problem was to find reasonably competent Germans who had not been affiliated or associated in some way with the Nazi regime.... All too often, it seems that the only men with the qualifications... are the career civil servants... a great proportion of whom were more than nominal participants (by our definition) in the activities of the Nazi Party."[53]

The Allies presided over the most effective period of Nazi prosecution from 1945 to 1949, while they were solely in command of the process. In 1949, however, Germany became responsible for the legal pursuit of its own criminals. The Nuremburg era for many Germans represented victor's justice and a retroactive application of laws that did not exist during the Reich. Indeed, one of the first acts of the new West German government was to prohibit such prosecutions. It did not help that the Americans reversed themselves on quite a few Nuremburg death sentences and even eventually released some criminals, several of whom were Einsatzgruppen commanders. Only a few of the Janowska or Lviv perpetrators were judged in this period. One of them was Karl Melchior, who had been recognized in Munich by a survivor. A German court sentenced him to life in prison in 1949. Both Johann Rauch of the Death Brigade and the JULAG commandant Josef Grzymek found themselves condemned to death in 1949, but in Poland, not Germany.

The legal machinery that brought the Janowska men to justice can trace its beginnings to two developments in the late 1950s and early 1960s. The first was the establishment in 1958 of a Central Office for the Investigation of Nazi Crime. After the combined trial of ten Einsatzgruppen members in Ulm that same year, German legal authorities recognized that the scale of Nazi crimes demanded the creation of a more efficient and organized system for investigation and prosecution. A small group of dedicated lawyers and researchers in the Central Office began to proactively pursue Nazis who might be at large in Germany. The group, based in a former women's prison in the Baroque town of Ludwigsburg, served as a clearinghouse for investigations, passing information on perpetrators on to state attorneys general. The tireless director Adalbert Rückerl kept the flames of justice alight for over twenty years, even when the mayor of Ludwigsburg objected to the "certain stench" that the Central Office left on his town.[54] In its first year, the little office of around twenty people initiated four hundred inquiries.[55]

The second key moment was, ironically, a concerted effort to forget rather than remember the crimes of the Third Reich. In 1960, some lawmakers realized the statute of limitations on manslaughter and murder or accessory to murder under Germany's legal code would soon save all Nazis from prosecution, making them essentially immune from prosecution in 1960 and 1965 respectively. Supporters of extending the period of limitations argued that many details of Nazi crimes were only now beginning to surface. Opponents suggested that few prosecutions were likely forthcoming given the passage of time (or, cynically, that without a statute of limitations the process would be "virtually endless").[56] Certainly, behind closed doors, many Germans hoped that legal bars to prosecution would end uncomfortable public reminders of Nazi crimes. A compromise measure added four more years to the clock, setting the statutory deadline at 1969.

A critical legal loophole now came into play. If investigators could identify crimes or suspects, even if their whereabouts were unknown, the statute of limitations could be interrupted. So, the Central Office and other organizations accelerated their efforts to collect and pore through documents from all over Europe, not infrequently with cooperation from Soviet Bloc countries. Their efforts resulted in almost nine thousand criminal cases opened from 1958 to 1969.[57] Not infrequently, denunciations or ill-advised statements by perpetrators themselves triggered investigations. In 1958, a jailhouse snitch revealed an Auschwitz perpetrator and led to the largest Nazi trial in German history.[58] Indeed, the period leading up to the *Lemberg Prozess* (Lviv Trial) witnessed a flurry of major trials: Eichmann (1961), Auschwitz (1963–65), Bełżec (1963–65), Treblinka (1964–65), and Sobibor (1965–66). The Lviv Trial has never received the attention of these others, however.

German investigators began focusing on Nazi crimes in Tarnopol, which led them to Lviv and Janowska in 1960. As investigators began their interviews, they unmasked one perpetrator after another and began to reveal the postwar paths of many Janowska men ... and at least one woman: Liesel Willhaus, the commandant's wife accused of shooting prisoners from the villa balcony. An arrest warrant was issued for her in 1964 under the "strong suspicion" that she had murdered at least fourteen prisoners out of a "lust to kill."[59] Liesel had continued her grifting after the war. She was convicted twice of operating gambling machines (which her new husband produced) without permission and of driving without a license.[60] Ever playing the con game, Liesel claimed that she had only heard of the goings-on in Janowska after the war, in the newspapers. She also claimed never to have met Fritz Gebauer or his wife.[61] Instead, she protested, "I had been fully occupied at that time with as a housewife, mother, and *Wehrmacht* volunteer worker."[62] Liesel Willhaus remained obstructive to the end but ultimately escaped prosecution due to "health reasons."[63]

The notorious killer Richard Rokita lived under false names until 1960 when authorities discovered and arrested him. He freely admitted that he had killed prisoners. "As an old man," he told investigators, "I have no interest in disputing anything that has happened. Understandably, I must acknowledge that I killed people in the camp. But, everything I did can only be understood in the context of the conditions."[64] By the time of the Lemberg Trial, however, Rokita was deemed unfit to appear in court due to age-related heart conditions. He would not be called to account for fifty separate charges.⁶⁵ Others, however, were not so fortunate. Police arrested Peter Blum and Adolf Kolonko in that same year, and Roman Schönbach, Martin Büttner, Hans Sobotta, and Paul Fox were arrested soon after. Fritz Gebauer was also arrested, but justice in his case would take longer to realize.

In the German policing system, defendants and witnesses were often brought face-to-face during the investigation process. The inquiries led to some truly surreal interactions. The most bizarre of these centered around Leon Wells. In 1964, he and German prosecutors visited some of the accused in the Hohenasperg prison on a hill above Ludwigsburg. Wells described the encounter in an article he wrote for the *New York Times*. His first appointment was with none other than Richard Rokita, the brutal SS man who had executed the camp orchestra. The man dressed in a prison uniform before him was "bent and pale" and "his flesh hung loosely on him." The prosecutor read Wells's deposition to the former Nazi who smirked back at Wells. Rokita remained obsequious. At one point, he interrupted, "with the look of a beaten dog," saying, "It could never have been forty people I shot. . . . I never shot more than seven or eight at a time by myself." His last words on the way back to his cell were: "I have lived an honest life, Herr Witness. I've always aimed at being the best kind of person a man can aim at being. And I have achieved my aim."

The next visitor brought before Wells was Walter Schallock, the commander of the Death Brigade. Unlike Rokita, the SK 1005 chief was not interested in currying favor. When he looked at Wells, "his lips pulled back in a snarl." He denied all charges, shouting and pounding his hands on the table. Then Schallock changed tactics, trying to convince Leon that "I was like a father to you" and that "if I had guarded you more carefully, you wouldn't have been able to escape," as if that had been some kind of favor. For Wells, it had been "terrifying to see a human being, even this one, so completely exposed." He left the prison feeling "utterly desolate."⁶⁶

After over six years of investigations, the collective trial of fifteen Lviv Nazis known as the Lviv Trial opened on October 25, 1966, in the center of Stuttgart. The trial would go on to last two years (a hundred forty-four days of court proceedings) and generate over ten thousand pages of courtroom testimony. Around two hundred fifty survivors would testify, coming from nine different countries around the globe.⁶⁷ International newspapers reported on the trial. German newspapers carried almost daily reports on the goings-on in the district court. It was a pivotal moment. Only a year before the trial started, a national poll found that 52 percent of Germans agreed with the following statement: "I think we should finally stop prosecuting people for crimes they committed many years ago. I think it would be good to close the book on the past."⁶⁸

The presiding judge, fifty-five-year-old Dr. Peter Pracht, had considerable experience in Nazi trials, having previously presided over the Tarnopol Trial of ten SS men in 1966. In January of that year, Pracht had been forced to dismiss a case against a Wehrmacht war criminal due to the machinations of the defense attorney.⁶⁹ In the upcoming Lviv Trial, he faced seven such defense attorneys, including one of the rockstars of the Nazi legal defense world: Rudolf Aschenauer. Aschenauer was a former Nazi who had worked in the Munich propaganda office where he had been described as "staunch, useful, and ready for action." The Americans categorized him as one step below a war criminal, but, by some "grotesque rationale," a denazification court in Munich classified him in the lowest category of those tainted by regime. Aschenauer had close ties to the Committee for Church Aid to Prisoners, an evangelical organization whose "main aim was to legally assist so-called destitute war criminals." As a result, Aschenauer quickly gained a large client list and became one of the most prolific specialists in defending Nazis.⁷⁰ He had mounted a vigorous defense of the brutal killer Otto Ohlendorf, commander of Einsatzgruppe D, whose crimes he described as "preventative measures to protect Germany from Bolshevism," and would go on to write for a neo-Nazi publication, *Nation Europa*.⁷¹ In Stuttgart, he represented Janowska guard Hans Sobotta and Sonderkommando 1005 man Ernst Preuss.

The law itself far surpassed unscrupulous lawyers as a challenge for the prosecutors. As we have seen, the statute of limitations placed the most easily prosecutable offenses like manslaughter off-limits and the rejection of ex-post-facto law (such as crimes against humanity) limited government attorneys to pre-1945 law. The only charges available, then, were accessory to murder and first-degree murder. The definition under German law (para. 211) was critical: "a murderer is anyone who kills a human being: from a lust for killing, to satisfy his sexual drives, from covetousness or other base motives, treacherously, cruelly, or by means endangering the community or in order to facilitate or conceal another crime."[72] The requirements of this charge hamstrung prosecutors, forcing them to prove not only the elements of the crime but also the mindset of the perpetrator. Naturally, most former Nazis were smart enough to avoid admitting to any of these "base motives"; if not, their lawyers, experienced men like Aschenauer, ensured that they did not incriminate themselves.

The reliance on prewar legal frameworks also hampered prosecution at its most basic level. Postwar courts often treated Holocaust-related crimes as normal homicides. However, when prosecuting these Nazi crimes, even the simplest of tasks became the most difficult. It was often extraordinarily hard to determine facts that would be the most elementary for a normal civilian crime. Concentration camp inmates had little access to calendars, let alone watches. Trials found them hard-pressed to remember specific dates and times, particularly years later. Often, the identity of the victim was unknown, even as eyewitnesses could clearly identify the killer. But if the victim could not be identified, was a crime committed? Sometimes, witnesses could not definitively prove that the person they saw shot or beaten to death was *actually* dead. Without the benefit of revised legal codes, the obstacles placed in the way of prosecution remained formidable, especially given that many prosecutors approached these Nazi investigations "wearily and without passion," in the words of Fritz Bauer, the prosecutor in the Frankfurt Auschwitz Trial. In addition, while the "obedience to orders" defense was rejected as invalid, commands from superiors could and were used in mitigation. The numbers show the unsatisfying effect of all these constraints on justice: between 1950 and 1962, 30,000 former Nazis found themselves in the sights of detectives. Only 43 percent of these ended in indictments. Just under 20 percent made it to a courtroom and a paltry 5 percent were convicted. Of these 1,399 convictions, only 155 Nazis received a murder conviction.[73]

The Lviv Trial thus started with the odds heavily stacked against the prosecution. The presiding judge managed a panel of five male and one female jurors: an engineer, a housewife, a retired bank employee, a civil servant, and two winery workers.[74] Judges in the German legal system are more active, questioning and even calling witnesses. Yet officials seemed to also have realized the pivotal importance of the trial. Unlike most German criminal trials, this one would be both recorded and transcribed.[75] There were losses from the beginning. "Poor health" kept Walter Schallock, Richard Rokita, and Liesel Willhaus out of the courtroom from the outset. Rokita escaped prosecution on at least fifty separate criminal charges; doctors had the gall to cite the "strain" from his previous prosecution in the Tarnopol Trial as a factor.[76] These three Janowska perpetrators never faced a judge.

Prosecutors presented a mass of evidence from historians, investigators, and 250 survivors and witnesses. As a result, the Lviv Trial produced moments of high drama as survivors confronted their tormentors after over twenty years. When a witness stated that he could recognize Peter Blum, even at night, the defendant shouted back in frustration, "Well, that beats everything!"[77] Another survivor identified Blum from the stand, shouting, "That is the redhead!" Blum merely smiled "maliciously" and repeated that the witness must be mistaken.[78] David Thürhaus, a survivor of the camp and the Death Brigade, also found Blum offensive. "Blum hasn't changed a bit as he sits there and grins insolently," he told the court. "He seems to be doing fine. He certainly got enough money when he was in the camp. Your honor, you can hardly punish him at all, because there isn't a harsh enough penalty for these people."[79]

Predictably, defense attorneys attacked the witnesses. After each survivor was questioned by the judge and the prosecutors, each of the eight lawyers had a chance to cross-examine witnesses. Consider the following exchange between Roman Schönbach's lawyer, Dr. Klaiber, and survivor Abraham Goldberg regarding his testimony about a killing he witnessed:

> KLAIBER: Mr. Witness, when did this incident you described take place? Can you give us a more specific time frame?
> GOLDBERG: It must have been November or December 1942.
> KLAIBER: Can you be more specific?
> GOLDBERG: I can't be more specific. You can see what happens, if after 20 years I write down a date. It is very hard to give a specific date in such things.
> KLAIBER: Was it before Christmas 1942?
> GOLDBERG: There wasn't any Christmas for us! So, I can't tell you.[80]

Attorneys also challenged survivors to identify SS ranks, pick perpetrators out of photo lineups when they were twenty years older, and generally attempted to discredit them with challenges on details at every point. Even Leon Wells—who had kept a diary, written a memoir, and testified at the 1961 Eichmann Trial—was not immune from these attacks on witness credibility. The professional Nazi defender Rudolf Aschenauer, in fact, directly attempted to point out contradictions between Wells's testimony in Israel and other statements. Another defense attorney claimed that "the testimony of the witness stands in stark contrast to the contents of his written statements." Of course, authorities had questioned Wells twelve times since 1957 and the disagreement seemed to center around the linguistic distinction between "personally known" and "recognition of his name."[81] Of course, this is not to say that witness testimony did not contain discrepancies, hearsay, and outright incorrect information. The problem lay more in that such errors tended to be used disproportionately to discredit eyewitness testimony.

Again, the unique circumstances of Holocaust-related crimes and the lack of any understanding of collective guilt demonstrated how unfair applying standard legal norms could be to the prosecution of former Nazis. The survivors recognized this themselves and it is apparent in their statements. Marian Rogowski told investigators that "I would only like to testify to what I actually saw and what is undeniably in my memory today. I do not want to testify about things I have heard."[82] Likewise, Bernard Nestler made it clear that "in the many intervening years, some things have disappeared from my memory. What I am stating here is what I have so clearly in my memory that I am prepared at any time to testify to it under oath."[83] Still, Peter Blum's attorney (like his colleagues on the defense team) argued that his client could not be convicted as contradictions between various witnesses made it impossible to prove his guilt.[84]

The defendants also took to the stand to explain themselves. One of the great benefits of trials like these is that we get to hear from the perpetrators themselves, even when much of the commentary is a smokescreen. Still, their responses give some insight into how they felt about their actions. Kolonko admitted to shooting a prisoner in the neck but claimed, "I had to do it. It was an order." An earlier testimony from 1960 was presented where he argued, "If one was part of this 'club,' you couldn't refuse orders or you would find yourself against the wall."[85] Of course, no credible evidence has ever been uncovered (by scholars or defense attorneys) of Germans being shot for individually refusing to kill Jews.

At times, the testimony became almost farcical. In January 1968, the prosecution called Otto Walter, a former SS man assigned to Janowska. His pretrial depositions had strongly incriminated Kolonko. Once on the stand, however, he appeared to suffer from amnesia, refusing to make any statements about crimes occurring in the camp. The judge intervened harshly, telling him to "get real!" Walter remained mainly uncooperative, telling a "very patient" court that "we even played soccer with the prisoners. In general, I didn't notice anything extreme going on." Judge Pracht replied acidly that "we have heard complaints from a few survivors of the Janowska camp that residence in the camp should not be reduced to soccer games."[86]

The defendants portrayed *themselves* as the victims of the terrible things they had to do while in the camp. In this, they mimicked the feelings of their commander, Heinrich Himmler, who had described the murder of the Jews as "a burdensome duty."[87] Roman Schönbach told the court that the killing of Jews in the camp was "terrible" and "got on his nerves." He explained, "I thought the same thing then as I do now: that what was going on with the Jews was simply monstrous." Describing his feelings after the liquidation of the Grodek-Jagiellonski camp, Schönbach stated that "after everything was done, I felt very depressed." Derisive laughter echoed in the courtroom. Kolonko described his participation in executions as "terrible" and "horrible for him." Judge Pracht, never one to mince words, responded, "Certainly, it must have been especially terrible for the victims." Kolonko responded, "I regret everything." In a fascinating exchange, Pracht continued, "That is too formal, excessively shallow, and general for me. Did you reflect on what you did when you shot another human being on orders? Did you only shoot in order not to be considered a pussy?" After some thought, Kolonko simply replied, "I didn't reflect on it."[88] Blum suggested his head injury sustained while with Warzok's group impaired his memory and further believed that "we were abused by our higher superiors."[89]

Other defendants resorted to blanket denial. Roman Schönbach dismissed every allegation, saying, "It wasn't me. . . . I never killed anyone."

A clearly annoyed Judge Pracht noted that it made no sense for him to give the same response to all eighteen charges against him. The combative Schönbach responded, "Then we'll just wait for the hearing of evidence."[90] Willy Schulze, another Janowska SS man who appeared not as a defendant but a witness, tried to dodge any discussion of criminality in the camp. Only "grudgingly" did he admit that the conditions were "gruesome" and that the SS did beat and mistreat prisoners.[91] Anton Löhnert denied knowledge of the fate of Lviv's Jews. He claimed to be "astounded that officials back then would have known." "I only knew," he testified, "that in our area the talk was of Lublin as a resettlement destination."[92] This claim is even more absurdly false given that Löhnert was one of the SS men specializing in Jewish affairs in the SS and police leaders' office. Löhnert also denied ever having shot during the liquidation of the Grodek-Jagiellonski camp, an incident that took center stage at the trial, though he admitted to being present with Willhaus in the house.

Hans Sobotta came closest to expressing some level of remorse or recognition of his guilt, telling the court that "it was my moral duty to decline these criminal orders." However, he was simply too weak to do so.[93] Only one defendant appeared genuinely sorry and apologized for his actions. Ernst Heinisch, who had served as the supply clerk among other things at Janowska, was the only one to confess. He "often attempted to circumvent orders but believed himself to be in a hopeless situation."[94]

The verdicts in the Lviv Trial could hardly be described as satisfying for those seeking justice, but they were not inconsequential either. The court found none of the Janowska SS men guilty of murder. The court held that "the primary perpetrators of the crimes committed by the defendants were Hitler, Göring, Himmler, Heydrich, and their close associates." The critical decision for the court then was to determine whether the accused were the perpetrators (*Täter*) of the crimes or simply accessories (*Gehilfe*) to those crimes. In explaining the legal standard, Judge Pracht wrote that "a subordinate is responsible as a perpetrator of a criminal act if he acts with criminal motives [*animus auctoris*]. On the other hand, if he is only carrying out the will of the order-giver, then he can only be punished as an accessory at most."[95] Thus, the reliance on base motives and proving the mindset of the perpetrator saved the Janowska men as all had claimed that any act they had committed had been under orders. In order to prove them guilty of murder, the prosecution would have had to prove that they also agreed with the motives behind the orders. This was next to impossible. For example, Roman Schönbach was found guilty of accessory to murder for the killing of a child under ten years old at the German Railway East subcamp. According to Schönbach, Willhaus had ordered him to go there, look for any hidden Jews, and kill any he found. The court judgment reflects the contradictions in the law and perhaps some of the frustration that Pracht seemed to display during the proceedings. Schönbach was to be punished as an accessory even though "it cannot be ignored that Schönbach enjoyed a very bad reputation as many witnesses have testified and that he allegedly brutally mistreated and arbitrarily killed prisoners in many instances which have not been charged." Further, "in spite of strong additional suspicion, it could only be established that, in carrying out Willhaus' orders, Schönbach supported the crime of another but did not commit the crime as his own." The court recognized that he was fully aware of the base motives behind the order and that the Jews were being killed simply because they were Jews. He had even admitted as much. However, because his own mindset could not be proved, only accessory to murder remained as a legal remedy.[96] Similarly, even though Blum "was one of the most heavily incriminated of the Janowska SS men, accused of countless murders and rumored to have a particularly brutal pattern of behavior," the court could not prove he acted as more than an accessory.[97]

In addition to this, the court wrestled with the evidence base. Despite accumulating mountains of evidence conclusively proving that the Janowska men had been stationed at the camp and involved deeply in all its operations, prosecutors struggled to prove individual events relying almost solely on eyewitness testimony. The court found the defendants not guilty on most of the charges. The explanations for the acquittals were similar. Sometimes, witness testimony faltered. In one instance, "the only witness to the crime contradicted his earlier statement, stating that he had not actually seen it with his own eyes, but rather had only heard about it. Because the court could not conclusively determine the identity of the perpetrator, he is not guilty due to lack of evidence."[98] Other times, the accusation could not be proven on the basis of only one eyewitness testimony. Or different defendants were accused of the same crimes. Or witnesses contradicted themselves. Or the court determined the evidence presented simply was not strong enough.

However, five of the eight Janowska ss men *were* convicted of accessory to murder and sentenced to prison time. Martin Büttner was found not guilty on all charges as was Ernst Preuss of Sonderkommando 1005. Paul Fox, brutal Janowska man and deputy commandant of the Jaktorów camp under Josef Grzimek, also escaped conviction. But Blum, Heinisch, Kolonko, Sobotta, and Schönbach were convicted for crimes in Lviv.

Table 4. Lviv Trial verdicts, 1968

DEFENDANT	CONVICTED	ACQUITTED	SENTENCE
Blum	1 count accessory to murder, 1 instance	18 counts	6 years, 6 months (erased by time served)
Büttner	Acquitted on all counts		
Fox	Acquitted on all counts		
Heinisch	4 counts accessory to murder, 4 instances	2 counts	8 years, 6 months
Kolonko	3 counts accessory to murder, at least 52 instances	9 counts	7 years
Preuss	Acquitted on all counts		
Schönbach	2 counts accessory to murder, at least 51 instances	11 counts	8 years
Sobotta	1 count accessory to murder, at least 50 instances	6 counts	2 years, 6 months (erased by time served)

While the results of the Lviv Trial were mixed, in the context of postwar justice, the trial could be considered fairly successful. That so many perpetrators from as obscure a place as Janowska even saw the inside of a courtroom was a great accomplishment. And the trial offered further opportunities for some limited accounting for Nazi crimes in the camp. The investigations that laid the groundwork for the Lviv Trial uncovered more Janowska perpetrators. Willy Schulze was charged but ultimately avoided prosecution due to "health issues" in 1970. Friedrich Heinen was convicted in 1978 and sentenced to life in prison. German authorities tried Hans Sobotta again, this time for crimes committed in Drohobycz, and he was sentenced to life in prison as well. The one-armed Werner Hahn was also charged but found unfit for trial. This leaves only two of the main Janowska perpetrators unaccounted for: Fritz Gebauer and Friedrich Warzok.

At the end of the war, Gebauer, the former commandant of the DAW, found himself in a makeshift Nazi unit in the Tyrol.[99] He made his way to the Soviet zone in East Germany where he linked up with his mother and wife. There he settled into civilian life, working for the Russians from whom he secured all-important identity papers. He worked building bridges and as a regional manager for a Soviet film distribution company before returning to work in manufacturing. Gebauer also did not let his ideology interfere with his advancement; he joined the East German Communist Party as well and soon became the section secretary in his factory. The former Nazi was so impressive that East German authorities began to consider him for the position of city secretary in Dessau, a city with a population of almost 100,000. But his success invited scrutiny. As the party would conduct background checks for such a position, Gebauer feared that his SS past would come to light with unpleasant consequences. So, he fled to the West in 1960 where he found another manufacturing job.[100] However, his success in escaping notice was short-lived. German authorities issued a warrant for his arrest in May 1961. An East German prosecutor noted helpfully that Gebauer had lied about his SS membership during his screening.[101] Officials held him in pretrial custody in Saarbrücken for four months before he was released as the court determined there was no risk of escape (despite the fact that Gebauer had done just that two years prior).[102] This caused outrage among survivors and the Association of Former Lwow Jews in Israel wrote directly to the Justice Minister in Saarbrücken that "it is unbelievable that the accused has been released from custody. This release ... is a grave offence against justice and an incomprehensible desecration of the dead who were murdered by Gebauer." For survivors, Gebauer's imprisonment was not about whether he might escape, but that he did not deserve to be free. "For the few survivors of this time," the association continued, "the name Gebauer personifies the people responsible for the annihilation of the Jews of Lviv."[103]

Despite this perhaps inauspicious beginning, prosecutors pursued charges against Gebauer in 1968. They charged him with 23 counts of murder during his tenure as commandant of the DAW. Also charged was his colleague Hugo Bleines, the factory manager. But this court was not as clear-eyed perhaps as that in Stuttgart, at least not initially. The judge set aside the case in a 270-page decision that delegitimized survivor testimony in excruciating detail. Regarding one charge, the court decided that "the assertion by the witness that he saw Gebauer—so he believed—going daily into the Janowska camp to get workers and to meet with Willhaus is unconvincing. It can only be that the witness incorporated rumors he had heard into his own testimony."[104] In another instance, the court concluded that "it is very doubtful whether any evidence can be produced proving that the blows by the rubber truncheon actually were responsible for [the prisoner's] death."[105] Displaying all the worst features of the German justice system, the court set aside the charges and declined to bring Gebauer to trial.

Perhaps most surprising is that the court seems to have been reacting to the prosecution's own wishes to not bring Gebauer to trial. In January 1967, the senior prosecutor wrote to the court requesting that the charges be dismissed. He wrote that he could not disprove Gebauer's claim that he had "merely kicked a Jew here and there, hit them a couple times, or boxed their ears. This would have been for reasons of work discipline. These measures would not have been injurious to the prisoners' health." Other allegations were classified as only manslaughter or attempted manslaughter, which statutes of limitations placed out of reach. Prosecutors seemed to accept that Gebauer was not a major figure in the Janowska camp as he was, in their view, a civilian "with no disciplinary power" and "merely the technical leader of the DAW." Gebauer simply was "not sufficiently suspect" and the lawyers thought it unlikely that a trial would result in his conviction.[106]

Thankfully, this reprieve did not last long and police rearrested Gebauer in December 1970. Prosecutors charged Gebauer with 22 counts of "malicious or brutal" murder aggravated by a motive of "lust to kill, greed, or base motives."[107] Ironically, Gebauer had gone from being a minor functionary to a master of life and death and received more serious charges than all the Janowska defendants in Stuttgart combined. The German monthly *Die Tat* published the details of all 22 indictments, calling them the "debit account of a cold-blooded murderer."[108] Again, survivors returned to court; this time, 55 from ten different nations testified against the "handkerchief killer."[109] Gebauer's trial lasted six months and consisted of 63 trial days. This time, Gebauer's luck ran out. The court found him guilty of three counts of murder. Specifically, it convicted him of 1) strangling a Jewish dentist for warming potatoes on a stove, 2) beating an Austrian Jewish musician to the ground and killing him by standing on his throat, and 3) together with the camp SS cook beating a Jewish prisoner to the ground and trampling him to death.[110] The court sentenced him to three life sentences on June 29, 1971. This might have been a satisfactory execution of justice, but there was a final twist in this story: Gebauer would not spend any time in prison. He was deemed not healthy enough for incarceration. A seething *Die Tat* scorned this "biological amnesty," noting that "under these circumstances, there can no longer be any talk of atonement for Nazi crimes. Prison sentences become a farce when they amount to an acquittal."[111] Hermann Langbein, a survivor and founder of the International Auschwitz Committee, bitterly observed that "the courts are often very generous in this regard." Medical documentation of unfitness for incarceration, he continued, constituted a popular method "by which Nazi criminals escape justice."[112] Fritz Gebauer died in 1979. He was the only Janowska commandant to stand trial for his crimes. Indeed, from 1949 to 2006, German courts convicted only 6,498 Nazis for their crimes.[113]

One other person of note also escaped justice due to health reasons. American authorities stripped Ukrainian policeman Ivan Kalymon of his citizenship in 2007 for lying about his participation in the Holocaust on his immigration documents. A deportation order was issued in 2011 but no country could be found to take him. Obstructive to the end, Kalymon denied any wrongdoing, stating, "They want to remove me, an old man. I never was arrested, pay my taxes. I don't know anyone as honest as me."[114] He was fortunate. Many of his fellow Ukrainian guards were not. Sixty-five former eastern European guards were tried and convicted by the Soviets, many of whom were executed.¹¹⁵

Friedrich Warzok, the last lord of Janowska, was declared officially dead in Berlin in 1950. His former captive Simon Wiesenthal and others were not so sure. In 1960, an Israeli investigator wrote to the Central Office in Ludwigsburg: "Based on conversations with witnesses about Warzok, I am convinced that we are dealing with a particularly cunning and crafty criminal who I would not put past a faked death certificate." He further asserted that "I am personally of the opinion that Warzok is hiding under an assumed name and is still alive."¹¹⁶ Simon Wiesenthal never stopped searching for the men of Janowska and reported a sighting of Warzok in 1966 in Hamburg.¹¹⁷ Perhaps he traveled over the well-worn path through Austria to Italy and then out of Europe. It is thought that the former Nazi escaped to Cairo, assisted by the movable wealth he had accumulated in the camp. The date and location of his death remain unknown.¹¹⁸ The man perhaps most responsible for the murder of the Jews of Lviv, Friedrich Katzmann, also evaded prosecution. After the war, he abandoned his wife and children, living under the name Bruno Albrecht in Darmstadt. The former ss and police leader for Lviv was never discovered by authorities. On his deathbed in 1957, he revealed his identity to a priest, leaving his ultimate judgment to a higher authority.

Ghosts in Transit: Janowska in Memory

Though its last inhabitants had been driven out in one way or another, Janowska remained.¹¹⁹ The camp's afterlife symbolizes in many ways the disappearance of the Holocaust from public memory in the city of Lviv. Indeed, the City of Lions is one in which memory is often hidden, buried, or painted over. As historian William J. Turkel has observed, "Every place is an archive that accumulates material traces of its past."¹²⁰ These traces tell a story, as do the ways in which they are cared for or abandoned. In the older parts of Lviv, the wearing away of more recent plaster reveals "ghost signs" in Yiddish and Polish. Routine maintenance on city streets uncovers face-down Jewish tombstones used as paving material. Locals also frequently unearth more grim reminders of the city's violent past. One journalist noted that "Lviv is a city where bones, not unlike the wartime history that left them here, cannot seem to stay buried."[121] Lost victims of the "bloodlands" are often discovered, with varying reactions depending on the possible circumstances of their lives and deaths: partisans killed by the Nazis, partisans killed by the Soviets, Poles and Ukrainians killed by the Nazis and Soviets, Poles and Ukrainians killed by each other, Jews killed by the Nazis (or Ukrainians or Poles). Each excavation has the potential to open old wounds. Though some care less than others; a retired telephone operator in the Lviv region lives in a house built on top of a suspected Gestapo mass grave. He shrugged and told a reporter, "It was a long time ago, and it doesn't bother me. Let them lay there. I'm not afraid of ghosts."[122]

Yet ghosts are indeed present in Lviv. This presence can be surprising. Simon Schama has noted that "in our mind's eye we are accustomed to think of the Holocaust as having no landscape—or at best one emptied of features and color, shrouded in night and fog, blanketed by perpetual winter, collapsed into shades of dun and gray."[123] Yet this is not so. The physical space of the Janowska camp exists in a variety of states, a reminder of a past that most of the locals have no reason to remember. Janowska never received the concerted attempts at preservation that Auschwitz or Majdanek benefited from. Perhaps this is because the overwhelming majority of Janowska's victims were Jews and almost no Jewish population remained in Lviv to advocate for the memorialization of Janowska. Like many things about the past, it remained physically visible but still mostly hidden.

Like the fog that often blankets the valley in which the camp sits, the history of Janowska the place is obscured by the passage of time. Photographs taken by the Soviets in 1944 reveal the camp at the end of its life. They show warehouse buildings destroyed and reduced to brick walls. Piles of enamelware, buckets, colanders, teapots, and other personal items were scattered around the compound. Shoes lay in heaps. The camp headquarters building showed signs of fire, with sooty smears around its windows. The guard towers remained standing as did the guard shack at the entrance to the inner precinct of the camp, where the roll-call square was. The Death Brigade's bone grinder sat abandoned on its damaged trailer. Further afield, the Soviets documented the black scars in the earth that marked the burial pits for the ashes of the victims.

In March 1945, a group of Janowska survivors including Samuel Drix returned to visit the camp. A Red Army unit had occupied the space and a Soviet officer had taken up residence in Willhaus's villa. The barracks and gallows were gone. "All that remained," Drix remembered, "was the latrine in which the floor was completely covered with hardened human excrement from which many shoes, among them children's shoes, were protruding." He was, perhaps unfairly in 1945, disappointed that the Russians had not made "the slightest effort . . . to preserve this place of martyrdom of so many thousands as a historical monument of inhumanity."[124] As at many former camps, practical considerations also determined the usage of space.

The Soviets first reused the site as a KGB prison for their own prisoners. This repurposing also demonstrated the deep distrust that the "liberators" had even for Nazi victims. In fact, the Soviet regime viewed those imprisoned by the Nazis with deep suspicion and the unfair judgment that captivity indicated complicity. The secret police apparatus used the site as a "filtration camp" so they could assess the reliability of people returning from Nazi camps. So, Mykola Petrenko, who had been held in Janowska in 1942 before being deported to Germany for forced labor, found himself imprisoned again in the camp, now under Russian control in 1945 before, again, being sent away for forced labor.[125] The KGB used the grounds of Janowska for this sorting until 1947 when the prison became part of Lviv Transit Prison No. 25. Under the Soviets, the site continued to function as a prison for mainly criminals and political offenders.[126] The newly independent Ukraine smoothly took ownership in 1999. In the valleys around the camp where so many had been murdered, the locals bred pigs and the police trained working dogs from 1982 to 2004.[127] When survivors approached to pay their respects, the dogs bayed and snarled at them.[128] Most of the DAW section of the camp was not included in the prison and returned to mainly residential use, with many of the factory buildings replaced by houses and apartment blocks.

Survivors of the camp did try to commemorate the site, though often from afar. They erected a small stone monument in the first two years after the war that evocatively referred to the "valley of tears" and called on God to "avenge their honor." It was later removed.[129] Alexander Schwarz emerged as one of the most prominent survivors dedicated to memorializing the camp.

He had arrived with his father during the Great Aktion of August 1942.[130] During an evening roll call, Peter Blum shot his father. Schwarz's time in the camp also included working in the Death Brigade. In October 1943, he and some comrades escaped from the Kleparów station. Schwarz survived the war in the forest eating berries and wild game. He then earned a PhD in Poland before moving to Germany in 1968. But he never forgot his roots in Lviv, and concern for both the living and the dead of Janowska moved him to establish the Janowska Camp Foundation in the 1990s.[131] He and another survivor raised funds for a simple monument that was placed in 1993, fifty years after the prisoner uprising. The text in English and Hebrew reads: "Let the memory of all the Nazi genocide victims in Janowska Death Camp remain forever, 1941–1943." The stone also references the Soviet-era death toll of two hundred thousand. An English and Ukrainian sign from 2003 commands: "Passerby, bow your head! In front of you see a spot of the former Janowska death camp. The ground is moaning. Here the innocent victims were tortured and tormented; here they were executed and sent to the gas chambers. May the memory of the innocently murdered live forever! Eternal malediction be upon executioners!" A plaque on the nearby Kleparów station commemorates the "about 500,000 [who] passed here in trains, from March 1942 till the beginning of 1943." In 2018, the Territory of Terror Museum in Lviv built a bus stop with an exhibition on the camp, and a project is underway to build a memorial park in the valley of death, though this has yet to be done as of the printing of this book.[132]

Much memorial work remains to be done around the former camp as well as in Lviv itself. Locals now live in the former camp headquarters building, which is still very much recognizable from its days as a place of terror. Remaining buildings from the DAW are lost within the modern residential neighborhood. Any extant features from the ZAL-L are off-limits as that part of the site remains in use today as Ukrainian Penal Colony No. 30. Life inside is decidedly bleak, as perhaps fitting for the prison's location.[133] A Council of Europe report condemned the "appalling material conditions" there in 2017.[134] Ironically, the prisoners in Penal Colony 30 labor at making the same kinds of products that DAW prisoners did. A sign on the wall outside advertises the prison's factory as an "outstanding" source of furniture and various metalworks.

Other important Holocaust sites in the city are gradually receiving more attention. In 2016, a memorial was erected near the remnants of the Golden Rose Synagogue. The site is an important and solemn installation, with marble stones displaying testimony from the time. Sadly, just steps away, the Golden Rose restaurant markets itself as a "Jewish-themed" establishment. Two menorahs flank the doors, above which the restaurant's name is written in Hebrew. It is nothing short of a monstrous caricature. Inside, Judaica covers the walls and a waiter arrives often with fake sidelocks. There are no prices; one must haggle for the prices in a none-too-subtle nod to antisemitic stereotypes.[135] One cannot miss the stark symbolism of the proximity of the restaurant to the ruins of the Golden Rose Synagogue. It easily encapsulates the complexity of the incomplete memory work in the city and in Ukraine as a whole. As recently as 2018, Ukrainian nationalists marched through the streets of Lviv to celebrate the 14th SS "Galizien" Division, and Holocaust memorials are frequently vandalized.[136] On the other hand, a museum located on the site of the former ghetto opened in 2016. It treats the Holocaust history of the city along with the Soviet period. In addition, the remarkable Lviv Center for Urban History has committed itself to presenting a complete and unblinking perspective on the city's past to its public and offers virtual tours of Jewish Lviv.

The blood spilled on the grounds of the camp, in the hills behind it, and on the streets of Lviv continues to haunt the families of survivors, of victims, of the perpetrators, and of the bystanders. In some instances, that haunting seems literal. In 2013, Julie Keefer visited the site. She had been born in Lviv in 1941 and survived hidden by Polish Catholics. Julie's grandfather had been imprisoned in Janowska. During her visit sixty-eight years after leaving Lviv, Julie met a woman who lived next door to the former camp, in the area of the DAW. With tears in her eyes, the woman said, "I live in that apartment building right near the prison. I hear chilling, ghostly sounds all the time. Terrible things were done by the Nazis who lived there. It's hard to sleep peacefully in that house."[137] That house could easily also be Lviv or Ukraine.

Conclusion

> Had these sands been miraculously endowed with the faculty of speech, they doubtless would have related countless Jewish tragedies that took place there. Next to Bełżec, these sands served as the largest mass grave of the Jews of Lvov.
> —Rabbi David Kahane, *Lvov Ghetto Diary*

In Julian Barnes's novel *The Sense of an Ending* (2011), the main character tells his history teacher that "history was the lies of the victors." His teacher replies, "as long as you remember that it is also the self-delusions of the defeated." By the end, however, the narrator reflects that history was more "memories of the survivors, most of whom are neither victorious nor defeated."[1] The story of the sixty acres at 134 Janowska Street embodies all these complexities, from the memories of survivors to the self-delusions of the defeated. It is a story not just of a place but also of the Holocaust writ large, an act that contains all the lessons of the larger play. It provides unique insights into how the Holocaust unfolded on the ground, in the lives of real people. This is the critical point: we cannot truly begin to understand a historical event until we walk in the paths of those who were there, not just in a figurative sense but in a physical one as well. Too often, we historians remain tethered to archival documents and do not venture into the remains of the worlds we study. The story of the camp illustrates the value of an intensive local focus, but one that does not lose sight of the broader implications.

Janowska may have been located in a backwater of the Nazi empire, but it played an essential and almost completely unrecognized part in the murder of over five hundred thousand human beings. The camp may well be the most important Holocaust site that most have never heard of. From its establishment during the violence of Nazi colonization of the East, Janowska played a central and unique role in the destruction of Galician Jews. One prominent historian has noted that "selections were generally carried out during ghetto-clearing while forced labour and mass murder by gassing took place in different places ... Only in Janowska did a large combined labour and extermination complex develop."[2] One must also consider the camp in its function as an accomplice in the murders of most of the Jews who died in the gas chambers of Bełżec. The camp served as a node for the mass extermination of communities throughout the region, connecting them, selecting workers, and loading trains for the final transit. Those workers pulled off the trains and out of the ghettos represent another function of the camp complex: to exploit the Jews for forced labor. It operated as a hub for construction and manufacturing, not just within the camp itself but also throughout Lviv and the surrounding region. Forced labor was always intimately connected with the Nazi genocidal project.

Ultimately, however, the shadow of death loomed largest over Janowska. The Nazis murdered perhaps as many as eighty thousand Jews there during the four years they occupied Lviv. This death toll would exceed that of the much more (in)famous Majdanek camp near Lublin, a place often considered as an extermination center alongside Auschwitz, Chelmno, and the Operation Reinhard camps. The Germans in Janowska killed in small, spontaneous actions as well as massive, well-organized operations. Indeed, when the gas chambers dedicated to Galicia closed, the Nazis seamlessly accelerated their usage of the camp as a dedicated extermination site. How this small place became such a lethal part of the Final Solution (and how it has been forgotten) has been an important element of this book.

But the victims of the camp cannot and should not be reduced to numbers or homicidal scorecards. They were people, individuals, each with a unique experience and history. Indeed, instead of noting that as many as eighty thousand were killed in Janowska, we might better say that the act of murdering a Jew was repeated eighty thousand times. The volume of sources from survivors, from memoirs to drawings to video testimony, gives us unprecedented insights into the ways in which individuals experienced life and death in the camp. We see how these people were forced to navigate the "choiceless choices" that the Holocaust created, and we uncover the details of their oppression. But the experience of Jews in the camp also reveals a larger truth about resistance. These men and women did not go like "lambs to the slaughter" as some have claimed. The history of Janowska shows the myriad ways in which prisoners fought back, to include the extraordinary heroism of rebellion and escape.

Ironically, the one organization that recognized the magnitude of Nazi crimes in the camp was the German judiciary. Janowska occupied the attention of the second largest Nazi trial in German history after the Frankfurt Auschwitz Trial. It left behind an incredibly detailed record of recordings and transcripts that really merits an entire book in its own right. The trial is far more, however, than the sum of its parts. It gives us not only a wealth of specific survivor testimony but also much of what we know about the perpetrators themselves. Those two years in Stuttgart and the many years preceding them laid bare the self-delusions of the defeated, both the SS men of the camp and the German nation as a whole. Through the treatment of Janowska and its crimes in the courts, we can take the measure of an incomplete and often disingenuous attempt at coming to terms with the past. At the same time, the story of the trial and the investigative process exposes the intimate and bizarre ways in which survivors and perpetrators interacted after the war as well as the courage it took for these former prisoners to confront their oppressors, in the street or in the courtroom. Indeed, the court judged the Janowska perpetrators in Stuttgart primarily on the basis of survivor testimony as few wartime documents from the camp itself have survived.

It is this element of experience that comes through so strongly when examining the Holocaust through the lens of the Janowska camp, that of space. We do not live our lives in the abstract and we do not remember them that way either. Our life experiences are firmly grounded in our geographies and our chronologies. Whether at the scale of our residence or city or nation, we encounter the world as a chain of places and times. We remember *where* we were when an event happened. Conversely, our surroundings play an active role in what happens to us. The Janowska camp, through its rich combination of textual and visual evidence, demonstrates this spatial truth in action. The urban geography of Lviv and the location of rail lines, for example, determined where the camp would be built, and the hills behind it, though deemed constricting for industry, became a perfect site for executions. Even at the scale of the individual, places in the camp took on contexts that could mean the difference between life and death. The newly arrived person who did not know that the Appellplatz was an easy shot from the Willhaus residence might not survive the first day, while seasoned prisoners knew to walk behind the barracks if possible. The very built environment of the camp took on emotional resonance. The laundry became in the minds of all the prisoners both a female area and a place of sexual violence and exploitation, forever bearing the mark of Peter Blum. For perpetrators, it represented a place of enjoyment and sexual gratification. Indeed, meanings could be complex. During the day, the latrines, though grotesque and filthy, were places of safety for prisoners, precisely because that filth dissuaded the ss from entering. Located out of the main sight lines of the camp, the latrine buildings functioned as places of commerce, communication, and fellowship. But, at night, when the prisoners were confined to their barracks, those same latrines became places of fear and death. The ss men enjoyed ambushing prisoners who attempted to relieve themselves there, often killing them.

Connections between people were just as important as those between people and their environment. Geography again plays a key role. As one of the very few truly urban camps in the East, most Janowska prisoners remained "at home." They were minutes from their pre-cataclysm lives. Families separated by the Nazis remained somewhat connected, for a time. This offered opportunities that other camp inmates did not have. As the central hub for the deportation of Jews in Galicia, Janowska brought together people from surrounding towns and villages, bringing with them their experiences and much-demanded information about the unfolding of the Holocaust around them. For a few prisoners, the camp served as a conduit to Auschwitz, Płaszów, and concentration camps within Germany itself.

Movement over space and time also critically influenced the perpetrators. Janowska shows the hidden connections between the ss men of the camp with one of the only social network analyses of the Holocaust. Reconstructing the paths of these men yields rare insights into their overlapping careers and experiences. A surprising number of the Janowska perpetrators shared similar geographic origins and assignments; many knew each other before arriving in Lviv. The threads of this web ran both ways as well. The men of the camp SS, though often of low rank, dispersed throughout Distrikt Galizien to command their own camps or ghettos. They brought with them both personal relationships and lessons learned about the business of genocide. Some, like Adolf Kolonko, returned "home" to Janowska as well. One potential result of this social network was the extreme brutality of these men. Another seems to be a kind of gruesome teamwork where these men reunited at various aktions and ghetto liquidations. Glimpses from surviving sources also suggest that some of these men maintained contact with each other after the war, raising fascinating questions about the nature of these relationships and what functions they may have served.

Above all, the Janowska camp stands as connective tissue, tying together grand plans and ideologies, regional peculiarities, and individual quirks and ambitions. As the subject of this book, it serves the same function for our understanding of the Holocaust. Through the lens of this camp, we can see how Nazi ideologies of antisemitism and colonial conquest at the highest echelons were filtered through changing situational constraints and demands at the local level of their execution. It also reveals the contradictions and power struggles between organizations and individuals in the Nazi system. Changes in the camp itself often reflected these debates. And, so, in the lives of survivors and perpetrators, we can see how the convictions and whims of so-called great men impacted the lives (and deaths) of actual human beings. All genocides are, in the end, local. This is not to discount the critical importance of ideology, power, and policy at a variety of scales; it is simply to acknowledge where these paths ultimately led. They led to the "between wire," to the gas chambers, to cramped cellars beneath barns, to courtrooms, and to the family memories of millions. It seems appropriate to conclude with the words of the Nobel Prize–winning Polish poet Czesław Miłosz, who himself helped rescue Jews in occupied Poland. He captured the task of the historian as well as the witness to history, saying, "You, who survived, received a mandate from all the others, who became quiet forever. You can only fulfil your responsibility by trying to reconstruct all that was, as it once was, rescuing the past from fabrications and legends."[3]

Notes

PROLOGUE

1. A note on nomenclature: I use "Lviv" as this is the current spelling of the city in Ukraine. If in a primary source or document, I use the extant name Lwów (Polish), Lemberg (German), or Lvov (Russian). I will generally use the Polish name of locations in the text as the region was Polish at the time; however, I will provide the Ukrainian name at the first mention. In addition, if I use the German name of a location in Poland or Ukraine, I will provide the current location name at first mention.
2. Chetverikov, "Geoinformational Determination," 98.
3. Center for Urban History of East Central Europe, "Former Beth Tahora."
4. Bartov, *Erased*, 16.
5. Matzevot translations by Howard Goldstein, "Jewish Roots in Ukraine," Facebook Group, accessed May 15, 2019.

INTRODUCTION

Epigraph: Lanzmann, *Shoah*, 70.
1. Honigsman, *The Catastrophy of Jewry in Lvov*, 7.
2. "Hirschhorn, Bernard Statement, 9 November 1948," StAL, EL 317 III, Bü 1524, 2–3.
3. "Bleines Hugo Statement, 21 October 1953," BA-ZS, B162/5763, 224.
4. "Hirschhorn, Bernard Statement, 9 November 1948," 3–4.
5. Richman, *Why?*, 10.
6. "Rosen, Chaim Statement, 11 September 1960," StAL, EL 317 III, Bü 1498, 99; "LG Saarbrücken Urteil gg. Fritz Gebauer, 29 June 1971," BA-ZS, B162/14465, 94–96.
7. Richman, *Why?*, 41.
8. "Hirschhorn, Bernard Statement, 9 November 1948," 4.
9. Yones, *Smoke in the Sand*, 170.

10. Friedman, "The Destruction of the Jews of Lwow," 265.
11. Kahane, *Lvov Ghetto Diary*, 16; Friedman, *Ich Träumte von Brot und Büchern*, 98; Maltiel-Gerstenfeld, *My Private War*, 61.
12. Milton and Stallard, *John Milton*, 23.
13. Ginsberg, "'Howl,'" in *Collected Poems*, 131.
14. Sandkühler, "Das Zwangsarbeitslager Lemberg-Janowska," 617.
15. "Rosen, Chaim, Statement, 11 September 1960," 102–3.
16. "Wells (Welizcker), Leon, Statement, 21 September 1944," BA-ZS: B162/29309, 353.
17. Wells, *The Janowska Road*, 158.
18. Sandkühler, "Das Zwangsarbeitslager Lemberg-Janowska," 616.
19. Center for Urban History of East Central Europe, "Former Tempel Synagogue."
20. Stromer, *Memoirs of an Unfortunate Person*, 112.
21. "Augenzeuge von 35 Mordtaten, Stuttgarter Zeitung, Nr. 287, 14 December 1966," YVA: RG-P13, file 189, 17.
22. "Rogowski, Marian Statement, 13 November 1963," StAL: EL 317 III, Bü 1516, 82.
23. Stromer, *Memoirs of an Unfortunate Person*, 127.
24. "Roger, Stanley Statement, 24 June 1964," StAL: EL 317 III, Bü 1516, 269.
25. "Porath, Zeev Statement, 8 June 1961," StAL: EL 48–2, Bü 397, 1347–48.
26. Arad, *Belzec, Sobibor, Treblinka*, 247.
27. "Wind, Josef Interview," William Breman Jewish Heritage Museum, Cuba Family Archives: Children of Holocaust Survivors Project (CHS) (1989), 16.
28. Drix, *Witness to Annihilation*, 81.
29. Borwicz, *The University of Criminals*, 38.
30. Agamben, *Homo Sacer*, 170.
31. Drix, *Witness to Annihilation*, 81.
32. "Wind, Josef Interview," 15.
33. "Lewinter, Herman," USC Shoah Foundation Institute: Interview #8443, Visual History Archive, 1995.
34. "Lubasz, Marcel Testimony," USHMM, RG 02.200, 1994, 2.
35. Friedländer, *The Years of Extermination*, xv–xvi.
36. Browning, "Evocation," 244.
37. I am not the first to observe the hybrid nature of the camp. Thomas Sandkühler has called the camp a "multi-functional camp" in Aktion Reinhard Sandkühler, "Das Zwangsarbeitslager Lemberg-Janowska," 615.
38. Sandkühler, "Das Zwangsarbeitslager Lemberg-Janowska," 606.
39. Desbois, *The Holocaust by Bullets*, 94.

40. Sandkühler, *"Endlösung" in Galizien*, 190–91. He suggests that "substantially" more Jews may have died in Janowska than at Majdanek, whose Jewish death toll he suggests was as high as eighty thousand.
41. Winstone, *The Dark Heart of Hitler's Europe*, 189.
42. Lower, *Hitler's Furies*, 133.
43. Sources for the numbers killed at Janowska from 1941 to 1944 are sparse, as are some of the records regarding numbers of Jews deported to Bełżec and Sobibor from Lviv. Indeed, even the starting number of Jews in Lviv is less than certain, given the refugee movement. Katzmann in his well-known report counted 254,989 Jews "resettled" from Lviv and 434,329 from the District. (See "Record of Soviet Military Court of the Carpathian Military Region against Prichodjko et al., 14 December 1966," BA-ZS: B162/29309, 75–76.) The Judenrat in Lwów reported 119,000 residents in October 1941, but historians have placed this number higher, such as 140,000 at the beginning of 1942. Both Nazi and Jewish sources are problematic in that they often do not account for those Jews not registered or those hiding in the ghetto. (See "Information of the Extraordinary State Commission on Atrocities of the German-Fascist Invaders in the Territory of Lvov Region, December 23, 1944," in *Nazi Crimes in Ukraine*, 213.)
44. Wiesenthal and Wechsberg, *The Murderers among Us*, 272.
45. Pohl, "The Murder of Ukraine's Jews," 23.
46. See Friedman, *Zaglada Zydów Lwowskich*; Aleksiun, "Philip Friedman"; Amar, *The Paradox of Ukrainian Lviv*; Honigsman, *The Catastrophy of Jewry in Lvov*; Sandkühler, *"Endlösung" in Galizien*; Yones, *Smoke in the Sand*; Sandkühler, "Das Zwangsarbeitslager Lemberg-Janowska"; and Mick, *Lemberg, Lwów, L'viv, 1914–1947*. Sandkühler has written the only lengthy and truly scholarly study of the camp, a book chapter in German. Additionally, Dieter Pohl covers it well in the context of the Holocaust in Galicia. Elsewhere, it receives mention but cursory analysis. Other works focus on the important topic of the larger unfolding of the Holocaust in Galicia (Pohl, Sandkühler), Lwów during the Holocaust (Honigsman, Yones), or as a multiethnic, multinational city (Amar, Mick). Amar's excellent study covers the history of the city from before World War II to the Soviet period. The book by Christoph Mick covers 1914–47 but does not mention the camp in any detail.
47. Brewer, "Microhistory," 104.
48. Friedländer, "An Integrated History of the Holocaust," 25.
49. Frydel, "The Ongoing Challenge," 624.
50. Friedländer, "An Integrated History of the Holocaust," 23.

1. CITY OF LIONS

Epigraph: Alfred Döblin, *Reise in Polen*, 1924, qtd. in Mick, *Lemberg, Lwów, L'viv, 1914–1947*, 209.

1. Reid, *Borderland*, 70.
2. Bechtel, "Lemberg/Lwów/Lvov/Lviv," 62.
3. Yones, *Smoke in the Sand*, 13.
4. Goldstein, *A Convenient Hatred*, 141.
5. Kubicek, *The History of Ukraine*, 40.
6. Roth, *The Radetzky March*, 129.
7. Mick, *Lemberg, Lwów, L'viv, 1914–1947*, 4.
8. Mick, 5.
9. Mick.
10. Reid, *Borderland*, 73.
11. Center for Urban History of East Central Europe, "Former Skarbek Theater," Lviv Interactive, accessed May 29, 2019.
12. Rubin, *Against All Odds*, 73.
13. Center for Urban History of East Central Europe, "Past, Present and Memory: Rediscovering Jewish Lviv," Lviv Interactive, 2016, accessed May 30, 2019.
14. Rubin, *Against All Odds*, 72.
15. Perlman, "Di Goldene Royz," 140.
16. Center for Urban History of East Central Europe, "Gimpel's Theater," Lviv Interactive, accessed May 30, 2019.
17. Rubin, *Against All Odds*, 10.
18. "Polska-Turcja 6:1," *Przeglad Sportowy* (Krakow), September 18, 1926, 1.
19. Amar, *The Paradox of Ukrainian Lviv*, 27.
20. Amar, 27.
21. Mick, *Lemberg, Lwów, L'viv, 1914–1947*, 9.
22. Mick, 10.
23. Wawro, *A Mad Catastrophe*, 154.
24. Wawro, 156.
25. Mick, *Lemberg, Lwów, L'viv, 1914–1947*, 64.
26. Viertel, *Das Unbelehrbare Herz*, 102, 119; Viertel, *The Kindness of Strangers*, 86.
27. Mick, *Lemberg, Lwów, L'viv, 1914–1947*, 41.
28. Borwicz, *The University of Criminals*, 154.
29. Schindler, *Fall of the Double Eagle*, 246.
30. Perlman, "Di Goldene Royz," 154.
31. Wawro, *A Mad Catastrophe*, 311.
32. Mick, *Lemberg, Lwów, L'viv, 1914–1947*, 70.

33. Mick, 72.
34. Amar, *The Paradox of Ukrainian Lviv*, 30.
35. Mick, *Lemberg, Lwów, L'viv, 1914–1947*, 147.
36. Mick, 158.
37. Mick, 159.
38. Wendland, "Neighbors as Betrayers," 145.
39. Viertel, *Das Unbelehrbare Herz*, 130.
40. Wendland, "Neighbors as Betrayers," 145.
41. Drix, *Witness to Annihilation*, 10.
42. Rubin, *Against All Odds*, 49.
43. "Stiffel, Frank Testimony, 4 February 1985," FVAHT: 963043.
44. Stachura, *Poland, 1918–1945*, 95.
45. Mick, *Lemberg, Lwów, L'viv, 1914–1947*, 217.
46. Rubin, *Against All Odds*, 40.
47. Mick, *Lemberg, Lwów, L'viv, 1914–1947*, 219.
48. "100 Jews Injured in Lemberg," *Palestine Post* (Jerusalem), November 30, 1932, 1; "More Trouble in Lemberg," *Palestine Post* (Jerusalem), December 15, 1932, 6; "The Riots in Poland-Sensational Discoveries in Lemberg," *Palestine Post* (Jerusalem), December 6, 1932, 2.
49. Drix, *Witness to Annihilation*, 10.
50. Lemkin, *Totally Unofficial*, 20.
51. Amar, *The Paradox of Ukrainian Lviv*, 78–79.
52. Mick, *Lemberg, Lwów, L'viv, 1914–1947*, 245.
53. Rubin, *Against All Odds*, 68.
54. "Unternehmen Tannenberg," *Der Spiegel*, August 13, 1979; "Translation of *Szkola Okuricienstwa*," STAL: EL 317 III, Bü 1720, 79–80.
55. Rubin, *Against All Odds*, 85.
56. Mick, *Lemberg, Lwów, L'viv, 1914–1947*, 259.
57. Zayarnyuk, *Lviv's Uncertain Destination*, 157.
58. Rubin, *Against All Odds*, 90.
59. Rubin, 93.
60. Arad, *The Holocaust in the Soviet Union*, 43.
61. "Poland under the Russians," *West Australian* (Perth), January 13, 1940, 8.
62. Zayarnyuk, *Lviv's Uncertain Destination*, 158.
63. Rubin, *Against All Odds*, 101.
64. Kochanski, *Eagle Unbowed*, 127.
65. Yones, *Smoke in the Sand*, 49.
66. Mick, *Lemberg, Lwów, L'viv, 1914–1947*, 267.

67. "Gebauer, Fritz Statement 4 May 1962," BA-ZS: B162/5764, 490–91; "Translation of *Szkola Okuricienstwa*," 15.
68. Drix, *Witness to Annihilation*, 5.
69. Kochanski, *Eagle Unbowed*, 119.
70. Beorn, *The Holocaust in Eastern Europe*, 83. The estimates range from 309,000 to 318,000 from Soviet convoy documents, to 316,000 to 323,000 from NKVD data, to 980,000 from the Polish Embassy in the USSR. This data comes from Wróbel, "Class War or Ethnic Cleansing," 27.
71. Amar, *The Paradox of Ukrainian Lviv*, 51.
72. Grünbart, "Das Blutbad von Lemberg," 20.
73. Gross, *Revolution from Abroad*, 154.
74. Kochanski, *Eagle Unbowed*, 129.
75. Wróbel, "Class War or Ethnic Cleansing," 21; Mick, "Incompatible Experiences," 341.
76. Mick, *Lemberg, Lwów, L'viv, 1914–1947*, 272.
77. Wells, *The Janowska Road*, 28–29.
78. Murray and Millett, *A War to Be Won*, 120.
79. Hastings, *Inferno*, 146; Murphy, *What Stalin Knew*, 218.
80. Struve, *Deutsche Herrschaft*, 247.
81. Struve, 252.
82. Grünbart, "Das Blutbad von Lemberg," 20.
83. Kaplan, *I Never Left Janowska*, 36.

2. EIN FURIOSO

Epigraph: Edmund Kessler, Lviv, in Kessler, *The Wartime Diary of Edmund Kessler*, 33.
1. Perlman, "Di Goldene Royz," 190.
2. Struve, *Deutsche Herrschaft*, 253.
3. Yones, *Smoke in the Sand*, 78.
4. Sandkühler, "Anti-Jewish Policy."
5. Mick, *Lemberg, Lwów, L'viv, 1914–1947*, 291.
6. Folkmann and Szende, *The Promise Hitler Kept*, 42.
7. "Translation of *Szkola Okuricienstwa*," 2.
8. "Goldberg, Abraham Trial Testimony, Band 77, 10 January 1967," StAL: EL 317 III, Bü 1578, 2443.
9. Redner, *Recollections*, 14–15.
10. Struve, *Deutsche Herrschaft*, 256.
11. Altenburger, "Oberfeldkommandantur 365."

12. Struve, *Deutsche Herrschaft*, 256.
13. Arad, *The Holocaust in the Soviet Union*, 116.
14. "Einsatzgruppen: Number of Jews Killed," *Holocaust Denial on Trial*, accessed July 9, 2019. https://www.hdot.org/debunking-denial/ezg5-number-killed/.
15. Lozowick, "Rollbahn Mord," 223.
16. Arad, *The Holocaust in the Soviet Union*, 90.
17. Struve, *Deutsche Herrschaft*, 247–48.
18. Rich, "Armed Ukrainians in L'viv," 271.
19. "Stiffel, Frank Testimony, 4 February 1985"; Rich, "Armed Ukrainians in L'viv," 271.
20. "Memo: Establishment and Financing of the Ukrainian Police in the Galician Districts of Lemberg, Stanislau, and Tarnopol, 29 July 1941," Government Exhibit P12: United States of America, Plaintiff, v. John Kalymon, a.k.a. Ivan, Iwan, John Kalymon/Kalymun, Defendant (2007), 3–4.
21. "Goldberg, Abraham Trial Testimony, Band 77, 10 January 1967," 2443; "Survivor Tells of Lemberg Massacres," *The Guardian*, February 4, 1960, Leo Baeck Institute: Abraham Goldberg Collection (AR 10769).
22. Kahane, *Lvov Ghetto Diary*, 6.
23. Mick, *Lemberg, Lwów, L'viv, 1914–1947*, 292.
24. Struve, *Deutsche Herrschaft*, 271, 311–12.
25. Kahane, *Lvov Ghetto Diary*, 86.
26. Lower, "Pogroms, Mob Violence and Genocide," 231.
27. Browning and Matthäus, *The Origins of the Final Solution*, 549.
28. See "Atrocities against Jews," USHMM, RG-60.0441, Film ID: 402.
29. "Gerner, Mendel Statement, 23 September 1944," BA-ZS: B162/29309, 211–12.
30. Beorn, *The Holocaust in Eastern Europe*, 137.
31. Redner, *Recollections*, 14.
32. Jack Fleischer, "Soviet Lays Waste to Abandoned Cities," *New York Times*, July 7, 1941, 2.
33. Struve, *Deutsche Herrschaft*, 394.
34. "Opfer russischer Massaker im Baltikum und Südrussland," USHMM: RG-60.0328, Film ID: 202B; "Opfer russischer Massaker im Baltikum und Südrussland (2)," USHMM: RG-60.1239, Film ID: 2887.
35. "Deutsche Wochenschau #566, 9 July 1941," USHMM: RG-60.0267, Film ID: 201.
36. "Excerpts from Four Policy Texts by Rosenberg's Office Regarding Propaganda and Public Relations Work with Reference to the Soviet Union (Typed, No Signature, Stamped 'Dienststelle Rosenberg'), No Date (Spring 1941)," in *The Political Diary of Alfred Rosenberg and the Onset of the Holocaust*, 373.

37. *Oxford English Dictionary.*
38. Struve, *Deutsche Herrschaft*, 394.
39. "Extract from Guidelines by Heydrich for Higher SS and Police Leaders in the Occupied Territories of the Soviet Union, July 2, 1941," in *Documents on the Holocaust*, 378.
40. "Teletype, Heydrich to Einsatzruppen Leaders, 29 July 1941," in *Die Einsatzgruppen in der Besetzten Sowjetunion, 1941/42: Die Tätigkeits-und Lageberichte des Chefs der Sicherheitspolizei und des SD*, ed. Peter Klein (Berlin: Edition Hentrich, 1997), 319.
41. Krausnick and Wilhelm, *Die Truppe des Weltanschauungskrieges*, 186–87.
42. Struve, *Deutsche Herrschaft*, 395–96.
43. Yones, *Smoke in the Sand*, 77–78.
44. Kessler, *The Wartime Diary of Edmund Kessler*, 9.
45. Connelly, "Nazis and Slavs," 31.
46. Sobieski, "Reminiscenses from Lwow, 1939–1945," 359.
47. "Porath, Zeev Statement, 6 June 1961," StAL: EL 48-2, Bü 397, 1319.
48. "Record of Soviet Commission for the Discovery and Investigation of German-Fascist Crimes in the City of Lemberg, 1–6 November 1944," BA-ZS: B162/29309, 5.
49. "Record of Soviet Commission," BA-ZS: B162/29309,
50. Vysotsky et al., *Nazi Crimes in Ukraine*, 209–10; "Modernism in Lviv," Lviv Interactive, Center for Urban History of East Central Europe, accessed July 20, 2019.
51. Kenez, "Pogroms and White Ideology in the Russian Civil War," 295.
52. Mick, *Lemberg, Lwów, L'viv, 1914–1947*, 294.
53. Yones, *Smoke in the Sand*, 92–93.
54. Kessler, *The Wartime Diary of Edmund Kessler*, 10.
55. Kessler, 48.
56. Snyder, *Bloodlands*, 196.
57. Lower, "Pogroms, Mob Violence and Genocide," 221.
58. For estimates of death tolls, see Lozowick, "Rollbahn Mord," 234; Kessler, *The Wartime Diary of Edmund Kessler*, 9; Yones, *Smoke in the Sand*, 77–78.
59. See EM 47, August 9, 1941. Here cited in Hlimka, "Ukrainian Collaboration in the Extermination of the Jews," 187.
60. Folkmann and Szende, *The Promise Hitler Kept*, 90.
61. Viktoria Sereda, "Gedenkstätte Im Wandel: Ein Spaziergang über den Prospekt Svobody (Freiheitsprospekt) in Lemberg," OST-WEST, *Europäische Perspektiven* 3 (2014).
62. Mick, *Lemberg, Lwów, L'viv, 1914–1947*, 300.
63. Sobieski, "Reminiscenses from Lwow, 1939–1945," 395.
64. Kahane, *Lvov Ghetto Diary*, 18.

65. Amar, *The Paradox of Ukrainian Lviv*, 90.
66. "Report: Das gewerbliche Genehmigungsverfahren und die Gewerbeplanung im Bereiche der Stadt Lemberg, 8 February 1942," DALO: R37-5-35, 90.
67. Zayarnyuk, *Lviv's Uncertain Destination*, 177.
68. Henry L. deZeng IV, Luftwaffe Airfields 1935–45: Poland, 2014.
69. Chetverikov and Babiy, "Methods of Creation," 71.
70. "Record of Soviet Commission for the Discovery and Investigation of German-Fascist Crimes in the City of Lemberg, 1–6 November 1944," 34.
71. Sandkühler, "Das Zwangsarbeitslager Lemberg-Janowska," 624.
72. Amar, *The Paradox of Ukrainian Lviv*, 92.
73. Mędykowski, *Macht Arbeit Frei?*, 195–96.
74. Longerich, *Heinrich Himmler*, 438.
75. Koonz, "On Reading a Document," 5.
76. Koonz, 8.
77. See "Memo: Members of SSPF Staff in Lemberg, LKA Baden-Württemberg to StA Saarbrücken, 27 January 1977," BA-ZS: B162/29259, 428.
78. "B., Ernst Statement, 1 June 1960," BA-ZS: B162/5102, 205–6.
79. Mazower, *Hitler's Empire*, 152.
80. Winstone, *The Dark Heart of Hitler's Europe*, 101, 103–4.
81. Amar, *The Paradox of Ukrainian Lviv*, 92.
82. Rubin, *Against All Odds*, 107.
83. Amar, *The Paradox of Ukrainian Lviv*, 132.
84. Mick, *Lemberg, Lwów, L'viv, 1914–1947*, 295.
85. Mick, 296.
86. "Memo: Flüchtigen ukr. Hilfspolizisten Artymon Szpaczynskyj, 8 May 1942," DALO: P-23-3-2, 4.
87. "Memo: Establishment and Financing of the Ukrainian Police in the Galician Districts of Lemberg, Stanislau, and Tarnopol, 29 July 1941."
88. See "Memo: Re: Detachment of Ukrainian Police Officials to Establish Ukrainian Auxiliary Police in Galicia District, 12 August 1941," Government Exhibit P14: United States of America, Plaintiff, v. John Kalymon, a.k.a. Ivan, Iwan, John Kalymon/Kalymun, Defendant. (2007).
89. See Rich, "Armed Ukrainians in L'viv: Ukrainian Militia, Ukrainian Police, 1941 to 1942."
90. Statiev, *The Soviet Counterinsurgency in the Western Borderlands*, 69.
91. *USA vs. John Kalymon*, No. No. 04–60003 Complaint, January 8, 2004 (United States District Court for the Eastern District of Michigan, Southern Division, March 29, 2007).

92. *USA vs. John Kalymon*, Trial Testimony-Cross Examination of Kalymon, September 22, 2006.
93. Rich, "Armed Ukrainians in L'viv: Ukrainian Militia, Ukrainian Police, 1941 to 1942," 276–77.
94. *USA vs. John Kalymon*, January 8, 2004.
95. *USA vs. John Kalymon*, January 8, 2004, Trial Testimony-Examination of Kalymon, September 22, 2006.
96. "Ahrens, Jack Interview, 11 May 1995," USHMM: RG-50.030*0311.
97. "Gilke, Georg Statement, 20 October 1964," StAL: EL 317 III, Bü 1502, 148.
98. "Rogowski, Marian Statement, 22 September 1961," StAL: EL 317 III, Bü 1502, 129.
99. Mick, "Incompatible Experiences," 352.
100. Struve, *Deutsche Herrschaft*, 416.
101. "Bescheinigung: Paula Günsberg, 12 August 1941," DALO: P-35-1-80, 1.
102. "Bescheinigung: Abteilung Möbeltransport, 20 October 1941," DALO: P-35-1-80, 3.
103. "Anzeige: 5th Kommissariate, 4 March 1942," USHMM, RG-31.001M, reel 2, R11.
104. Honigsman, *The Catastrophy of Jewry in Lvov*, 8; Yones, *Smoke in the Sand*, 100–102.
105. Sinnreich, "Victim and Perpetrator Perspectives," 118.
106. "Chronicle, Parnas's Appeal on the Contribution Imposed on the Jewish Community, July 28, 1941," LAMOTH: RG-89.73.
107. "Nazis Impose $4,000,000 Collective Fine on Jews in Lemberg," JTA *Daily News Bulletin* (New York), August 13, 1941, 1–2.
108. "Notice to Jewish Population Regarding Fur Aktion, 4 January 1942," USHMM, RG-15.069M: Teka Lwowska (Sygn. 229/75).
109. "Porath, Zeev Statement, 6 June 1961," 1319.
110. "Bericht des SS-und Polizeiführers über die Vernichtung der Juden Galiziens (Katzmann Bericht) Reproduced by T. Friedman, October 1963," USHMM: 1.2 .7.8/82187874_0_1–82188051_0_1/its Digital Archive.
111. Kahane, *Lvov Ghetto Diary*, 27.
112. Redner, *Recollections*, 18.
113. "Translation of *Szkola Okuricienstwa*," 49.
114. "Ahrens, Jack Interview, 11 May 1995."
115. "Poster: Anordnung Nr. 6, Stadthauptmann Kujath, 8 August 1941," Biblioteka Narodowa-Warsaw: DŻS IA 7 Cim.
116. "Ullrich, Albert Statement, 26 January 1950," USHMM, RG-17.003M, reel 116.
117. Redner, *Recollections*, 9.
118. Allen, *The Fantastic Laboratory of Dr. Weigl*, 138.
119. Friedman, "The Jewish Ghettos of the Nazi Era," 62.

120. Friedman, 66–67.
121. Friedman, 81–82.
122. Drix, *Witness to Annihilation*, 32.
123. Angrick, "Forced Labor along the 'Straße der SS,'" 83.
124. Angrick, 84.

3. THE DEVIL'S WORKSHOP

Epigraph: Anna Cwirn, Statement, March 8, 1963, StAL: EL 317 III, Bü 1516.

1. For Gebauer's official date of assignment (August 1), see "Memo, Sta Blank, 19 October 1953," BA-ZS: B162/5763, 110.
2. Perlman, "Di Goldene Royz," 213; Sandkühler, "Das Zwangsarbeitslager Lemberg-Janowska," 607.
3. Drix, *Witness to Annihilation*, 76; Gundula Werger, "Denk Ich an Lemberg," *Die Welt* (July 19, 2004); "Gebauer, Fritz Statement, 2 April 1962," BA-ZS: B162/20041, 1039.
4. Benz, Distel, and Königseder, *Der Ort des Terrors Geschichte der Nationalsozialistischen Konzentrationslager*, 93.
5. Poprzeczny, *Odilo Globocnik*, 224.
6. Enno, *Die Wirtschaftlichen Unternehmungen der SS*, 58–59.
7. Wachsmann, *Kl*, 160.
8. "Affidavit Concerning Oswald Pohl's Personality and Character-Heinrich Hoepker, 21 June 1947," HLS Nuremberg Trials Project: HLSL Document #4921: Harvard Law School Library, 4.
9. "Affidavit Concerning Oswald Pohl's Family Home and the Treatment of Inmate-Workers There-Katherina Katzmayr, 16 July 1947," HLS Nuremberg Trials Project: HLSL Document #4936: Harvard Law School Library, 3.
10. Niemann, *A Nazi in the Family*, 119; "Beweiserherbungen, Oberstaatsanwalt Saarbrücken, 12 March 1965," BA-ZS: B162/5766, 722.
11. Niemann, *A Nazi in the Family*, 121.
12. "Lg Saarbrücken Urteil Gg. Fritz Gebauer, 29 June 1971," 14.
13. Enno, *Die Wirtschaftlichen Unternehmungen der SS*, 62.
14. Kranjc, *To Walk with the Devil*, 124.
15. Arad, *Belzec, Sobibor, Treblinka*, 14–15.
16. "LG Saarbrücken Urteil gg. Fritz Gebauer, 29 June 1971," 12, 15.
17. Hoess, *Commandant of Auschwitz*, 227–28.
18. Sandkühler, "Das Zwangsarbeitslager Lemberg-Janowska," 607.
19. "Gebauer, Fritz Statement, 17 May 1961," BA-ZS: B162/5764, 421.
20. Mann, *The Dark Side of Democracy*, 181.

21. Mann, 195–96.
22. Party number: 388264, SS number: 5549. "Note, StA Blank, 18 June 1959," BA-ZS: B162/5763, 22; "Gebauer SS Personnel Card," YVA: RG-068, file 117.
23. "Gebauer, Fritz Statement, 17 May 1961."
24. "Gebauer, Fritz Statement, 2 April 1962," 1038.
25. After the war, Gebauer claimed to have been a member of SS-Standarte 58. (See "Gebauer, Fritz Statement, 17 May 1961," 421.) However, given that that unit was headquartered in Köln on the other side of Germany, it is likely that he misremembered the number.
26. Promotion date: January 30, 1943. "LG Saarbrücken Urteil gg. Fritz Gebauer, 29 June 1971," 8–9; "Note, StA Blank, 18 June 1959," 22.
27. "Gebauer, Fritz Statement, 17 May 1961," 422.
28. "Translation of *Szkola Okuricienstwa*," 29.
29. "Translation of *Szkola Okuricienstwa*," 23.
30. "Goldberg, Abraham Trial Testimony, Band 77, 10 January 1967," 2450.
31. "LG Saarbrücken Urteil gg. Fritz Gebauer, 29 June 1971," 11.
32. "Hirschhorn, Bernard Statement, 9 November 1948," 1.
33. "Letter, II. StA Werner to Oberstaatsanwalt-Saarbrücken, 30 May 1961," BA-ZS: B162/5764, 410.
34. "Gebauer, Fritz Statement, 2 April 1962," 1039.
35. One scholar notes that Mohwinkel left in November 1941, which is consistent with other evidence placing him as commandant effective December 1, 1941. See Poprzeczny, *Odilo Globocnik*, 224; Benz, Distel, and Königseder, *Der Ort des Terrors Geschichte der Nationalsozialistischen Konzentrationslager*, 7, 93.
36. Mędykowski, *Macht Arbeit Frei?*, 44–45.
37. Pohl, *Nationalsozialistische Judenverfolgung in Ostgalizien*, 422.
38. Kahane, *Lvov Ghetto Diary*, 50; "Schreiber, Benjamin Statement, 5 March 1964," StAL: EL 317 III, Bü 1497, 155; Yones, *Smoke in the Sand*, 87.
39. "Hirschhorn, Bernard Statement, 9 November 1948," 2.
40. "Hirschhorn, Bernard Statement," 2.
41. "Ferber, Itzchak Statement, 31 October 1963," BA-ZS: B162/5768, 1316.
42. "Goldberg, Abraham Statement, 29 June 1962," BA-ZS: B162/5765, 609/32; "Schreiber, Benjamin Statement, 2 November 1962," BA-ZS: B162/5765, 602.
43. Pick, *Simon Wiesenthal*, 57.
44. "Kerner, Arnold Statement, 17 May 1972," BA-ZS: B162/28734.
45. "Gebauer, Fritz Statement, 2 April 1962," 1040; "LG Saarbrücken Urteil gg. Fritz Gebauer, 29 June 1971," 15.
46. Sandkühler, "Das Zwangsarbeitslager Lemberg-Janowska," 607.

47. "Gebauer, Fritz Statement, 2 April 1962," 1040.
48. "LG Saarbrücken Urteil gg. Fritz Gebauer, 29 June 1971," 15; Sandkühler, "Das Zwangsarbeitslager Lemberg-Janowska," 607.
49. Auerbach, "Die Einheit Dirlewanger," 250.
50. Bell, *Besieged*, 190; Lewy, *Perpetrators*, 46.
51. This should not be confused with the Bełżec extermination center, which had not yet been built. Very little has been written about the activities of the Dirlewanger Battalion during its time in the Generalgovernment. Most literature focuses on Dirlewanger himself and his unit's later actions in antipartisan warfare in the Soviet Union. See Winstone, *The Dark Heart of Hitler's Europe*, 189.
52. Richman, *Why?*, 11.
53. "Hirschhorn, Bernard Statement, 9 November 1948," 2–3.
54. Hoess, *Commandant of Auschwitz*, 110.
55. "Ferber, Itzchak Statement, 31 October 1963," 1316.
56. "Hirschhorn, Bernard Statement, 9 November 1948," 2.
57. "Translation of *Szkola Okuricienstwa*," 17.
58. Richman, *Why?*, 3.
59. Mędykowski, *Macht Arbeit Frei?*, 138.
60. "Translation of *Szkola Okuricienstwa*," 21.
61. Pohl, *Nationalsozialistische Judenverfolgung in Ostgalizien*, 423.
62. "Gebauer, Fritz Statement, 17 May 1961," 425.
63. "Richman, Leon Statement, 14 June 1960," BA-ZS: B162/5764, 31, 33; "Translation of *Szkola Okuricienstwa*," 16.
64. "Additional Melchior Trial Witness Statements, 28 August 1949," BA-ZS: B162/5763, 120.
65. Matthäus and Böhler, *War, Pacification, and Mass Murder, 1939*, 39.
66. "Kolonko, Adolf Trial Testimony, Band 2," StAL: EL 317 III, Bü 1572, 47–50.
67. "Verzeichnis Der Zwangsarbeitslager des SSPF Im Distrikt Galizien, 1941–1943, Staatsanwaltschaft Stuttgart, 15 June 1967," USHMM: 1.2.7.8/82187532_0_1–82187628_0_1/its Digital Archive.
68. Black, "Foot Soldiers of the Final Solution," 6.
69. Beorn, *The Holocaust in Eastern Europe*, 125.
70. Kay, "The Purpose of the Russian Campaign," 116.
71. Archival source: ГДА СБУ.-Ф. 5.-Спр. 67855.-Т.17.-Арк. 89, cited in "Аскари Янівського Табору," Музей "Територія Терору," accessed December 11, 2020.
72. Black, "Foot Soldiers of the Final Solution," 16–17.
73. Black, 7.
74. Black, 15.

75. Black, 29–30.
76. Black, "Police Auxiliaries for Operation Reinhard," 347.
77. "KdS Lemberg, Besprechungs Niederschrift, 15 December 1941," DALO: P-23–4, 1.
78. Паripя, "Yevreys'ke Hetto," 148.
79. The periodization here is clear regarding the establishment of the ZAL-L. However, in the minds of survivors, distinctions are not often as clear. I have endeavored to ensure that the evidence provided here does concern the DAW, though at times it is impossible to determine whether it occurred before or after May 1942.
80. "Gebauer, Fritz Statement, 26 November 1962," BA-ZS: B162/5765, 609. While it might seem odd that Gebauer would be supplying footwear to the Reichsbank, this is what he claimed in his statement. The circumstances of this (and its veracity) remain unclear.
81. It is possible that that he *was* in the SS but attempted to deny this. However, the authorities identified him as a civilian in 1967. (See "Verzeichnis der Zwangsarbeitslager des SSPF im Distrikt Galizien, 1941–1943, Staatsanwaltschaft Stuttgart, 15 June 1967.") "Biedermann, Richard Statement, 12 November 1953," BA-ZS: B162/5763, 80.
82. "Gebauer, Fritz Statement, 26 November 1962," 609.
83. "Gebauer, Fritz Statement, 24 July 1962," BA-ZS: B162/20039, 516.
84. "Gebauer, Fritz Statement, 17 May 1961," 425.
85. "Gebauer, Fritz Statement, 27 July 1962," BA-ZS: B162/20039, 536.
86. "Melchior, Karl Statement, 22 April 1960," StAL: EL 317 III, Bü 1505, 62.
87. "Gebauer, Fritz Statement, 17 May 1961," 424.
88. "Hirschhorn, Bernard Statement, 9 November 1948," 3.
89. "Löbel, Adolf (Carlos Brosek) Statement, Undated," BA-ZS: B162/5768, 1298b.
90. "Gruss, Roszka Statement, 12 February 1948," BA-ZS: B162/5763.
91. "Goldberg, Abraham Statement, 9 October 1961," BA-ZS: B162/20039, 268–69.
92. "Boni, Kasimir Statement, 20 September 1944," BA-ZS: B162/29309, 156–57.
93. "Hirschhorn, Bernhard Statement, 9 February 1948," StAL EL 317, III Bü 1524, 3–4.
94. "Translation of *Szkola Okuricienstwa*," 25.
95. Kaplan, *I Never Left Janowska*, 43.
96. "Translation of *Szkola Okuricienstwa*," 24.
97. "Bleines Hugo Statement, 21 October 1953," 224.
98. Wells, *The Janowska Road*, 58, 63–65.
99. "Hirschhorn, Bernard Statement, 9 November 1948"; "Translation of *Szkola Okuricienstwa*"; Richman, *Why?*.
100. "Hirschhorn, Bernard Statement, 9 November 1948," 5.
101. Richman, *Why?*, 26.

102. "Mandel, Irving Statement, 18 May 1960," BA-ZS: B162/5764, 371.
103. This number increased from spring 1942 onward. "LG Saarbrücken Urteil gg. Fritz Gebauer, 29 June 1971," 31.
104. "LG Saarbrücken Urteil gg. Fritz Gebauer, 29 June 1971," 37–38.
105. "Translation of *Szkola Okuricienstwa*," 24.
106. Richman, *Why?*, 9, 17.
107. "Translation of *Szkola Okuricienstwa*," 26.
108. "Hirschhorn, Bernard Statement, 9 November 1948," 4.
109. "Translation of *Szkola Okuricienstwa*," 26.
110. "Mandel, Irving Statement, 18 May 1960," 372–73.
111. "Schächter, Wolf Statement, 27 September 1944," BA-ZS: B162/29309, 335.
112. Richman, *Why?*, 10.
113. "LG Saarbrücken Urteil gg. Fritz Gebauer, 29 June 1971," 19; "Kraus, Jakob Statement, 11 October 1962," BA-ZS: B162/5765, 366–67; "Gebauer, Fritz Statement, 2 April 1962," 1040; Kaplan, *I Never Left Janowska*, 42–43.
114. Kaplan, *I Never Left Janowska*, 42–43.
115. Kaplan, 47.
116. "Gebauer, Emmi Statement 4 July 1961," BA-ZS: B162/5764, 449; "Gebauer, Fritz Statement, 26 November 1962," 609/11.
117. "Melchior, Amalie Statement, 13 November 1953," BA-ZS: B162/20038, 138.
118. "Löbel, Adolf (Carlos Brosek) Statement, Undated," 1300.
119. Borwicz, *The University of Criminals*, 62–63.
120. Kaplan, *I Never Left Janowska*, 47.
121. Wachsmann, *Kl*, 375.
122. "LG Saarbrücken Urteil gg. Fritz Gebauer, 29 June 1971," 95.
123. "Wust, Fritz Statement, 11 September 1962," BA-ZS: B162/5765, 577.
124. "Additional Melchior Trial Witness Statements, 28 August 1949," 123.
125. Wells, *The Janowska Road*, 88.
126. "Gebauer, Fritz Statement, 24 July 1962," 529.
127. "Gebauer, Fritz Statement, 17 May 1961," 425.
128. "Gebauer, Fritz Statement, 2 April 1962," 1040.
129. Wells, *The Janowska Road*, 87.
130. Wells, 87; "Translation of *Szkola Okuricienstwa*," 73.
131. "LG Saarbrücken Urteil gg. Friedrich Heinen, 10 July 1978," BA-ZS: B162/14582, 26.
132. "Beweiserherbungen, Oberstaatsanwalt Saarbrücken, 12 March 1965," 744.
133. "Beweiserherbungen," 698–99.
134. Sandkühler, "Das Zwangsarbeitslager Lemberg-Janowska," 610.
135. Niemann, *A Nazi in the Family*, 84.

136. "Document No-1216: Report on an Inspection Tour of SS Industrial Enterprises (Kurt May), 11 June 1942," HLS Nuremberg Trials Project: Harvard Law School Library, 3.

4. A TRAGIC LIFE

Epigraph: Meeting of Lviv Nazi administrators, January 10, 1942 ("Aktenvermerk-Besprechung Am 9.1.1942 Betr. Aussiedlung der Juden aus Lemberg, 10 January 1942"), StAL, P37-4-140, 61.

1. "Memo-Errichtung eines Judenwohnbezirkes in Lemberg, 7 October 1941," DALO: P23-3-1, 21.
2. Sandkühler, "Anti-Jewish Policy," 111.
3. Sandkühler, 111.
4. "Express Letter by Reinhard Heydrich to the Einsatzgruppen on the 'Jewish Question in the Occupied Territory,' September 21, 1939," in *War, Pacification, and Mass Murder, 1939*, 105.
5. Polonsky, "Introduction," 10–11.
6. Mędykowski, *Macht Arbeit Frei?*, 195–96.
7. Honigsman, *The Catastrophy of Jewry in Lvov*, 12.
8. Michman, *The Emergence of Jewish Ghettos*, ff. 115.
9. "Memo: Errichtung eines Judenwohnbezirkes in Lemberg, 7 October 1941," DALO: P-23-3-1, 21.
10. "Letter, Stadtgesundheitsamt Lemberg to Stadtbauamt, 10 November 1941," DALO: P37-4-140, 68.
11. "Meeting Summary: Construction of a Jewish Residential District in the City of Lemberg, 6 November 1941," DALO: 32-2-155, 30.
12. "Memo: Distrikt Gov Lasch to SSPF Katzmann, 6 November 1941," DALO: 32-2-155, 4.
13. "Poster: Bekanntmachung-Bildung eines Jüdischen Wohnbezirkes, 8 November 1941," Steegh/Teunissen map collection, Dordrecht/Holland.
14. "Memo: Jewish Community in Lemberg to Distrikt Gov Lasch, 10 November 1941," DALO: 32-2-155, 1.
15. "Memo," 7.
16. "Letter, Stadthauptmann, Bauverwaltung to Wirtschaftsabteilung, Betrifft: Einfriedigung Wohnbezirk Der Juden, 2 December 1941," DALO: P37-4-140, 68.
17. "Poster: Bekanntmachung-Bildung eines Jüdischen Wohnbezirkes, 8 November 1941."
18. Alex Kozlowski, "Olec-as Told to Anne Marie Davies," USHMM, RG-2015.165.1, 4.
19. "Goldberg, Abraham Trial Testimony, Band 77, 10 January 1967," 2443–44.

20. "Porath, Zeev Statement, 6 June 1961," 1319.
21. Kessler, *The Wartime Diary of Edmund Kessler*, 54.
22. Kessler, 10–11.
23. "Lewi, Meier Statement, 22 September 1944," USHMM: 1.2.7.7/82183313_0_1–82183317_0_1/its Digital Archive.
24. Amar, *The Paradox of Ukrainian Lviv*, 106.
25. Wawrzeniuk, "'Lwów Saved Us,'" 15.
26. "Jewish Population of Europe in 1933: Population Data by Country," United States Holocaust Memorial Museum, accessed January 13, 2016.
27. Kessler, *The Wartime Diary of Edmund Kessler*, 10.
28. Trunk, *Judenrat*, 51.
29. "Memo: Jewish Community in Lemberg to Distrikt Gov Lasch, 25 November 1941," DALO: 32-2-155, 25–26.
30. "Memo: Umsiedlung, 12 May 1942," DALO: P37-4-140, 30.
31. "Memo: Jewish Community in Lemberg to Distrikt Gov Lasch, 25 November 1941," 25–26.
32. Kessler, *The Wartime Diary of Edmund Kessler*, 63.
33. See "Kirschner, Richarda Statement, 16 September 1944," BA-ZS: B162/29309, 260; "Blai, Abraham Statement, 19 September 1944," BA-ZS: B162/29309, 169; "Blai, Barbara Statement, 19 September 1944," BA-ZS: B162/29309, 174.
34. Trunk, *Judenrat*, 110.
35. Kahane, *Lvov Ghetto Diary*, 19.
36. "Aktenvermerk-Besprechung Am 9.1.1942 Betr. Aussiedlung der Juden aus Lemberg, 10 January 1942," 61–62.
37. "Instructions Re: Jewish Labor Operations, Dr. Höller, 25 March 1942," DALO: P37-4-140, 41.
38. Kahane, *Lvov Ghetto Diary*, 83.
39. Kessler, *The Wartime Diary of Edmund Kessler*, 52.
40. Trunk, *Judenrat*, 103.
41. These numbers come primarily from Folkmann (survivor memoir) and Honigsman (an archivally sourced but somewhat amateurish historical account). See Honigsman, *The Catastrophy of Jewry in Lvov*, 15; Folkmann and Szende, *The Promise Hitler Kept*, 51.
42. Honigsman, *The Catastrophy of Jewry in Lvov*, 15.
43. "Mitteilungen des Judenrates in Lemberg für die jüdische Gemeinde, 1 March 1942," DALO: P35-6-250, 7–8.
44. Drix, *Witness to Annihilation*, 35.
45. Kozlowski, "Olec-as Told to Anne Marie Davies," 7.

46. Rifkind and Freeman, *The Nobel Prize Winning Discoveries in Infectious Diseases*, 67.
47. Barnes, *Diseases and Human Evolution*, 256.
48. Rifkind and Freeman, *The Nobel Prize Winning Discoveries in Infectious Diseases*, 68.
49. Drix, *Witness to Annihilation*, 36.
50. "Mitteilungen des Judenrates in Lemberg für die jüdische Gemeinde, 1 March 1942," 5.
51. Redner, *Recollections*, 16.
52. "Former Jewish Hospital," Lviv Interactive, Center for Urban History of East Central Europe, accessed November 1, 2019; Kahane, *Lvov Ghetto Diary*, 21.
53. "Mitteilungen des Judenrates in Lemberg für die jüdische Gemeinde, 1 March 1942," 5–6.
54. "Sawitzky, Leon and Ella Testimony, 4 November 1984," FVAHT: 982266.
55. "Weigl, Rudolf," The Righteous Among the Nations Database, Yad Vashem, 2019, accessed November 1, 2019; "How Scientists Created a Typhus Vaccine in a 'Fantastic Laboratory,'" *Fresh Air*, NPR, June 26, 2015.
56. "Nazis Recall Jewish Scientists from Ghetto to Develop Anti-Typhus Vaccine," *JTA Daily News Bulletin*, February 24, 1942, 3.
57. "Sonderbefehl: Massnahmen gegen Hundetollwut, 7 May 1942," DALO: P-23-3-2, 6.
58. Yones, *Smoke in the Sand*, 111.
59. "Mitteilungen des Judenrates in für die jüdische Gemeinde, 1 March 1942," 7.
60. Drix, *Witness to Annihilation*, 36.
61. Burleigh, *The Third Reich*, 639.
62. Leidinger, "Das Schicksal der polnischen Psychiatrie unter deutscher Besatzung im zweiten Weltkrieg," S73. See also the Wacyk case, BA-ZS B162–25034.
63. "Zimmerman, Leopold Statement, 1 February 1965," BA-ZS: B162/20039.
64. Yones, *Smoke in the Sand*, 111; Honigsman, *The Catastrophy of Jewry in Lvov*, 16.
65. "Hirschhorn, Bernhard Statement, 9 February 1948," 4.
66. "Translation of *Szkola Okuricienstwa*," 39.
67. "Gogolowska, Stanislawa Statement, 12 March 1947," BA-ZS: B162/5768, 1258–59.
68. "Gogolowska, Stanislawa Statement, 31 January 1965," BA-ZS: B162/29309, 226; "Mikolajewski (Lurie), Wlodzimierz Statement, 5 March 1963," StAL: EL 317 III, Bü 1516, 5–6.
69. "Goldberg, Abraham Trial Testimony, Band 77, 10 January 1967," 2457–58.
70. "Translation of *Szkola Okuricienstwa*," 31.
71. "Wieselberg, Teresa Statement, 10 March 1963," StAL: EL 317 III, Bü 1516, 28–29; Drix, *Witness to Annihilation*, 97.
72. "Bialecki (Altmann), Thedor (Salomon) Statement, 24 February 1960," BA-ZS: B162/5764, 218.

73. Kahane, *Lvov Ghetto Diary*, 33.
74. Folkmann and Szende, *The Promise Hitler Kept*, 109–10.
75. "Ahrens, Jack Interview, 11 May 1995."
76. "Zarwyn, Berthold," USC Shoah Foundation Institute: Interview #41186, Visual History Archive, 1998; "Szor, Leopold," USC Shoah Foundation Institute: Interview #5248, Visual History Archive, 1998.
77. Kahane, *Lvov Ghetto Diary*, 17.
78. Yones, *Smoke in the Sand*, 104–5.
79. The dating of these decisions remains the subject of some debate, with some scholars suggesting an April or May time frame.
80. Browning and Matthäus, *The Origins of the Final Solution*, 495.
81. See Dannecker memo of January 21, 1941, in Browning, *Nazi Policy, Jewish Workers, German Killers*, 20.
82. As articulated in Christopher R. Browning, "Hitler, Antisemitism, and the Final Solution," *Antisemitism Studies* 7, no. 1 (2023).
83. "Translation of Document 710-PS: Letter from Goering to Heydrich Concerning Solution of Jewish Question, 31 July 1941," in *Trials of War Criminals before the Nuremberg Military Tribunals*.
84. Browning, "Hitler, Antisemitism, and the Final Solution," 95.
85. Kampe, "Die Wannsee-Konferenz," 99.
86. Gerlach, "The Wannsee Conference," 797.
87. Gerlach, 798.
88. See chart in Beorn, *The Holocaust in Eastern Europe*, 205–6.
89. Testimony of Stanisław Kozak in Kuwałek, *Death Camp in Bełżec*, 41.
90. Poprzeczny, *Odilo Globocnik*, 117.
91. Browning and Matthäus, *The Origins of the Final Solution*, 841.
92. Testimony of Stanisław Kozak in Kuwałek, *Death Camp in Bełżec*, 40–41.
93. Testimony of Stanisław Kozak in Kuwałek, 52, 74.
94. Rieß, "Christian Wirth," 239.
95. "alle Juden umgelegt werden sollten," in Rieß, "Christian Wirth," 242–44; Arad, *Belzec, Sobibor, Treblinka*, 17.
96. Kuwałek, *Death Camp in Bełżec*, 57, 59.
97. Arad, *Belzec, Sobibor, Treblinka*, 45.
98. "Government Exhibit P64: Report on Sweeps for Jews (5th Commissariat), 20 March 1942," United States of America, Plaintiff, V. John Kalymon, a.k.a. Ivan, Iwan, John Kalymon/Kaylmun, Defendant (2007).
99. "Government Exhibit P65: Report on Jewish Operation (Headquarters of the Ukrainian Police) on 25 March 1942," United States of America, Plain-

tiff, V. John Kalymon, a.k.a. Ivan, Iwan, John Kalymon/Kaylmun, Defendant (2007).

100. "Government Exhibit P67: Report on the Jewish Operation on 27 March 1942," United States of America, Plaintiff, V. John Kalymon, a.k.a. Ivan, Iwan, John Kalymon/Kaylmun, Defendant (2007).

101. Statement of Michał Kuśmierczyk in Kuwałek, *Death Camp in Bełżec*, 97.

102. Statements of Andrzej Jonkoa and Alojzy Berezowski in Kuwałek, *Death Camp in Bełżec*, 120.

103. Kuwałek, 121.

104. "Übersetzung aus dem Hebräischen-aus dem Buch 'Encyclopedia der Jüdischen Diaspora,' Serie Polen, Band Tarnopol," USHMM: 1.2.7.1/82291075_0_1– 82291086_0_1/its Digital Archive, 233.

105. Kuwałek, *Death Camp in Bełżec*, 124–26.

106. Tregenza, "Belzec Death Camp," 1100–1.

107. "Chyrowski, Jerzy Statement, 31 January 1961," StAL: EL 317 III, Bü 1505, 139.

108. "Szpilka, Klara Statement, 21 January 1964," StAL: EL 317 III, Bü 1516, 135.

109. "Goldberg, Abraham Trial Testimony, Band 77, 10 January 1967," 2459.

110. Drix, *Witness to Annihilation*, 38.

111. Kahane, *Lvov Ghetto Diary*, 47.

112. "Manusevich, David Statement, 13 September 1944," BA-ZS: B162/29309, 293.

113. Arad, *Belzec, Sobibor, Treblinka*, 349–50.

114. "Translation of Document M-173 'Israelistisches Wochenblatt,'" 1228.

115. Sandkühler, "Anti-Jewish Policy," 115.

116. Kaienburg, "Jüdische Arbeitslager," 15.

117. "Bericht des SS-und Polizeiführers über die Vernichtung der Juden Galiziens (Katzmann Bericht) Reproduced by T. Friedman, October 1963."

118. Sandkühler, "Das Zwangsarbeitslager Lemberg-Janowska," 610.

119. Mędykowski, *Macht Arbeit Frei?*, 225.

120. Longerich, *Heinrich Himmler*, 562.

121. "Dienstanweisung für den jüdischen Ordnungsdienst in Lemberg, 26 January 1942," DALO: P-23-3-1, 100.

122. "Government Exhibit P62: Jewish Council Report on Jewish Resettlement, 26 March 1942," United States of America, Plaintiff, V. John Kalymon, a.k.a. Ivan, Iwan, John Kalymon/Kaylmun, Defendant (2007).

123. "Mitteilungen des Judenrates in Lemberg für die jüdische Gemeinde, 1 March 1942," 2.

124. Drix, *Witness to Annihilation*, 38.

125. "Trial of Adolf Eichmann, Session 22, 1 May 1961," Nizhkor Project, http://www.nizkor.org/hweb/people/e/eichmann-adolf/transcripts/Sessions/Session-022-03.html
126. Tomaszewski, "Der Psychologe Tadeusz Tomaszewski," 147.
127. "SSPF Memo: Jewish Labor Force, 6 November 1942," BA-ZS: B162/4358, 84; "Chyrowski, Jerzy Statement, 31 January 1961," 321.
128. "Wells (Welizcker), Leon Statement, 21 September 1944," 353.
129. Yones, *Smoke in the Sand*, 166; Arad, *The Holocaust in the Soviet Union*, 278.
130. "Government Exhibit P87: Report on the Jewish Operation on 24 June 1942 (5th Commissariat)," United States of America, Plaintiff, V. John Kalymon, a.k.a. Ivan, Iwan, John Kalymon/Kaylmun, Defendant (2007); "Government Exhibit P86: Report on Jewish Operation (Headquarters of the Ukrainian Police) on 25 June 1942," United States of America, Plaintiff, V. John Kalymon, a.k.a. Ivan, Iwan, John Kalymon/Kaylmun, Defendant (2007). For more on the NSKK's participation in the Holocaust in Lviv, see Hochstetter, *Motorisierung und "Volksgemeinschaft"*, 468.
131. Arad, *The Holocaust in the Soviet Union*, 278; Yones, *Smoke in the Sand*, 166. The Kalymon trial placed the number at around 1,000, but they may have been relying only on the numbers reported by the Ukrainian police who reported "1,921 Jews and 45 beggars," see "Government Exhibit P86: Report on Jewish Operation (Headquarters of the Ukrainian Police) on 25 June 1942."
132. "Richman, Leon Statement, 14 June 1960," 351.
133. Wells, *The Janowska Road*, 119.
134. Reder, *Belzec*, 115.
135. Kahane, *Lvov Ghetto Diary*, 57.
136. "Document 2233-PS: Excerpts from the Diary of Hans Frank, Governor General of the Occupied Polish Territories, 25 October 1939–3 April 1945," in *Trials of the War Criminals*, 541.
137. Kahane, *Lvov Ghetto Diary*, 57.
138. Pohl, *Nationalsozialistische Judenverfolgung in Ostgalizien*, 218.
139. "Keren, Christine Interview, 10/25/2007," USHMM, RG-50.030*0520, 2007.349.
140. Kahane, *Lvov Ghetto Diary*, 65.
141. Redner, *Recollections*, 24, 50–51.
142. "Report: Kdo d. ukr. Polizei, 21 August 1942," YVA: RG-M52, file 252, 524.
143. "Report: Kdo d. ukr. Polizei, 22 August 1942," YVA: RG-M52, file 252, 528.
144. *USA vs. John Kalymon*.
145. Kahane, *Lvov Ghetto Diary*, 66.
146. Kahane, 66.

147. Longerich, *Heinrich Himmler*, 620; Pohl, *Nationalsozialistische Judenverfolgung in Ostgalizien*, 220–21.
148. "Rogowski, Marian Statement, 13 November 1963," 82.
149. "Drix, Samuel, Tagebuch, 1942–1943," StAL: EL 317 III, Bü 1721, 9.
150. Folkmann and Szende, *The Promise Hitler Kept*, 114.
151. Kahane, *Lvov Ghetto Diary*, 63.
152. Bloxham, *The Final Solution*, 233.
153. Browning, *Ordinary Men*, xv.

5. CERBERUS AWAKENS

Epigraph: Borwicz, *The University of Criminals*, 21.

1. Lower, *Hitler's Furies*, 69. Historian Thomas Sandkühler reports that Willhaus was officially named commandant on July 1, 1942, but Gebauer testified that Willhaus began construction of the ZAL at the end of May, beginning of June. It is quite possible that both are true and that the official appointment lagged behind the de facto assuming of the role, or that the appointment was delayed until the ZAL actually existed. See Sandkühler, "Das Zwangsarbeitslager Lemberg-Janowska," 611; "Gebauer, Fritz Statement 4 May 1962," 493.
2. "Gebauer, Fritz Statement 4 May 1962," 493; "Gebauer, Fritz Statement, 17 May 1961," 426.
3. "Rokita, Richard Statement, 27 April 1966," StAL: EL 317 III, Bü 1516, 3.
4. "Rycevskij, Miroslav Statement, 27 January 1967," BA-ZS: B162/29309, 313.
5. "Gebauer, Fritz Statement, 26 November 1962," 509.
6. "Translation of *Szkola Okuricienstwa*," 40–43.
7. "Kolonko, Adolf Statement, 16 September 1960," StAL: EL 317 III, Bü 1505, 157.
8. "Translation of *Szkola Okuricienstwa*," 40; "Porath, Zeev Statement, 6 June 1961," 1322; Henryk Griffel, Reinforcing Member for Reinforced Concrete Structures, Poland 1938.
9. "Translation of *Szkola Okuricienstwa*," 40.
10. "Porath, Zeev Statement, 8 June 1961," 1352.
11. "Porath, Zeev Statement, 6 June 1961," 1323–24.
12. "Porath, Zeev Statement, 7 June 1961," StAL: EL 48-2, Bü 397, 1331.
13. "Report of Berlin Document Center on Gustav Willhaus, 4 November 1959," BA-ZS: B162/5726, 22.
14. "Willhaus SS Marriage Application, 11 July 1935," YVA: RG-068, file 850, 14.
15. Willhaus held Party number 1292975 and SS number 40675. See Lower, *Hitler's Furies*, 67; "Report of Berlin Document Center on Gustav Willhaus, 4 November

1959," 22; "Letter: Gustav Willhaus to SS Rassen u. Siedlungsamt, Saarbrücken, 17 June 1935," YVA: RG-068, file 850, 50.
16. "Riedel SS Marriage Application, 11 July 1935," YVA: RG-068, file 850, 36.
17. Pohl, *Nationalsozialistische Judenverfolgung in Ostgalizien*, 423.
18. Lower, *Hitler's Furies*, 68.
19. "Adolf Hitler an das Saarvolk: Schenkt eure Treue dem neuen Reich!," Berlin, March 2–4, 1935.
20. "Letter: Gustav Willhaus to SS Rassen u. Siedlungsamt, Saarbrücken, 12 February 1935," YVA: RG-068, file 850, 65.
21. "Letter: Sippenamt Berlin to SS-Oberabschnitt Südwest, 24 August 1936," YVA: RG-068, file 850, 59.
22. Lower, *Hitler's Furies*, 68.
23. Altenburger, "Infanterie-Regiment 32."
24. Pohl, *Nationalsozialistische Judenverfolgung in Ostgalizien*, 423.
25. "Gutschek, Todej Andrejewitsch Statement, 1 August 1967," BA-ZS: B162/29309, 244; "Weniger, Rachel Statement, 14 September 1944," BA-ZS: B162/29309, 375; "Willhaus SS Marriage Physical, 20 September 1935," YVA: RG-068, file 850, 33.
26. Wells, *The Janowska Road*, 87.
27. "Blai, Abraham Statement, 19 September 1944," 168.
28. "Stromer, Marek Testimony, 17 August 1983," FVAHT: 801243.
29. "Weniger, Rachel Statement, 14 September 1944," 375.
30. "Record of Soviet Commission for the Discovery and Investigation of German-Fascist Crimes in the City of Lemberg, 1–6 November 1944," 28.
31. "Rogowski, Marian Statement, 22 September 1961," 143.
32. Wachsmann, *Kl*, 110.
33. Lower, *Hitler's Furies*, 67.
34. Drix, *Witness to Annihilation*, 173.
35. Lower, *Hitler's Furies*, 133.
36. Adolf Kolonko comment in "Hansberg, Elizabeth Statement, 18 September 1964," StAL: EL 317 III, Bü 1502, 119.
37. Borwicz, *The University of Criminals*, 39.
38. "'A Plan for a Residential Building'-Zeev Porath," GFHM: Catalog Nr. 4265; "Hansberg, Elizabeth Statement, 7 May 1963," StAL: EL 317 III, Bü 1502, 15.
39. "Korn, Moische Statement, 13 September 1944," BA-ZS: B162/29309, 263.
40. Yones, *Smoke in the Sand*, 200.
41. "Hansberg, Elizabeth Statement, 1 September 1962," StAL: EL 317 III, Bü 1502, 5.
42. Adolf Kolonko comment in "Hansberg, Elizabeth Statement, 18 September 1964," 119.

43. "Rogowski, Marian Statement, 13 November 1963," 85.
44. Based on forty-two men who had biographical origin details.
45. Lumans, "The Military Obligation," 305.
46. Swanson, "Minority Building in the German Diaspora," 153.
47. Janjetović, "The Role of the Danube Swabians in the History of the Serbs," 203.
48. Swanson, "Minority Building in the German Diaspora," 156.
49. Swanson, 160.
50. "Blum, Peter Statement, 8 September 1960," StAL: EL 317 III, Bü 1505, 307.
51. Lumans, "The Military Obligation of the Volksdeutsche," 312.
52. Lumans, 316.
53. Investigators examining him for a claim of refugee status discovered a "round scar on his left upper arm" which was likely where he removed this tattoo. See "Blum Application for IRO Assistance, 16 August 1949," USHMM: 3.2.1.1./78945202_0_1–78945202_0_4/its Digital Archive.
54. See SS-FHA, OrgAbt, TgbNr. 1620/42 geh.v.17.3.1942 quoted in "Truppenübungsplatz der Waffen-SS Debica 'Heidelager,'" Lexikon der Wehrmacht, Andreas Altenburger, accessed October 10, 2023, https://www.lexikon-der-wehrmacht.de/Karte/TruppenubungsplatzeSS/TruppenubungsplatzeSSDebica.htm.
55. See photos in Hembera, "Ermittlungsakten Aufgeschlagen."
56. Vernehmung Alois K. vom 16.10.1967, in BArch, B 162/5288, Bl. 1185 in Hembera, "Ermittlungsakten Aufgeschlagen."
57. "Blum, Peter Trial Testimony, Band 2," StAL: EL 317 III, Bü 1572, 43.
58. "Blum, Peter Statement, 8 September 1960," 307.
59. "Schönbach, Roman Trial Testimony, Band 6/K," StAL: EL 317 III, Bü 1572, 125–29.
60. "Schönbach, Roman Statement, 21 February 1962," StAL: EL 48/2, Bü 397, 1584.
61. Black, "Rehearsal for 'Reinhard'?," 207.
62. Black, "Indigenous Collaboration in the General Government," 244.
63. Black, "Rehearsal for 'Reinhard'?," 212–13.
64. Black, 222.
65. Black, "Indigenous Collaboration in the General Government," 249.
66. Black, 244.
67. In his testimony, Schönbach states that he drove for a Sturmbannführer Binner. "Schönbach, Roman Trial Testimony, Band 6/K."
68. Gilbert, *The Routledge Atlas of the Holocaust*, 40; Benz, Distel, and Königseder, *Der Ort des Terrors Geschichte der Nationalsozialistischen Konzentrationslager*, 594.
69. "Schönbach, Roman Statement, 21 February 1962," 1585.
70. Hoess, *Commandant of Auschwitz*, 48.

71. "Schönbach, Roman Statement, 21 February 1962," 1585–86.
72. Borwicz, *The University of Criminals*, 38.
73. Wachsmann, *Kl*, 21.
74. Longerich, *Heinrich Himmler*, 573–74.
75. Sandkühler, *"Endlösung" in Galizien*, 142ff.
76. Browning, *Remembering Survival*, 4.
77. Wachsmann, *Kl*, 411.
78. Wachsmann, 207.
79. Wells, *The Janowska Road*, 79, 66–67.
80. "Goldberg, Abraham Trial Testimony, Band 77, 10 January 1967," 2465.
81. Drix, *Witness to Annihilation*, 115.
82. "Barth, Pinkas Statement, 2 March 1960," BA-ZS: B162/5764, 250.
83. Hoess, *Commandant of Auschwitz*, 75.
84. Wells, *The Janowska Road*, 62.
85. "Manusevich, David Statement, 13 September 1944," 293–94.
86. Folkmann and Szende, *The Promise Hitler Kept*, 66.
87. "Orenstein, Karol Statement (Undated)," StAL: EL 317 III, Bü 1497, 263.
88. Borwicz, *The University of Criminals*, 27.
89. "Osterweil, Mozes Statement, 17 May 1963," StAL: EL 317 III, Bü 1516, 37–38.
90. "Nestler, Bernard Statement, 17 January 1964," StAL: EL 317 III, Bü 1516, 107.
91. "Orenstein, Karol Statement (Undated)," 263–64.
92. "Szor, Leopold Affidavit, 15 June 1960," BA-ZS: B162/5764, 355.
93. Borwicz, *The University of Criminals*, 27.
94. Folkmann and Szende, *The Promise Hitler Kept*, 67.
95. "Trial of Adolf Eichmann, Session 22, 1 May 1961."
96. "Kruszewski, Emil Statement, 22 April 1964," StAL: EL 317 III, Bü 1498, 365; "Kruszewski, Emil Statement, 16 May 1972," BA-ZS: B162/28734, 273–74.
97. "Gutschek, Todej Andrejewitsch Statement, 1 August 1967," 237.
98. Kahane, *Lvov Ghetto Diary*, 53.
99. Sandkühler, "Das Zwangsarbeitslager Lemberg-Janowska," 623–24.
100. It is unclear which of several Schuchardt firms this truck belonged to.
101. Drix, *Witness to Annihilation*, 130.
102. "Zimmerman, Leopold Statement, 30 July 1969," BA-ZS: B162/28733, 88.
103. "Eichenholz, Lidia," USC Shoah Foundation Institute: Interview #5248, Visual History Archive, 1995.
104. "Korn, Moische Statement, 13 September 1944," 263.
105. "Blum, Peter Statement, 28 January 1963," StAL: EL 317 III, Bü 1497, 3.
106. "Szpilka, Klara Statement, 21 January 1964," 136.

107. "Blum, Peter Statement, 8 September 1960," 315.
108. "Weniger, Rachel Statement, 14 September 1944," 373; "Winter, Klara Statement, 22 September 1944," BA-ZS: B162/29309, 390.
109. Kahane, *Lvov Ghetto Diary*, 47, 91.
110. "Weniger, Rachel Statement, 14 September 1944," 375–76.
111. "Kruszewski, Emil Statement, 3 January 1962," StAL: EL 317 III, Bü 1498, 373; "Zicher, Symon Statement, 12 October 1947," BA-ZS: B162/20039, 409.
112. "Thürhaus, David Statement, 15 October 1963," StAL: EL 317 III, Bü 1523, 53.
113. "Blum, Peter Statement, 8 September 1960," 315.
114. "Osterweil, Mozes Statement, 17 May 1963," 38.
115. "Wieselberg, Teresa Statement, 10 March 1963," 27.
116. "Stromer, Marek Testimony, 17 August 1983."
117. "Weniger, Rachel Statement, 14 September 1944," 373.
118. "Winter, Markus Statement, 24 September 1944," BA-ZS: B162/29309.
119. "Wieselberg, Teresa Statement, 10 March 1963," 27.
120. Bräu, "The Economic Consequences," 437; "SSPF Memo: Jewish Labor Force, 6 November 1942," 81–82; Scherner and White, *Paying for Hitler's War*, 9.
121. SSPF Lemberg Memo 688/42, October 23, 1942, in "Beweiserherbungen, Oberstaatsanwalt Saarbrücken, 12 March 1965," 701.
122. "Bleines Hugo Statement, 21 October 1953," 224.
123. "Memo: HSSPF Galizien to Konfektions Fabrik, 7 January 1943," StAL: EL 317 III, Bü 1686, 44.
124. Wells, *The Janowska Road*, 135.
125. Segev, *Simon Wiesenthal*, 46.
126. Zayarnyuk, *Lviv's Uncertain Destination*, 183.
127. Sandkühler, "Das Zwangsarbeitslager Lemberg-Janowska," 623.
128. "Lubasz, Marcel Statement, 31 January 1965," BA-ZS: B162/4357, 34–35.
129. Andreas Rorowski, "Ruhrgebiets-Geschichte: Vom Kutschenbauer zum Autogiganten," *Westdeutsche Allgemeine Zeitung*, March 17, 2018, https://www.waz.de/staedte/bochum/ruhrgebiets-geschichte-vom-kutschenbauer-zum-auto giganten-id213743545.html.
130. "Orenstein, Karel Statement (Undated)," StAL: EL 317 III, Bü 1498, 19.
131. Drix, *Witness to Annihilation*, 64–65.
132. "Bachmann, Fred Statement, 26 September 1944," BA-ZS: B162/29309, 161.
133. "Übersetzung aus dem Hebräischen-Aus dem Buch 'Encyclopedia der Jüdischen Diaspora,' Serie Polen, Band Tarnopol," 232.
134. Arad, *Belzec, Sobibor, Treblinka*, 129.
135. Miedziński, "Nicht Schematische Erinnerungen des Großvaters," 28.

136. Miedziński, 28.
137. Jäcklein, "The Train Journey to Belzec," 232–35.
138. Miedziński, "Nicht Schematische Erinnerungen des Großvaters," 29.
139. Dean and Megargee, *Encyclopedia of Camps and Ghettos II*, 793.
140. "Porath, Zeev Statement, 8 June 1961," 1344.
141. Dean and Megargee, *Encyclopedia of Camps and Ghettos II*, 750–51, 754, 756, 807–8.
142. Dean and Megargee, 782.
143. A brief accounting is as follows, assuming an initial ghetto population of 160,000. The main distinction between the two estimates here, each based primarily on numbers from major killing actions, is the number killed during the ghetto liquidation in 1943. However, if one assumes a 20 percent death rate in the ghetto itself (which was the rough death rate in the Warsaw and Łódź ghettos), that still leaves almost 30,000 unaccounted for in the low estimate, while accounting for the majority remaining in the higher estimate. If the death rate in the ghetto was lower, that would add to the numbers remaining. The 41,500 number also does not include day-to-day deaths in the camp, executions of Jews not from the Lviv ghetto, executions of non-Jews, executions of Jews captured in the city, and executions of POWs and others on the site of the camp or under the auspices of its personnel (SK 1005 in the Lyczaków forest, for example). Given this accounting, it is not at all difficult to project the actual death toll at the camp to be substantially higher than 41,500. As noted earlier, Sandkühler has put the death toll equal or greater than Majdanek.
144. Sandkühler, "Das Zwangsarbeitslager Lemberg-Janowska," 619.
145. Winstone, *The Dark Heart of Hitler's Europe*, 189.
146. Wachsmann, *Kl*, 286.
147. Megargee, *Encyclopedia of Camps and Ghettos I*, 281, 293, 445.
148. Sandkühler, "Das Zwangsarbeitslager Lemberg-Janowska," 628.
149. Drix, *Witness to Annihilation*, 232.
150. "Children Shot for Sport, Reds Charge," *Washington Post*, 20 January 1945, 2.
151. "Dansches, Rudolf Statement, 2 January 1947," USHMM, RG-15.156M.
152. Solarewicz, "Helft Uns die Erinnerung zu Bewahren," 33.
153. "Lubasz, Marcel Testimony," 2.
154. Harran, *The Holocaust Chronicle*, 335.
155. "Beglückter, Jakob Statement, 29 February 1960," BA-ZS: B162/5764, 261.
156. Leopold Zimmerman in "Record of Soviet Military Court of the Carpathian Military Region against Prichodjko et al., 14 December 1966," 75–76.
157. "Wells (Welizcker), Leon Statement, 21 September 1944," 353.

158. Solarewicz, "Helft Uns die Erinnerung zu Bewahren," 34.
159. "Sobotta, Hans Statement, 4 June 1961," StAL: EL 317 III, Bü 1498.
160. "Trial of Adolf Eichmann, Session 22, 1 May 1961."
161. Awtuszewska-Ettrich, "Płaszów-Stammlager," 237.
162. Arad, *Belzec, Sobibor, Treblinka*, 51–52.
163. "Chyrowski, Jerzy Statement, 31 January 1961," 333–35; "Drix, Samuel Statement, 11 April 1969," BA-ZS: B162/28733, 71–72.
164. "Thürhaus, David Statement, 15 October 1963," 53.
165. "Zimmerman, Leopold Statement, 1 February 1965," 423.
166. "Zimmerman, Leopold Statement, 1 February 1965," 424; "Record of Soviet Commission for the Discovery and Investigation of German-Fascist Crimes in the City of Lemberg, 1–6 November 1944," 42.

6. BEHIND THE WIRES

Epigraph: Borwicz, *The University of Criminals*, 85.

1. Levi, *Survival in Auschwitz*, 51.
2. Yones, *Smoke in the Sand*, 188.
3. Wells, *The Janowska Road*, 63–64.
4. "Jüdische Frauen als Zielscheiben, Stuttgarter Zeitung, Nr. 166, 22 July 1967," YVA: RG-P13, file 189.
5. "Zimmerman, Leopold Statement, 30 July 1969," 88.
6. "Drix, Samuel, Tagebuch, 1942–1943," 15.
7. Drix, *Witness to Annihilation*, 62, 92.
8. Shenfeld, "The Recollections of Stepan Yakimovich Shenfeld [1943]," 92.
9. "Javorskij, Michail Statement, 13 September 1944," BA-ZS: B162/29309, 250.
10. "Gutschek, Todej Andrejewitsch Statement, 1 August 1967," 235.
11. "Szal, Abraham, Statement, 14 November 1962," BA-ZS: B162/5765, 609/28.
12. Wachsmann, *Kl*, 122.
13. Wachsmann, 122.
14. Sandkühler, "Das Zwangsarbeitslager Lemberg-Janowska," 623.
15. Drix, *Witness to Annihilation*, 82.
16. "Bogucki, Eugen Statement, 31 May 1972," BA-ZS: B162/28734, 212.
17. Wachsmann, *Kl*, 123.
18. "Porath, Zeev Statement, 7 June 1961," 1336.
19. "Porath, Zeev Statement, 24 April 1964," StAL: EL 317 III, Bü 1516, 205.
20. "Spinner, Aron (Leib)," USC Shoah Foundation Institute: Interview # 3522, Visual History Archive, 1995.

21. Drix, *Witness to Annihilation*, 136.
22. "Drix, Samuel, Tagebuch, 1942–1943."
23. "Translation of *Szkola Okuricienstwa*," 54, 64.
24. "Blum, Peter Statement, 28 January 1963," 3.
25. Kahane, *Lvov Ghetto Diary*, 91.
26. Borwicz, *The University of Criminals*, 82.
27. "Kolonko, Adolf Statement, 10 January 1963," StAL: EL 317 III, Bü 1523, 8.
28. "Kolonko, Adolf Statement, 10 January 1963," 8; "Porath, Zeev Statement, 6 June 1961," 1324–35.
29. "Porath, Zeev Statement, 6 June 1961," 1326.
30. "Letter, Simon Wiesenthal, 12 September 1960," StAL: EL 317 III, Bü 1505, 195.
31. "Drix, Samuel, Tagebuch, 1942–1943," 76.
32. Levi, *Survival in Auschwitz*, 90.
33. Richman, *Why?*, 43–45.
34. Richman, 26.
35. Richman, 44.
36. "Translation of *Szkola Okuricienstwa*," 52.
37. "Translation of *Szkola Okuricienstwa*," 24.
38. Borwicz, *The University of Criminals*, 40; Drix, *Witness to Annihilation*, 82.
39. "Translation of *Szkola Okuricienstwa*," 52.
40. "Translation of *Szkola Okuricienstwa*," 36–37.
41. Richman, *Why?*, 55.
42. "Translation of *Szkola Okuricienstwa*," 52.
43. "Szor, Leopold."
44. See "Translation of *Szkola Okuricienstwa*," 65–66; "Haffner, Dorothy Statement, 12 June 1964," StAL: EL 317, III Bü 1502, 94; "Mikolajewski (Lurie), Wlodzimierz Statement, 5 March 1963," 4.
45. "Translation of *Szkola Okuricienstwa*," 65–66.
46. "Bogucki, Eugen Statement, 31 May 1972," 211.
47. "Eichmann Court Hears of Nazi Effort to Hide Massacres," *The Times* (London), May 3, 1961, 10.
48. "Zimmerman, Leopold Statement, 1 February 1965," 416.
49. "Drix, Samuel, Tagebuch, 1942–1943," 19.
50. Hoess, *Commandant of Auschwitz*, 79.
51. Kessler, *The Wartime Diary of Edmund Kessler*, 59–60.
52. Drix, *Witness to Annihilation*, 122, 169.
53. "Weinberg, Jozef Statement, 8 January 1964," StAL: EL 317 III, Bü 1516, 99.

54. Segal, *Chaim Heißt Leben*, 79.
55. "Ash, Felix Video Interview, 1980," Ash Family Private Collection.
56. Levi, *Survival in Auschwitz*, 150.
57. Drix, *Witness to Annihilation*, 14.
58. Kaplan, *I Never Left Janowska*, 71.
59. Drix, *Witness to Annihilation*, 126.
60. "Beer, Aba," USC Shoah Foundation Institute: Interview #53564, Visual History Archive, 1981.
61. Ringelblum and Sloan, *Notes from the Warsaw Ghetto*, 310.
62. John Cox quoted in Beorn, *The Holocaust in Eastern Europe*, 227.
63. Levi, *Survival in Auschwitz*, 89.
64. As summarized in Marrus, "Jewish Resistance to the Holocaust," 93. See Rings, *Life with the Enemy*.
65. Bluhm, "How Did They Survive?," 96.
66. Richman, *Why?*, 21.
67. Drix, *Witness to Annihilation*, 72.
68. "Drix, Samuel, Tagebuch, 1942–1943," 43–44.
69. Richman, *Why?*, 15.
70. "Trial of Adolf Eichmann, Session 23, 2 May 1961," Nizhkor Project, http://nizkor.com/hweb/people/e/eichmann-adolf/transcripts/Sessions/Session-023-03.html; Angrick, *"Aktion 1005"*, 1196.
71. Kahane, *Lvov Ghetto Diary*, 102–3, 112, 116.
72. "The Janovska Camp at Lvov," Teaneck NJ: Ergo Media, 1993, video recording.
73. "Schlechter, Emanuel," *Biblioteka Polskiej Piosenki*, September 28, 2017, https://bibliotekapiosenki.pl/osoby/Schlechter_Emanuel.
74. Yones, *Smoke in the Sand*, 196–97.
75. Kahane, *Lvov Ghetto Diary*, 112.
76. Perlman, "Di Goldene Royz," 205.
77. "Translation of *Szkola Okuricienstwa*," 56.
78. "Münzer, Leopold," Virtual Shtetl, POLIN Museum of the History of Polish Jews, 2017, accessed March 15, 2020, https://sztetl.org.pl/en/biographies/3370-munzer-leopold.
79. "The Polish Pianist Artur Hermelin (1901–1942) by Hanna Palmon (Undated)," YVA: RG-O88, file 42.
80. Gilbert, "Music in the Nazi Ghettos and Camps," 440.
81. It is also possible that this was an original composition. "The Polish Pianist Artur Hermelin (1901–1942) by Hanna Palmon (Undated)," 11.
82. "Drix, Samuel, Tagebuch, 1942–1943," 79.

83. Wiesenthal and Wechsberg, *The Murderers among Us*, 280.
84. "Blai, Barbara Statement, 19 September 1944," 175.
85. Drix, *Witness to Annihilation*, 159.
86. Kahane, *Lvov Ghetto Diary*, 101.
87. "Official Camp Orchestras in Auschwitz," Holocaust Music, World ORT, accessed March 16, 2020, http://holocaustmusic.ort.org/places/camps/death-camps/auschwitz/camp-orchestras/.
88. Redzik, "The Janowska Hell," 215.
89. Drix, *Witness to Annihilation*, 105–6.
90. Fackler, "Cultural Behaviour and the Invention of Traditions," 625.
91. Kassow, *Who Will Write Our History?*, 6–7.
92. "Porath, Zeev Statement, 18 May 1972," BA-ZS: B162/28734, 265.
93. "Porath, Zeev Statement, 7 June 1961," 1336.
94. "Seweryn, Alma Testimony," USHMM, RG-15.084M, AZIH 301/605 (Testimonies-Relacje).
95. Richman, *Why?*, 42.
96. Segal, *Chaim Heißt Leben*, 79.
97. "Translation of *Szkola Okuricienstwa*," 52.
98. Wells, *The Janowska Road*, 292.
99. Stromer, *Memoirs of an Unfortunate Person*, 172–73.
100. "Spinner, Aron (Leib)."
101. "Porath, Zeev Statement, 24 April 1964," 205.
102. "Lewinter, Herman," USC Shoah Foundation Institute: Interview #8443, Visual History Archive, 1995.
103. "Hirschhorn, Bernhard Statement, 9 February 1948," 5.
104. "Translation of *Szkola Okuricienstwa*," 45–46.
105. "Translation of *Szkola Okuricienstwa*," 30.
106. Drix, *Witness to Annihilation*, 94–95.
107. "Gebauer, Fritz Statement, 26 November 1962," 609.
108. Drix, *Witness to Annihilation*, 95.
109. Folkmann and Szende, *The Promise Hitler Kept*, 141.
110. Vysotsky et al., *Nazi Crimes in Ukraine*, 212.
111. Kahane, *Lvov Ghetto Diary*, 107.
112. "Translation of *Szkola Okuricienstwa*," 46.
113. "Gutschek, Todej Andrejewitsch Statement, 1 August 1967," 243.
114. "Wiesen, Ida Statement, 5 July 1970," BA-ZS: B162/5768, 1311–12a.
115. "Beer, Aba."

116. "Rogowski, Marian Statement, 22 September 1961," 137.
117. "The Janovska Camp at Lvov."
118. "Chamaides, Heinrich Statement, 13 September 1944," USHMM: 1.2.7.7/82183301_0_1–82183305_0_1/its Digital Archive.
119. "The Janovska Camp at Lvov"; "Lubasz, Marcel Testimony," 3–4.
120. Werger, "Denk Ich an Lemberg."
121. "Translation of *Szkola Okuricienstwa*," 57.
122. "Rogowski, Marian Statement, 13 November 1963," 80; "Rogowski, Marian Statement, 22 September 1961," 148–49.
123. "Translation of *Szkola Okuricienstwa*," 88–89.
124. Borwicz, *The University of Criminals*, 36–37.
125. Stromer, *Memoirs of an Unfortunate Person*, 195–96.
126. "Translation of *Szkola Okuricienstwa*," 77.
127. Gawron, "Michał Maksymilian Borwicz," 116–17.
128. Perlman, "Di Goldene Royz," 220–21.
129. "The Janovska Camp at Lvov."
130. "Translation of *Szkola Okuricienstwa*," 78.
131. "Additional Melchior Trial Witness Statements, 28 August 1949," 124.
132. "Translation of *Szkola Okuricienstwa*," 78.
133. Drix, *Witness to Annihilation*, 138.
134. Sandkühler, "Das Zwangsarbeitslager Lemberg-Janowska," 614.
135. Borwicz, *The University of Criminals*, 56,58.
136. Borwicz, 71.

7. HERE BE MONSTERS

Epigraph: Levi, *The Reawakening*, 228.
1. "Der Hinrichtung Entgangen," *Die Mahnung*, May 15, 1971; "Gogolowska, Stanislawa Statement, 12 March 1947," 1258.
2. "Gogolowska, Stanislawa Its Documents," USHMM: 6.3.3.2/td 983883/109487746/its Digital Archive.
3. Améry, *At the Mind's Limits*, 27–29.
4. "Krebs, Zygmunt Statement, 14 September 1961," STAL: EL 317 III, Bü 1498, 223.
5. "Entenberg, Meier Statement, 8 April 1947," USHMM: 1.2.7.7/82183195_0_1–82183196_0_1/its Digital Archive.
6. "Memo: Identification of Prisoner-Hügel, Michael, Detachment a, 7708 War Crimes Group, 31 January 1947," USHMM, RG-15.156M, 474.
7. "Goldberg, Abraham Statement, 29 June 1962," 608/33–34.
8. Wells, *The Janowska Road*, 139.

9. Borwicz, *The University of Criminals*, 42.
10. "Drix, Samuel, Tagebuch, 1942–1943," 43.
11. "Drix, Samuel, Tagebuch, 1942–1943," 43.
12. "Rogowski, Marian Statement, 13 November 1963," 80.
13. "Translation of *Szkola Okuricienstwa*," 67.
14. "Kruszewski, Emil Statement, 22 April 1964," 115.
15. "Manusevich, David Statement, 13 September 1944," 296; "Wind, Joseph Statement, 25 September 1944," USHMM: 1.2.7.7/82183306_0_1–82183312_0_1/its Digital Archive.
16. "Osterweil, Mozes Statement, 17 May 1963," 35.
17. "Weinberg, Jozef Statement, 8 January 1964," 100.
18. Borwicz, *The University of Criminals*, 31–32.
19. "Schättinger, Sonja Statement, 28 February 1964," StAL: EL 317 III, Bü 1516, 156.
20. "Jüdische Frauen als Zielscheiben, Stuttgarter Zeitung, Nr. 166, 22 July 1967."
21. "Wahllos Menschen erschossen," Stuttgarter Zeitung, Nr. 77, 4 April 1967, YVA: RG-P13, file 189, 16.
22. "Wegen Zwei Kartoffeln Erschossen, Stuttgarter Zeitung, 16 November 1967," YVA: RG-P13, file 189.
23. "Chamaides, Henry Statement, 10 June 1964," StAL: EL 317 III, Bü 1516, 275–76.
24. "Korn, Severn Statement, 21 September 1944," BA-ZS: B162/29309, 276.
25. "Wells, Leon Weliczker," USC Shoah Foundation Institute: Interview # 23410, Visual History Archive, 1996.
26. "Rosen, Chaim Statement, 11 September 1960," 112–13.
27. "Translation of *Szkola Okuricienstwa*," 79.
28. "Haffner, Dorothy Statement, 12 June 1964," 92.
29. Kahane, *Lvov Ghetto Diary*, 90.
30. Lower, *Hitler's Furies*, 134–35.
31. Rycevskij and others sometimes misidentified the weapon used. Rycevskij said it was a machine gun. "Rycevskij, Miroslav Statement, 27 January 1967," 315.
32. "Barth, Pinkas Statement, 21 April 1964," StAL: EL 317 III, Bü 1502, 67–68.
33. Kahane, *Lvov Ghetto Diary*, 90. See also Wiesenthal and Wechsberg, *The Murderers among Us*, 276.
34. Lower, *Hitler's Furies*, 155.
35. "Hansberg, Elizabeth Statement, 1 September 1962," 189; "Hansberg, Elizabeth Statement, 18 September 1964," 116.
36. "Rogowski, Marian Statement, 22 September 1961," 84.
37. Lower, *Hitler's Furies*, 159, 166.
38. Améry, *At the Mind's Limits*, 36.

39. Lower, *Hitler's Furies*, 158.
40. Borwicz, *The University of Criminals*, 41.
41. "Rosen, Chaim Statement, 23 September 1959," BA-ZS: B162/5763, 175.
42. "Blai, Abraham Statement, 19 September 1944," 175.
43. "Urteil gg. Röder u.a, LG Stuttgart vom 29.4.1968, Ks 5/65," in *Justiz und NS-Verbrechen. Sammlung Deutscher Strafurteile wegen Nationalsozialistischer Tötungsverbrechen 1945–1999*, vol. 28, 727.
44. Schroer, "Civilization, Barbarism, and the Ethos of Self-Control," 41.
45. Wachsmann, *Kl*, 105.
46. Wachsmann, 155.
47. "LG Saarbrücken Urteil gg. Friedrich Heinen, 10 July 1978," 6–9.
48. Borwicz, *The University of Criminals*, 40–41. Wachsmann points out a similar case with Gustav Sorge in Sachsenhausen; see Wachsmann, *Kl*, 222–23.
49. "Children Shot for Sport, Reds Charge," 2.
50. "Hirschhorn, Bernard Statement, 9 November 1948," 3–4. See also "Finkelstein, Sol Statement, 23 June 1964," StAL: EL 317 III, Bü 1497, 272.
51. "Jolles, Bronislawa Statement, 13 January 1960," BA-ZS: B162/5763, 188.
52. "Lg Saarbrücken Urteil Gg. Fritz Gebauer, 29 June 1971," 59–60.
53. "Porath, Zeev Statement, 9 June 1961," StAL: EL 48-2, Bü 397, 1365.
54. "Rosen, Chaim Statement, 11 September 1960," 109.
55. "The Janovska Camp at Lvov."
56. Häkkänen, "Murder by Manual and Ligature Strangulation," 74–75.
57. "Schächter, Wolf Statement, 27 September 1944," 334.
58. "Heilpern, Julian Statement, 14 June 1960," StAL: EL 317 III, Bü 1505, 23.
59. Heinen, Biermann, Brumbauer. See "Porath, Zeev Statement, 8 June 1961," 1357; "Porath, Zeev Letter 30 November 1960," StAL: EL 317 III, Bü 1505, 507; "Korn, Moische Statement, 13 September 1944," 264.
60. "Poplawski, Tadeusz Statement, 17 April 1964," StAL: EL 317 III, Bü 1516, 298.
61. "Borwicz, Michel Statement, 13 March 1963," StAL: EL 317 III, Bü 1523, 5.
62. "Hier spricht Augenzeuge Wiesenthal, Stuttgarter Zeitung, Nr. 293, 21 December 1966," YVA: RG-P13, file 189.
63. "Katz, Aron Statement, 11 March 1961," StAL: EL 317 III, Bü 1523, 123.
64. "Halbkram, Maria Statement, 27 September 1967," BA-ZS: B162/5768, 1276.
65. "Schächter, Wolf Statement, 27 September 1944," 336.
66. "Excerpt, Irena Szajewicz Diary from Żydowski Instytut Historyczny, 7 July 1961," BA-ZS: B162/5764, 442.
67. "The Janovska Camp at Lvov."
68. Kahane, *Lvov Ghetto Diary*, 110–11.

69. One of the rabbis from Jaworow was named Feibisch. This event appears in Kahane, *Lvov Ghetto Diary*; "The Janovska Camp at Lvov." "Gerner, Mendel Statement, 23 September 1944"; Drix, *Witness to Annihilation*.
70. "Katz, Aron Statement, 11 March 1961," 123–25.
71. See Wells, *The Janowska Road*, 74; "Translation of *Szkola Okuricienstwa*," 26; "Chamaides, Henry Statement, 10 June 1964"; Borwicz, *The University of Criminals*, 62; "Record of Soviet Commission for the Discovery and Investigation of German-Fascist Crimes in the City of Lemberg, 1–6 November 1944," 27.
72. "Wells, Leon Weliczker Statement, 16 June 1961," StAL: EL 317 III, Bü 1505, 443.
73. Beorn, *The Holocaust in Eastern Europe*, 130.
74. Heinrich Himmler, "Document 1919-Ps: Himmler's Speech at Posen, 4 October 1943," in *Trials of the Major War Criminals before the International Military Tribunal: Documents and Other Material in Evidence, 1850-Ps to 2233-Ps*, 146.
75. These camps were often of a relatively similar size, though populations increased throughout the war.
76. Pohl, "Die großen Zwangsarbeiterlager," 426, 437.
77. Wachsmann, *Kl*, 115.
78. See, for example, the work of Thomas Kühne. Kühne, *Kameradschaft*.
79. "Lieber zur Front als ins Judenlager, Stuttgarter Nachrichten, Nr. 193, 17 August 1967," YVA: RG-P13, file 189; "Ehemalige Bahnpolizisten als Zeugen, Stuttgarter Zeitung, Nr. 188, 17 August 1967," YVA: RG-P13, file 189.
80. "Osterweil, Mozes Statement, 17 May 1963," 38.
81. Améry, *At the Mind's Limits*, 31.
82. Nutkiewicz, "Shame, Guilt, and Anguish in Holocaust Survivor Testimony," 21.
83. Sinnreich, "The Rape of Jewish Women During the Holocaust," 108.
84. Katz, "Thoughts," 297.
85. Halbmayr, "Sexualized Violence," 30. See also the work of Hájková, "Sexual Barter in Times of Genocide."
86. Beorn, "Bodily Conquest," 196.
87. Brown, *The Reaper's Garden*, 107.
88. "Porath, Zeev Statement, 7 June 1961," 1334–35.
89. "Verzeichnis der Zwangsarbeitslager des SSPF im Distrikt Galizien, 1941–1943, Staatsanwaltschaft Stuttgart, 15 June 1967."
90. Chalmers, "Jewish Women's Sexual Behaviour and Sexualized Abuse During the Nazi Era," 189.
91. "Charatan, Ludwig Statement, 30 January 1948," USHMM: 1.2.7.7/82183197_0_1/ its Digital Archive.
92. "Lewinter, Herman."

93. "Spinner, Paula Statement, 12 February 1948," USHMM: 1.2.7.7/82183202_0_1–82183203_0_1/its Digital Archive.
94. "Czerner, Rudolf Statement, 27 November 1958," BA-ZS: B162/5726, 8.
95. "Jolles, Bronislawa Statement, 13 January 1960," 189.
96. See "Drix, Samuel, Tagebuch, 1942–1943," 61–63; "Wind, Joseph Statement, 25 September 1944"; "Bachmann, Fred Statement, 26 September 1944," 164.
97. "Korn, Moische Statement, 13 September 1944," 265; "Korn, Severn Statement, 21 September 1944," 277.
98. "Winter, Klara Statement, 24 September 1944," BA-ZS: B162/29309, 394–95.
99. "Sta Lübeck-Sachvermerk, 3 April 1970," BA-ZS: B162/28733, 160.
100. "Rogowski, Marian Statement, 22 September 1961," 150–51.
101. Probably one of the reasons that Heinen stands out is that he actually went on trial, and so witnesses focused on his crimes. "Porath Letter, 30 November 1960," StAL: EL 317 III, Bü 1505, 507.
102. "Drix, Samuel, Tagebuch, 1942–1943," 82–83; "LG Saarbrücken Urteil gg. Friedrich Heinen, 10 July 1978," 67–69.
103. Chalmers, "Jewish Women's Sexual Behaviour and Sexualized Abuse During the Nazi Era," 189.
104. Levi, *Survival in Auschwitz*, 26–27.
105. Kaplan, *I Never Left Janowska*, 53.
106. "Blum, Peter Statement, 8 September 1960," 314–15; "Halbkram, Maria Statement, 8 May 1972," BA-ZS: B162/28734, 308.
107. "Winter, Klara Statement, 24 September 1944," 68; "Weniger, Rachel Statement, 14 September 1944," 375.
108. "Halbkram, Maria Statement, 27 September 1967," 1274.
109. "Fox war der Schlimmste," *Stuttgarter Zeitung*, 15 December 1967, YVA: RG-P13, file 189.
110. "Gutschek, Todej Andrejewitsch Statement, 1 August 1967," 242.
111. "Halbkram, Maria Statement, 27 September 1967," 1276.
112. "Porath Letter, 30 November 1960," 503.
113. "Blum, Peter Protokoll, 9 June 1961," StAL: EL 48/2, Bü 397, 1249.
114. "Porath, Zeev Statement, 6 June 1961," 1327; "Blum, Peter Statement, 28 January 1963," 3.
115. "Translation of *Szkola Okuricienstwa*," 76–77.
116. "Schal, Karol Statement, 21 September 1944," BA-ZS: B162/29309, 339.
117. "Translation of *Szkola Okuricienstwa*," 69.
118. Solarewicz, "Helft Uns die Erinnerung zu Bewahren," 34.

119. "Thürhaus, David Statement, 15 October 1963," 57–58; "Wells (Welizcker), Leon Statement, 22 September 1944," BA-ZS: B162/29309, 358; Wells, *The Janowska Road*, 190.
120. "Urbach, Gisela Statement, 11 May 1971," BA-ZS: B162/5768, 1343.
121. Katz, "Thoughts," 295.
122. Wells, *The Janowska Road*, 88.
123. "Translation of *Szkola Okuricienstwa*," 54.
124. Leon Wells, "Living Ghosts of the Concentration Camps," *New York Times*, January 26, 1964, SM 13.
125. Levenkron, "Death and the Maidens," 19–20.
126. See "Registration Cards for Jews from Lviv Ghetto," USHMM, RG-31.098M 1997.A.0297; "Translation of *Szkola Okuricienstwa*," 50.
127. Wells, *The Janowska Road*, 181. Other survivors state variously that she was shot because a Pole had kissed her hand and that she was planning to escape. "Gogolowska, Stanislawa Statement, 12 March 1947," 1265; "Hirschhorn, Bernhard Statement, 9 February 1948," 14.
128. "Kohn, Rosa Statement, 27 November 1958," BA-ZS: B162/5726, 5.
129. Adolf Hitler, "'Fortsetzung meiner Antwort an die marxistischen Staatsretter im Untersuchungsausschuß' Rede auf NSDAP-Versammlung in München, 28 January 1928," in *Vom Weimarer Parteitag bis zur Reichstagswahl, Juli 1926-Mai 1928*, ed. Clemens Vollnhals and Bärbel Dusik (Munich: K.G. Saur, 1992), 646.
130. Mühlhäuser, "Between 'Racial Awareness' and Fantasies of Potency," 88.
131. Katz, "Thoughts," 297.
132. Wells, *The Janowska Road*, 88.
133. Katz, "Thoughts," 293.
134. Katz, 294.
135. Browning, *Remembering Survival*, 191.

8. THE SPIDER'S WEB

Epigraph: Guare, *Six Degrees of Separation*, 48–49.
1. "ADGB Trade Union School History of Use," Bauhaus Denkmal Bundesschule Bernau bei Berlin, 2020, accessed May 17, 2020, https://www.bauhaus-denkmal-bernau.de/en/trade-union-school/usage-history.html; "Kolonko, Adolf Trial Testimony, Band 2," 47–49.
2. Matthäus and Böhler, *War, Pacification, and Mass Murder, 1939*, 39; Barbier, *Spies, Lies, and Citizenship*, 294, 5.
3. Kwiet, "Paul Zapp," 254.
4. Golfard, *The Diary of Samuel Golfard*, 164.

5. "Interrogation of Fritz Liebl, Member of Einsatzkommando 3/I, by SS and Police Investigators, December 1939," in *War, Pacification, and Mass Murder, 1939*, 109.
6. These were Richard Dyga, Johann Salzborn, Ernst Pramor, and Erich Minkus.
7. Borwicz, *The University of Criminals*, 21.
8. Tukey, *Exploratory Data Analysis*, vi.
9. Chronakis, "From the Lone Survivor to the Networked Self," 59.
10. Raab, "More Than Just a Metaphor," 326.
11. Raab, 321.
12. Wölfer, Faber, and Hewstone, "Social Network Analysis in the Science of Groups," 46.
13. Winstone, *The Dark Heart of Hitler's Europe*, 189.
14. Bennett, *The Nazi, the Painter and the Forgotten Story*, 1407.
15. "Schönbach, Roman Trial Testimony, Band 6/K," 126–27.
16. "Fox, Paul Statement, 2 October 1961," StAL: EL 48/2, Bü 397, 1549; "Sobotta, Hans Statement, 31 May 1961," StAL: EL 317 III, Bü 1498, 289.
17. He claimed that he did not serve there until the summer of 1942, but this is unlikely as he received a War Merit Cross (*Kriegsverdienstkreuz*) from the SSPF in Lviv in January 1942. See "Beweiserherbungen, Oberstaatsanwalt Saarbrücken, 12 March 1965," 727.
18. Kolonko further alleged that Rokita was the deputy commandant of the "Soviet prisoner of war camp." This seems unlikely, though he may have held some related role. Rokita himself admitted serving in Trawniki, but claimed this was in 1943. "Kolonko, Adolf Statement, 16 September 1960," 155; Sandkühler, *"Endlösung" in Galizien*, 435; Shenfeld, "The Recollections of Stepan Yakimovich Shenfeld [1943]," 2.
19. "Kolonko, Adolf Statement, 9 December 1960," StAL: EL 48/2, Bü 398, 1698.
20. Browning and Matthäus, *The Origins of the Final Solution*, 32, 34.
21. They were Kolonko, Mellar, Schönbach, Sobotta, Siller, Thomanek, Lambor, Fox.
22. Black, "Rehearsal for 'Reinhard'?," 208.
23. "Fox, Paul Statement, 2 October 1961," 1550.
24. "Fox, Paul Statement, 2 October 1961," 1549–51.
25. Dean and Megargee, *Encyclopedia of Camps and Ghettos II*, 849.
26. Golfard, *The Diary of Samuel Golfard*, 166.
27. Pohl, *Nationalsozialistische Judenverfolgung in Ostgalizien*, 414.
28. Golfard, *The Diary of Samuel Golfard*, 66–67.
29. Golfard, 73.

30. Druck, *Swastika over Jaworow*, 16. https://www.jewishgen.org/yizkor/Yavoriv1/Yavoriv1.html; "Kruszewski, Emil Statement, 22 April 1964," 115.
31. "Verzeichnis der Zwangsarbeitslager des SSPF im Distrikt Galizien, 1941–1943, Staatsanwaltschaft Stuttgart, 15 June 1967."
32. "Kolonko, Adolf Statement, 16 September 1960," 159.
33. Dean and Megargee, *Encyclopedia of Camps and Ghettos II*, 778; "Record of Soviet Commission for the Discovery and Investigation of German-Fascist Crimes in Grodek, 8/12 October 1944," BA-ZS: B162/29309, 61.
34. "Kolonko, Adolf Statement, 10 January 1963," 3; "Kolonko, Adolf Statement, 16 September 1960," 159–61; "Kolonko, Adolf Statement, 14 June 1960," StAL: EL 317 III, Bü 1505, 128–29.
35. "Kriminalkommissariat Waldshut Memorandum to Staatsanwaltschaft Waldshut, 5 July 1960," StAL: EL 317 III, Bü 1505, 35. The Holzmann company was contracted for multiple Nazi projects including the Atlantic Wall and building projects across eastern Europe. The company also used thousands of forced laborers. See Pohl, *Philipp Holzmann*.
36. "Kolonko, Adolf Statement, 16 September 1960," 163; "Hansberg, Elizabeth Statement, 18 September 1964," 118.
37. "Löhnert, Anton Statement, 18 October 1960," StAL: EL 317 III, Bü 1523, 37.
38. "Kolonko, Adolf Statement, 13 October 1960," StAL: EL 48/2, Bü 398, 1775; "Porath Letter, 30 November 1960," 501.
39. "Kolonko, Adolf Statement, 10 January 1963," 5.
40. "Hochberg, Ptachia Letter, 5 April 1961," StAL: EL 317 III, Bü 1505, 187.
41. "Sobotta, Hans Statement, 4 June 1961," 14.
42. "Kolonko, Adolf Statement, 10 January 1963," 5.
43. "Noch einmal auf Befehl gemordet?, Stuttgarter Zeitung, Nr. 270, 24 November 1966," YVA: RG-P13, file 189.
44. "Abschrift-Handakten des StA Lübeck, 17 April 1970," BA-ZS: B162/28733, 191; "Sachverhaltdarstellung StA Waldhsut, 26 June 1961," BA-ZS: B162/259075, 11.
45. "Löhnert, Anton Statement, 18 October 1960," 37.
46. "Hochberg, Ptachia Letter, 5 April 1961," 187.
47. "Kolonko, Adolf Statement, 16 September 1960," 169.
48. "Kraus, Jakob Statement, 11 October 1962," 565.
49. Karten, "The Bitter End," 193.
50. Jaskot, "The Architecture of the Holocaust," 4.
51. Kühne, "Male Bonding and Shame Culture," 65.
52. Raab, "More Than Just a Metaphor," 331.
53. McDoom, "Antisocial Capital," 868.

9. HOLOKAUSTOS

1. The first wave was the Einsatzgruppen killings in 1941 and the second was the major reduction of ghetto populations and large aktions in 1942. Raul Hilberg identified the first two waves or sweeps.
2. Longerich, *Heinrich Himmler*, 583.
3. "Chyrowski, Jerzy Statement, 31 January 1961," 345.
4. Kahane, *Lvov Ghetto Diary*, 105–6.
5. "Gauben, Chaim Statement, 19 September 1944," BA-ZS: B162/29309, 210.
6. Wells, *The Janowska Road*, 122.
7. Bem, *Sobibor Extermination Camp, 1942–1943*, 181–82.
8. "Chyrowski, Jerzy Statement, 31 January 1961," 333.
9. Folkmann and Szende, *The Promise Hitler Kept*, 145.
10. "Lageplan des Judenlagers R-W Lemberg," DALO: P37-4-188.
11. Sandkühler, "Das Zwangsarbeitslager Lemberg-Janowska," 613.
12. Folkmann and Szende, *The Promise Hitler Kept*, 143; "Polish UNWWC Report on Joseph Grzymek," USHMM: 1.2.7.8/82188094_0_1–82188097_0_1/its Digital Archive; "Goldmann-Giliead, Michael Statement, 28 October 2015," USHMM: RG-50.030.0832, 84.
13. "Amtliches Fernsprechbuch für den Distrikt Galizien (1942)," DALO, 19; Sandkühler, "Das Zwangsarbeitslager Lemberg-Janowska," 626.
14. Angrick, "Annihilation and Labor," 218; Pohl, *Nationalsozialistische Judenverfolgung in Ostgalizien*, 253.
15. "Urteil gg. Hildebrand, Friedrich, Lg Bremen, 12 May 1967," BA-ZS: B162/14277, 64; Stroop, *The Stroop Report*, 4.
16. Stroop, *Żydowska Dzielnica Miezkaniowa W Warsawie Już Nie Istnieje!*, 13; Pohl, *Nationalsozialistische Judenverfolgung in Ostgalizien*, 256.
17. Katzmann, *Rozwiazania Kwestii Żydowskiej W Distrykcie Galicja*, 122.
18. "Urteil Gg. Röder U.A., Lg Stuttgart Vom 29.4.1968, Ks 5/65," 728.
19. "Drix, Samuel, Tagebuch, 1942–1943," 96.
20. *USA vs.John Kalymon*.
21. "Eissmann, Jehuda Statement, 10 May 1972," BA-ZS: B162/28734, 298.
22. Yones, *Smoke in the Sand*, 176–77.
23. Katzmann, *Rozwiazania Kwestii Żydowskiej W Distrykcie Galicja*, 136.
24. Folkmann and Szende, *The Promise Hitler Kept*, 168.
25. Katzmann, *Rozwiazania Kwestii Żydowskiej W Distrykcie Galicja*, 136.
26. Katzmann, 180.
27. "Drix, Samuel, Tagebuch, 1942–1943," 95–96.

28. "Trial of Adolf Eichmann, Session 23, 2 May 1961."
29. "Zimmerman, Leopold Statement, 30 July 1969," 88.
30. "Katz, Aron Statement, 11 March 1961," 123.
31. Pohl, *Nationalsozialistische Judenverfolgung in Ostgalizien*, 263.
32. Stroop, *Żydowska Dzielnica Miezkaniowa W Warsawie Już Nie Istnieje!*, 12.
33. Katzmann, *Rozwiazania Kwestii Żydowskiej W Distrykcie Galicja*, 123–24.
34. "Drix, Samuel, Tagebuch, 1942–1943," 97–98.
35. "Spinner, Aron (Leib)."
36. "Letter: Rudolf Brandt to Gustav Willhaus, 12 April 1943," IfZ: MA 297/1.
37. "Letter: SS-Personalhauptamtes to Rudolf Brandt, 6 March 1943," IfZ: MA 297/1.
38. "Letter: Rudolf Brandt to Gustav Willhaus, 23 July 1943," IfZ: MA 297/1.
39. "Letter: Gustav Willhaus to Rudolf Brandt, 17 July 1943," IfZ: MA 297/1.
40. Wiesenthal and Wechsberg, *The Murderers among Us*, 277.
41. "Letter: StA Sichting to StA München I, 25 July 1960," BA-ZS: B162/5725, 5; Lepre, *Himmler's Bosnian Division*, 38.
42. "LG Saarbrücken Urteil gg. Friedrich Heinen, 10 July 1978," 26.
43. Friedman, *Ich Träumte*, 64; "Geller, Baruch Statement, 20 March 1960," BA-ZS: B162/5764, 262; "Schächter, Wolf Statement, 27 September 1944," 337
44. "Translation of *Szkola Okuricienstwa*," 88.
45. Spector, "Aktion 1005," 158.
46. See, for example, the detailed report of December 8, 1942. "Memorandum to the President of the United States, Congress Weekly, 8 December 1942," FDRPL: Selected Digitized Correspondence of Eleanor Roosevelt, 1933–1945.
47. Spector, "Aktion 1005," 158.
48. Terry, "Covering Up Chelmno," 203.
49. Berger, *Experten der Vernichtung*, ii.
50. Montague, *Chełmno and the Holocaust*, 116.
51. Terry, "Covering up Chelmno: Nazi Attempts to Obfuscate and Obliterate an Extermination Camp," 200–201.
52. Montague, *Chełmno and the Holocaust*, 116; Wachsmann, *Kl*, 314.
53. Berger, *Experten der Vernichtung*, ii.
54. Spector, "Aktion 1005," 161.
55. Angrick, *"Aktion 1005"*, 2, 774–76.
56. "Record of Soviet Commission for the Discovery and Investigation of German-Fascist Crimes in the City of Lemberg, 1–6 November 1944," 13.
57. "Walter Friedrich Karl Schallock Vita Compiled by Rüdiger Schallock, 12 June 2020," Unpublished, author collection.
58. Wells, "Living Ghosts of the Concentration Camps," SM13.

59. Wells, *The Janowska Road*, 165; "Wells (Welizcker), Leon Statement, 21 September 1944," 354.
60. "Walter Friedrich Karl Schallock Vita Compiled by Rüdiger Schallock, 12 June 2020"; "Correspondence with Rüdiger Schallock, 23 August 2020," Author's personal collection.
61. Angrick, *"Aktion 1005"*, 2, 778.
62. Pohl, *Nationalsozialistische Judenverfolgung in Ostgalizien*, 379; Klemp, *Nicht Ermittelt*, 249–50.
63. Browning, *Nazi Policy, Jewish Workers, German Killers*, 119.
64. "Trial of Adolf Eichmann, Session 23, 2 May 1961."
65. "Chamaides, Heinrich Statement, 13 September 1944."
66. "Feinsilber, Abraham Statement, 30 May 1972," BA-ZS: B162/28734, 215.
67. "Wells (Welizcker), Leon Statement, 21 September 1944," 354.
68. "Thürhaus, David Ben Statement, 22 May 1972," BA-ZS: B162/28734, 261–62.
69. Wells, *The Janowska Road*, 161.
70. Levi, *Survival in Auschwitz*, 88.
71. "Translation of *Szkola Okuricienstwa*," 86–87.
72. "Büttner, Martin Statement, 27 March 1963," StAL: EL 317 III, Bü 1498, 35.
73. "Thürhaus, David Statement, 15 October 1963," 49; Wells, *The Janowska Road*, 194.
74. Wells lists them as: Leichengräber, Schlepper, Träger, Reinigungsleute [stackers and layerers], [bone carriers], Aschebrigade, Streukolonne. Wells, *The Janowska Road*.
75. "Manusevich, David Statement, 13 September 1944," 299.
76. "Korn, Moische Statement, 13 September 1944," 267; Sobieski, "Reminiscenses from Lwow, 1939–1945," 359.
77. Vysotsky et al., *Nazi Crimes in Ukraine*, 222.
78. "Sie nannten mich Oberteufel, Stuttgarter Nachrichten, Nr. 145, 22 June 1967," YVA: RG-P13, file 189, 15.
79. "Chamaides, Heinrich Statement, 13 September 1944"; "Wells (Welizcker), Leon Statement, 22 September 1944."
80. "Eichmann Court Hears of Nazi Effort to Hide Massacres," 10.
81. Angrick, *"Aktion 1005"*, 2, 1186.
82. "Trial of Adolf Eichmann, Session 23, 2 May 1961"; Wells, *The Janowska Road*, 146.
83. Wells, *The Janowska Road*, 150–51.
84. "Trial of Adolf Eichmann, Session 23, 2 May 1961."
85. "Eichmann Court Hears of Nazi Effort to Hide Massacres," 10.
86. Wells, *The Janowska Road*, 180.

87. "Korn, Moische Statement, 13 September 1944," 136.
88. "Trial of Adolf Eichmann, Session 23, 2 May 1961."
89. "Spinner, Aron (Leib)."
90. Angrick, *"Aktion 1005"*, 2, 783–84.
91. "Wells (Welizcker), Leon Statement, 22 September 1944," 355–56.
92. "Appendix II, Translation of Lothar Wendel Statement Re: SK1005 (Undated)," USHMM, RG-15.155M, 760.
93. Wells, *The Janowska Road*, 180.
94. "'Blutrünstig' klingt zu bescheiden, Stuttgarter Zeitung, Nr. 153, 7 July 1967," YVA: RG-P13, file 189.
95. "Zimmerman, Leopold Statement, 1 February 1965," 415.
96. "Ash, Felix Statement, 23 November 1964," StAL: EL 317 III, Bü 1497, 306; "Wells (Weliczker), Leon Statement, 11 April 1949," StAL: EL 317 III, Bü 1513, 28.
97. Wells, *The Janowska Road*, 141.
98. "Eichmann Court Hears of Nazi Effort to Hide Massacres," 10.
99. "Wells (Weliczker), Leon Statement, 11 April 1949," 28.
100. "Eichmann Court Hears of Nazi Effort to Hide Massacres," 10.
101. "Thürhaus, David Statement, 15 October 1963," 57.
102. "Ramelow, Klaus-Joachim Statement, 18 November 1947," BA-ZS: B162/29309, 133.
103. "Blai, Barbara Statement, 19 September 1944," 175.
104. Angrick, *"Aktion 1005"*, 2, 781.
105. Wells, *The Janowska Road*, 161.
106. "Wind, Josef Interview," 14.
107. "Translation of *Szkola Okuricienstwa*," 87.
108. "Ash, Felix Video Interview, 1980."
109. Wells, *The Janowska Road*, 182, 196.
110. "Thürhaus, David Statement, 15 October 1963," 57–58.
111. Wells, "Living Ghosts of the Concentration Camps," SM13; "Schallock gab sich wie ein Vater, Stuttgarter Stadt-Nachrichten, Nr. 139, 15 June 1967," YVA: RG-P13, file 189, 13.
112. "Ash, Felix Video Interview, 1980."
113. "Trial of Adolf Eichmann, Session 23, 2 May 1961."
114. Wells, "Living Ghosts of the Concentration Camps," SM13.
115. "Korn, Moische Statement, 13 September 1944," 268–69.
116. "Trial of Adolf Eichmann, Session 23, 2 May 1961."
117. Tenenbaum, *Underground*, 317.
118. "Ash, Felix Statement, 23 November 1964," 307.

119. Wells, *The Janowska Road*, 186–87.
120. "Ash, Felix Statement, 23 November 1964," 305–6.
121. Angrick, *"Aktion 1005"*, 2.
122. Levi, *Survival in Auschwitz*, 89–90.
123. "Trial of Adolf Eichmann, Session 23, 2 May 1961."
124. Angrick, *"Aktion 1005"*, 2, 1180–81.
125. Wells, *The Janowska Road*, 200.
126. "Manusevich, David Statement, 13 September 1944," 299; "Wells (Welizcker), Leon Statement, 22 September 1944," 360.
127. Pohl, *Nationalsozialistische Judenverfolgung in Ostgalizien*, 381.
128. Pohl, "Die großen Zwangsarbeiterlager," 428.
129. Schulz and Zinke, *Die Generale der Waffen-SS und der Polizei*, 613.
130. "Theobald Thier Spruchkämmer Tübingen, 24 January 1952," StA-S: Wü 13 T 2 Nr. 2682/079, 11–12; Katzmann, *Rozwiazania Kwestii Żydowskiej W Distrykcie Galicja*.
131. Pohl, *Nationalsozialistische Judenverfolgung in Ostgalizien*, 353.
132. Sandkühler, "Das Zwangsarbeitslager Lemberg-Janowska," 615.
133. Poprzeczny, *Odilo Globocnik*, 105.
134. Uhl et al., *Die Organisation des Terrors*, 527.
135. Wells, *The Janowska Road*, 211.
136. Borwicz, *The University of Criminals*, 53.
137. "Beglückter, Jakob Statement, 29 February 1960," 261.
138. "Lubasz, Marcel Testimony," 3–4.
139. Drix, *Witness to Annihilation*, 160; "Zimmerman, Leopold Statement, 1 February 1965," 416; "Trial of Adolf Eichmann, Session 23, 2 May 1961."
140. "Beglückter, Jakob Statement, 29 February 1960," 261.
141. "The Janovska Camp at Lvov."
142. Borwicz, *The University of Criminals*, 73.
143. Borwicz, 91.
144. Borwicz, 98–99.
145. Mailänder, "A Specialist," 47.
146. "Bitsch, Zbignew Statement, 12 September 1944," BA-ZS: B162/29309, 206.
147. "Melchior, Karl Statement, 22 April 1960," 62–63.
148. Tenenbaum, *Underground*, 310.
149. Borwicz, *The University of Criminals*, 23.
150. "Katz, Aron Statement, 11 March 1961," 120–21.
151. "Bitsch, Zbignew Statement, 12 September 1944," 206.

152. "Mit Fernglas Massaker beobachtet, Stuttgarter Nachrichten, Nr. 206, 1 September 1967," YVA: RG-P13, file 189.
153. "Hat auch die Schutzpolizei geschossen?, Stuttgarter Zeitung, Nr. 183, 11 August 1967," YVA: RG-P13, file 189.
154. "Kolonko, Adolf Statement, 16 September 1960," 180–81.
155. "Kolonko, Adolf Statement, 14 June 1960," 120–23.
156. Tenenbaum, *Underground*, 310.
157. "Kolonko, Adolf Statement, 16 September 1960," 181.
158. "Blai, Barbara Statement, 19 September 1944," 175; "Kolonko, Adolf Statement, 16 September 1960," 181; "Misiewicz, Ignacy Statement, 1 October 1960," StAL: EL 317 III, Bü 1505, 259.
159. "Melchior, Karl Statement, 22 April 1960," 63.
160. "Kolonko, Adolf Statement, 14 June 1960," 122–23.
161. "Chamaides, Heinrich Statement, 13 September 1944."
162. "Wells, Leon Weliczker."
163. Wells, *The Janowska Road*, 194–95.
164. "Korn, Moische Statement, 13 September 1944."
165. "Wells, Leon Weliczker."
166. "Ash, Felix Audio Interview, 1980," Ash Family Private Collection.
167. Wells, *The Janowska Road*, 213-.
168. "Wind, Josef Interview."
169. Megargee, *Encyclopedia of Camps and Ghettos I*, 884.
170. "Kuryniec, Rebeka Testimony," USHMM, RG-15.084M, AZIH 301/1173 (Testimonies-Relacje).
171. "Nichtenhauser, Alfred Statement, 31 May 1961," StAL: EL 48/2, Bü 397, 1297–98; "Javorskij, Michail Statement, 13 September 1944," 252; "Kolonko, Adolf Statement, 14 June 1960," 123.
172. E. C., "Russians About to Cross Polish Frontier," *The Palestine Post* (Jerusalem), January 3, 1944, 4.
173. Glantz and House, *When Titans Clashed*, 188.
174. "Kuryniec, Rebeka Testimony."
175. "Lehmann, Helene Statement, 6 December 1960," StAL: EL 317 III, Bü 1505, 371; "Wind, Joseph Statement, 25 September 1944."
176. Segev, *Simon Wiesenthal*, 70.
177. "Wiesenthal, Simon," USC Shoah Foundation Institute: Interview #35104, Visual History Archive, 1997; Segev, *Simon Wiesenthal*, 58.
178. "Blum, Alina Statement, 3 June 1961," StAL: EL 48/2, Bü 397, 1311.
179. Segev, *Simon Wiesenthal*, 59.

180. "Lehmann, Helene Statement, 6 December 1960," 374.
181. "Haftbefehl für Peter Blum, 15 June 1965," StAL: EL 317 III, Bü 1497, 332.
182. "Kolonko, Adolf Statement, 13 October 1960," 183–84.
183. Awtuszewska-Ettrich, "Płaszów-Stammlager," 277.
184. "Memo: Joseph Grzymek, Polish Representative, UNWCCC (Undated)," USHMM, RG-15.155M, 757.
185. "Nichtenhauser, Alfred Statement, 31 May 1961," 397.
186. "Lehmann, Helene Statement, 6 December 1960," 375.
187. "Wiesenthal, Simon."

10. TESTIFY FOR US ALL

Epigraph: Stromer, *Memoirs of an Unfortunate Person*, 28.

1. "Righteous among the Nations: Kalwiński Family," Yad Vashem, 2017, accessed February 10, 2017, http://db.yadvashem.org/righteous/family.html?language=en&itemId=4039691.
2. "Arrest Documents for Max Ringer, 21 May 1944," USHMM, 1995.A.1086 (reel 29-R77, 01, D1258).
3. Wiesel, *And the Sea Is Never Full*, 405.
4. David B. Green, "1944: Russian Troops Seize Lwow from Nazis, Find the Jews Gone," *Haaretz*, July 26, 2016, https://www.haaretz.com/jewish/1944-russian-troops-seize-lwow-1.5415470.
5. "Ahrens, Jack Interview, 11 May 1995."
6. "Ahrens, Jack Interview, 27 January 1999," USHMM, RG-50.549.02*0037, 1999.A.0046.
7. Drix, *Witness to Annihilation*, 216.
8. Kessler, *The Wartime Diary of Edmund Kessler*, 21.
9. "Wind, Josef Interview."
10. Wells, *The Janowska Road*, 244–45.
11. "Wolf, Isaac Interview, 1 September 1946," Paul V. Galvin Library, Illinois Institute of Technology: Voices of the Holocaust-David Boder Interviews.
12. Sorokina, "People and Procedures," 121.
13. "Record of Soviet Commission for the Discovery and Investigation of German-Fascist Crimes in the City of Lemberg, 1–6 November 1944"; "Record of the Inspection of the Work Camp on Janowska Street, 14 September 1944 (Soviet Extraordinary State Commission)," BA-ZS: B162/29309.
14. Zorgdrager and Driebergen, *The Jews of Lemberg*, 79.
15. Judt, *Postwar*, 43.
16. Judt, 31.

17. "Letter, Kriminalrat Scharf (Hessisches LKA) to ZS-Ludwigsburg, 12 August 1960," BA-ZS: B162/5725, 7; "Hansberg, Elizabeth Statement, 1 September 1962," 181.
18. "Warzok, Antonie Statement, 26 October 1967," StAL: EL 317 III, Bü 1497, 2.
19. "LG Saarbrücken Urteil gg. Fritz Gebauer, 29 June 1971," 6.
20. "Blum, Peter Trial Testimony, Band 2," 45; "Blum, Peter Statement, 8 September 1960," 321.
21. "LG Saarbrücken Urteil gg. Friedrich Heinen, 10 July 1978," 11.
22. "Urteil gg. Röder u.a., LG Stuttgart vom 29.4.1968, Ks 5/65," 724.
23. "Kolonko, Adolf Statement, 16 September 1960," 149.
24. Judt, *Postwar*, 17, 19, 21–22, 39.
25. Judt, 25.
26. Judt, 14–16.
27. "Warzok, Antonie Statement, 26 October 1967," 2–3.
28. "Letter, Israeli Police (Haifa) to ObStA Schüle, 22 March 1960," BA-ZS: B162/5764, 255.
29. "Blum Application for IRO Assistance, 16 August 1949."
30. Wiesenthal and Wechsberg, *The Murderers among Us*, 280–81.
31. "Government Exhibit 11: U.S. Displaced Persons Commission Report, 29 March 1949," United States of America, Plaintiff, V. John Kalymon, a.k.a. Ivan, Iwan, John Kalymon/Kaylmun, Defendant (2007); "Government Exhibit 10: Region Iv, Cic Worksheet, 23 March 1949," United States of America, Plaintiff, V. John Kalymon, a.k.a. Ivan, Iwan, John Kalymon/Kaylmun, Defendant (2007).
32. Steinacher, "'A Man with a Wide Horizon,'" 229.
33. "Blum, Peter Statement, 9 September 1960," StAL: EL 317 III, Bü 1505, 331.
34. "Federmann, Philipp Statement, 28 February 1962," StAL: EL 48/2, Bü 397, 1415.
35. "Monz, Willi Statement, 4 May 1962," BA-ZS: B162/4358, 508.
36. "Dantsches, Rudolf Statement, 29 March 1949," BA-ZS: B162/20038, 21.
37. "Anklageschrift gg. Karl Melchior, Schwurgericht, LG München I, 29 July 1949," BA-ZS: B162/5763, 26.
38. "Wells (Weliczker), Leon Statement, 11 April 1949," 26–27.
39. "Letter from Johann Rauch's Sister, 8 August 1948," StAL: EL 317 III, Bü 1513, 203.
40. Wells, *The Janowska Road*, 297–300; "Schallock gab sich wie ein Vater, Stuttgarter Stadt-Nachrichten, Nr. 139, 15 June 1967," 13; "Five Nazis, Polish Collaborators Sentenced to Death for Murdering Jews During War," JTA *Daily News Bulletin* (New York), July 20, 1949.
41. Beevor, *The Fall of Berlin, 1945*, 311.
42. "Ernst Wilhelm Borchert," DEFA Film Library, accessed 25 October 2020, https://ecommerce.umass.edu/defa/people/36732.
43. Weckel, "The Mitläufer in Two German Postwar Films," 68.

44. Judt, *Postwar*, 57.
45. Judt, 56; Herf, *Divided Memory*, 204.
46. "Urteil gg. Röder u.a., LG Stuttgart vom 29.4.1968, Ks 5/65," 709.
47. "Schallock Fragebogen, 12 January 1949," BA-K: Z42, 1113599; "Walter Friedrich Karl Schallock Vita Compiled by Rüdiger Schallock, 12 June 2020."
48. Kellenbach, *The Mark of Cain*, 39.
49. Wilke, "Renten für SS-Veteranen," 61.
50. Wilke, 69.
51. Judt, *Postwar*, 58.
52. Wittmann, *Beyond Justice*, 26.
53. Judt, *Postwar*, 56.
54. Dietrich Strothmann, "Dem Grauen auf der Spur: Dreiundzwanzig Jahre lang war die Aufklärung von Nazi-Verbrechen seine tägliche Arbeit," *Die Zeit*, no. 11 (March 9, 1984). https://www.zeit.de/1984/11/dem-grauen-auf-der-spur/komplettansicht.
55. Rückerl, *The Investigation of Nazi Crimes, 1945–1978*, 52.
56. Wittmann, *Beyond Justice*, 50.
57. Eichmüller, "Die Strafverfolgung," 626.
58. Wittmann, *Beyond Justice*, 57.
59. "Haftbefehl für Elizabeth Hansberg, 10 September 1964," BA-ZS: StAL EL 317 III Bü 1502, 108.
60. "Hansberg, Elizabeth Strafregister, Saarbrücken, 13 December 1961," StAL: EL 317 III, Bü 1502, 146.
61. "Hansberg, Elizabeth Statement, 5 October 1962," BA-ZS: B162/5765, 575.
62. "Hansberg, Elizabeth Statement, 1 September 1962," 175.
63. "Das Urteil erst in einem Jahr-in Stuttgart beginnt heute der Lemberg-Prozeß / Sechzehn Angeklagte," *Frankfurter Allgemeine Zeitung* (Frankfurt), October 25, 1966, 9.
64. "Rokita, Richard Statement, 13 October 1964," StAL: EL 317 III, Bü 1516, 313–14.
65. "LG Stuttgart gg. Rokita Einstellung, 20 January 1965," StAL: EL 317 III, Bü 1536, 1.
66. Leon Wells, "Living Ghosts of the Concentration Camps," *New York Times*, January 26, 1964, 13.
67. "Protokoll des Lemberger-Prozesses umfasst fast zehntausend Seiten, Die Welt, Nr. 101, 30 April 1968," YVA: RG-P13, file 189, 20; "Das Urteil erst in einem Jahr-in Stuttgart beginnt heute der Lemberg-Prozeß / Sechzehn Angeklagte," 9.
68. Bergmann, *Antisemitismus*, 282.
69. Mauz, "'Als Anwalt,'" 71.
70. Earl, "'Bad Nazis and Other Germans,'" 68.

71. Westemeier, *Himmlers Krieger*, 480–81; "Läuft Bestens," 60.
72. Wittmann, *Beyond Justice*, 44.
73. Wittmann, 15–16.
74. "Urteil gg. Röder u.a., LG Stuttgart, 9 May 1968," StAL: EL 317 III, Bü 1536, 3.
75. "Lemberg-Prozeß auf Tonband," *Frankfurter Allgemeine Zeitung* (Frankfurt), October 26, 1966, 7; "Protokoll Des Lemberger-Prozesses umfasst fast zehntausend Seiten, Die Welt, Nr. 101, 30 April 1968," 20.
76. "LG Stuttgart gg. Rokita Einstellung, 20 January 1965," 1.
77. "'Wahllos Menschen erschossen,' Stuttgarter Zeitung, Nr. 77, 4 April 1967," 16.
78. "Nach dem Mord gelacht, Stuttgarter Zeitung, Nr. 52, 3 March 1967," YVA: RG-P13, file 189, 24.
79. "Sie nannten mich Oberteufel, Stuttgarter Nachrichten, Nr. 145, 22 June 1967," 15.
80. "Goldberg, Abraham Trial Testimony, Band 77, 10 January 1967."
81. "Nach der eigenen Leiche gesucht, Stuttgarter Zeitung, Nr. 134, 14 June 1967," YVA: RG-P13, file 189, 17.
82. "Rogowski, Marian Statement, 22 September 1961," 145.
83. "Nestler, Bernard Statement, 17 January 1964," 108.
84. "Plädoyers der Verteidiger im Lemberg-Prozeß," *Frankfurter Allgemeine Zeitung* (Frankfurt), March 22, 1968, 8.
85. "Noch einmal auf Befehl gemordet?, Stuttgarter Zeitung, Nr. 270, 24 November 1966."
86. "'Mit Häftlingen sogar Fussball gespielt,' Stuttgarter Zeitung, 4 January 1968," YVA: RG-P13, file 189.
87. Rhodes, *Masters of Death*, 168.
88. "Noch einmal auf Befehl gemordet?, Stuttgarter Zeitung, Nr. 270, 24 November 1966."
89. "Schlußworte im Lemberg-Prozeß," *Frankfurter Allgemeine Zeitung* (Frankfurt), April 20, 1968, 7.
90. "Noch einmal auf Befehl gemordet?, Stuttgarter Zeitung, Nr. 270, 24 November 1966."
91. "Hat auch die Schutzpolizei geschossen?, Stuttgarter Zeitung, Nr. 183, 11 August 1967," 16.
92. "Vernichtung von Juden war kein Geheimnis, Stuttgarter Zeitung, Nr. 164, 20 July 1967," YVA: RG-P13, file 189, 17.
93. "Schlußworte im Lemberg-Prozeß," 7.
94. "Schlußworte im Lemberg-Prozeß," 7.
95. "Urteil gg. Röder u.a., LG Stuttgart vom 29.4.1968, Ks 5/65," 709.

96. "Urteil gg. Röder u.a.," 744.
97. "Urteil gg. Röder u.a.," 747.
98. "Urteil gg. Röder u.a.," 774.
99. "Gebauer, Fritz Statement, 17 May 1961," 423.
100. "LG Saarbrücken Urteil gg. Fritz Gebauer, 29 June 1971," 6–7.
101. "Letter, Generalsaatsanwalt der DDR Jahnke to ZS, 11 August 1961," BA-ZS: B162/5764, 447.
102. "Letter, Oberstaatsanwalt Saarbrücken to ZS-Ludwigsburg, 8 October 1963," BA-ZS: B162/5765, 624.
103. "Letter, Association of Former Lwow Jews in Israel to Justizminister, Saarbrücken, 4 September 1963," BA-ZS: B162/5765, 617.
104. "Beschluss des Landgerichts Saarbrücken gg. Fritz Gebauer, 14 September 1968," BA-ZS: B162/5767, 1141–42.
105. "Beschluss des Landgerichts Saarbrücken gg. Fritz Gebauer, 14 September 1968," 1089.
106. "Letter, Oberstaatsanwalt Saarbrücken, 24 January 1967," BA-ZS: B162/5767, 938–49.
107. "Anklageschrift gg. Fritz Gebauer, Grosse Strafkammer, LG Saarbrücken, 14 October 1969," BA-ZS: B162/5768, 1232.
108. "Schuldkonto eines kaltblütigen Mörders," *Die Tat*, 26 September 1970, 1349.
109. "Die Tat: Karl Sauer 'Der Halstuchmörder vom Janowski-Lager' 8 August 1970," BA-ZS: B162/5769.
110. "Anklageschrift gg. Fritz Gebauer, Grosse Strafkammer, LG Saarbrücken, 14 October 1969," 1232–35.
111. "'Nulltarif' für NS-Verbrecher: Gebauer 'sühnt' zu Hause," *Die Tat*, July 10, 1971.
112. "Justiz," 66–67.
113. Bönich, "Amnesie und Amnestie," 49.
114. Krishnadev Calamur, "Man Tied to Nazis Dies in Michigan at Age 93," *National Public Radio*, July 9, 2014, https://www.npr.org/sections/thetwo-way/2014/07/09/330193311/man-tied-to-nazis-dies-in-michigan-at-age-93.
115. Паріря, "Yevreys'ke Hetto," 141.
116. "Letter, Israeli Police (Haifa) to Obsta Schüle, 22 March 1960," 255.
117. Segev, *Simon Wiesenthal*, 236.
118. Golfard, *The Diary of Samuel Golfard*, 168.
119. "Ghosts in Transit," in Schama, *Landscape and Memory*, 26.
120. Turkel, "Every Place Is an Archive."
121. Kramer, "Where Bones, and History, Won't Stay Buried," *New York Times*, May 14, 2015.

122. Kramer.
123. Schama, *Landscape and Memory*, 27.
124. Drix, *Witness to Annihilation*, 232.
125. "Janowska Forced Labour Camp," 49.
126. Zorgdrager and Driebergen, *The Jews of Lemberg*, 79.
127. "Correspondence with Oleksandr Pahiria (Territory of Terror Museum), 9 December 2020," author's personal collection.
128. Werger, "Denk Ich an Lemberg."
129. "Photograph: A Memorial Stone Erected by Members of the Holocaust Survivor Community in Lvov," GFHM: Catalog Nr. 43537, translation by Gershom Gorenberg.
130. "Schwarz, Alexander Statement, 26 September 1969," BA-ZS: B162/28733, 92.
131. Perlman, "Di Goldene Royz," 225.
132. "Janowska Forced Labour Camp," 56–57.
133. "Ukraine: Monitoring Visit in Lviv Prison," *Prison Insider*, 2017, accessed October 11, 2023, https://www.prison-insider.com/en/articles/ukraine-visite-de-controle-et-du-mpn-a-la-prison-de-lviv.
134. Report to the Ukrainian Government on the Visit to Ukraine Carried out by the European Committee for the Prevention of Torture and Inhuman or Degrading Treatment or Punishment (CPT) from 8 to 21 December 2017, CPT/Inf (2018) 41, 6 (Strasbourg: Council of Europe, 2018).
135. See Alex Schmidt, "Reflections from a Jew at a Mock-Jewish Restaurant," *National Public Radio*, 2019, https://www.npr.org/sections/codeswitch/2019/12/28/403012038/reflections-from-a-jew-at-a-mock-jewish-restaurant?t=1606563036009.
136. "Nazi Symbols, Salutes on Display at Ukrainian Nationalist March," *Times of Israel*, April 30, 2018, https://www.timesofisrael.com/nazi-symbols-salutes-on-display-at-ukrainian-nationalist-march/.
137. "Visit to L'viv: Janowska," Echoes of Memory, United States Holocaust Museum, 2018, accessed August 10, 2020, https://www.ushmm.org/remember/holocaust-reflections-testimonies/echoes-of-memory/visit-to-lviv-janowska.

CONCLUSION

1. Barnes, *The Sense of an Ending*, 55, 115.
2. Pohl, "Die großen Zwangsarbeiterlager," 427.
3. Gawron, "Michał Maksymilian Borwicz," 116.

Bibliography

ARCHIVES

BA-ZS. Bundesarchiv Zentralen Stelle zur Aufklärung nationalsozialistischer Verbrechen, Ludwigsburg, Germany
FDRPL. Franklin Delano Roosevelt Presidental Library, Hyde Park, New York
FVAHT. Fortunoff Video Archive for Holocaust Testimonies, Yale University, New Haven Connecticut
GFHM. Ghetto Fighters' House Museum, Israel
Harvard Law School Library
IfZ. Institut für Zeitgeschichte, Munich, Germany
Leo Baeck Institute, New York
William Breman Jewish Heritage Museum, Atlanta, Georgia
Los Angeles Museum of the Holocaust, Los Angeles
National Library of Poland, Warsaw, Poland
StAL. Staatsarchiv Ludwigsburg, Ludwigsburg, Germany
DALO. State Archive of Lviv Region, Lviv, Ukraine
Paul V. Galvin Library, Illinois Institute of Technology, Chicago
USHMM. United States Holocaust Memorial Museum, Washington DC
Visual History Archive, Shoah Foundation Institute, University of Southern California, Los Angeles
YVA. Yad Vashem, Jerusalem, Israel
JewishGen Press Yizkor Book Project

UNPUBLISHED
Ash Family Collection
Porath Family Collection
Lewinter Family Collection
Niemann Family Collection
Schallock Family Collection

MEMOIRS

Despite a relative lack of scholarly work on Janowska, there are quite a gew memoirs of survivors who spent time in the camp and/or in Lviv during the Holocaust.

Borwicz, Michał Maksymilian. *The University of Criminals: The Janowska Camp in Lviv, 1941–1944*. Edited by Jacek Tokarski and Leon Perlman. Krakow: Wysoki Zamek, 2014.

Drix, Samuel. *Witness to Annihilation: Surviving the Holocaust, a Memoir*. Washington DC: Brassey's, 1994.

Druck, Samuel. *Swastika over Jaworow*. Translated by Samuel Kreiter. New York: First Jaworower Independent Association, 1984. https://www.jewishgen.org/yizkor/Yavoriv1/Yavoriv1.html.

Folkmann, Adolf, and Stefan Szende. *The Promise Hitler Kept*. New York: Roy, 1945.

Golfard, Samuel. *The Diary of Samuel Golfard and the Holocaust in Galicia*. Edited by Wendy Lower. Lanham: Altamira in association with United States Holocaust Memorial Museum, 2011.

Kahane, David. *Lvov Ghetto Diary*. Translated by Jerzy Michalowicz. Amherst: University of Massachusetts Press, 1990.

Kaplan, Helene C. *I Never Left Janowska*. New York: Holocaust Library, 1989.

Kessler, Renata ed. *The Wartime Dary of Edmund Kessler: Lwow, Poland, 1942–1944*. Boston: Academic Studies Press, 2010.

Lemkin, Raphael. *Totally Unofficial: The Autobiography of Raphael Lemkin*. New Haven CT: Yale University Press, 2013.

Maltiel-Gerstenfeld, Jacob. *My Private War: One Man's Struggle to Survive the Soviets and the Nazis*. London: England Vallentine Mitchell, 1993.

Reder, Rudolf. *Belzec*. Edited by Michael Jacobs. Krakow: Fundacja Judaica w Krakowie, 1999.

Redner, Marek. *Recollections on the Life and Martyrdom of Jewish Medical Doctors in the Lvov Ghetto, 1944–1949*. Translated by A. S. Redner. Edited by Isabel Alcoff. Jerusalem: Yad Vashem, 2003.

Richman, Leon. *Why? Extermination Camp Lwów (Lemberg), 134 Janowska Street, Poland: A Documentary by an Inmate*. New York: Vantage, 1975.

Stromer, Moty. *Memoirs of an Unfortunate Person*. New York: Yad Vashem, 2008.

"Translation of *Szkola Okuricienstwa* by Stanislawa Gogolowska, Wydanictwo Lubelskie, 1964." StAL: EL 317 III, Bü 1720.

Wells, Leon Weliczker. *The Janowska Road*. New York: MacMillan, 1963.

Wiesenthal, Simon, and Joseph Wechsberg. *The Murderers among Us: The Wiesenthal Memoirs*. New York: McGraw-Hill, 1967.

PUBLISHED WORKS

Agamben, Giorgio. *Homo Sacer: Sovereign Power and Bare Life*. Translated by Daniel Heller-Roazen. Stanford CA: Stanford University Press, 1995.

Aleksiun, Natalia. "Philip Friedman and the Emergence of Holocaust Scholarship: A Reappraisal." In *Simon Dubnow Institute Yearbook*, edited by Dan Diner, 333–46. Göttingen: Vandenhoeck & Ruprecht, 2012.

Allen, Arthur. *The Fantastic Laboratory of Dr. Weigl: How Two Brave Scientists Battled Typhus and Sabotaged the Nazis*. New York: W. W. Norton, 2014.

Altenburger, Andreas. "Infanterie-Regiment 32." *Lexikon der Wehrmacht*, accessed November 22, 2019. http://www.lexikon-der-wehrmacht.de/Gliederungen/Infanterieregimenter/IR32.htm.

———. "Oberfeldkommandantur 365." *Lexikon der Wehrmacht*, accessed July 9, 2019. http://www.lexikon-der-wehrmacht.de/Gliederungen/Kommandantur/OFK365-R.htm.

Amar, Tarik Cyril. *The Paradox of Ukrainian Lviv*. Ithaca NY: Cornell University Press, 2015.

Améry, Jean. *At the Mind's Limits: Contemplations by a Survivor on Auschwitz and Its Realities*. Translated by Sidney Rosenfeld and Stella P. Rosenfeld. Bloomington: Indiana University Press, 1980.

Angrick, Andrej. *"Aktion 1005"-Spurenbeseitigung von NS-Massenverbrechen, 1942–1945*. Vol. 2. Göttingen: Wallstein Verlag, 2018.

———. "Annihilation and Labor: Jews and Thoroughfare Iv in Central Ukraine." In *The Shoah in Ukraine: History, Testimony, Memorialization*, edited by Ray Brandon and Wendy Lower, 190–223. Bloomington: Indiana University Press, 2008.

———. "Forced Labor along the 'Straße der ss.'" In *Forced and Slave Labor in Nazi-Dominated Europe: Symposium Presentations*, 83–93. Washington DC: Center for Advanced Holocaust Studies, United States Holocaust Memorial Museum, 2004.

Arad, Yitzhak. *Belzec, Sobibor, Treblinka: The Operation Reinhard Death Camps*. Bloomington: Indiana University Press, 1987.

———. *The Holocaust in the Soviet Union*. Lincoln: University of Nebraska Press, 2009.

Arad, Yitzhak, Israel Gutman, and Abraham Margaliot, eds. *Documents on the Holocaust: Selected Sources on the Destruction of the Jews of Germany and Austria, Poland, and the Soviet Union*. Jerusalem: Yad Vashem, 1999.

Auerbach, Hellmuth. "Die Einheit Dirlewanger." *Vierteljahrshefte für Zeitgeschichte* 10, no. 3 (1962): 250–63.

Awtuszewska-Ettrich, Angelina. "Płaszów-Stammlager." In *Der Ort des Terrors: Geschichte der nationalsozialistischen Konzentrationslager*, edited by Wolfgang Benz and Barbara Distel, 235–87. München: C. H. Beck, 2008.

Barbier, Mary. *Spies, Lies, and Citizenship: The Hunt for Nazi Criminals*. Lincoln NE: Potomac Books, 2017.

Barnes, Ethne. *Diseases and Human Evolution*. Albuquerque: University of New Mexico Press, 2006.

Barnes, Julian. *The Sense of an Ending*. London: Random House, 2011.

Bartov, Omer. *Erased: Vanishing Traces of Jewish Galicia in Present-Day Ukraine*. Princeton NJ: Princeton University Press, 2007.

Bechtel, Delphine. "Lemberg/Lwów/Lvov/Lviv: Identities of a 'City of Uncertain Boundaries.'" *Diogenes* 53, no. 2 (2006): 62–71.

Beevor, Antony. *The Fall of Berlin, 1945*. New York: Viking, 2002.

Bell, J. B. *Besieged: Seven Cities under Siege*. New York: Routledge, 2017.

Bem, Marek. *Sobibor Extermination Camp, 1942–1943*. Translated by Tomasz Karpiński and Natalia Sarzyńska-Wójtowicz. Radom: Drukarnia BIGA-DRUK, C. Wałachowski, J. Leszczyński s.c., 2015.

Bennett, G. H. *The Nazi, the Painter and the Forgotten Story of the SS Road and the Forgotten Story of the SS Road*. London: Reaktion, 2013.

Benz, Wolfgang, Barbara Distel, and Angelika Königseder. *Der Ort des Terrors Geschichte der nationalsozialistischen Konzentrationslager*. Vol. 7. München: C. H. Beck, 2008.

———. *Der Ort des Terrors Geschichte der nationalsozialistischen Konzentrationslager*. Vol. 9. München: C. H. Beck, 2009.

Beorn, Waitman Wade. "Bodily Conquest: Sexual Violence in the Nazi East." In *Mass Violence in Nazi-Occupied Europe*, edited by Alex J. Kay and David Stahel, 195–215. Bloomington: Indiana University Press, 2018.

———. *The Holocaust in Eastern Europe: At the Epicenter of the Final Solution*. London: Bloomsbury Academic, 2018.

Berger, Sara. *Experten der Vernichtung: Das T4-Reinhardt-Netzwerk in den Lagern Belzec, Sobibor und Treblinka*. Hamburg: Hamburger Edition, 2013.

Bergmann, Werner. *Antisemitismus in öffentlichen Konflikten: Kollektives Lernen in der Politischen Kultur der Bundesrepublik, 1949–1989*. Frankfurt: Campus Verlag, 1997.

Black, Peter. "Foot Soldiers of the Final Solution: The Trawniki Training Camp and Operation Reinhard." *Holocaust and Genocide Studies* 25, no. 1 (2011): 1–99.

———. "Indigenous Collaboration in the General Government: The Case of the Sonderdienst." In *Constructing Nationalities in East Central Europe*, edited by Pieter M. Judson and Marsha L. Rozenblit, 243–66. New York: Berghahn, 2009.

———. "Police Auxiliaries for Operation Reinhard: Shedding Light on the Trawniki Training Camp through Documents from Behind the Iron Curtain." In *Secret Intelligence and the Holocaust: Collected Essays from the Colloquium at the City University of New York Graduate Center*, edited by David Bankier, 327–66. New York: Enigma, 2006.

Black, Peter R. "Rehearsal for 'Reinhard'? Odilo Globocnik and the Lublin Selbstschutz." *Central European History* 25, no. 2 (1992): 204–26.

Bloxham, Donald. *The Final Solution: A Genocide*. New York: Oxford University Press, 2009.

Bluhm, Hilde O. "How Did They Survive? Mechanisms of Defense in Nazi Concentration Camps (1948)." *American Journal of Psychotherapy* 53, no. 1 (1999): 123–25.

Bönich, Georg. "Amnesie und Amnestie." *Der Spiegel*, January 9, 2006, 49–57.

Bräu, Ramona. "The Economic Consequences of German Occupation Policy in Poland." In *Paying for Hitler's War: The Consequences of Nazi Hegemony for Europe*, edited by Jonas Scherner and Eugene N. White, 427–50. New York: Cambridge University Press, 2016.

Brewer, John. "Microhistory and the Histories of Everyday Life." *Cultural and Social History* 7, no. 1 (2010): 87–109.

Brown, Vincent. *The Reaper's Garden: Death and Power in the World of Atlantic Slavery*. Cambridge MA: Harvard University Press, 2008.

Browning, Christopher R. "Evocation, Analysis, and the 'Crisis of Liberalism.'" *History and Theory* 48, no. 3 (2009): 238.

———. "Hitler, Antisemitism, and the Final Solution." *Antisemitism Studies* 7, no. 1 (2023): 80–99.

———. *Nazi Policy, Jewish Workers, German Killers*. Cambridge: Cambridge University Press, 2000.

———. *Ordinary Men: Reserve Police Battalion 101 and the Final Solution in Poland*. New York: Harper Perennial, 1998.

———. *Remembering Survival: Inside a Nazi Slave-Labor Camp*. New York: W. W. Norton, 2010.

Browning, Christopher R., and Jürgen Matthäus. *The Origins of the Final Solution: The Evolution of Nazi Jewish Policy, September 1939–March 1942*. Lincoln: University of Nebraska Press, 2004.

Burleigh, Michael. *The Third Reich: A New History*. New York: Hill and Wang, 2000.

Calamur, Krishnadev. "Man Tied to Nazis Dies in Michigan at Age 93." *National Public Radio*, July 9, 2014, accessed November 28, 2020. https://www.npr.org/sections/thetwo-way/2014/07/09/330193311/man-tied-to-nazis-dies-in-michigan-at-age-93.

Center for Urban History of East Central Europe. "Former Beth Tahora." Lviv Interactive, accessed May 17, 2019. https://lia.lvivcenter.org/en/objects/beit-tahora/.

———. "Former Jewish Hospital." Lviv Interactive, accessed November 1, 2019. https://lia.lvivcenter.org/en/objects/ukrainky-1/.

———. "Former Skarbek Theater." Lviv Interactive, May 29, 2019, https://lia.lvivcenter.org/en/objects/ukrainky-1/.

———. "Former Tempel Synagogue." Lviv Interactive, accessed May 17, 2019. https://lia.lvivcenter.org/en/objects/tempel-synagogue/.

———. "Gimpel's Theater." Lviv Interactive, accessed May 30, 2019. https://lia.lvivcenter.org/en/themes/?ci_themeid=86.

———. "Modernism in Lviv." Lviv Interactive, accessed July 20, 2019. http://modernism.lvivcenter.org/#/en/map/object/2536/photo/0.

———. "Past, Present and Memory: Rediscovering Jewish Lviv." Lviv Interactive, 2016. https://lia.lvivcenter.org/en/storymaps/jewish-lviv/.

Chalmers, Beverley. "Jewish Women's Sexual Behaviour and Sexualized Abuse During the Nazi Era." *Canadian Journal of Human Sexuality* 24, no. 2 (2015): 184–96.

Chetverikov, B. "Geoinformational Determination of the Change Boundaries of New Jewish Cemetery in Lviv." *Suchasni dosiahnennia heodezychnoi nauky ta vyrobnytstva: zbirnyk naukovykh prats* 2, no. 34 (2017): 98–101.

Chetverikov, B., and L. Babiy. "Methods of Creation of Historical Situation Plan Concentration Camp 'Stalag-328' (Citadel) in Lviv (Ukraine) on the Base Archval Aerial Image." Сучасні досягнення геодезичної науки та виробництва 28, no. 2 (2014): 71–73.

Chronakis, Paris Papamichos. "From the Lone Survivor to the Networked Self: Social Networks Meet the Digital Holocaust Archive." *Quest: Issues in Contemporary Jewish History, Journal of Fondazione* CDEC 13 (August 2018): 52–84.

Connelly, John. "Nazis and Slavs: From Racial Theory to Racist Practice." *Central European History* 32, no. 1 (1999): 1–33.

Dean, Martin, and Geoffrey P. Megargee, eds. *Encyclopedia of Camps and Ghettos 2: Ghettos in Occupied German-Occupied Eastern Europe*. Vol. A. Bloomington: Indiana University Press, 2012.

———. *Encyclopedia of Camps and Ghettos 2: Ghettos in Occupied German-Occupied Eastern Europe*. Vol. B. Bloomington: Indiana University Press, 2012.

De Mildt, D. W., and C. F. Rüter, eds. *Justiz und NS-Verbrechen. Sammlung Deutscher Strafurteile wegen Nationalsozialistischer Tötungsverbrechen 1945–1999*. Vol. 28. Amsterdam: University Press Amsterdam, 2003.

Desbois, Patrick. *The Holocaust by Bullets: A Priest's Journey to Uncover the Truth Behind the Murder of 1.5 Million Jews*. New York: Palgrave Macmillan, 2008.

Earl, Hilary. "'Bad Nazis and Other Germans': The Fate of SS-Einsatzgruppen Commander Martin Sandberger in Postwar Germany." In *A Nazi Past: Recasting German*

Identity in Postwar Europe, edited by David A. Messenger and Katrin Paehler, 57–81. Lexington: University Press of Kentucky, 2015.

Eichmüller, Andreas. "Die Strafverfolgung Von NS-Verbrechen Durch Westdeutsche Justizbehörden Seit 1945." *Vierteljahreshefte für Zeitgeschichte* 56, no. 4 (2008): 621–40.

"Einsatzgruppen: Number of Jews Killed." *Holocaust Denial on Trial*, accessed July 9, 2019. https://www.hdot.org/debunking-denial/ezg5-number-killed/.

Enno, Georg. *Die wirtschaftlichen Unternehmungen der SS*. Stuttgart: Deutsche Verlags-Anstalt, 1963.

Fackler, Guido. "Cultural Behaviour and the Invention of Traditions: Music and Musical Practices in the Early Concentration Camps, 1933–6/7." *Journal of Contemporary History* 45, no. 3 (2010): 601–27.

Friedländer, Saul. "An Integrated History of the Holocaust: Possibilities and Challenges." In *Years of Persecution, Years of Extermination: Saul Friedländer and the Future of Holocaust Studies*, edited by Christian Wiese and Paul Betts, 21–30. London: Bloomsbury, 2010.

———. *The Years of Extermination: Nazi Germany and the Jews, 1939–1945*. New York: Harper Collins, 2007.

Friedman, Benedikt. *Ich Träumte von Brot und Büchern: zornige Erinnerungen eines jüdischen Österreichers*. Vienna: Promedia, 1992.

Friedman, Philip. "The Destruction of the Jews of Lwow." In *Roads to Extinction: Essays on the Holocaust*, edited by Ada June Friedman, 244–321. New York: Jewish Publication Society, 1980.

———. "The Jewish Ghettos of the Nazi Era." *Jewish Social Studies* 16 (January 1954): 61–88.

———. *Zaglada Zydów Lwowskich*. Łódz: Centralna Żyd. komisja historyczna w Polsce, 1945.

Frydel, Tomasz. "The Ongoing Challenge of Producing an Integrated Microhistory of the Holocaust in East Central Europe." *Journal of Genocide Research: Special issue on The Holocaust/Genocide Template in Eastern Europe* 20, no. 4 (2018): 624–31.

Gawron, Edyta. "Michał Maksymilian Borwicz." In *The University of Criminals: The Janowska Camp in Lviv, 1941–1944*, edited by Michał Maksymilian Borwicz, Jacek Tokarski, and Leon Perlman, 116–21. Krakow: Wysoki Zamek, 2014.

Gerlach, Christian. "The Wannsee Conference, the Fate of German Jews, and Hitler's Decision in Principle to Exterminate All European Jews." *The Journal of Modern History* 70, no. 4 (1998): 759–812.

Gilbert, Martin. *The Routledge Atlas of the Holocaust*. 3rd ed. New York: Routledge, 2002.

Gilbert, Shirli. "Music in the Nazi Ghettos and Camps." In *The Routledge History of the Holocaust*, edited by Jonathan C. Friedman, 436–51. New York: Routledge, 2011.

Ginsberg, Allen. *Collected Poems: 1947–1980*. New York: Harper and Row, 1984.

Glantz, David M., and Jonathan M. House. *When Titans Clashed: How the Red Army Stopped Hitler*. Lawrence: University Press of Kansas, 1995.

Goldstein, Phyllis. *A Convenient Hatred: The History of Antisemitism*. Brookline MA: Facing History and Ourselves, 2012.

Gross, Jan Tomasz. *Revolution from Abroad: The Soviet Conquest of Poland's Western Ukraine and Western Belorussia*. Princeton NJ: Princeton University Press, 1988.

Grünbart, Moritz. "Das Blutbad von Lemberg: Ein Erlebnisbericht von Moritz Grünbart." *Der Spiegel*, no. 11 (3 March 1960): 20–21.

Guare, John. *Six Degrees of Separation*. London: Methuen Drama, 2010.

Hájková, Anna. "Sexual Barter in Times of Genocide: Negotiating the Sexual Economy of the Theresienstadt Ghetto." *Signs* 38, no. 3 (2013): 503–33.

Häkkänen, Helinä. "Murder by Manual and Ligature Strangulation: Profiling Crime Scene Behaviors and Offender Characteristics." In *Criminal Profiling: International Theory, Research, and Practice*, edited by Richard N. Koscis, 73–88. Totowa NJ: Humana, 2007.

Halbmayr, Brigitte. "Sexualized Violence against Women During Nazi 'Racial' Persecution." In *Sexual Violence against Jewish Women During the Holocaust*, edited by Sonja M. Hedgepeth and Rochelle G. Saidel, 29–44. Waltham MA: Brandeis University Press, 2010.

Harran, Marilyn J., ed. *The Holocaust Chronicle*. Lincolnwood IL: Publications International, 2003.

Hastings, Max. *Inferno: The World at War, 1939–45*. New York: Alfred A. Knopf, 2011.

Hembera, Melanie. "Ermittlungsakten Aufgeschlagen: Aufklärung und Strafverfolgung von NS-Verbrechen an den Häftlingen des jüdischen Zwangsarbeitslagers Pustków." *Mitteilungen aus dem Bundesarchiv-Sonderheft: Die Außenstelle Ludwigsburg* 2 (2008): 83–93.

Herf, Jeffrey. *Divided Memory: The Nazi Past in the Two Germanys*. Cambridge MA: Harvard University Press, 1997.

Hlimka, John Paul. "Ukrainian Collaboration in the Extermination of the Jews During the Second World War: Sorting out the Long-Term and Conjunctural Factors." In *The Fate of the European Jews, 1939–1945: Continuity or Contingency?*, edited by Jonathan Frankel, 170–89. New York: Oxford University Press, 1997.

Hochstetter, Dorothee. *Motorisierung und "Volksgemeinschaft," Das nationalsozialistische Kraftfahrkorps (NSKK) 1931–1945*. Studien Zur Zeitgeschichte. Vol. 68. Berlin: De Gruyter, 2009.

Hoess, Rudolf. *Commandant of Auschwitz*. Translated by Constantine FitzGibbon. London: Weidenfeld & Nicholson, 2000.

Honigsman, Y. A. *The Catastrophy of Jewry in Lvov*. Lvov: Solom-Aleichem Jewish Society of Culture, 1997.

Jäcklein, Josef. "The Train Journey to Belzec: Schutzpolizei Zugwachtmeister Jäcklein's Report." In *"The Good Old Days": The Holocaust as Seen by Its Perpetrators and Bystanders*, edited by Ernst Klee, Willi Dressen, and Volker Riess, 232–35. New York: Free Press, 1991.

Janjetović, Zoran. "The Role of the Danube Swabians in the History of the Serbs: A Heterodox View." *Tokovi istorije* 22, no. 3 (2014): 197–212.

"Janowska Forced Labour Camp: Industry of Terror; Exhibition Catalogue." Edited by Territory of Terror Memorial Museum. Lviv: Ukrainian Jewish Encounter, 2019. https://bit.ly/3PPfIgw.

Jaskot, Paul B. "The Architecture of the Holocaust." 2016 Joseph and Rebecca Meyerhoff Annual Lecture. Washington DC: United States Holocaust Memorial Museum, 2017.

Judt, Tony. *Postwar: A History of Europe since 1945*. New York: Penguin, 2005.

"Justiz: Alte Kameraden." *Der Spiegel*, no. 26 (June 28, 1982): 63–68.

Kaienburg, Hermann. "Jüdische Arbeitslager an der 'Strasse der SS.'" *Zeitschrift für Sozialgeschichte des 20. und 21. Jahrhunderts* 11, no. 1 (1999): 13–35.

Kampe, Norbert. "Die Wannsee-Konferenz." In *Die Wannsee-Konferenz und der Völkermord an den europäischen Juden*, edited by Christa Schikorra, 98–119. Berlin: Jütte-Messedruck Leipzig GmbH, 2006.

Karten, Itche. "The Bitter End." In *Le-Zekher Kehilat Bobrka U-Benoteha (Boiberke Memorial Book)*, edited by Sharaga Feivel Kallay, 193. Jersualem: Sivan Press and Association of Former Residents of Bobrka and Vicinity, 1964.

Kassow, Samuel D. *Who Will Write Our History? Emanuel Ringelblum, the Warsaw Ghetto, and the Oyneg Shabes Archive*. Bloomington: Indiana University Press, 2007.

Katz, Steven T. "Thoughts on the Intersection of Rape and Rassenschande During the Holocaust." *Modern Judaism* 32, no. 3 (2012): 293–322.

Katzmann, Friedrich. *Rozwiazania Kwestii Żydowskiej W Distrykcie Galicja*. Edited by Andrzej Żbikowski. Warsaw: Instytut Pamięci Narodowej, 2001.

Kay, Alex J. "The Purpose of the Russian Campaign Is the Decimation of the Slavic Population by Thirty Million: The Radicalisation of German Food Policy in Early 1941." In *Nazi Policy on the Eastern Front, 1941: Total War, Genocide, and Radicalization*, edited by Alex J. Kay, Jeff Rutherford, and David Stahel, 101–29. Rochester NY: University of Rochester Press, 2012.

Kellenbach, Katharina von. *The Mark of Cain: Guilt and Denial in the Post-War Lives of Nazi Perpetrators.* Oxford: Oxford University Press, 2013.

Kenez, Peter. "Pogroms and White Ideology in the Russian Civil War." In *Pogroms: Anti-Jewish Violence in Modern Russian History,* edited by John Klier and Shlomo Lambroza, 293–313. Cambridge: Cambridge University Press, 1992.

Klemp, Stefan. *Nicht Ermittelt: Polizeibataillone und die Nachkriegsjustiz-ein Handbuch.* Essen: Klartext Verlag, 2005.

Kochanski, Halik. *Eagle Unbowed: Poland and the Poles in the Second World War.* Cambridge MA: Harvard University Press, 2014.

Koonz, Claudia. "On Reading a Document: ss-Man Katzmann's 'Solution of the Jewish Question in the District of Galicia.'" Raul Hilberg Lecture, 2005.

Kranjc, Gregor Joseph. *To Walk with the Devil: Slovene Collaboration and Axis Occupation, 1941–1945.* Toronto: University of Toronto Press, 2013.

Krausnick, Helmut, and Hans-Heinrich Wilhelm. *Die Truppe des Weltanschauungskrieges: Die Einsatzgruppen der Sicherheitspolizei und des SD, 1938–1942.* Stuttgart: Deutsche Verlags-Anstalt, 1981.

Kubicek, Paul. *The History of Ukraine.* Westport CT: Greenwood, 2008.

Kühne, Thomas. *Kameradschaft: Die Soldaten des nationalsozialistischen Krieges und das 20. Jahrhundert.* Göttingen: Vandenhoeck & Ruprecht, 2006.

———. "Male Bonding and Shame Culture: Hitler's Soldiers and the Moral Basis of Genocidal Warfare." In *Ordinary People as Mass Murderers: Perpetrators in Comparative Perspectives,* edited by Olaf Szejnmann Claus-Christian W. Jensen, 55–77. New York: Palgrave MacMillan, 2008.

Kuwałek, Robert. *Death Camp in Bełżec.* Translated by William Brand. Lublin: Państwowe Muzeum na Majdanku, 2016.

Kwiet, Konrad. "Paul Zapp–Vordenker Und Vollstrecker Der Judenvernichtung." In *Karrieren der Gewalt: Nationalsozialistische Täterbiographien,* edited by Klaus-Michael Mallmann and Gerhard Paul, 252–63. Darmstadt: Wissenschaftliche Buchgesellschaft, 2013.

Lanzmann, Claude. *Shoah: An Oral History of the Holocaust.* New York: Pantheon, 1985.

Läuft Bestens. "Mit Einer Nach Aa-Ansicht 'Unpolitischen' Visite in Chile Will Ein Rechtslastiger 'Freundeskreis' Die Pinochet-Diktatur Aufwerten." *Der Spiegel* 42 (1977): 60.

Leidinger, Friedrich. "Das Schicksal Der Polnischen Psychiatrie Unter Deutscher Besatzung Im Zweiten Weltkrieg." *Psychiat Prax* 41, no. 1 (2014): S69–S75.

Lepre, George. *Himmler's Bosnian Division: The Waffen-SS Handschar Division, 1943–1945.* Atglen PA: Schiffer Military History, 1997.

Levenkron, Nomi. "Death and the Maidens: 'Prostitution,' Rape, and Sexual Slavery During World War II." In *Sexual Violence against Jewish Women During the Holocaust*, edited by Sonja M. Hedgepeth and Rochelle G. Saidel, 13–28. Waltham MA: Brandeis University Press, 2010.

Levi, Primo. *The Reawakening*. Translated by Stuart Wolf. New York: Touchstone, 1965.

———. *Survival in Auschwitz: The Nazi Assault on Humanity*. New York: Touchstone, 1996.

Lewy, Guenter. *Perpetrators: The World of the Holocaust Killers*. New York: Oxford University Press, 2017.

Longerich, Peter. *Heinrich Himmler: A Life*. New York: Oxford University Press, 2012.

Lower, Wendy. *Hitler's Furies: German Women in the Nazi Killing Fields*. New York: Houghton Mifflin Harcourt, 2013.

———. "Pogroms, Mob Violence and Genocide in Western Ukraine, Summer 1941: Varied Histories, Explanations and Comparisons." *Journal of Genocide Research* 13 (2011): 217–46.

Lozowick, Yaacov. "Rollbahn Mord: The Early Activities of Einsatzgruppe C." *Holocaust and Genocide Studies* 2, no. 2 (1987): 221–41.

Lumans, Valdis. "The Military Obligation of the Volksdeutsche of Eastern Europe Towards the Third Reich." *East European Quarterly* 23, no. 3 (1989): 305–25.

Mailänder, Elissa. "A Specialist: The Daily Work of Erich Muhsfeldt, Chief of the Crematorium at Majdanek Concentration and Extermination Camp, 1942–44." In *Destruction and Human Remains: Disposal and Concealment in Genocide and Mass Violence*, edited by Jean-Marc Dreyfus and Élisabeth Gessat-Anstett, 46–68. Manchester, UK: Manchester University Press, 2014.

Mann, Michael. *The Dark Side of Democracy: Explaining Ethnic Cleansing*. New York: Cambridge University Press, 2005.

Marrus, Michael R. "Jewish Resistance to the Holocaust." *Journal of Contemporary History* 30, no. 1 (1995): 83–110.

Matthäus, Jürgen, and Frank Bajohr, eds. *The Political Diary of Alfred Rosenberg and the Onset of the Holocaust*, Documenting Life and Destruction: Holocaust Sources in Context. Lanham MD: Rowman & Littlefield, 2015.

Matthäus, Jürgen, and Jochen Böhler, eds. *War, Pacification, and Mass Murder, 1939: The Einsatzgruppen in Poland*. Lanham: Rowman & Littlefield, 2014.

Mauz, Gerhard. "'Als Anwalt Darf Man Nicht Zimperlich Sein.'" *Der Spiegel* 46 (1964): 71.

Mazower, Mark. *Hitler's Empire: How the Nazis Ruled Europe*. New York: Penguin, 2008.
McDoom, Omar Shahabudin. "Antisocial Capital: A Profile of Rwandan Genocide Perpetrators' Social Networks." *Journal of Conflict Resolution* 58, no. 5 (2014): 865–93.
Mędykowski, Witold. *Macht Arbeit Frei? German Economic Policy and Forced Labor of Jews in the General Government, 1939–1943*. Boston: Academic Studies Press, 2018.
Megargee, Geoffrey P., ed. *Encyclopedia of Camps and Ghettos I: Early Camps, Youth Camps, and Concentration Camps and Subcamps under the SS-Business Administration Main Office (WVHA)*. Vol. A. Bloomington: Indiana University Press, 2009.
———. *Encyclopedia of Camps and Ghettos I: Early Camps, Youth Camps, and Concentration Camps and Subcamps under the SS-Business Administration Main Office (WVHA)*. Vol. B. Bloomington: Indiana University Press, 2009.
Michman, Dan. *The Emergence of Jewish Ghettos during the Holocaust*. Cambridge: Cambridge University Press, 2011.
Mick, Christoph. "Incompatible Experiences: Poles, Ukrainians and Jews in Lviv under Soviet and German Occupation, 1939–44." *Journal of Contemporary History* 46, no. 2 (2011): 336–63.
———. *Lemberg, Lwów, L'viv, 1914–1947: Violence and Ethnicity in a Contested City*. West Lafayette IN: Purdue University Press, 2016.
Miedziński, Tomasz. "Nicht schematische Erinnerungen des Großvaters." Translated by Krzysztofa Marzec-Gacka. In *Unter deutscher Besatzung*, edited by Magda Cieszkowska, Rafał Degiel, and Agnieszka Dzierżanowska, 26–31. Warsaw: Stiftung Polnisch-Deutsche Aussöhnung, 2014.
Milton, John, and Matthew Stallard, eds. *John Milton, Paradise Lost: The Biblically Annotated Edition*. Macon GA: Mercer University Press, 2011.
Montague, Patrick. *Chełmno and the Holocaust: The History of Hitler's First Death Camp*. Chapel Hill: University of North Carolina Press, 2012.
Mühlhäuser, Regina. "Between 'Racial Awareness' and Fantasies of Potency: Nazi Sexual Politics in the Occupied Territories of the Soviet Union, 1942–1945." In *Brutality and Desire: War and Sexuality in Europe's Twentieth Century*, edited by Dagmar Herzog, 197–220. New York: Palgrave Macmillan, 2009.
Murphy, David E. *What Stalin Knew: The Enigma of Barbarossa*. New Haven CT: Yale University Press, 2005.
Murray, Williamson, and Allan Reed Millett. *A War to Be Won: Fighting the Second World War, 1937–1945*. Cambridge MA: Harvard University Press, 2001.
Niemann, Derek. *A Nazi in the Family*. London: Short, 2015.
Nutkiewicz, Michael. "Shame, Guilt, and Anguish in Holocaust Survivor Testimony." *Oral History Review* 30, no. 1 (2003): 1–22.

Oxford English Dictionary. Oxford: Oxford University Press, 2000.

Perlman, Leon. "Di Goldene Royz: A Survey of the Polish-Jewish Community of Lviv (1256–1943)." In *The University of Criminals: The Janowska Camp in Lviv, 1941–1944*, edited by Michał Maksymilian Borwicz, Jacek Tokarski, and Leon Perlman, 122–206. Krakow: Wysoki Zamek, 2014.

Pick, Hella. *Simon Wiesenthal: A Life in Search of Justice*. Boston: Northeastern University Press, 1996.

Pohl, Dieter. "Die großen Zwangsarbeiterlager der SS-und Polizeiführer für Juden im Generalgouvernement, 1942–1945." In *Die nationalsozialistischen Konzentrationslager: Entwicklung und Struktur*, edited by Ulrich Herbert, Karin Orth, and Christoph Dieckmann, 415–37. Göttingen: Wallstein Verlag, 1989.

———. "The Murder of Ukraine's Jews under German Military Administration and in the Reich Commissariat Ukraine." In *The Shoah in Ukraine: History, Testimony, Memorialization*, edited by Ray Brandon and Wendy Lower, 23–76. Bloomington: Indiana University Press, 2008.

———. *Nationalsozialistische Judenverfolgung in Ostgalizien, 1941–1944: Organisation und Durchführung eines staatlichen Massenverbrechens*. München: R. Oldenbourg, 1996.

Pohl, Manfred. *Philipp Holzmann: Geschichte eines Bauunternehmens, 1849–1999*. Munich: C. H. Beck, 1999.

Polonsky, Antony. "Introduction." In *The Wartime Diary of Edmund Kessler: Lwow, Poland, 1942–1944*, edited by Renata Kessler, 3–14. Boston: Academic Studies Press, 2010.

Poprzeczny, Joseph. *Odilo Globocnik, Hitler's Man in the East*. Jefferson NC: McFarland, 2004.

Raab, Jörg. "More Than Just a Metaphor: The Network Concept and Its Potential in Holocaust Research." In *Networks of Nazi Persecution: Bureaucracy, Business, and the Organization of the Holocaust*, edited by Gerald D. Feldman and Wolfgang Seibel, 321–39. New York: Berghahn, 2005.

Redzik, Adam. "The Janowska Hell." In *The University of Criminals: The Janowska Camp in Lviv, 1941–1944*, edited by Michał Maksymilian Borwicz, Jacek Tokarski, and Leon Perlman, 207–27. Krakow: Wysoki Zamek, 2014.

Reid, Anna. *Borderland: A Journey through the History of Ukraine*. Boulder CO: Westview, 1999.

Report to the Ukrainian Government on the Visit to Ukraine Carried out by the European Committee for the Prevention of Torture and Inhuman or Degrading Treatment or Punishment (Cpt) from 8 to 21 December 2017. Strasbourg: Council of Europe, 2018.

Rhodes, Richard. *Masters of Death: The SS-Einsatzgruppen and the Invention of the Holocaust.* New York: Vintage, 2003.

Rich, David Alan. "Armed Ukrainians in L'viv: Ukrainian Militia, Ukrainian Police, 1941 to 1942." *Canadian-American Slavic Studies* 48, no. 3 (2014): 271–87.

Rieß, Volker. "Christian Wirth–Der Inspekteur Der Vernichtungslager." In *Karrieren der Gewalt: Nationalsozialistische Täterbiographien,* edited by Klaus-Michael Mallmann and Gerhard Paul, 239–51. Darmstadt: Wissenschaftliche Buchgesellschaft, 2013.

Rifkind, David, and Geraldine L. Freeman. *The Nobel Prize Winning Discoveries in Infectious Diseases.* London: Elsevier Academic, 2005.

Ringelblum, Emanuel, and Jacob Sloan, eds. *Notes from the Warsaw Ghetto: The Journal of Emmanuel Ringelblum.* New York: McGraw-Hill, 1958.

Rings, Werner. *Life with the Enemy: Collaboration and Resistance in Hitler's Europe, 1939–1945.* London: Weidenfeld and Nicholson, 1982.

Roth, Joseph. *The Radetzky March.* Translated by Joachim Neugroschel. New York: Overlook, 1995.

Rubin, Arnon. *Against All Odds: Facing Holocaust; My Personal Recollections.* Tel Aviv: Tel Aviv University Press, 2005.

Rückerl, Adalbert. *The Investigation of Nazi Crimes, 1945–1978: A Documentation.* Hamden CT: Archon, 1979.

Sandkühler, Thomas. "Anti-Jewish Policy and the Murder of the Jews in the District of Galicia. 1941–1942." In *National Socialist Extermination Policies: Contemporary German Perspectives and Controversies,* edited by Ulrich Herbert, 104–27. New York: Berghahn, 2000.

———. "Das Zwangsarbeitslager Lemberg-Janowska, 1941–1944." In *Die Nationalsozialistischen Konzentrationslager: Entwicklung und Struktur,* edited by Ulrich Herbert, Karin Orth, and Christoph Dieckmann, 606–35. Göttingen: Wallstein Verlag, 1998.

———. *"Endlösung" in Galizien: Der Judenmord in Ostpolen und die Rettungsinitiativen von Berthold Beitz, 1941–1944.* Bonn: Dietz, 1996.

Schama, Simon. *Landscape and Memory.* New York: Vintage, 1995.

Scherner, Jonas, and Eugene N. White, eds. *Paying for Hitler's War: The Consequences of Nazi Hegemony for Europe.* New York: Cambridge University Press, 2016.

Schindler, John R. *Fall of the Double Eagle: The Battle for Galicia and the Demise of Austria-Hungary.* Lincoln NE: Potomac, 2015.

Schroer, Timothy L. "Civilization, Barbarism, and the Ethos of Self-Control among the Perpetrators." *German Studies Review* 35, no. 1 (2012): 33–54.

Schulz, Andreas, and Dieter Zinke, eds. *Die Generale der Waffen-SS und der Polizei.* Vol. 5. Bissendorf: Biblio-Verlag, 2011.

Segal, Chaim. *Chaim Heißt Leben: Ein Jüdisches Schicksal in Boryslaw und ein Neuanfang in Hofgeismar*. Hofgeismar: Verein für Hessische Geschichte und Landeskunde e.V. Kassel 1834, 2012.

Segev, Tom. *Simon Wiesenthal: The Life and Legends*. New York: Doubleday, 2010.

Shenfeld, Stepan. "The Recollections of Stepan Yakimovich Shenfeld [1943]." Translated by Christopher Morris and Joshua Rubenstein. In *The Unknown Black Book: The Holocaust in the German-Occupied Soviet Territories*, edited by Joshua Rubenstein and Ilya Altman, 89–99. Bloomington: Indiana University Press, 2008.

Sinnreich, Helene. "The Rape of Jewish Women During the Holocaust." In *Sexual Violence against Jewish Women During the Holocaust*, edited by Sonja M. Hedgepeth and Rochelle G. Saidel, 108–33. Waltham MA: Brandeis University Press, 2010.

———. "Victim and Perpetrator Perspectives of World War II–Era Ghettos." In *The Routledge History of the Holocaust*, edited by Jonathan C. Friedman, 115–24. New York: Routledge, 2011.

Snyder, Timothy. *Bloodlands: Europe between Hitler and Stalin*. New York: Basic, 2012.

Sobieski, Zygmunt. "Reminiscenses from Lwow, 1939–1945." *Journal of Central European Affairs* 6 (1947): 350–74.

Solarewicz, Stanisław. "Helft Uns die Erinnerung zu Bewahren." Translated by Krzysztofa Marzec-Gacka. In *Unter deutscher Besatzung*, edited by Magda Cieszkowska, Rafał Degiel and Agnieszka Dzierżanowska, 32–34. Warsaw: Stiftung Polnisch-Deutsche Aussöhnung, 2014.

Sorokina, Marina. "People and Procedures: Toward a History of the Investigation of Nazi Crimes in the USSR." Translated by David Habecker. In *The Holocaust in the East: Local Perpetrators and Soviet Responses*, edited by Michael David-Fox, Peter Holquist and Alexander M. Martin, 118–41. Pittsburgh PA: University of Pittsburgh Press, 2014.

Spector, Schmuel. "Aktion 1005: Effacing the Murder of Millions." *Holocaust Genocide Studies* 5, no. 2 (1990): 157–73.

Stachura, Peter D. *Poland, 1918–1945: An Interpretive and Documentary History of the Second Republic*. London: Routledge, 2004.

Statiev, Alexander. *The Soviet Counterinsurgency in the Western Borderlands*. Cambridge: Cambridge University Press, 2010.

Steinacher, Gerald. "'A Man with a Wide Horizon': The Postwar Professional Journey of SS Officer Karl Nicolussi-Leck." In *A Nazi Past: Recasting German Identity in Postwar Europe*, edited by David A. Messenger and Katrin Paehler, 225–48. Lexington: University Press of Kentucky, 2015.

Stroop, Jürgen. *The Stroop Report*. Edited and Translated by Sybil Milton. New York: Pantheon, 1979.

———. *Żydowska Dzielnica Miezkaniowa W Warsawie Już Nie Istnieje!* Edited by Andrzej Żbikowski. Warsaw: Instytut Pamięci Narodowej, 2009.

Struve, Kai. *Deutsche Herrschaft, Ukrainischer Nationalismus, antijüdische Gewalt: der Sommer 1941 in der Westukraine*. Berlin: De Gruyter Oldenbourg, 2015.

Swanson, John C. "Minority Building in the German Diaspora: The Hungarian-Germans." *Austrian History Yearbook* 36 (2005): 148–66.

Tenenbaum, Joseph. *Underground: The Story of a People*. New York: Philosophical Library, 1952.

Terry, Nicholas. "Covering Up Chelmno: Nazi Attempts to Obfuscate and Obliterate an Extermination Camp." *Dapim: Studies on the Holocaust* 32, no. 3 (2018): 188–205.

Tomaszewski, Tadeusz. "Der Psychologe Tadeusz Tomaszewski schildert in seinem Tagebuch am 2. und 9. 1941 Die Verfolgung und Erschiessung von Juden in Lemberg." In *Polen: Generalgouvernement, August 1941–1945*, vol. 9, edited by Klaus-Peter Friedrich. Munich: Oldenbourg Verlag, 2014.

Tregenza, Michael. "Belzec Death Camp." In *The Nazi Holocaust: Historical Articles on the Destruction of European Jews: The "Victims of the Holocaust,"* edited by Michael Robert Marrus, 1085–1114. Westport: Meckler, 1989.

Trials of the War Criminals before the International Military Tribunal: Documents and Other Material in Evidence, 1850-PS to 2233-PS. Vol. 29. Washington DC: GPO, 1948.

Trials of War Criminals before the Nuremberg Military Tribunals (Einsatzgruppen and RuSHA Cases), Vol. IV, 132–33. Washington DC: GPO, 1949.

Trunk, Isaiah. *Judenrat: The Jewish Councils in Eastern Europe under Nazi Occupation*. Lincoln: University of Nebraska Press, 1996.

Tukey, John W. *Exploratory Data Analysis*. London: Addison-Wesley, 1977.

Turkel, William J. "Every Place Is an Archive: Environmental History and the Interpretation of Physical Evidence." *Rethinking History* 10, no. 2 (2006): 259–76.

Uhl, Matthias, Thomas Pruschwitz, Martin Holler, Jean-Luc Leleu, and Dieter Pohl, eds. *Die Organisation des Terrors: Der Dienstkalender Heinrich Himmlers, 1943–1945*. München: Piper, 2020.

"Vernichtung von Juden war kein Geheimnis, Stuttgarter Zeitung, Nr. 164, 20 July 1967." YVA: RG-P13, File 189.

Viertel, Salka. *Das Unbelehrbare Herz*. Frankfurt Am Main: Eichborn, 2011.

———. *The Kindness of Strangers*. New York: Holt, Rinehart, and Winston, 1969.

Vysotsky, A. F., A. L. Kopylenko, F. A. Lopushansky, and V. V. Sokolov, eds. *Nazi Crimes in Ukraine, 1941–1944: Documents and Materials*. Kiev: Naukova Dumka, 1987.

Wachsmann, Nikolaus. *Kl: A History of the Nazi Concentration Camps*. New York: Farrar, Straus and Giroux, 2015.

Wawro, Geoffrey. *A Mad Catastrophe: The Outbreak of World War I and the Collapse of the Habsburg Empire*. New York: Basic, 2014.

Wawrzeniuk, Piotr. "'Lwów Saved Us': Roma Survival in Lemberg 1941–44." *Journal of Genocide Research* (2018): 1–24.

Weckel, Ulrike. "The Mitläufer in Two German Postwar Films." Article. *History & Memory* 15, no. 2 (2003): 64–93.

Wendland, Anna Veronika. "Neighbors as Betrayers: Nationalization, Remembrance Policy, and the Urban Public Sphere in L'viv." In *Galicia: A Multicultured Land*, edited by C. M Hann and Paul R. Magocsi, 139–59. Toronto: University of Toronto Press, 2005.

Westemeier, Jens. *Himmlers Krieger: Joachim Peiper und Die Waffen-SS in Krieg und Nachkriegszeit*. Paderborn: Schöningh Ferdinand GmbH, 2019.

Wiesel, Elie. *And the Sea Is Never Full: Memoirs, 1969–*. Translated by Marion Wiesel. New York: Alfred A. Knopf, 1999.

Wilke, Karsten. "Renten für SS-Veteranen. Die 'Hilfsgemeinschaft Auf Gegenseitigkeit' in Der FrüHen Bundesrepublik." *Mittelweg 36 Zeitschrift des Hamburger Instituts für Sozialforschung* 5 (2015): 59–71.

Winstone, Martin. *The Dark Heart of Hitler's Europe: Nazi Rule in Poland under the General Government*. London: I. B. Tauris, 2015.

Wittmann, Rebecca. *Beyond Justice: The Auschwitz Trial*. Cambridge MA: Harvard University Press, 2005.

Wölfer, Ralf, Nadira S. Faber, and Miles Hewstone. "Social Network Analysis in the Science of Groups: Cross-Sectional and Longitudinal Applications for Studying Intra-and Intergroup Behavior." *Group Dynamics: Theory, Research, and Practice* 40, no. 4 (2015): 45–61.

Wróbel, Piotr J. "Class War or Ethnic Cleansing." *Polish Review* 59, no. 2 (2014): 19–42.

Yones, Eliyahu. *Smoke in the Sand: The Jews of Lvov in the War Years, 1939–1944*. Jerusalem: Gefen, 2004.

Zayarnyuk, Andriy. *Lviv's Uncertain Destination: A City and Its Train Terminal from Franz Joseph I to Brezhnev*. Toronto: University of Toronto Press, 2020.

Zorgdrager, Heleen, and Michiel Driebergen. *The Jews of Lemberg: A Journey to Empty Places*. Translated by Jantine van der Knaap and Kristie Szalanski. Dorset: Vallentine Mitchell.

Пагіря, Олександр. "Yevreys'ke Hetto Ta Natsyst·S'kyy Kontstabir U L'vovi (Za Dokumentamy Hda Sbu)." In Українсько-Єврейське Співжиття Під Час Голокосту. За Матеріалами Західної України, edited by А. Боляновський, 138–60. Дніпро-Львів: Український інститут вивчення Голокосту 'Ткума', Інститут українознавства ім, 2019.

Index

aktion(s), 37–38, 93, 101–5, 107, 128, 194, 202, 205–7, 267
Améry, Jean, 166, 171, 179
antisemitism, 16, 20–23, 39, 43, 178, 267; and ideology, 20, 119, 240; and pogroms, 19; and policy, 22, 46; and propaganda, 241; and stereotypes, 49, 262
Appellplatz, 121, 124, 176, 266; and forced labor, 170; and Janowska, 114, 146; murders on, 146; and SS officers, 146; and sexual violence, 182; and Sobibor uprising, 222; and Zwangsarbeitslager-Lemberg (ZAL-L), 5, 169
Aschenauer, Rudolf, 247–48, 250
Ash, Feliks, 150, 217, 219–20, 226, 227
Ash Brigade, 216
Asocial Aktion, 97, 131
August Aktion, 103, 106, 145, 148
Auschwitz Trial, 11, 248, 265
Axer, Henryk, 161
Axer, Richard "Rysiek," 145, 157, 160, 162

Bełżec, 100, 104, 263; aktion at, 106; and deportations, 86, 97–98, 103, 132, 133, 148, 207; as extermination center, 95–96, 131, 136; and gas chambers, 7, 10, 98, 99, 101, 134, 137, 204, 264; and Janowska, 102; and labor camps, 60; and Lviv, 138, 211; murders at, 131, 145; station, 97; and trial, 245; and victims, 99, 128, 131, 138
Bitsch, Zbigniew, 225
Bleines, Hugo, 4, 63, 68–69, 73–74, 129, 256
Blitz Aktion, 102
Blöbel, Paul, 31, 211–12, 214, 220–21, 237
Blum, Peter, 115, 125, 138, 145, 237–39, 246; antisemitism of, 178; and early life, 115; and family, 238–39; and Great Aktion, 128; and Holocaust survivors, 138, 169; and Janowska, 119, 168–69; and Lviv ghetto, 138; and Lviv Trial, 249, 251, 253–54; as murderer, 174–75, 178, 230, 261; and sexual violence, 183–84, 229, 266; as SS officer, 116, 127; and Waffen-SS, 117, 191
Borszczów, 133
Borwicz, Michał, 74, 114; and Bienenstock, 162; and camp resistance, 223, 225; and Janowska, 167, 171, 222; as survivor, 74, 167; torture of, 173; and *The University of Criminals*, 109, 141, 190; and vitamin work, 125; and Zegota, 161

brigades, 226; cemetery, 6, 126; cleaning, 208; compulsion, 123; concrete, 145; construction, 124, 143; cripples, 170; labor, 130, 144, 150; laundry, 145; prisoner, 9–10, 68, 129–30; punishment, 123; singing, 215; Wire, 111; work, 143, 146, 169, 222–23
brutality, 58; competitive, 177; excessive, 177, 267; and Janowska, 120, 130, 141, 166–67, 177–79, 201; and Nazis, 206
Browning, Christopher, 95, 107, 123, 187
Buber, Martin, 18
Büttner, Martin, 167, 169, 174, 181–82, 195, 197, 214, 238, 246, 254

camp orchestra, 143, 153–54, 175, 215, 225, 246
Carpathian oil company, 221
children: and August Aktion, 103–4; and clinic, 18; and gas chambers, 74; and Great Aktion, 6; and Janowska camp, 102–3, 204–5; Jewish, 2, 5–6, 48; and March Aktion, 207–8; and mass murder, 217; orphaned, 238; as victims of the Holocaust, 19, 74, 94, 102–4, 107, 131, 136–37, 174–75, 181, 204–8, 217, 228; and Warsaw ghetto, 156
Cohen, Joseph, 90
corpse(s), 176, 215; and Dachau concentration camp, 23; and Death Brigade, 210; disposal of, 98, 126, 150, 152, 211, 220–21, 226; in Galicia, 221; and Lviv, 28, 196; at prisons, 32
Czechoslovakia, 36, 128, 237

Death Brigade (Janowska SK 1005), 210, 212, 218–19, 228, 242, 246; and Alexander Schwarz, 261; and body disposal, 184; and bone-grinder, 259; and bone-grinder operator, 235; and burning sites, 7, 215; and David Manusevich, 240; and David Thürhaus, 249; and Janowska, 213, 216, 221, 226; and Johann Rauch, 217, 220, 240, 244; and Leon Wells, 214, 218, 220, 226, 246; and Lviv, 214; and Lyczakow forest camp, 223; and Moische Korn, 235; and music, 226–27; and prisoners, 217; and rabbis, 152; and revolt, 233; and routine, 216; and Schutzstaffel (SS), 220, 221, 226. See also Sonderkommando 1005 (SK1005)
Dębica, 116, 117, 191–92
deportation(s), 105–6, 257; and Adolf Hitler, 94; and aktions, 93, 101, 103, 131; and Bełżec, 86; and Distrikt Galizien, 137–38; and Galicia, 266; and ghettos, 99; and Janowska, 130, 137, 139, 207; and Jewish Council, 101; and Jews, 6, 86, 93, 128, 130, 137; and Lviv, 27, 98–99, 101, 103–4, 123; and Nazis, 93–94, 139; network of, 10; and sexual violence, 185; and Soviet Union, 26; and trains, 97
Deutsche Ausrüstungswerke (DAW), 3, 54, 58–61, 63, 65, 71, 74, 77, 91, 110–11, 118, 122, 260; and anti-Jewish policy, 54; and Berlin, 57, 110; and Chaim Rosen, 173; and commandants, 66; and construction, 239; and German Equipment Works (Lviv), 53; and guard force, 64; and Gustav Willhaus, 77, 201; and the Holocaust, 9, 54; and Janowska camps, 79, 129, 197, 223–24; and Jews, 3, 59, 72; and Lublin, 55–56,

340 Index

60; and Lviv, 60, 79, 261–62; and origins, 54; and prisoners, 70–71, 111; and Zwangsarbeitslager-Lemberg (ZAL-L), 121, 169, 177, 190, 197. *See also* Deutsche Ausrüstungswerke-Lemberg (DAW-L); Gebauer, Fritz; Schutzstaffel (SS)

Deutsche Ausrüstungswerke-Lemberg (DAW-L), 3, 54–56, 60, 62, 64, 74, 76–77; as closed camp, 95; and daily life, 66; and employees, 72; and German civilians, 73; and Gustav Willhaus, 109; and Helene Kaplan, 59; and hybridity, 9; and women, 72; and World War II, 67

Dirlewanger Brigade, 193

disease, 49, 83, 88–89, 158, 218

Distrikt Galizien, 40, 59, 79–80, 107, 122, 131, 134, 188, 211; and anti-Jewish policy, 45; and concentration camps, 189; and Death Brigade, 216; and doctors, 49, 90; and ghettos, 133, 206, 267; and Heinrich Himmler, 100; and highway, 50; and Jews, 137, 202–3, 208; and killing sites, 138; and Nazi authority, 42; and police, 109; and SS officers, 43, 190, 193, 201; and workers, 101

Drix, Samuel: and camp guards, 123; and family, 25; and ghettos, 99, 207; and Janowska, 106, 134, 145, 150, 152, 155, 260; and Leon Wells, 234; and Lviv, 22–23, 87, 99, 101; as physician, 88, 90, 130, 143, 158; and sexual violence, 182; and violence, 149

Drohobycz, 197, 255

Durchgangstrasse IV (DG IV), 10, 50, 76, 100, 106, 122, 126, 194, 205, 222

Eastern Front, 20, 41, 95, 172, 203

Eichmann Trial, 12, 101, 149, 250

Eismann, Yehuda, 223

escape: and Auschwitz, 54; and Death Brigade, 7, 246; and Janowska, 65, 80, 130, 147, 157, 159–60, 162, 167, 203, 255–56; and Jews, 38, 120, 130, 132, 142, 196, 223, 225–26, 234, 265

execution(s), 261; and Adolfo Kolon-cko, 251; and Death Brigade, 214; and Janowska, 8–9, 68, 135, 137–39, 161–62, 168, 175, 186, 201, 207, 228, 231; and JULAG, 205; and Leon Wells, 240; and Lviv, 27, 217, 266; and Piaski, 159; and the Sands, 121, 125, 135, 154; and Schutzstaffel (SS), 216

expropriation, 47–48, 86, 118, 127, 143

Final Solution: and ghettos, 133; and Janowska, 129, 137, 202, 264; and Lviv, 45, 100; and Nazi authorities, 133, 203; and Odilo Globocnik, 55; and Reinhard Heydrich, 36, 49, 95, 211

1st Gebirgsjäger Division, 29

Folkmann, Adolf, 30, 40, 92, 107, 124, 125, 205, 206

forced labor, 54, 61, 76, 103, 110, 117, 133; and DAW camps, 55, 65; and Distrikt Galizen, 59; and Janowska, 122–24, 260, 264; and Lipowa DAW camp, 60; and Nazi policy, 86

forced labor camps, 118, 134, 195; construction of, 100; and Janowska, 9, 80; and Lviv, 2, 9, 242; and Tarnopol, 197, 199; and Zwangsarbeitslager-Lemberg (ZAL-L), 4

14th SS Galizien Division, 230, 262

14th Waffen-SS Grenadier Division, 230
Fox, Paul, 125, 168, 190, 192–93, 198, 200, 207, 246, 254
Friedman, Philip, 12
funereal building, 1
Fur Aktion, 47–48

Galicia (Western Ukraine), 5; and Austrian Empire, 17; and concentration camps, 197, 211; and Eastern region, 39, 211; and gas chambers, 264; and the Holocaust, 10–11, 42, 197, 201, 203; and *Judenrein*, 128; and Jews, 16, 19, 131, 135, 200–202, 208, 266; and Lviv, 18, 50, 211; and Nazi policy, 13; and Poland, 21, 185; and Prince Danylo, 15; and Soviet Union, 20; and violence, 44, 211
Gebauer, Fritz: and arrest, 246; and Chaim Rosen, 173; and Deutsche Ausrüstungswerke (DAW), 53, 57, 62, 67–68, 72, 74, 76, 79, 91, 131, 146, 162, 201; and Deutsche Ausrüstungswerke-Lemberg (DAW-L), 55, 59–62, 64, 66, 73, 75; and Eugenia Maas, 4; and Friedrich Katzmann, 77, 106, 110; and Friedrich Warzock, 255; and Gisela Urbach, 185; and Gustav Willhaus, 91, 106, 109, 110, 112–13, 122, 167, 174; and Helene Kaplan, 183; and Hugo Bleines, 256; and imprisonment, 256; and Janowksa, 158, 255–57; and Janowksa Street, 54, 66; and Karl Melchior, 162, 171; and Leon Wells, 185; and Liesel Willhaus, 245; life of, 56; and Lviv, 3, 58, 63–64; and murder, 173, 176; and Nazi Party, 57, 89; and Roman Kampf, 69, 147; and Schutzstaffel (SS), 72, 147; and trial of, 75, 109, 256–57; and violence, 176–77; and Willi Monz, 239–40; and Zwangsarbeitslager-Lemberg (ZAL-L), 70–71, 109, 111, 236
the General Government, 89; and August Aktion, 103; and concentration camps, 80, 224; and Distrikt Galizien, 40, 42, 45, 59, 101, 107, 211; and Emissionsbank, 129; and Final Solution, 137; and forced labor, 60; and Friedrich Krüger, 212; and Hans Frank, 80, 237; and Heinrich Himmler, 138, 203, 206, 222; and Holocaust survivors, 70; and Nazi policy, 13, 76; and Odilo Globocnik, 55; and Operation Reinhard, 96; and overlord, 43; and Soviet Union, 97; and Ukrainian police, 44
German 1st Mountain Division, 24, 33
German (language), 12, 81, 119, 127, 257; newspapers, 115, 247
German Moloch, 5
Germany, 11, 63, 74, 85, 92, 112, 116, 126, 208, 235, 238, 265; and administrators, 80; and Adolf Hitler, 40; and Alfred Rosenberg, 49; and Army, 24, 27, 29–30, 32–35, 37, 48, 89–90, 104, 130, 209, 212; and August Aktion, 148; and Austria, 20; authorities, 38; and Bomlitz, 44; and bureaucracy, 43; and citizens, 90; and concentration camps, 4, 37, 54, 62, 68, 71, 96, 179, 185, 266; and courts, 257; and culture, 154; and Death Brigade, 210, 244; and Deutsche Ausrüstungswerke (DAW), 72–73; and East Germany,

237, 255; and economy, 6, 9; and Egon Höller, 86; and Einsatzgruppe D, 247; and empire, 64; and ethnic Germans, 115–18, 189; and Europe, 94, 178; and Galicia, 43–44; and German Equipment Works, 53; and government, 192, 241–42; and Holocaust, 186, 241–42; and hospitals, 90; and Hungary, 115–16, 178, 183–84; and infrastructure, 193, 253; and jails, 217; and Janowska camp, 130, 241–42, 245–46, 260; and Jews, 45–46, 49, 72, 104, 123, 128, 178, 185, 204, 236, 243; and Josef Grzimek, 23; and Karl Lasch, 80; and killing sites, 5; and legal system, 247–49, 255–56; and Leon Wells, 185, 246; and Lviv, 37, 46, 65, 80, 126, 129, 175; and nationalism, 56; and Nazis, 11, 13, 96, 112, 178, 185, 229, 238–47; and occupation (of Ukraine), 32, 36, 39–41; and Philipp Holzmann, 194; and Poland, 27, 43, 63, 115, 261; and police, 44, 66, 79, 132, 233, 242, 245–46; and Roman Kamf, 148; and Schutzstaffel (SS), 72, 112, 206; and Sicherheitsdienst (SD), 104; and *Stadthauptmann*, 82, 86; and Ukraine, 96, 229; and Ukrainian police, 43–44, 104–5; and violence, 39, 45; and Wannsee, 101; and World War I, 112; and World War II, 13, 27, 203, 225–29, 234; and Wrocław, 42
Gestapo, 36, 59, 93, 234, 259; and August Aktion, 104; and Great Aktion, 5; and Heinrish Müller, 210, 217; and Janowska camp, 222; and Jews, 37, 105; and Lviv, 212; and murder, 37; and prison, 228; and sexual violence, 183; and Soviet Secret Police (GPU), 26; and torture, 166; and Ukrainian police, 38, 47, 104; and Walter Schallock, 242

ghettoization, 48–49, 79, 81–82, 85, 87
ghettos, 62, 72, 103, 107, 149, 158; and aktions, 102, 104–5, 128, 131, 204; benches, 23; and Borysław, 133; and community, 47; and concentration camps, 203; creation of, 80; and Distrikt Galizien, 206, 208, 267; and Final Solution, 133; and Friedrich Katzmann, 206–8; and Germans, 85, 102; and Gestapo, 104; and Gustav Willhaus, 194; and Holocaust, 151; Holocaust memorials to, 262; and Janowska, 4, 89–90, 99, 114, 131, 138, 160, 194, 207–8; and Jewish Council, 83–84, 86–88, 90, 92; and JULAG, 204–5; Kraków, 49; and liquidation of, 133, 144, 194, 197, 205–6, 213, 221, 264, 267; Łodz, 94; Lviv, 8, 10, 24, 50, 46, 48–50, 79, 81–84, 87, 90, 92, 97, 138, 162, 189–90, 193, 203–5, 208, 224, 233, 263; and March Aktion, 98, 101–3, 207; and Paul Fox, 193; and Radom, 42, 190; and Rudolf Weigl, 89, 104; and Rysiek Axer, 157; and sexual violence, 180; and Ukrainian police, 105, 146, 206; and violence, 83; Warsaw, 150, 156, 206, 221; and Zwangsarbeitslager-Lemberg (ZAL-L), 197
Gleiwitz, 23
Globocnik, Odilo, 58, 95, 100, 106, 117, 192; and Christian Wirth, 96; and Distrikt Lublin, 60; as Schutzstaffel (SS) officer, 55, 118

Goebbels, Joseph, 35, 49
Great Aktion (1942), 5–7, 79, 101, 104, 106, 128, 131, 135, 195, 261
Gródek-Jagielloński, 190, 194–95, 197, 203, 251–52
Grzimek, Jozef, 23, 189, 193, 204–5, 207, 254

Hasmonea Lwów sports club, 18
Hebrew, 1, 12, 261–62
Heereskraftfahrzeugpark (HKP) 547, 42, 53, 130
Heinen, Friedrich, 168, 173–75, 177, 181–82, 201, 237, 255
Heydrich, Reinhard, 36, 38, 49, 64, 80, 94–95, 211, 252
Himmler, Heinrich: and Adolf Eichmann, 94; and anti-Jewish policy, 76; and Auschwitz, 211; and Bełziec, 138; and culpability, 243; and Distrikt Galizien, 100, 203; and Durchgangstrasse IV (DG IV), 50; and Einsatzgruppen, 36; and Friedrich Katzmann, 42, 208; and ghettos, 206; and Great Aktion, 106; and Janowska, 143, 172; and Jewish resistance, 222; and JULAG, 204; and Lviv, 38, 76, 123; as murderer, 94, 206, 251; and Odilo Globocnik, 95, 106, 117, 192; and Reichsführer SS, 210, 221; and Schutzstaffel (SS), 54, 172, 208–9; and Sobibor, 222; and Soviet Union, 64; and Third Reich, 54, 243; trial of, 251–52; and Wehrmacht, 116
Hirshhorn, Bernard, 4, 59, 67–69, 71, 91, 126
Hitler, Adolf, 252; and allegiance, 138; defeat of, 239; and deportations,

94; and Gustav Willhaus, 113; and Heinrich Himmler, 50, 94, 243; and Italy, 217; and Janowska, 60, 252; and Jewish Question, 93; and Lviv, 40; and Poland, 37; and Prison Aktion, 36; and racial ideology, 186; and Saarbrücken, 112
Hitlerism, 24
Hitler Youth, 112, 117
Holocaust, 129, 145, 239, 248, 250; and awareness of, 210; and Babi Yar, 31, 210–11; and concentration camps, 110, 165, 171; and Distrikt Galizien, 190; experience of, 165, 197; and Galicia (Ukraine), 9–11, 42, 201, 203; and ghettos, 213; and Great Aktion, 135; and historians, 134, 142, 150; and Janowska camp, 2, 9–10, 79, 130, 139, 141–42, 191, 197, 202, 205, 264–67; and Jewish Council, 92; and Jews, 5; and Lviv, 5, 12–15, 42, 89, 200, 258–59; and mass shootings, 31; and memorials, 262; and Nazis, 84, 107, 139, 178; perpetrators of, 189, 237; and "place," 120; and resistance, 162; and sexual violence, 179–80, 186–87; and sites, 2, 262–64; and slave labor camp, 122; and Soviet Union, 44, 235; and survivors, 18, 151, 236; and Ukrainian police, 44, 257; and victims, 211; and violence, 26, 174, 176
Holocaust survivors: and Arnon Rubin, 18; and Auschwitz, 182; and David Kahane, 152; and Death Brigade, 240; and deportations, 98; and Deutsche Ausrüstungswerke-Lemberg (DAW-L), 74, 167; and extermination camps, 134; and Frie-

drich Warzok, 229; and Fritz Gebauer, 58, 60–61, 69, 75, 146, 173; and ghetto, 149; and Gustav Willhaus, 113, 125, 171; and Helene Kaplan, 72; and Hilde Bluhm, 151; and humiliation, 128, 181; and International Auschwitz Committee, 257; and Janowska, 41, 128, 143, 157–58, 169, 197, 218, 240, 261; and Karl Melchior, 243–44; and Leon Wells, 113; and Liesel Willhaus, 114; and Lviv, 32; and mass shootings, 135; and memoirs, 7; and Michał Borwicz, 190; and Nazis, 32; and Peter Blum, 138, 178, 249; and Philip Friedman, 12; and Ravensbrück camp, 180; and recollections, 61, 75, 125, 128, 149–50, 158, 221, 224; and the Sands, 135; and sexual violence, 184; and skilled laborers, 71; and testimony, 102, 141, 175, 256, 265; and violence, 124–25; and Zwangsarbeitslager-Lemberg (ZAL-L), 7–8, 70, 113

Jäcklein, Josef, 132–33
Jaktorów camp, 44, 193, 198, 207, 222, 254
Janow-Lwowski, 133
Janowska camp, 2, 12, 31, 54, 79; and afterlife, 258–62; and aktions, 7, 103–4, 106; and Appellplatz, 114; and Asocial Aktion, 131; and Bełżec, 10, 137; and body disposal, 211–12; and Buchenwald, 178; and construction, 67, 124; and current day, 2; and daily life, 176; and death toll, 2, 138, 208, 217, 264; and Distrikt Galizien, 107, 122, 133, 201–2; and documentation, 13; and empire, 8, 9, 50, 178, 263; and Gestapo, 93; and ghettos, 4, 86, 88, 160, 208; and hybridity, 121; and Jewish clothing, 128, 129; and Jewish intellectuals, 153–54; and Jewish labor, 86, 100, 126, 197, 213; and Jewish victims, 51, 99–105, 131, 138, 153, 179, 204, 217–19, 224, 264–66; and kapos, 144; as killing center, 111, 134–36, 138–39, 158; liquidation of, 161, 221, 222, 226, 227, 228, 231; and murders, 89, 101–2, 130, 135–36, 138–39, 169, 171, 177, 187, 211–12, 216, 223, 253; and music, 154–55; and opening, 60; and perpetrator network, 197–202; and perpetrators, 122, 138, 195, 237–39, 249, 252–53; and physical reality, 203; and Piaski, 83, 138; and Polish victims, 90; and prisoner society, 142, 147; and rabbis, 175; and sexual violence, 165, 179–82, 186–88; and slave labor, 50, 122, 123; and Soviet inspection, 235; and Soviet use, 259–60; and staff, 191; and Stanisława Gogolowska, 165; and surveillance, 152; survivors of, 72, 124, 141, 156, 165–66, 169, 176, 179, 190, 193, 233–34, 236, 240, 261–62; as transit camp, 130–33; as transit prison, 260; and trials of perpetrators, 11, 166, 241–45, 249–58; and Ukrainian victims, 90; and urban geography, 265, 266. *See also* Death Brigade (Janowska SK 1005); Deutsche Ausrüstungswerke-Lemberg (DAW-L); Jewish resistance; Lviv Trial; Nazi Party; Schutzstaffel (SS); Zwangsarbeitslager-Lemberg (ZAL-L)

Janowska Street, 53, 54, 74; and German military, 24, 29, 42; and Jews, 14, 153; and Schutzstaffel (SS), 51; and Steinhaus company, 56; and survivors, 6, 263

Jehovah's Witnesses, 54

Jewish Council (Judenrat), 71; and Aid Committee, 91; and Adolf Rothfeld, 82; and ghetto, 84, 86, 88, 92; and Holocaust, 92; and hospitals, 88; and Housing Office, 83; and Janowska, 90, 204; and Jewish Labor Office, 3; and Jewish registration, 79; and Josef Parnas, 46–47; and Lviv, 84; and March Aktion, 101; and Nazi authorities, 101, 133, 204; and services, 87; and subdivisions, 47; and Złoczów, 210

Jewish resistance, 6, 8, 13, 209, 212; armed, 151, 160; artistic, 153, 155; defensive, 157; diversity of, 150–51; and Janowska, 148, 150, 159, 161–63, 223–24, 265; and mass revolts, 151, 159, 162, 222–24, 228, 233; symbolic, 152; and Warsaw ghetto, 206–7, 221

Jewish tombstones (*matzevot*), 1–2, 6, 120, 126, 216, 258

Judaism, 18, 152

JULAG, 204, 205, 208; and Jewish resistance, 206; and Jozef Grzymek, 189, 230, 244

July Days (pogrom), 31–32, 36, 45, 53

justice (postwar), 246; and constraints, 248; and Friedrich Warzok, 210; and German justice system, 241, 243, 255–57; and Janowska perpetrators, 11, 239, 244; and Lviv Trial, 252, 254; and Simon Wiesenthal, 234

Kahane, Rabbi David, 107, 145, 159; and Aktions, 106, 128; and Carl Wöbke, 104; and deportations, 105; and diary, 156, 263; and extermination camps, 99; and Gestapo, 93; and ghettos, 92, 204; and Gustav Willhaus, 170, 175; as historian, 18; as Holocaust survivor, 152–53, 263; and Jewish property, 48; and Leon Wells, 156; and Lviv, 37, 85, 92, 103; and music, 155; and Ukrainian police, 33

Kalymon, Ivan, 44, 46, 102, 104, 206, 239, 257

Kampf, Roman, 69–70, 145–48

Kaplan, Helene, 28, 59, 68, 72, 74–75, 150, 183

Katz, Aron, 225

Katz, Steven, 187

Katzmann, Friedrich: and anti-Jewish policy, 42, 76; and Asocial Aktion, 97; and Deutsche Ausrüstungswerke (DAW), 110; and Durchgangstrasse IV (DG IV), 100, 106; and ghettos, 221; and Gustav Willhaus, 75–77, 110, 113, 172, 195–96, 201, 208–9; and Janowska, 100, 117, 122, 200–201, 206, 211; and Judenrat, 47; and JULAG, 204–6, 208; and Lviv, 76, 80–81, 190, 195, 208, 211–12, 234; as murderer, 207; and Nazi authorities, 122; and prosecution, 258; as Schutzstaffel's (SS), 42, 48–49, 59, 178; and slave labor camps, 106, 122; and Ukrainian police, 104; and Zwangsarbeitslager (ZAL), 109; and Zwangsarbeitslager-Lemberg (ZAL-L), 209

Kessler, Edmun, 29, 39, 85–86, 149, 235

346 Index

Kleparów station, 4, 7, 10, 25, 27, 29, 70, 97, 105, 106, 110, 120, 124, 125, 131–32, 148, 229, 261
Kolomea, 132–33
Kolonko, Adolf, 64, 200, 213; and Allgemeine-SS, 63; and August Aktion, 145; and Deutsche Ausrüstungswerke (DAW), 65, 73, 111; and Gustav Willhaus, 195–96; and Janowska Camp, 117, 189–90, 192, 194, 196–98, 225–26, 251, 267; and Jewish prisoners, 5, 161, 194; and Lviv, 196; as murderer, 5, 174, 182, 196, 250; and Peter Blum, 239, 246, 251, 254; and prosecution, 250–51, 254; and Richard "Rysiek" Axer, 145; and Roman Schönbach, 117, 174, 192, 200; as Schutzstaffel (SS) officer, 5, 73, 114, 192; and Silesia, 63; and Ukrainians, 196; and US Army, 237; and Zwangsarbeitslager-Lemberg (ZAL-L), 190
Korn, Moische, 127, 215–16, 219, 227, 235
Kraków, 77, 81, 162, 213, 221; and ghetto, 49; and Hans Frank, 40; and Holocaust victims, 116; and Jagiellonion University, 37; and Montelupich prison, 231; and Płaszów concentration camp, 230; and Pustków camp, 117
Kroch, Izak, 1

labor, 3, 27, 59, 62, 114, 127, 130, 145, 179; brigades, 144, 150; and concentrations camps, 57, 100, 109, 121, 157, 191, 193–94, 197; force, 61, 71; free, 134; and Jaktorów, 193; and Janowska, 134, 155; Jewish, 10–11, 45, 82, 85–86, 92, 95, 101, 103–4, 110, 117–18, 129, 205, 264; menial, 70; physical, 143; sites of, 10; skilled, 60, 71, 86, 142; slave, 3–4, 8–9, 50, 54, 100, 106, 121–24, 125–26, 129–31, 139, 190; and Tarnopol, 197; unskilled, 142. *See also* forced labor
Lasch, Karl, 42; and Adolf Rothfeld, 85; and anti-Jewish policy, 46, 81; and Breslau (Wrocław), 42; and Distrikt Galizien, 80; and Friedrich Katzmann, 42, 81; and ghettos, 49; and Lviv, 82; and Otto Wächter, 43; and Radom, 49; and Ukraine, 44
Levi, Primo, 130, 142, 146, 150–51, 165, 182, 214
Lewinter, Herman, 8, 127, 156
Löhnert, Anton, 138, 195–96, 213, 242, 252
Lubasz, Bronia, 8
Lubasz, Marcel, 8, 160, 223
Ludwigsburg, 244, 246, 258
Lueg auto company, 129–30
Lviv, 1, 16, 26, 28, 31, 36–37, 44, 153, 158–59, 197, 202, 267; and Aktions, 102–3, 106–7; and anti-Jewish policy, 9, 45, 76, 79; and Bełżec, 99, 128, 138, 145; and Death Brigade, 214; and Deutsche Ausrüstungswerke (DAW), 53, 56, 60, 63, 65–66, 77; and Distrikt Lublin, 44; and Forced Labor Camp-Lviv, 2, 9, 60; and gas chambers, 99; and German Army, 130; and German Equipment Works, 53; and German population, 29–30, 35, 44, 58, 129, 228, 230; and Gestapo, 37, 40, 211–12; ghetto, 24, 46, 49–50, 79, 81, 84–85, 87, 90–91, 138, 189–90,

Lviv (cont.)
  193–94, 203–4, 224; and the Holocaust, 12–13, 15, 18, 135, 200; and Jewish Council, 47, 92; and Jewish Labor Office, 3; and Jewish population, 2, 4–5, 7–9, 14–16, 18–21, 23–25, 33–34, 39, 44–47, 50, 60, 72, 75, 80–83, 94, 97–100, 103, 106, 132, 135, 203–6, 208, 211, 233–35, 239, 252, 256, 258–59, 262; and JULAG, 230; and labor camps, 242; and Lviv Flying Club, 41; and Lviv Opera House, 17, 25–26, 103; and Lviv Philharmonic, 154; and Nazis, 32, 38, 41–42, 48, 79, 90, 100–101, 129, 138, 160, 195–96, 229, 246, 264; and newspapers, 20; and occupation of, 40–41; and Philip Friedman, 12; and Poland, 21–22; Police, 100; and police academy, 43; and Polonization, 17; Polytechnic University, 111; and prisons, 28, 32; and railways, 95–96, 131, 175; and Schutzstaffel (SS) officers, 51, 63, 97, 117, 146, 191; and slave labor, 123, 129; and Soviet Union, 25–27, 30–31, 229, 238; and transit prisons, 260; and typhus vaccine, 89; and urban geography, 265; and Wannsee Conference, 95, 100; and Warsaw, 162, 206, 221; and Wehrmacht, 113; and women's camps, 148. *See also* Janowska camp
Lviv Trial, 11–12, 241, 245–49, 252, 254–55
Lwow, 125, 154, 255
Lychakivska Penal Colony Number 30, 2
Lyczakow forest camp, 223

Maas, Eugenia, 4, 75
Majdanek camp, 177; and death toll, 11, 134; and gas chambers, 224; and Janowska, 135, 190; and Lublin, 228, 264; and Michał Borwicz, 109; and preservation, 259; and prisoners, 222; size of, 58
March Aktion, 97–99, 101, 103, 127, 131, 207
Maria Zankovetska Theatre, 1
mass executions, 5, 128, 212
mass shootings, 5, 31, 60, 136, 170–72, 206, 217, 220, 223, 227, 245; and Adolf Kolonko, 192, 225, 250; and Babi Yar, 31, 211; and Gustav Willhaus, 175, 181, 193, 196; and Janowska camp, 10, 103, 136–38, 154; and Jews, 10, 103, 133, 213; and Leon Wells, 135; and Lviv, 54, 137–38; and Makdanek, 11, 134; and Piaski, 83, 159, 174, 208; and Płaszów camp, 169; and shooting pits, 145, 160, 163, 208; and Ukrainian police, 104, 162; and Waffen-SS, 116; and Zwangsarbeitslager-Lemberg (ZAL-L), 184
matzevah, 2
May Aktion, 102
Mickiewicz, Adam, 17
Miedzieński, Tomasz, 132, 133
Mohwinkel, Wolfgang, 59, 61–62; and Janowska, 58–59; and Lipowa, 54, 59, 118; and Lublin, 56, 59, 61; and Lviv, 56, 60; as Schutzstaffel (SS) officer, 53, 61
Moloch, 5
Monz, Willie, 63, 239–40
Mósciska, 133
Munich, 236, 239–40, 244, 247

music, 17, 36; German, 183, 225, 239; jazz, 160; Jewish musicians, 18, 48, 153–56, 226–27, 257; and Nazis, 69; and Peter Blum, 116; and Richard Rokita, 48, 143; and Roman Kampf, 146

Mutual Aid Organization for Former Waffen-SS Member (HIAG), 242–43

National Socialist Motor Corps (NSKK), 102, 104

Nazi crimes: and Adolf Kolonko, 190; and atonement, 257; and Bełżec, 60; concealment of, 31, 210, 216; and complicity, 243; documentation of, 157; and geography, 169; and Hans Sobotta, 255; investigation of, 235, 244; at Janowska, 156; and Leopold Zimmerman, 149; and Liesel Willhaus, 170; and Lviv, 203, 265; and Kulparkow, 90; and Paul Blobel, 237; and prosecution of, 244, 247–48, 250–52, 254–55, 257, 265; and punishment, 257; recollection of, 158; and Samuel Drix, 182; and Schutzstaffel (SS), 60, 242; and sexual crimes, 186; and Tarnopol, 245; and Waffen-SS, 242; witnesses to, 219

Nazi Party, 55, 64, 112, 152, 166, 240; actions of, 7–8, 13–14, 31, 49, 76, 94–95, 123, 134, 178, 210, 214, 218, 225, 237; and administrators, 4, 35, 38, 40–42, 43, 45, 48, 50, 54, 57–60, 75, 79–81, 84, 89, 101, 103, 112, 117, 122, 138, 192, 212, 218, 250, 255; and Adolf Hitler, 186, 239; and Aktions, 103–4; and *amidah*, 151; and anti-Jewish policy, 9, 59, 175, 209; and antisemitism, 171, 267; and Askaris, 64; and colonial policy, 49–50, 119, 210; and concentration camps, 2, 7, 9, 13–14, 16, 65, 69, 72–73, 75, 101–6, 110, 115–116, 119, 121–123, 129, 133–35, 139, 142–43, 151–52, 157, 159–60, 165–66, 178, 194, 201, 212, 216, 219, 221–22, 224, 228, 263, 266; and denazification, 241–42; and empire, 119, 188, 263; and genocide, 107, 121, 137, 141, 150, 157, 192, 203, 237–38, 261, 264; history of, 1, 24, 27, 32, 38–43, 45, 47, 82, 84, 86–90, 93, 100, 107, 138, 229, 246, 262; ideology of, 57, 125, 143, 186–87, 189; and Jewish Council, 84, 92, 204; and Jewish Question, 210; and Jewish resistance, 206, 223–24; and JULAG, 205; and murder, 83, 102, 131; and Nazi-Soviet pact, 24; and newspapers, 112; and paramilitary formations, 119; and Peter Blum, 127; and Piaski, 83; and pogroms, 33, 39, 135; and Poland, 30, 96, 117, 221; and propaganda, 35, 39; prosecution of, 243–48, 250, 257–58, 265; and *Rheinfront*, 112; and sexual violence, 183; and Soviet Union, 28, 230, 235–36, 259–60; and synagogues, 39; and Ukrainians, 12, 53, 65, 77, 105

Nazi propaganda, 35, 39, 57, 235, 241, 247

Nuremburg Trial, 237

Operation Reinhard, 11, 96–97, 100, 211, 264

Organization of Ukrainian Nationalists (OUN), 22, 44

physicians: concentration camp, 91, 159, 161, 249; and Distrikt Galizien, 90; Jewish, 18, 34, 38, 88, 89–90, 158;

physicians (*cont.*)
and Joachim Reichler, 89; and Maximilian Kurzrock, 158; and Nazi ideology, 143; prisoner, 71; and Samuel Drix, 143; and Wilhelm Dopheide, 49

Piaski (sands), 4–5, 83, 135, 159

Płazów, 74, 169, 183, 189, 230, 266

pogroms, 19–21, 30–31, 33–36, 38, 39–40, 135

Poland, 15, 17–20, 233, 235; and anti-Polish policy, 45; and Army, 21; and Catholics, 262; and citizens, 47–48, 60, 83, 118; and Council to Aid Jews, 161; and culture, 22; and Czesław Miłosz, 267; and Delegatura, 99–100; and Gustav Willhaus, 209; and intelligentsia, 37–38; and Jews, 47, 83, 107, 118, 152; and Jozef Grzimek, 189; and laborers, 72, 95–97; and LOT airline, 41; and Lviv, 24, 27, 31–32, 34, 43, 83, 89–90; and nationalists, 36; and Nazis, 192; and Polish Radio, 154; and Polish supremacy, 15; and politics, 22, 36; and Polonization, 22; and prisoners, 126; and Przemyśl, 230; and resistance, 26; and Roman Schönbach, 117–18; and Soviet occupation, 23–26; and Ukraine, 16, 44; and universities, 23. *See also* Polish (language)

police, 55, 161, 172, 220, 240, 256; and Adolf Kolonko, 190; and Death Brigade, 227–28; and Friedrich Katzmann, 75, 178, 208, 221; and Friedrich Krüger, 212; and Fritz Weise, 79–80; German, 42, 132–33, 205, 217, 222, 225–26, 242, 252; German military, 33–34, 63–64, 230, 233; and German *Schutzpolizei* (city police), 66; and Gestapo, 222; and ghettos, 204; and Gisela Urbach, 185; and Gustav Willhaus, 75, 109, 208; and Janowska, 218; Jewish, 47, 82, 92, 100–101, 205; and Lviv, 22, 26, 36, 44, 79, 100, 117, 214, 224, 227–28, 258; and Nazis, 27, 48, 133, 260; and Odilo Globocnik, 95–96, 118; and Peter Blum, 246; and Poland, 22; Soviet, 26; Ukrainian, 33–34, 38–39, 43–46, 66, 83, 89, 97, 102, 104–5, 160, 206, 239, 257; and Walter Schallock, 213; and Willi König, 215

Polish (language), 5, 12, 40, 63, 81, 124, 258

Prison Aktion, 31, 35–36

prisoner functionaries, 63, 69, 123, 126, 143, 146

prisoners, 4, 251–52; and Adolf Kolonko, 5, 161, 250; and Aid Committee, 91; and Auschwitz, 149, 154; and concentration camps, 5, 9–10, 13, 110, 134; and Dachau, 123; and Death Brigade, 212–20, 223; and death runs, 135; and deportation, 6; and Deutsche Ausrüstungswerke (DAW), 62–65, 72, 74, 91, 110, 162; and Deutsche Ausrüstungswerke-Lemberg (DAW-L), 66–74; and disease, 10; and Eichmann Trial, 12; escapes of, 203; female, 180–82; and Fritz Gebauer, 57–58, 62, 91, 167–68, 175–76, 256; and ghetto, 90, 207; and graves, 236; and Gustav Willhaus, 75, 121, 124, 128, 196; and Jaktorów, 193; and Janowska, 41, 57–58, 105, 115, 119, 123–27, 132–33, 135, 139, 141, 143–44,

147–49, 151, 153–60, 163, 166–74, 178–79, 193, 202, 207–8, 210, 213–14, 227–31, 234, 266; and Kleparów freight station, 120, 124–25; as laborers, 54, 114, 127–30, 139; and Leon Richman, 102; and Leon Wells, 137, 152, 176; and Lipowa DAW camp, 60; and Lviv, 8–9, 13, 26, 28, 60–62, 111, 129, 145–46; murder of, 10, 28, 32, 113, 136, 245, 253; and music, 155; and Paul Fox, 125; political, 32, 138; and prisoner society, 142, 148; and prisoners of war, 41–42, 64, 94, 192; and resistance, 150–52, 157, 225–26, 261, 265; and Richard Rokita, 168; and Roman Kampf, 145–48; and slave labor, 8; and Sobibor uprising, 222; and STALAG 328, 41; torture of, 171, 173–74, 180–88; and Treblinka, 222; and violence, 166, 180, 257; and "vitamin work," 124; and Zeev Porath, 6; and Zwangsarbeitslager (ZAL), 111; and Zwangsarbeitslager-Lemberg (ZAL-L), 4, 7, 224

Professor Aktion, 215

rabbis, 93, 174, 175, 178; and David Kahane, 18, 33, 37, 85, 92, 93, 99, 263; and Death Brigade, 152; and Rabbi Feibish, 153; and Stephen Wise, 210

rape: and Holocaust, 179; and Janowska, 179–80, 187–88; mass, 184; and sexual violence, 179–80, 183; sites of, 181; systematic, 165; as torture, 166

Rauch, Johann, 213, 215, 217, 220, 240–41, 244

Redner, Marek, 30, 34, 48–49, 104

Rogowski, Marian, 45, 106, 159, 168, 250

Rokita, Richard, 239, 249; and ghettos, 194; and Gustav Willhaus, 148, 168; and Janowska, 48, 106, 153; and Leon Wells, 185; as murderer, 7, 150, 160, 245–46; and music, 153–54; and Roman Kampf, 146–48; as Schutzstaffel (SS) officer, 6, 110, 143, 225, 246; and sexual violence, 185; and Tarnopol, 197, 199; and torture, 182; and Zwangsarbeitslager (ZAL), 192

Rosen, Chaim, 4–5, 169, 173

Rosenberg, Alfred, 35, 49

Roth, Joseph, 16

Rothfeld, Adolf, 46–47, 82, 85

Rothkirch, Edwin Graf von, 31

Rückerl, Adalbert, 244

Sammelplatz, 5–7

Schallock, Walter, 219–21, 249; and Death Brigade, 184, 212, 216, 218, 246; and Gestapo, 212; and Janowska, 212, 218, 242; and Johann Rauch, 213; and Leon Wells, 215

Schönbach, Roman, 199–200; arrest of, 246; and Gródek-Jagielloński, 190, 195; and Janowska, 119, 125, 175, 192, 196, 239; and Janowska Street, 117; lawyer of, 249; and Lublin, 118; as murderer, 168–69, 174, 207–8; prosecution of, 249, 251–54; release of, 237; and violence, 125

Schutzpolizei, 44, 66, 81

Schutzstaffel (SS), 23, 43, 53, 96, 119, 121, 129, 141–43, 221, 239; and Adolf Kolonko, 5, 111, 114, 189–90, 267; and Aktions, 98, 131, 195; and Allgemeine-SS, 117; and anti-Jewish policy,

Schutzstaffel (SS) (cont.)
47, 54, 59, 103, 203–4; and concentration camps, 7, 54–55, 60, 62, 72–73, 110, 124, 126, 129, 136, 162, 172, 182, 219, 230; and forced labor, 51, 100; and Janowska camp, 10, 237; and Jews, 5, 31, 47, 51, 53, 69, 122–23, 136, 143, 146, 151, 154–56, 166, 210, 213, 214, 233, 250, 257; and officers, 3, 31, 42, 50, 55–58, 62, 66, 68, 70, 73–77, 91, 105–6, 110–12, 114, 125, 146–48, 153, 173, 175–76, 192–97, 200–209, 211–13, 216, 222, 234, 236, 238, 246, 251, 255; and operations, 67, 130, 159–60, 162, 167, 215–21; and sexual violence, 161, 181–88; and social network, 13; and survivors, 72, 145, 173, 214; and torture, 166, 171–72, 179, 181–82, 220, 266; and Ukrainian police, 97, 102, 104, 206; and Ukrainians, 38, 83, 110, 135, 138, 146, 196; and violence, 6–7, 23, 37–38, 67–68, 94, 105, 110, 137–38, 145, 149, 155–57, 159, 161, 165, 167–68, 177–78, 181, 190–91, 207, 215, 222–25, 233, 252–54, 257; and women's camps, 161, 207. *See also* Lviv; Waffen-SS; Zwangsarbeitslager-Lemberg (ZAL-L)
Schwarz Aktion, 205
Schwarzarbeitern, 4, 68–71, 73
2nd SS Panzer Division, 64
Selbstschutz (Self-Defense), 117–18, 192, 193, 200
sexualized violence, 142, 179–82
sexual violence, 13, 141–42, 179–80, 183, 187–88, 266
6th SS Mountain Division, 236
Sobibor extermination center, 65, 96, 132, 204, 211

Sobibor Trial, 245
Sobibor uprising, 222
Sobieski III, Jan, 17, 40
Sobotta, Hans: and Gródek-Jagielloński, 195; and Janowska, 136–37, 193, 196, 247, 252; and Lublin, 192; and Paul Fox, 190, 192, 246; prosecution of, 254–55; as Schutzstaffel (SS) officer, 193, 196; and Selbstschutz, 192
social networks, 197–202
Sonderkommando 1005 (SK1005), 211, 237, 240, 242, 247, 254. *See also* Death Brigade (Janowska SK 1005)
Sonderkommandos, 98; Auschwitz, 213; and liquidation, 219, 227; and Sonderkommando 4a, 31, 36; and Sonderkommando 4b, 36; and Sonderkommando 1005, 211, 237, 240, 242, 247, 254
Soviet crimes, 39
Soviet Extraordinary State Commission (ESC), 235
Soviet Union: and Adolf Hitler, 94; and Alfred Rosenberg, 35; and anti-Jewish violence, 39; and Austro-Hungarian Empire, 20; and counteroffensives, 72; and East Germany, 255; and Eichmann Trial, 12; and Einsatzgruppen, 36; and Germans, 12, 68, 99, 238; and Germany, 35, 64, 68, 238; government, 68; and Heinrich Himmler, 64; and hinterland, 80; and Holocaust, 262; and invasion of, 193; and Janowska, 53, 64, 193–94, 211, 221, 235–36, 259–61; and Jews, 35, 93, 95, 97–98, 235; and Leon Wells, 102; and Lviv, 22, 24, 30,

98, 229; and Michail Javorskiij, 143; and military, 21; and murders, 259; and Nazis, 230, 238; and occupation of Lviv, 24–28, 31; and Peter Blum, 229; and Poland, 24–26; and *Pravda*, 100; and prisoners of war, 41, 94, 192; and prisons, 33–34; and Red Army, 235, 241; and Reinhard Heydrich, 36; and Second Polish Republic, 21; and Soviet Bloc, 245; and Ukraine, 21, 44; and Ukrainian guards, 257–58; and Ukrainian Jews, 11; as victims, 32; and Walter Schallock, 211–12; and Wehrmacht, 55

SS-und Polizeiführer (SSPF), 42, 48–49, 55, 59, 76, 119, 222

Stars of David, 1

Steinhaus Company 25, 27, 56

Stets'ko, Yaroslav, 32

Stroop, Jürgen, 205–8

Tarnopol, 24, 100, 131, 197, 199, 205, 213, 222

Tarnopol Trial, 245, 247, 249

Technical Office, 4, 111, 126, 142, 144–45, 156–57, 162

Tempel Progressive synagogue, 5, 39

testimony: of Abraham Goldberg, 99, 249; of Adolf Kolonko, 192; and Anton Löhnert, 252; of Bernard Hirschhorn, 71; and Elie Wiesel, 234; eyewitness, 253; of Fritz Gebauer, 71, 109, 257; and Georg Gilke, 45; and Gustav Willhaus, 169, 171; of Holocaust survivors, 13, 102, 141, 165, 167, 171, 179, 228, 234, 246, 256, 262, 265; and Janowska, 141, 156, 165, 176, 179, 188, 246, 265; of Klara Szpilka,

99; of Leon Wells, 101, 226, 250; of Leopold Zimmerman, 135; and Lviv, 153, 246; of Marian Rogowski, 250; and Martin Büttner, 167; and Nazi trials, 250, 253; and Otto Walter, 251; perpetrator, 98; and Peter Blum, 183–84; and Roman Schönbach, 253; of Rosa Kohn, 186; and sexualized violence, 180; and Simon Wiesenthal, 174; of Stanisława Gogolowska, 90, 111, 165; of Ukrainians, 162; video, 24; of Yankel Schudrich, 153

13th Croatian Waffen-SS Division, 236

13th Waffen-SS Mountain Division, 209

torture, 38, 168; and Gestapo, 166; and Gustav Willhaus, 91, 168, 174; and Heinrich Himmler, 172; and Holocaust, 162, 168; and Jaktorów, 193; and Janowska, 124, 141, 165, 168, 176, 182, 187–88, 261; mental, 124; and Michał Borwicz, 173; physical, 124; of prisoners, 141, 149; and Reinhard camps, 179; and Schutzstaffel (SS), 166; and victims, 171

Trawniki, 64–66, 95–96, 98, 189–90, 192, 198–99, 224

Treblinka, 96, 156, 177, 211, 222, 245

Trestle Aktion, 83, 101

typhus, 49, 68, 85, 88–89, 91, 104, 125, 158

Ukraine: and anti-Jewish policy, 33–34, 68; and ethnic minorities, 64; as foremen, 68; and Germans, 41, 43–44; and guards, 96, 125, 135, 138, 162, 166, 176, 194, 214; and Janowska camp, 90, 143, 176, 228; and Jews, 15–16, 18, 33–35, 37–38, 83, 110, 122, 126, 162, 194; and Lviv, 12, 17–18, 38, 90;

Ukraine (cont.)
and militia, 32, 47, 161, 196; and nationalists, 16, 29–30, 32, 34, 38, 262; and Nazis, 32, 43, 53, 146, 259; and Organization of Ukrainian Nationalists (OUN), 22; and Poland, 20–22, 40, 143; and police, 39–40, 44–46, 66, 83, 89–90, 97, 102, 104–5, 160, 206, 239, 257; as prisoners, 228; and rail lines, 88; and Schutzstaffel (SS), 230; and Soviet Union, 20–22, 26; and students, 19–20; and Ukrainian Communist Party, 25; and Ukrainian Military Organization (UMO), 22; and Ukrainian Nachtigall Battalion, 32; and United Ukrainian American Relief Committee, 239; and violence, 33–34, 39; and volunteer guards, 65. *See also* Galicia (Western Ukraine)

Ukrainian (language), 5, 12, 44

Vienna, 5, 17–18, 20–21, 40, 186
violence: and anti-Jewish violence, 39; ethnic, 233; female perpetrators of, 171; and Fritz Gebauer, 167, 177; and General Government, 43; and ghetto benches, 23; and ghettos, 83; and Gustav Willhaus, 112, 168, 201; and Heinrich Himmler, 206; and Holocaust, 110, 174; and Janowska, 14, 119, 124, 141–42, 149, 165–66, 178, 188, 190, 193, 208; and July Days, 45, 53; and Lviv, 15–16, 21, 26, 33–34, 81; mass, 35; mob, 31; and Nazis, 41, 160, 264; and pogroms, 31–32; and Prison Aktion, 36; sexualized, 179–82; transgressive, 175; and Ukrainians, 19, 176

Wachsmann, Nikolaus, 177
Wächter, Otto, 43, 49
Waffen-SS, 36, 62–63, 113, 116–18, 173, 191, 230, 242
Walter, Otto, 251
Warzok, Friedrich, 176, 197, 200, 209–10, 222, 224–25, 228–30, 236, 238, 255, 258
Wehrmacht, 44, 245; and corruption, 67; and Gustav Willhaus, 113; and Heinrich Himmler, 116; and Jews, 31; and Lviv, 30, 33, 37; and prisoner brigades, 130; and prisoner of war camp STALAG 328, 41; soldiers, 47, 242; and Soviet territory, 28, 55; and Ukrainians, 29; and violence, 33; and war criminals, 247
Wells (Weliczker), Leon, 75, 157, 167, 176, 235–36; and Adolf Eichmann, 101, 149; and Appellplatz, 124; and David Kahane, 156; and Death Brigade, 184, 212–15, 217–20, 226; and deposition, 246; and family, 25, 27, 84, 204, 235; and ghettos, 103, 207; and Gustav Willhaus, 75, 169; and Holocaust survivors, 137; and Janowska, 125, 127, 129, 137, 142, 156, 185–86, 217; and Jewish Question, 123; and Johann Rauch, 240; and Lviv, 135, 159, 233–34; and Majdanek, 222; and memoir, 250; and Kleparów, 125; and resistance, 228, 240; and Richard Rokita, 185, 246; and Soviet Union, 102; and Walter Schallock, 246; and Yom Kippur, 152; and Zwangsarbeitslager-Lemberg (ZAL-L), 113
West German, 243
West Prussia, 42, 208

West Wall, 117
Wiesenthal, Simon, 11–12, 60, 129, 145, 154, 174–75, 229–31, 234, 258
Willhaus, Gustav, 89, 124, 128, 153, 183, 266; and Adolf Kolonko, 195–96; and antisemitism, 143; and David Kahane, 175; and Death Run, 68; and Deutsche Ausrüstungswerke (DAW), 121; and Deutsche Ausrüstungswerke-Lemberg (DAW-L), 75–76, 91, 109–12; and early life, 112; and family, 74, 170; and Friedrich Katzmann, 76–77, 109–10, 113, 178, 195–96, 201, 208; and Friedrich Warzok, 197, 209; and ghettos, 103, 144; and Gródek-Jagielloński, 194, 252; and Henryk Griffel, 111; and Janowska, 106, 125–26, 130, 148, 157–59, 165, 167–72, 174–76, 201, 206, 209, 256; and Jewish resistance, 162; and Liesel Willhaus, 114, 169–71, 245, 249; and Lviv, 76, 158, 196, 208; and March Aktion, 103; and Majdanek camp, 177; as murderer, 130, 161, 169–70, 174; and Nazi trials, 253, 256; and Paul Fox, 200; and Roman Kampf, 146, 148; as Schutzstaffel (SS) officer, 62, 176; and slave labor, 122; and Soviet Union, 260; and Tarnopol, 245; and torture, 89, 169, 177; and Waffen-SS, 62, 75–76, 113, 236; and Wehrmacht, 113; and Zwangsarbeitslager (ZAL), 66, 71, 79, 109, 111, 121, 193, 195; and Zwangsarbeitslager-Lemberg (ZAL-L), 91, 209
Wind, Joseph, 7, 32, 228, 235
Winstone, Martin, 134
Wirth, Christian, 96, 98
women, 2, 5–6, 21, 54, 62, 74, 114, 128, 136, 248; and concentration camp staff, 42, 73, 128; and Death Brigade, 217–18; and deportations, 104–5; and Janowska camp, 7, 179, 188, 265; Jewish, 2, 5–6, 33, 35, 48, 94, 104, 131, 163, 183–84, 218; and Nazis, 35, 42, 73; as perpetrators of violence, 127, 170–71; and prisoners, 146, 158, 161, 180, 183–86, 188; and Schutzstaffel's (SS) and sexual violence, 179–88, 266; as victims of the Holocaust, 5–8, 94, 101–2, 163, 169, 173, 179–84, 196, 205, 207; and women's camps, 8, 120, 144, 148, 157–58, 161, 207, 223; and women's prisons, 244
World War I, 18, 19, 30, 38, 96, 112, 212, 221
World War II, 11–13, 16, 24, 115, 172, 241

Yanivski cemetery, 1

Zamarstynówka Street, 5, 88
Zimmerman, 69–70
Zimmerman, Leopold, 127, 135, 142, 145–47, 149, 207
Zwangsarbeitslager-Lemberg (ZAL-L), 2, 4, 70, 113, 122, 146, 169, 193, 209, 261; and Adolf Folkmann, 205; and Chaim Rosen, 5; and Einsatzgruppen, 176–77; and Gródek-Jagielloński, 197; and hybridity, 9, 139; and Jews, 6, 203; and murder, 203; and Nazis, 7, 193, 224; and oppression, 193; and prisoners, 111, 224; and torture, 184; and women's section, 184. *See also* Deutsche Ausrüstungswerke-Lemberg (DAW-L); Janowska camp